DIRECT AND OBLIQUE INTENTION IN THE CRIMINAL LAW

Direct and Oblique Intention in the Criminal Law

An inquiry into degrees of blameworthiness

ITZHAK KUGLER
Faculty of Law
The Hebrew University of Jerusalem

Ashgate

Published by
Ashgate Publishing Limited
Gower House
Croft Road
Aldershot
Hampshire GU11 3HR
England

Ashgate Publishing Company
131 Main Street
Burlington, VT 05401-5600 USA

Ashgate website: http://www.ashgate.com

British Library Cataloguing in Publication Data
Kugler, Itzhak
   Direct and oblique intention in the criminal law : an
   inquiry into degrees of blameworthiness
   1. Criminal intent 2. Criminal liability
   I. Title
   345'.04

Library of Congress Control Number: 2001099672

ISBN 0 7546 2248 7

Printed and bound in Great Britain by MPG Books Ltd, Bodmin, Cornwall

Contents

Preface

In 1982, as a first year student at the Faculty of Law at the Hebrew University of Jerusalem, I had the pleasure of attending the fascinating course in criminal law delivered by Professor Mordechai Kremnitzer. The fact that Professor Kremnitzer emphasised issues of justice and policy, coupled with the fact that a year earlier I had attended, as a Philosophy student at the same university, the stimulating course *Introduction to Moral and Political Philosophy* given by Professor David Heyd, helped me to see the strong connections between moral and political philosophy and many criminal law issues. I felt that research in specific criminal law issues can be more thorough and fruitful with the help of relevant philosophical materials.

In 1985 I was a law clerk to Justice Aharon Barak at the Supreme Court of Israel. One of the cases on which I worked was a case of criminal libel. The Israeli offence of criminal libel requires for conviction that the defamatory material be published with intent to injure (the good name of another person). One of the questions that was raised in the case was whether, in order to be convicted of criminal libel, the publication must be done out of a desire to injure (i.e. the actor must have direct intention), or whether oblique intention (i.e. knowledge that it is practically certain that the publication will injure, which is not accompanied by a desire to injure) should also suffice for conviction. When I started to think about this question I felt that in order to deal with it adequately a more basic question should be addressed, namely why, in this offence, recklessness as to the injury (i.e. knowingly taking an unjustified risk that the injury will ensue) does not suffice for conviction. I thought that the answer to this last question would assist in deciding whether in criminal libel oblique intention should suffice for conviction. Of course I immediately saw that this line of thinking is also relevant for many other offences that require intention for conviction. These thoughts led me to see the importance of the issue of oblique intention and I decided to keep researching it and thinking about it even after the judgment in the mentioned case was delivered. The idea that acting with intent to cause a certain result is more culpable than acting with recklessness with regard to the same result is a common idea. Therefore it is natural to raise the possibility that the requirement of intention in certain offences is based on the desire to require a high degree of culpability in the context of those offences. But is it correct that causing a result purposely is more culpable than causing it recklessly? At the time I started to think about this question, I was also taking a seminar on moral philosophy at the Department of Philosophy at the Hebrew University (delivered by Professor Heyd). One of the topics of that seminar was the double effect theory, and this enabled me to see the potential links between the legal question I was thinking about and this philosophical theory. Naturally I decided to explore these links. However, the rationale related to degrees of moral culpability is not the only possible rationale for requiring intention in criminal offences. Indeed, after thinking about the rationale for requiring intention in criminal libel I concluded that there are various potential reasons for requiring intention in that offence, some of which are not connected to degrees of moral culpability. This was also the case when I thought about some other specific offences that require intention for conviction. I also felt that some of these potential reasons for requiring intention (as well as certain other ideas relevant to the research) came to my mind only by virtue of my investing time and energy in thinking seriously about various specific offences, and studying their context and history. These thoughts led me to two conclusions. First, that when exploring the issue of intention, one should be open to dealing with this issue not only from the viewpoint of degrees of culpability but also from other perspectives. Second, that research in criminal law should not be limited to the "general part". Doing serious research on specific offences may yield many insights that possibly will not be revealed when thinking only about the "general part"; and the conclusions that may be drawn from research on specific offences may be of considerable importance not only for understanding these offences but also for the "general part".

This book is the product of my research on the issues of direct and oblique intention in the criminal law. However, I must emphasise that it includes only part of my thinking about these issues, for in this book the discussion deals with the topic of intention only from the viewpoint of degrees of moral blameworthiness. I leave it for another occasion to publish my thoughts on the topic of intention that are not directly related to degrees of moral culpability.

Structure of the book

This book examines the issues of direct and oblique intention in the criminal law. The question of oblique intention is whether to convict of "intention crimes" (i.e. crimes in the context of which recklessness is not sufficient for conviction) those people who act with mere oblique intention with respect to the proscribed result (i.e. those people who act not *in order* to cause the result, but who are practically certain that the result will ensue). In chapter 1 of the book (the Introduction) I introduce the question of oblique intention as it is raised in courts and as it is raised when legislators prepare criminal codes. Then I suggest that in order to deal adequately with this question a more basic question needs to be addressed, namely: What, if any, is the justification for distinguishing in the criminal law between direct intention and recklessness? The answer to this last question is important not only because of its contribution to dealing with the question of oblique intention, but also in itself – because it may help legislators when deliberating whether, in certain contexts, to require "intention" for conviction. The issue of the justification for distinguishing between intention and recklessness in the criminal law, and the implications of this issue for the question of oblique intention, are explored throughout the book, from the viewpoint of degrees of moral culpability.

A legislator who believes that a person who causes a bad result purposely is more morally blameworthy than one who causes the same result recklessly may be motivated by this belief to grade offences based on the distinction between intention and recklessness. But even the acceptance of this belief does not explain the enactment of "basic crimes of intention" (i.e. offences in the context of which intention is required for the very penalisation of the conduct and in which reckless actors are not exposed at all to criminal liability). Since it is more difficult to understand and justify the existence of "basic crimes of intention" than the practice of grading offences along the distinction between intention and recklessness, the book is divided into two parts: Part One (chapters 2-10) deals with grading offences, and Part Two (chapters 11-13) with "basic crimes of intention".

In chapter 2 I challenge the common saying that "intention is a more culpable state of mind than recklessness" by bringing counter-examples in which an actor who causes a certain result purposely is less morally culpable than an actor who causes the same result recklessly. In light of these examples I suggest that we should ask whether causing a result purposely is more culpable than causing it recklessly, when all other things, *including the motives,* are equal. The answer to this question is not simple. A question similar to it (in some respects) is discussed in moral philosophy, in the context of the discussion about the doctrine of the double effect. I turn to the debate concerning this doctrine in order to see what we can infer from it to our issue. Chapter 3 deals with the debate, in moral philosophy, concerning the doctrine of the double effect. The discussion describes, elaborates and analyses the debate and adds several insights as well. In order to understand the debate adequately we should first capture the difference between consequentialism and deontological ethics, and understand the nature of deontological constraints. The discussion first deals with these topics, and then addresses the debate about the doctrine of the double effect. It suggests, inter alia, several ways to understand the existence of the deontological constraints, and several ways to understand the doctrine of the double effect. The discussion also suggests that the question as to which explanation for the said doctrine is embraced may have practical implications. Chapter 4 brings us back to criminal law. The discussion here carefully explores the conclusions that may be drawn from the debate about the doctrine of the double effect in relation to the issue of degrees of culpability in the criminal law. The reason why this exploration should be careful is that there are differences between the context in which the said doctrine is discussed and the context of degrees of culpability in the criminal law, so that the views that a person holds concerning the said doctrine do not automatically dictate what this person should think concerning degrees of culpability in the criminal law. The main questions in this chapter are whether the existence of a desire to cause the result increases the culpability of the actor, and what the implications of the answer to this question are for the issue of oblique intention. While chapters 3 and 4 revolve around the element of desire, chapter 5 examines the possibility that intention is more culpable than recklessness not because of the desire to cause the result, but because of another mental element that distinguishes between intention and recklessness. The discussion examines several options (e.g. that in cases of direct intention the actor does not have a hope that the result will not ensue and therefore he is more culpable than a reckless actor), and their implications for the issues of direct and oblique intention in the criminal law. Chapter 6 examines the idea that the moral culpability of the actor increases in proportion to the degree of probability with which the result is foreseen. The discussion examines various possible justifications for this idea, and also explores the implications of the various justifications for the issues of direct and oblique intention in the criminal law.

The discussion in chapters 3-6 assumes that the adoption of the position that when all other things are equal, *including the motives,* a person who causes a result purposely is more morally culpable than a person who causes the same result recklessly, justifies the grading of offences based on the distinction between intention and recklessness. Chapter 7 reconsiders this assumption. In this chapter I suggest and develop the argument that because many factors other than that of intention versus recklessness (and which are no less important than this factor) are taken (and should be taken) into consideration in the sentencing stage, there is much to be said against grading offences based on the distinction between intention and recklessness. Another point that is raised and justified in this chapter is that a rational legislator is not logically obliged to adopt the same scheme concerning intention in the context of all offences. Chapter 8 addresses the option of grading offences not by distinguishing between intention and recklessness, but by using a moral formula (i.e. by providing that conviction of the aggravated offence be conditioned upon the actor being highly culpable). The discussion deals with the pros and cons of this option, and also examines whether special considerations apply in the context of homicide.

Chapter 9 brings us back to the idea of grading offences based on the distinction between intention and recklessness. In this chapter I suggest and examine a different way from that examined in the previous chapters to justify the grading of offences based on the distinction between intention and recklessness. This justification is not built on the view that there is an intrinsic moral difference between intention and recklessness when all other things (including the motives) are equal. Rather, it is based on the idea that in the context of certain offences there is an empirical correlation between the existence of intention and being highly culpable, due to an empirical correlation between the existence of intention and the existence of factors which increase the culpability of the actor. The implications for the issue of oblique intention of enacting "intention crimes" on the basis of this justification are also examined, as well as the question whether in the context of this justification special considerations apply in the context of homicide. Chapter 10 summarises briefly the conclusions of the discussion in Part One of the book.

Part Two of the book is devoted to the phenomenon of "basic crimes of intention". Even embracing the view that actors who act with intent to cause the result are more culpable than those who act recklessly cannot, by itself, justify the enactment of "basic crimes of intention", for such enactment means that in the context of those crimes the reckless actor is completely exempted from criminal liability. The existence of such crimes seems, *prima facie,* very problematic. Nonetheless, in Part Two (chapters 11-13) I suggest, develop, and discuss two possible justifications for enacting such crimes. I also examine what the law of cases of oblique intention should be in the context of such crimes. The discussion in chapter 11 is based on the acceptance of "a principle of threshold of culpability" according to which an agent must be *sufficiently* morally culpable in order to permit the imposition of criminal liability. I suggest that a legislator who adopts this principle and who believes that "intention is more culpable than recklessness" may come to the conclusion that in the context of certain offences that do not protect very important interests, those who act with recklessness generally do not reach the threshold of culpability that is required to permit the imposition of criminal liability, as harm is only done to interests that are not very important. In chapter 12 I suggest a further possible justification for requiring intention in basic crimes. This justification is based on the idea that when the imposition of punishment is based on retribution, rather than on deterrence, an especially high degree of culpability should be required to justify the imposition of punishment. If we accept this view and we also think that "intention is more culpable than recklessness", then we have a *prima facie* reason for requiring intention in contexts in which the punishment is based on retribution. Chapter 13 summarises briefly the conclusions of the discussion in Part Two of the book.

Acknowledgements

I am enormously grateful to Professor Mordechai Kremnitzer and Professor David Heyd for their helpful comments on the draft of this book. I am also very grateful to Daniel Ohana and Yael Wyant for their careful language editing, and to the British Friends of the Hebrew University for financial support of the research.

My greatest debt is to my wife, Tzippi, and to my sons, Lior and Tomer. They tolerated my spending too many hours in my study, and only by virtue of their love and patience could I finish this work. The book is dedicated to them.

Some of the ideas and arguments presented in this book appeared earlier (in Hebrew) in my doctoral dissertation which was submitted to the Hebrew University of Jerusalem in 1993, and in subsequent publications of mine in Israel.

INTRODUCTION

Chapter 1

The Problem of Oblique Intention in the Criminal Law

1.1   Crimes of Intention

Many offences that contain a result element can be committed "intentionally or recklessly". The traditional definition of recklessness is a subjective one: recklessness means the conscious taking of an unjustified risk. A person acts with recklessness as to a consequence if, when he acts, he actually foresees that there is a risk that that consequence may possibly result from his act, and it is unreasonable for him to take the risk of it occurring.[1] The Draft Criminal Code for England and Wales defines recklessness in the same manner. Clause 18 of the draft Code provides that a person acts "recklessly" with respect to a result when he is aware of a risk that it will occur; and it is, in the circumstances known to him, unreasonable to take the risk.[2] In this book, the term "recklessness" will be used in this sense.

There are, however, offences that are defined so as to require an "intention" to cause a specified result (we can call them "intention-crimes"). Recklessness does not suffice for conviction in these crimes. This means that in these crimes, an actor who foresees the possibility that the result will ensue will not be convicted unless he also wants it to ensue.[3]

We can distinguish between two types of "intention-crimes". First, the legislator may use the distinction between intention and recklessness in order to grade offences. For example: he may enact an offence of recklessly causing bodily harm, that is punishable by a maximum of five years imprisonment, and enact another offence of intentionally causing bodily harm that is punishable by a maximum of twenty years imprisonment. In this case, the "intention-crime" is an aggravated offence. Second, the legislator may enact an offence in which intention is required as a prerequisite for the criminalisation of the actor's conduct. In this context, when he only acts with recklessness, the actor is entirely exempted from criminal liability.[4] I will call offences of this type "basic intention-crimes".

The element of "intention to cause a result" may appear not only in offences the actus reus of which includes the forbidden result (as in the case of "intentionally causing bodily harm"), but also in so-called "ulterior intent" offences. Here the crime is defined in such a manner that the mens rea includes an intention to produce some further consequence beyond the actus reus of the crime in question. In these offences, it is irrelevant whether the further consequence actually occurs. The structure of these crimes is "doing x with intent to cause y". Here too, recklessness as to the further consequence does not suffice to establish liability.[5] Ulterior intent offences, like result crimes of intention, can also be divided into two categories: offences in which intent is required as a prerequisite for the criminalisation of the conduct in question (so that recklessness as to the further consequence does not suffice to establish liability) and offences in which the "ulterior intent" is used by the legislator to create an aggravated offence.

1.2   Direct Intention

In "intention-crimes", a conviction may ensue if the accused acted with the intention of causing the proscribed result. This means that the accused will be convicted if, when he acted, he foresaw the possibility that his act would bring about the proscribed consequence and he also desired, wished, that this consequence would occur.[6] The consequence need not be desired as an end in itself; it may be desired as a means to another end.[7] For example, if a person causes the death of his relative in order to receive an inheritance, he is considered, from the perspective of the law, to act with intent to cause his death, although for him the death is only desired as a means to a further end (to receive the inheritance), so that he may be convicted of an offence conditioned upon an intention to cause death. This interpretation of "intention-crimes" as encompassing cases of desiring a result as a means to a further end, also accords with everyday speech. Indeed, everyone would say that the person in such a case intended the death. This last point has led some scholars to suggest that we should define "intention" without using the notion of desire or wish because sometimes when we act in order to achieve a certain result which is only needed by us as a means to another end, we may be very sorry that we have to cause that result. If a person causes the death of his dog in order to put it out of its pain, he may be very sad when he is acting. In this case we say that he intends to kill the dog, since he acts in order to kill it, in spite of the fact that he is very sorry that he must cause the death of the dog. The fact that in these kinds of cases the actor is sad and sorry has led some scholars to suggest that we cannot say that in such cases there is a desire or wish that the result (e.g. the death of the dog) ensue. And this, in turn, has led them to claim that intention should not be defined in terms of desire or wish.[8]   There are several proposals for defining intention without using the notions of desire and wish. For example: A person acts with intent to bring about a consequence if he acts with the *purpose* of bringing it about,[9] or: A person acts with intent to cause a result if he acts *in order* to cause it.[10] In response to the arguments above, some maintain that even in such cases as the killing of the dog, the actor wants to bring about the death of the dog. This is because the death of the dog is perceived by the actor as the lesser of two evils; this means that in the circumstances, he prefers to kill the dog and thus acts in order to kill it, which means that he wants to kill it.[11] Others maintain that there are two senses to the term "want" in ordinary speech. Sometimes we use "want" in a broad sense, according to which the actor in the example above wants to kill the dog; and sometimes we use "want" in a narrower sense, according to which the actor does not want to kill the dog.[12] This may lead some to prefer that intention be defined in the criminal law without the term "want" or "desire", in order to avoid possible difficulties that may emerge if juries or judges understand the term "want" in the narrower sense, which is not suitable for interpreting intention in "intention-crimes".[13]

I think that in undertaking a theoretical analysis of intention, we should not avoid using the notion of wanting a result. It seems that a person who acts in order to cause some result must want (at least in the broader sense discussed above) that result to ensue, otherwise we would not say that he acts *in order* to achieve it. Thus, when we try to explain more fully what is going on in the world when somebody acts with intent to cause a certain result, the account that mentions the actor wanting (at least in the broader sense) the result to ensue is a better one. But when we are defining intention in a criminal code for daily usage in the courts, it may be best not to use the terms "want" or "desire" in order to prevent mistakes by judges or jurors. Thus, the definition of the Draft Criminal Code for England and Wales of 1989, according to which a person acts intentionally with respect to a result when he acts in order to bring it about, is a good one.[14] But in this book, which is not a criminal code, I will continue to use the terms "want" and "desire" when appropriate.

A person sometimes acts with two or more intentions. The general rule is that an actor can be convicted of a "crime of intention" if he intends to cause the proscribed result, even if he intends to cause other results as well. There is no requirement that the proscribed result be his only purpose or even his dominant one.[15] Thus, for example, in order to obtain a blackmail conviction, it is enough to show that *one* of the objectives of the accused in making the demand was to make a gain for himself or another.[16]

To sum up: In order to convict an accused of a crime of intention, the prosecution must prove that the accused acted with intent to cause the proscribed result. A person acts with intent to cause the proscribed result if he acts in order to bring about that result, regardless of whether he wants the result as an end in itself or as a means to another end. It is not required that the proscribed purpose be the sole or even the dominant purpose of the actor. If the accused did not act in order to achieve the proscribed result but only foresaw it as possible or probable, he may not be convicted of an "intention-crime".

A person who acts in order to achieve a result is sometimes referred to in the literature as a person acting with a *direct* intention. The adjective "direct" is added in order to distinguish between the kind of intention discussed thus far, and another kind of intention which is sometimes called (by jurists and philosophers) *oblique* or *indirect* intention. I will now turn to "oblique intention".

1.3   Oblique Intention

1.3.1   *Cases of Foresight of Certainty*

Sometimes a person acts without a purpose to achieve the proscribed result (even not as a means to another end), but is aware that there is a practical certainty (and not merely a probability or a high probability) that the proscribed result will ensue. Should this person be convicted of an "intention-crime"? On the one hand, this person resembles the reckless actor since he does not act *in order* to cause the proscribed result, so that he should not be convicted of an "intention-crime". On the other hand, this person takes a course of action that is worse than the taking of an unjustified risk, as he, unlike the reckless actor, is *sure* that his act will bring about the forbidden result. And since he nevertheless acts, despite this assurance, we might want to treat him more severely than we treat the reckless actor. This may lead us to suggest that he should be convicted of a "crime of intention". Consider the following two examples:

1. A is a friend of a prisoner and wants to help him to escape from prison. He knows that every day between 4:00 and 5:00 in the afternoon the prisoners go for a stroll in the prison courtyard. He sets a time bomb to explode at 4:30. The explosion will make a hole in the wall of the prison, which will enable his friend to escape. In this case, A acts both in order to cause an explosion and to make a hole in the wall. These results are needed by him as means to achieve a further result, namely, his friend's escape from prison (he told his friend in advance about the plan so that he will not be too close to the wall at the time of the explosion and so that he will be prepared to escape immediately afterwards). Suppose now that A is aware that the courtyard will be very crowded so that it is practically certain that the explosion will cause grievous bodily harm to one of the prisoners, and that this actually happens. Note that this anticipated harm to one of the prisoners is not needed by him as a means to his end: he does not act *in order* to achieve it. Now, suppose that in a certain criminal code there are two offences of causing grievous bodily harm. The aggravated one requires intention and the lesser one requires recklessness. Should we convict him of the aggravated offence? The same example, with modifications, may apply to a criminal code which conditions liability for murder on an intention to kill and liability for manslaughter on recklessness as to the death of a person.

2. Suppose that we have an offence of doing an act with intent to impede the apprehension of another person who committed an offence. This is a "basic crime of intention" since where there is only recklessness as to the impediment of the apprehension there is no crime at all. Suppose that a hotel proprietor, in the ordinary course of business, provides accommodation for one night to a person whom he knows to be someone who committed an offence. The proprietor is only interested in obtaining advance payment for the night; he has no interest whatsoever in impeding the apprehension. The impediment is not even needed by him as a means to get his money. Suppose further that the

proprietor is practically certain, at the time he accepts the offender, that providing him with the room will impede his apprehension. Does he perpetrate the above mentioned offence?

1.3.2 *The Problem of Oblique Intention in Interpreting Current Criminal Offences*

In countries where there is no statutory definition of "intention" for the purpose of criminal offences, cases of "practical certainty" confront courts as a problem concerning the proper interpretation of criminal offences. The various tools generally employed in interpreting laws can be used in confronting this problem. First, there is the linguistic question. If you think that in English a person who does not act *in order* to cause a certain result cannot be said to act with intent to cause that result, even if he is aware that his act would certainly cause that result, and if additionally you also believe that courts should never apply criminal offences to cases that are not covered by the language of these offences, then you should reach the conclusion that a person acting with "foresight of certainty" (who does not act in order to bring about the forbidden result) should not be convicted of a crime that requires acting "with intent" to cause the result, even if considerations of justice and policy dictate otherwise.[17] But if you think that cases of "foresight of certainty" (where there is no desire to cause the relevant result) are included in English in "acting with intent" to cause a result (at least in a broader sense of "acting with intent") or, in the alternative, if you reject that thought, but nevertheless believe that courts are entitled to stretch the language of the law in interpreting criminal offences when considerations of justice or policy necessitate such course of action, then the path is cleared to consider the view that in all (or, in the alternative, in some) "intention-crimes" courts should convict not only in cases of acting in order to cause the result but also in cases of "foresight of certainty" (which is not accompanied by a desire to cause the result).[18]

Another factor that can be taken into consideration when interpreting a "crime of intention" is the intention of the legislator. Did the legislator who enacted the said offence intend that a person who had "foresight of certainty" (without desire) be convicted? Did he intend that such a person be acquitted? Or, perhaps, he intended that the reckless actor be acquitted and that the one who acted in order to cause the result be convicted, but simply did not think separately about cases of "foresight of certainty" (without desire). Even those who do not think that the legislative intent is a decisive factor in interpreting laws may be open to considering it among other considerations.

If we assume that courts have the right to interpret "intention-crimes" as applying to cases of "foresight of certainty" (without desire), then considerations of justice and policy enter into consideration. Here three main possibilities arise. The first possibility is to say that justice and policy dictate that no conviction of a "crime of intention" obtain in the absence of desire. For if the legislator decided that recklessness should not suffice for conviction in those crimes, then presumably he had a good reason. And the reason for not convicting in cases of recklessness applies in the same manner to cases of "foresight of certainty". So the law should be the same for all crimes of intention: no conviction in cases of "foresight of certainty". The second possibility is to say that considerations of justice and policy lead to the conclusion that we should apply all crimes of intention to cases of "foresight of certainty". Even if we assume that the legislator had good reasons for not convicting in cases where there is only foresight of possibility or probability, cases of foresight of certainty are essentially different and should be equated with cases of desire for the purposes of all crimes of intention. A third possibility is to say that the law as to cases of "foresight of certainty" should vary from crime to crime. According to this possibility, there is no one sweeping theoretical argument which dictates that cases of "foresight of certainty" always be treated, in the context of criminal offences, as cases of desire, or, for that matter, that these cases should never be treated alike. Rather, the right solution is to specifically consider in every crime of intention what the law should be as to cases of "foresight of certainty".[19] This approach has its own price, as it undermines unity and predictability in the system, though we may be ready to pay it if we think that such an approach is more justifiable than the other two insofar as justice and policy are concerned. Authors differ in their opinions as to what courts should do in cases of oblique intention. There are those who support applying all crimes of intention to cases of "foresight of certainty"[20] and there are those who would not apply any crime of intention to cases of "foresight of certainty".[21] Others think that the law of oblique intention may vary from offence to offence.[22] Other positions can be found as well.[23]

Since there is a debate as to whether "foresight of certainty" should be equated with "acting in order to cause the result", and since there is also a view according to which the law of "foresight of certainty" should vary from one "intention-crime" to another, many feel that we should have a term of art to designate cases of foresight of certainty (without desire). Hence, it is common to refer to cases of foresight of certainty (without purpose) as cases in which there is *oblique* intention, or *indirect* intention, as opposed to *direct* intention which is defined in terms of desire or purpose. In this book I will use the term "oblique intention".[24]

1.3.3 How to Deal with the Problem of Oblique Intention in Interpreting Current Criminal Offences

So what should the law be concerning oblique intention? I think that in addressing this question it may be fruitful to think first about the reason for having "crimes of intention" in the first place. Suppose a court has to construe a statutory "basic crime of intention".[25] If the legislator required intention it seems that he intended that recklessness not suffice for conviction. Let us assume that the legislator did not think about the case of foresight of certainty when he enacted this offence. He intended that there not be a conviction when the actor acts with foresight of possibility or probability, and that there be a conviction in cases of desire, but he simply did not think about the cases of "foresight of certainty" (without desire). Let us assume further that the court has the right to apply "crimes of intention" to cases of oblique intention (i.e. there is no prohibition against stretching the language of offences a little or, alternatively, the suggested application does not involve stretching the language of the law). It seems that it is useful, in such a case, to ask first why the legislator decided that in this offence recklessness should not suffice for conviction. Since, as will be explained in chapter 2, in "basic offences" recklessness should as a matter of policy generally suffice for conviction (and indeed usually suffices for conviction under conventional law), we should inquire why in the "basic crime of intention" under discussion the legislator decided that recklessness should not suffice. If we have an answer to this question, then we can proceed to deal with the question of oblique intention. If we find that the reason for exempting the reckless actor from liability in the offence before us is A, then we can ask what A implies for cases of oblique intention. Does reason A equally apply to cases of foresight of certainty as it does to cases of recklessness? If so, we have a very good reason to decide that the actor who has foresight of certainty should be exempted from liability. But if we find that the logic underlying reason A does not apply to cases of foresight of certainty, then we have a good reason to apply the offence under discussion to cases of oblique intention. Now, it might be the case that there are various potential reasons for exempting reckless people from criminal liability, and consequently it might be the case that the reason for which the legislator required intention varies from offence to offence. It might also be the case that some reasons for exempting reckless people are applicable to cases of oblique intention, while others are not applicable to them. If so, we have a good reason for taking the view that the law of cases of oblique intention should vary from offence to offence, following the reason lying behind the requirement of intention in the crime under discussion. We should also be aware of the possibility that in discussing the implications of reason A for cases of oblique intention we might find out that the case of oblique intention is an intermediate one, between direct intention and recklessness. If this should be the case, we may think that the court will have to use its discretion or, in the alternative, that it will have to acquit, as the logic underlying the crime under discussion does not necessarily dictate a conviction, in which case the accused should have the benefit of the doubt.

The above method of interpretation may also be used when the legislator distinguishes between intention and recklessness in grading offences. If there is a crime of recklessly causing x, and an aggravated one of intentionally causing x, then we can try to understand why the legislator thought that the punishment for causing the result intentionally should be more severe than the punishment for causing the result recklessly. The answer to this question may be of help in deciding whether one who acts with oblique intention should be convicted of the aggravated crime or the lesser one.

Of course, I am aware of the fact that the aforementioned approach is not the only reasonable one. For example: Some may think that courts should not be confined to the reasons which originally led the legislator to require intention and that they should have the right to develop their own philosophy regarding questions of policy and justice that arise in cases of oblique intention. I am also aware of the fact that it may sometimes be impossible to discover what actually led the legislator to require intention in the offence under discussion and that in such cases the court can but speculate on the question. Nevertheless, I think that the above method is good, at least as a starting point, when proceeding to interpret a crime of intention.

1.3.4 *The Problem of Oblique Intention in Legislating a Criminal Code*

The issue of oblique intention may arise not only within the courts but also within the legislative process. Suppose that we are asked to compose a new criminal code made up of both a general and a special part. What should we do concerning the mental element? Let us concentrate on crimes in which negligence as to the proscribed result should not suffice for conviction. One possibility is to decide that in all those crimes recklessness as to the proscribed result should suffice for conviction. There would be no crimes of intention in the code. In such a case, the question what to do with cases of oblique intention will not arise at all. But suppose we come to the conclusion that we should have some crimes of intention in our code. This means that our code will include some crimes in which recklessness does not suffice for conviction. Then we have to decide what to do with cases of oblique intention. Here three possibilities arise. First we can decide that in all "intention-crimes" oblique intention will suffice for conviction. Second, we can decide that liability for "intention-crimes" will not obtain in cases of oblique intention. Or, third, we can decide that oblique intention will suffice as to *some* "intention-crimes". If we adopt the first position, then the term "intention" can be defined in the general part as including not only direct intention but also oblique intention, so that the term "intention" may be used in all "intention-crimes". If we adopt the second position, then the term "intention" can be defined in the general part as including only direct intention, so that the term "intention" may be used in all "intention-crimes". But if we adopt the third position, then two separate terms should appear in the general part: one for offences in which only direct intention suffices and one for offences in which both kinds of intention suffice. After defining the two terms, we will then have to decide as to every crime of intention, which of the two terms should be used.

The Model Penal Code adopts the third position.[26] In section 2.02(2) we find definitions of four kinds of culpability: purpose, knowledge, recklessness, and negligence. A person acts purposely with respect to a result of his conduct if it is his conscious object to cause such a result. A person acts knowingly with respect to a result if he is aware that it is practically certain that his conduct will cause such a result. So acting purposely is acting with "direct intention" and acting "knowingly" is acting with "oblique intention". The Code also defines recklessness[27] and negligence. Section 2.02(3) provides that when the culpability sufficient to establish a material element of an offence is not prescribed by law, such an element is established if a person acts purposely, knowingly or recklessly with respect thereto. Section 2.02(5) provides, inter alia, that when recklessness suffices to establish an element such element also is established if a person acts purposely or knowingly, and that when acting knowingly suffices to establish an element such element also is established if a person acts purposely.

The Code thus distinguishes between two kinds of offences in which recklessness as to a result does not suffice for conviction. In some offences only "purpose" (direct intention) suffices. In others, acting "knowingly" (with oblique intention) suffices. In the second kind of offences, direct intention also suffices, as specified in section 2.02(5).[28] And, indeed, in the special part of the Model Penal Code you can find offences of the two kinds.[29]

In England, the Draft Criminal Code Bill of 1985 adopted a similar position. It provides in section 22 that a person acts "purposely" in respect to an element of an offence when he wants it to exist or to occur, and "intentionally" when he either wants it to exist or to occur, or is aware that it exists or is almost certain that it exists or will exist or occur.[30] This means that in crimes where recklessness with respect to the result does not suffice for conviction there is sometimes a requirement of "purpose" with respect to the result, i.e. a requirement of direct intention, and sometimes a requirement of "intention" with respect to the result, i.e. a requirement that can be satisfied either by direct intention or by oblique intention. In the Report of the Criminal Code team it is explained that the term "purposely" is needed to enable the enactment of offences in which only *direct* intention should suffice for conviction. The Report mentions as examples several offences (that are not included in the special part of the draft Bill) concerning which it was held or proposed in the past that oblique intention does not suffice for conviction.[31]

The Draft Criminal Code for England and Wales of 1989 does not include the term "purpose" in the list of fault terms appearing in the general part. Clause 18 mentions only two fault terms with respect to results: "intentionally" and "recklessly". According to this clause a person acts "intentionally" with respect to a result "when he acts either in order to bring it about or being aware that it will occur in the ordinary course of events". At first glance, it seems that the framers of the Draft Code were sure that there would never be an offence with respect to which it would be appropriate to only hold direct intention as sufficient for conviction. But this is not the case. As the commentary on the Draft Criminal Code explains, the fault terms provided for under clause 18 are neither exclusive nor binding. Future legislation, like the Code itself, may use fault terms other than those defined by the clause. Future legislation can also modify the meaning of any of the Code terms for the purpose of specific offences. This means, the commentary continues, that clauses 18 and 20 "require the draftsman of any future offence to give active consideration to the question of fault" without, however, dictating the outcome of that consideration. Thus, the commentary clarifies that if a number of offences in the special part of the Code had required "purpose" (i.e. direct intention) for conviction, this term and its definition would very likely have been included in the Code's list of fault terms. However, the commentary explains, "purpose" did not prove necessary for the definitions of offences proposed for inclusion in the Code, as first enacted. Nevertheless, the commentary continues, the list of fault terms defined at clause 18 is not a closed one, and additions may be made in the future, if that would prove useful for the Code as a whole.[32] Note also that clause 18 does not apply to "pre-Code offences".[33]

In Canada, the proposed draft Criminal Code of 1987 contains three fault terms concerning consequences: purpose, recklessness and negligence. Purpose as to a consequence is defined so as to include not only direct intention but also oblique intention.[34] This means that all offences in the draft Code requiring purpose can be satisfied by oblique intention, and not only by direct intention. Although future legislation can always derogate from this principle, nothing in the commentary is said about this. Hence, it is reasonable to assume that the framers of this draft Code thought that there should be no offence concerning which only direct intention (as opposed to oblique intention) should suffice for conviction.

1.3.5   *How to Deal with the Problem of Oblique Intention in Legislating a Criminal Code*

So what position should the legislator of a criminal code take concerning oblique intention? I think that in addressing this issue, it is desirable for the legislator to follow a method similar to the one discussed above regarding the interpretation of current "intention-crimes". As will be explained in chapter 2, recklessness should generally suffice for conviction in "basic crimes". This means that when those who prepare the code are dealing with the formulation of a basic crime they should begin with the presumption that recklessness as to the forbidden result should suffice for conviction. A decision that in a certain offence recklessness should not suffice for conviction, and that only intention should suffice, should only be taken if there is a special reason to support it. If the framers of the code cannot clearly explain to themselves why, in the crime under discussion, recklessness should not suffice, they should determine that recklessness suffices. But if they find a reason to require intention (desire) as to a certain crime, then they should also ask themselves a further question: What are the implications of this reason for cases of oblique intention? Does the reason for exempting the reckless actor (as opposed to the one who wants the result to ensue) from criminal liability dictate that the one who has oblique intention should also be exempted? If the answer is "yes" then the framers should decide that for that offence only direct intention suffices for conviction. But if the reason for exempting the reckless actor does not apply to cases of oblique intention – or, in other words, if the reason for convicting the actor who has direct intention also applies to cases of oblique intention – then the framers should determine that in that offence oblique intention (and not only direct intention) suffices for conviction. A similar method can be used in grading offences. Suppose the framers want to create two offences, one of recklessly causing x and one of intentionally (i.e. with direct intention) causing x, with a harsher punishment being provided for the latter offence. Before doing so, they have to explain to themselves what is the rationale for such grading in liability. Indeed if they do not have a good reason for such a grading in liability, why differentiate between the intentional actor and the reckless one? Once the underlying justification for the grading is elucidated, they have to ask themselves another question: What does the reason that led to the grading imply for cases of oblique intention? According to the logic underlying the grading, does oblique intention resemble direct intention or recklessness? The answer to this question should determine whether causing x with oblique intention should be included within the aggravated offence or the lesser one.

Now if there are various potential reasons for requiring intention in criminal offences, it might be the case that the suggested process will lead to the conclusion that the law as to cases of oblique intention should vary from one crime of intention to the other, corresponding with the reason invoked for requiring intention in the crime under discussion. If this is the case, then the framers should include in the general part of the code two different terms for intention as to results: one for offences in which only direct intention suffices, and another for offences in which either direct intention or oblique intention suffices. These terms could then be used in specific offence definitions. Note that the fact that the law of cases of oblique intention may vary from offence to offence does not present a problem of lack of predictability, as the solution for cases of oblique intention will clearly appear in the various offence definitions.

If, in contrast to the above assumption, there is only one reason for requiring intention in criminal offences, then this will presumably lead us to the conclusion that the law as to cases of oblique intention will be the same for all crimes of intention. Alternatively, it may be the case that, although there are various reasons for requiring intention in criminal offences, all of them lead to the same conclusion concerning cases of oblique intention. If, after considering all of the offences in the code, the framers come to the conclusion that the law as to cases of oblique intention should be the same for all crimes of intention, they will not have to include in the general part more than one term for intention as to results.

I am aware of the fact that the method suggested here for dealing with oblique intention when framing a criminal code is not the only reasonable one. Still, I believe that it is a good one. I am also aware that even if we use this method in framing a code, it will not always be very simple to derive the right solution to cases of oblique intention from the reason for requiring intention. Sometimes things will prove to be more complex. Nonetheless, I think it is desirable to adopt the above method, at least as a starting point for the discussion of each specific offence. Sometimes this method will plainly yield the solution to the question of oblique intention. In other cases complexities may arise; yet even in these cases the suggested method will help us to understand the roots of the complexity and, in turn, to better deal with it. In this book, I will use the above method. The purpose of this book is to explore what the law as to cases of oblique intention should be. In order to deal with this question theoretically and freely, I decided not to write as dealing with the problem of how to interpret "crimes of intention" in this or that country. When interpreting a statute one sometimes must take into consideration the language of the statute and perhaps the actual intention of the legislator. So in order to concentrate on considerations of justice and policy, I decided to ask what the framers of a completely new criminal code should do concerning cases of oblique intention. And when dealing with this question I will adopt the method suggested above. Of course, although the book is written with the legislator in mind, courts may use it when interpreting "crimes of intention".

From what I have said above, it is clear that a key issue in this book will be whether there are reasonable reasons at all to enact "crimes of intention" in the first place. Since I will deal with this question extensively, this book should be viewed as not only about "oblique intention" but also about criminal intention in general. But here I have to clarify that I am not going to deal with all the potential reasons for requiring intention in criminal offences. When asking why distinguish between intention and recklessness the first answer that comes to mind is related to degrees of blameworthiness. It is sometimes said that a person who intends to cause the proscribed result is more blameworthy than the person who acts with recklessness. In this book I will limit myself to the subject of degrees of blameworthiness. I do believe there are other potential reasons for distinguishing between intention and recklessness that are not related to degrees of blameworthiness, but I will not deal with them in this book. It is also worth mentioning that I am not dealing with "intention" as to the circumstances of criminal offences but only with intention as to consequences.

Before concluding this introduction I would like to refer to the issue of the degree of probability. I have assumed thus far that in order for an actor who does not want a result to ensue to be considered as acting with oblique intention, it is not enough that he foresee the result as probable or even highly probable. Only foresight of practical certainty should suffice. It seems that many scholars share this view, although in the past some thought that probability or high probability is enough.[35] Williams, for example, maintains that foresight of a high probability should not suffice,[36] even if the actor is "almost certain" that the result will ensue.[37] He does not require absolute certainty but thinks that practical certainty,[38] that can also be called virtual certainty,[39] or human certainty,[40] or moral certainty,[41] should suffice. Practical certainty, he explains, is present when the outcome is so certain that nothing short of a "miracle" (i.e. a wholly extraordinary chance) can prevent it;[42] it is a degree of probability so high that common sense would view it as certain (mere philosophical doubt, or the intervention of extraordinary chance, is to be ignored).[43] The Model Penal Code, like Williams, requires that the actor be aware that it is practically certain that his conduct will cause the result.[44]

In this book I will accept the definition of oblique intention as foresight of practical certainty (and not merely of high probability) that the result will ensue. I will understand it as present when there is such a high degree of probability that ordinary people treat it in their everyday life as absolute certainty. Although a philosopher may doubt whether the sun will rise tomorrow, ordinary people behave as if there is absolute certainty that the sun will rise. Although objectively there is a difference between absolute certainty and practical certainty, psychologically there is no difference between them in the minds of ordinary people in their regular affairs.

I do not deny that there might be an offence for the purpose of which we should equate foresight of a high degree of probability with direct intention. But I prefer to concentrate in this book on foresight of practical certainty, because I want to proceed step by step and not jump from one question to another. Foresight of practical certainty can be viewed by some as being different in quality from foresight of possibility (which is enough for recklessness) and therefore it has a higher chance of being equated with direct intention than foresight of high probability, which differs from foresight of possibility only in degree. Therefore in this book I will concentrate on foresight of practical certainty.

Notes

1   Smith and Hogan (1999) 61. Under current English law there is also another kind of recklessness, the Caldwell-type recklessness. This kind of recklessness can be established even when the actor is not actually aware of the risk. The English law now is that some offences of recklessness require subjective recklessness while others are satisfied by Caldwell-type recklessness. See Smith and Hogan (1999) 60-63, 66-67. Smith and Hogan recommend that the current English law be modified to adopt the position that there is only one type of recklessness – the subjective one (ibid., at 67).

2   Law Commission: *A Criminal Code for England and Wales* (1989), Law Com No 177.

3   I will refer later to cases in which the actor does not want the proscribed result to ensue but foresees it as practically certain and not only as a possibility.

4   For example: According to clause 67(1) of the Draft Criminal Code for England and Wales (1989) a pregnant woman is guilty of an offence if she intentionally causes her own miscarriage (otherwise than in accordance with the provisions of the Abortion Act 1967). But if she only acts recklessly, there is no crime at all.

5   On crimes of ulterior intent see Smith and Hogan (1999) 70-71. An example would be the offence of doing an act with intent to impede the apprehension of a person who has committed an arrestable offence (Smith and Hogan (1999) 162). I am not dealing in this book with crimes of ulterior intent in which the ulterior intent is to perform a subsequent act, such as entering a building as a trespasser with intent to steal anything in the building.

6   For the definition of intention by using the terms of desire and wish, see for example Williams (1965) 10; Williams (1987) 417-418.

7   Williams (1961) 35; Williams (1965) 14; Gordon (1978) 222-223.

8   See Goff (1988) 42; Stannard (1986) 69; Hall (1960) 111-112; Card, Cross and Jones (1998) 45.

9   Card, Cross and Jones (1998) 46; Stannard (1986) 69; Dennis (1987) 54; Dennis (1988) 650; Cross (1967) 223.

10   Dennis (1987) 54; Fried (1978) 22. See also Duff (1989) 78.

11   Williams (1983a) 74; Williams (1987) 418 (Williams says here that the replacement of "desire" with "purpose" doesn't change anything because purpose implies desire).

12   Duff (1989) 78. Cf. Audi (1973) 389-392.

13   See Duff (1989) 78.

14   Clause 18 of the draft Code. (Here I only deal with "direct intention". I will deal later with the case of foresight of the result as certain without acting in order to achieve it). The Model Penal Code also avoids using the terms "want" or "desire" in its definitions of the mental elements applying to results. It says that a person acts purposely with respect to a result when it is his conscious object to cause such a result. See Model Penal Code (1985), section 2.02(2)(a).

15   LaFave and Scott (1986) 223; Williams (1961) 50.

16   Smith and Hogan (1999) 610. For applying the same rule to another offence see ibid., at 166. There can be exceptions to the rule mentioned in the text. The legislator may

require explicitly in the definition of a certain offence that the intent to cause a certain result should be the sole intention of the actor in doing what he has done (or in another offence he may require that the purpose of causing a specific result should be the dominant purpose of the actor in doing what he did). For American codes that required in the past that the proscribed intent be the only intent of the actor in an offence that required intent to prevent apprehension of an offender see Model Penal Code and Commentaries (1980) Part 2, vol. 3, at p. 229. For the possibility of requiring in an offence that the actor published materials with the predominant purpose of insulting the feelings of religious believers see: The Law Commission, Working Paper No. 79, *Offences against Religion and Public Worship* (1981) 114. Moreover, it seems that the courts may create exceptions to the general rule by interpreting a certain "crime of intention" as requiring that the proscribed purpose be the dominant (or the sole) purpose of the actor, even when the language of the statute speaks of intent to cause a result, without mention of this additional requirement. Cf. Williams (1961) 50.

17   The linguistic question whether cases of "foresight of certainty" (unaccompanied by purpose) constitute cases in which there is intention is debated among both jurists and philosophers. Some maintain that the term intention encompasses cases of "foresight of certainty" while others reject this view. Others think that there are two senses in ordinary speech to the term "intention" and that cases of "foresight of certainty" are only covered by the broad sense of intention. Others suggest that we have to distinguish between sentences in which "intention" appears according to their structure. For example: If a person puts a time bomb not in order to cause the death of a person but with the practical certitude that his act will bring about the death of a person, then we cannot say that he puts the bomb "with intent" to cause the death of a person. However if the bomb does cause the death of a person, then we can say that the above actor caused the death intentionally. This short summary does not exhaust all of the existing views on the subject; nor does it cover all the ways in which the word "intention" appears in sentences. I will not discuss the linguistic question further, as this question is without importance for the discussion in this book which concentrates on considerations of justice and policy.

18   Note that where there is a desire to cause the result, the conviction is not dependent on the result being foreseen with a degree that is higher than a mere possibility. If the actor acts in order to bring about the result there is intention, even if he thinks that the chances of succeeding in causing the result are very low. See for example Smith and Hogan (1999) 54.

19   A variation of this position is that the general rule should be that "intention-crimes" apply to cases of "foresight of certainty" but that courts have the discretion not to apply this rule to specific exceptional offences.

20   Smith seems to imply this in Smith (1978) 21. Cf. Feller (1970) 358-359.

21   Cf. Dennis (1987) 54-55.

22   In Williams (1983a) at 86, it is said that although the general rule should be that "foresight of certainty" be equated with intention, the courts should have the right not to apply the rule where it runs contrary to the purpose of the law or justice. Also in Williams (1987) at 435-437 it is said that courts should generally interpret a requirement of intent to include "foresight of certainty", but exceptionally, where justice so requires, to exclude it. He also gives three examples of exceptional contexts in which intention should not be interpreted to include foresight of certainty. See also Card, Cross and Jones (1998) 55.

23   For example: In the past, it was sometimes suggested that "intention" in criminal offences (or at least in some of them) should be interpreted to include not only foresight of practical certainty but also foresight of high probability or even foresight of probability (as distinguished from mere possibility). This position was also taken on occasion by the courts in England. See for example Buzzard (1978) 5-13; Smith and Hogan (1983) 47-51. Another example may be found in current English law. Until recently the leading case was *Nedrick*, which seemed to say that foresight of virtual certainty (without purpose) is not by itself intention, though the jury *may* (but not must) nevertheless infer from this foresight that the accused acted with intention. See *Nedrick* (1986) 83 Cr App R 267. The problem here is that it is not clear exactly what the jury have to try to infer from the facts under consideration. For if there is no purpose, and if foresight of certainty is not equated with intention, what is the mysterious ingredient the jury is supposed to look for in order to conclude that there is an intention in the case before them? This ingredient was not defined in *Nedrick*. As commented in Card, Cross and Jones: "The courts have not stated what the mystery ingredient is that can be inferred from foresight so as to convert foresight (which is not intention) into intention". See Card, Cross and Jones (1998) 53. I share the view of many scholars that *Nedrick* was highly problematic. See Card, Cross and Jones ibid.; Ashworth (1995a) 172; Smith (1986) 182; Williams (1987) 434. Recently the House of Lords delivered a judgment on the intention issue in *Woollin* [1999] AC 82. The House of Lords decided that, in cases in which there is no purpose to cause the result and the result is foreseen as virtually certain to ensue, the law is not that the jury may *infer* intention from foresight of certainty, but that it is entitled to *find* intention (ibid. at 96). But, in spite of the replacement of "inferring" with "finding", the legal situation is still problematic, for the House of Lords did not provide that in a case of foresight of certainty (when there is no purpose to cause the result) the jury is *bound* to find intention. It seems from the judgment that even after *Woollin* the jury is *entitled* (and not bound) to find intention, which implies that the jury is also entitled *not* to find it. As J.C. Smith puts it: "The *Nedrick* formula, however, even as modified ('entitled to find'), involves some ambiguity with the hint of the existence of some ineffable, undefinable, notion of intent, locked in the breasts of the jurors" (Smith (1998) 891). One might suggest that the House of Lords refrained from equating foresight of certainty with intention, in order to give the jury some moral discretion so that it not be compelled to convict of "intention-crimes" in those exceptional cases where such a conviction is not justified, in spite of the actor's foresight of certainty (cf. Horder (1995) 687. See Ashworth (1999) 182). But if this is the case, then the law should be formulated in terms that make it clear to the jury that it is given moral discretion and not in terms that imply that it is required to determine whether a mysterious and undefinable mental state exists. On *Woollin* see also Wilson (1999).
It should also be noted that in *Woollin* Lord Steyn remarked that "intent" does not necessarily have precisely the same meaning in every context in the criminal law, and that the focus of the appeal in *Woollin* is the crime of murder. This leaves open the possibility that in the context of crimes other than murder the legal meaning of intention will be different from that provided in *Woollin* (see Smith (1998) 892).
Finally I should add that it seems that in *Re A (children) (conjoined twins: surgical separation)* [2000] 4 All ER 961, Ward LJ (and probably Brooke LJ as well) understood *Woollin* as establishing that in murder foresight of virtual certainty *constitutes* intention (i.e. that in murder "intention" includes not only purpose but also foresight of virtual certainty, and there is no room, in cases of foresight of virtual

certainty, for jury discretion concerning the existence of intention). See ibid. at 1012 and 1029.

24   Following Williams (1987) 420-421. Some use the term "oblique intention" as also encompassing cases where the actor does not want the result but foresees it as probable or highly probable. But I will only use the term "oblique intention" for cases of foresight of "virtual certainty" or "practical certainty" and not for cases of foresight of probability or high probability.

25   My discussion here relates to a jurisdiction that does not have a statutory definition of "intention".

26   Model Penal Code (1985).

27   The definition of recklessness in the Model Penal Code differs slightly from the one I adopted at the beginning of this chapter (which is based on the English tradition and the Draft Criminal Code for England and Wales of 1989). In the Model Penal Code, the risk that the result will ensue has to be substantial and the disregard of the risk has to involve a *gross* deviation from the standard of conduct that a law-abiding person would observe in the actor's situation. See Model Penal Code (1985), section 2.02(2)(c). In this book I will use the term "recklessness" as defined earlier, at the beginning of this chapter (following the English tradition).

28   This clarification is not redundant because in many cases a person acting with direct intention does not foresee the result as certain but only as possible. It is also worth mentioning that section 1.13(11) provides that acting "with purpose" has the same meaning as acting "purposely", and that section 1.13(13) provides that acting "with knowledge" has the same meaning as acting "knowingly". This means that the two kinds of offences exist not only in the realm of offences conditioned upon the actual occurrence of a result but also in the realm of "ulterior intent" crimes.

29   Examples can be found infra in chapter 2 (note 15) and in section 11.4 (example C, and at note 31). See also chapter 11, at note 45.

30   Draft Criminal Code Bill (1985).

31   Law Commission: Codification of the Criminal Law, A Report to the Law Commission (1985) p. 65.

32   Law Commission: A Criminal Code for England and Wales, vol. 2, Commentary on Draft Criminal Code Bill (1989) p. 191.

33   As explained ibid.

34   See Report on Recodifying Criminal Law (1987), clause 2(4)(b) at p. 23. The draft code provides that a person acts purposely as to a consequence if he acts in order to effect : (A) that consequence; or (B) another consequence which he knows involves that consequence. The commentary (at p. 24) explains that option B is intended to cover cases of oblique intention. Note that the formulation of option (B) is such that it may extend the notion of "oblique intention" to cases that are not covered by the definition I have used thus far. By the definition I have used thus far, "oblique intention" exists when at the time of his action, a person foresees it as practically certain that the proscribed result will ensue from his action (and he does not act *in order* to bring it about). If the actor does not want to bring about a result *y* and at the time he acts he only foresees a probability that *y* will occur, then he is only reckless. Now, suppose an actor is doing something in order to cause a result *x,* and he knows there is only a 50% chance that he will succeed in bringing it about. Suppose also that when he acts he knows that *if x* happens, it is practically certain that *y* will also happen (*y* is the proscribed result in the offence under discussion). Should we treat this person as having oblique intention for purposes of criminal law or should we treat him as

acting with recklessness? By the definition of oblique intention used thus far, this person is only reckless. He does not act *in order* to cause *y* (but only in order to cause *x*, which is not the proscribed result) and when he acts he knows that there is, at most, only a 50% chance that *y* will be caused by his action. The definitions of oblique intention from the Model Penal Code and from the English draft codes of 1985 and 1989 mentioned above also require that when the actor acts he foresee the proscribed result as practically certain (or almost certain), so that the case described above would not fall under these definitions. But the definition of the proposed Canadian Code seems to imply that the case above is a case of oblique intention and that a person who acts with the above state of mind should be convicted of any offence in which oblique intention suffices for conviction. Smith thinks that such a person should indeed be treated as having an oblique intention and he also says that according to the Canadian clause this person is indeed deemed to have an oblique intention. See Smith (1990) 86, 88. Since inclusion of the case above in the definition of "oblique intention" is disputed, I will only deal in this book with oblique intention as I have defined it thus far. It is better to proceed step by step, and explore first what the law should be in clear cases of "oblique intention" and only later deal with the cases discussed above. So in this book I will continue to use the term "oblique intention" in the same sense that I have used it thus far.

35 See supra note 23.
36 Williams (1987) 421; Williams (1978) 589.
37 Williams (1987) 422.
38 Williams (1987) 421; Williams (1983a) 85; Williams (1978) 588.
39 Williams (1987) 422; Williams (1983a) 85; Williams (1978) 588.
40 Williams (1983a) 85.
41 Williams (1965) 35; Williams (1961) 40. For moral certainty see also Smith (1978) 21.
42 Williams (1965) 35.
43 Williams (1961) 40. See also Williams (1987) 421.
44 Model Penal Code (1985), section 2.02(2)(b).

PART ONE

Chapter 2

Intention and Degrees of Blameworthiness – An Introductory Discussion

2.1 Distinguishing between the Use of Intention to Grade Crimes and Basic Crimes of Intention

What should the legislator do concerning cases of oblique intention? In chapter 1, I suggested that he should first ask himself whether it is appropriate to enact "crimes of intention" in the first place. Why should we treat intention and recklessness differently? Wouldn't it be better if recklessness sufficed for all crimes?[1] If the legislator has a reason to require direct intention for a certain offence, then he can proceed to inquire as to the implications for oblique intention. The first potential reason that comes to mind for treating direct intention and recklessness differently in criminal offences has to do with degrees of moral blameworthiness. It is common to say that a person who acts in order to cause a proscribed result is more blameworthy than a person who only takes an unjustified risk that the same result will ensue (i.e., who is reckless). But even if we assume that there is a difference between the blameworthiness of a person acting with direct intention and that of a person acting with recklessness – and even if we also assume that this difference can justify the grading of offences along the lines drawn by the distinction between direct intention and recklessness – we still have to ask ourselves whether there is a valid reason to enact *basic* crimes of intention. Many think that the main purpose of the criminal law is to protect against harms by general deterrence. In order to protect against harms the legislator enacts criminal offences that contain a prohibition against doing certain acts, together with a threat of punishment. The legislator hopes that people will be deterred by the threat of punishment and act accordingly. If this is the case, it seems that recklessness should suffice for conviction in "basic crimes". The legislator must not only deter people who are going to cause harms purposely but also people who are going to take unjustified risks of causing harms. Take, for example, the offence of "causing bodily harm to a person". If in a certain country there is no offence of causing bodily harm recklessly (but only an offence of causing it intentionally) then the criminal law of that country does not act as a deterrent against acting recklessly as to causing bodily harm, and consequently the protection afforded to the value of bodily integrity is not sufficient in that country. A person who plans to clear his roof and, in the process, to throw heavy stones on the street with the awareness that by doing so he might cause bodily harm to people walking on the street, will not feel threatened by the criminal law, and this might lead him to act in the described manner and to cause bodily harm. Thus, in order to adequately protect the bodily integrity of people, we need to have an offence of causing bodily harm recklessly. It seems that the argument above applies (at least at first glance) to all crimes the definition of which contains an actual or potential result element. The goal of ensuring adequate protection against harms will only be achieved if people are deterred both from causing them purposely and from causing them recklessly.[2] Of course, even if the main purpose of the criminal law is general deterrence, justice and fairness require that we not convict and punish morally innocent people, even if doing so would contribute in some way to an increase in general deterrence.[3] Hence the common idea that criminal liability should generally not attach unless the actor has a culpable state of mind when he is acting.[4] But it seems that the reckless actor, who knowingly takes an unjustified risk that the result will ensue, is sufficiently morally blameworthy, to permit conviction and punishment for the purpose of general deterrence.[5] Hence, the very common idea that recklessness should suffice for conviction in "basic crimes".[6] Indeed, in some criminal codes the general part contains a provision to the effect that when the definition of an offence does not specify the mental element required, recklessness suffices for conviction.[7] Such provisions seem to proceed on the assumption that recklessness is the mental element that should suffice in most offences. It follows from the discussion above that even if we assume that there is more moral blameworthiness in acting with direct intention than in acting with recklessness, the idea of having *basic* crimes of intention is highly problematic, and it is perfectly reasonable to have a criminal code with no basic crimes of intention at all.[8] The situation is different, however, in deliberating whether to grade offences according to the distinction between intention and recklessness. Here the discussion starts with the assumption that liability in cases of recklessness will be provided for, so that a deterrent against acting recklessly will be secured. The idea of grading would then be designed to merely provide for an increase in punishment for acting with intention. It is a common idea that in using their discretion in sentencing specific offenders, judges take (and should take) into consideration the degree of the moral blameworthiness of the offender, as the severity of punishment should be proportional to the degree of the offender's moral culpability.[9] If we accept this idea, then it also seems reasonable to suggest that the legislator grade offences by degrees of blameworthiness and that the penalty for more heinous acts be more severe than the penalty for less heinous acts.[10] So, if we believe that those who act with direct intention are morally more blameworthy than those who act recklessly, then we might want to grade offences according to the distinction between intention and recklessness. Because it is easier to understand why the distinction between intention and recklessness would be used for the purpose of grading offences than to understand why "basic crimes of intention" would be enacted, I will deal first with the issue of grading and leave the issue of "basic crimes of intention" to Part Two of the book. So my discussion in the first part will be devoted to the question whether the legislator should grade offences according to the distinction between direct intention and recklessness, and if so – what he should do concerning cases of oblique intention.

2.2 Examples of the Use of Intention in Grading Offences

Before I proceed further in the discussion, I would like first to bring some examples where the distinction between intention and recklessness is used to grade offences. The Draft Criminal Code for England and Wales of 1989 has two separate offences of causing serious personal harm to another. One offence deals with cases where the forbidden result is intentionally caused and the other with cases where it is caused recklessly. The maximum punishment provided for the first offence is higher than that provided for the second one.[11] In Canada, the proposed draft Criminal Code of 1987 distinguishes, inter alia, between the crime of purposely causing the death of another person (Murder) and the crime of recklessly causing the same result (Manslaughter).[12] The first one is considered more serious and is intended to carry a higher penalty than the second.[13] In the Model Penal Code,[14] a person who starts a fire or causes an explosion *with the purpose* of destroying a building or occupied structure of another is guilty of a felony of the second degree under section 220.1(1)(a), while according to section 220.1(2)(b), a person who purposely starts a fire or causes an explosion and thereby *recklessly* places a building or occupied structure of another in danger of destruction, is only guilty of a felony of the third degree.[15]

2.3 Subjecting to Scrutiny the Idea that Acting with Intention is More Blameworthy than Acting with Recklessness

I now return to the question whether the legislator should grade offences according to the distinction between direct intention and recklessness, and if so – what he should do concerning cases of oblique intention. The first potential reason that leaps to mind for grading offences according to the distinction between direct intention and recklessness relates to degrees of moral blameworthiness. In this book I will concentrate on this potential rationale. As I said earlier (supra in 2.1), if it is correct that causing a certain proscribed result intentionally is morally more blameworthy than causing it recklessly, then it seems reasonable to grade offences according to this difference. So the first question to be addressed is whether it is a well founded assumption that the person who acts with direct intention is morally more culpable than the person who acts with recklessness.[16] I now turn to this question.

It is common to find in the literature the idea that there is more moral blameworthiness in causing a proscribed result intentionally than in causing it recklessly.[17] But is this correct? I will now subject this idea to critical scrutiny by adducing a number of hypothetical situations in which the reckless actor appears to be morally more culpable than the one who acts with intent to bring about the proscribed result. I will advance three sets of two imaginary cases in order to make my point. Of course, in each set the amount of harm caused (and foreseen) by the defendant in the two cases will remain constant. That means that I will not deal, for example, with the case in which a person recklessly causes a grievous bodily harm that is much more serious than the grievous bodily harm intentionally caused by another person. Nor will I invoke the case in which a person recklessly causes damage of $100,000 to the property of another to show that this person is more culpable than the one who intentionally causes damage of $100 to the property of another. I will not use such examples because, as the latter two cases illustrate, though the first person may be considered more blameworthy than the second, this does not further us in our inquiry, because the difference in the amount of the damage caused (or in the severity of the bodily harm) explains why the reckless actor is considered more blameworthy.

1. John takes a gun and shoots at his little son in order to kill him and, in this way, to relieve him of the extreme pain he has to endure on account of an incurable disease (suppose there is no other way of relieving him of the pain). The son is killed.

    Sam wants to practice in marksmanship. He puts an apple on the head of his little son and shoots with a gun intending to hit the apple but knowing that there is a substantial risk that he will miss and kill his son. He misses and kills him.

2. Sally is brutally raped by a man. The rape destroys her life, and changes it from happy to miserable. The rapist is caught and prosecuted but is acquitted on a procedural technicality. After the trial, the rapist is interviewed in the newspapers and ridicules Sally. He tells lies, describes her as licentious, and claims that she actually seduced him. Sally decides to take revenge by causing grievous harm to the rapist's leg. She takes a gun and shoots at his leg in order to cause it grievous harm, and succeeds in doing so.

    Sara makes a $100 bet with a friend that she can shoot towards a doorstep with a person standing on it and hit the step without causing the person any harm. She takes a gun and shoots towards a step with a person standing on it (the person does not know anything about what is going to happen). She hopes that no harm will be caused but she knows that there is a substantial risk that grievous harm will be caused to the person's leg. Indeed, this is what happens.

3. A person dies and his son inherits two objects of equal monetary value. The first object is a manuscript of a book about the life of George, a famous individual. George knows that the manuscript is full of lies and that, if published, it would destroy both his family life and professional career. By the law of the land, he is unable to prevent the publication of the book by legal means. Though he may receive compensation afterwards, it will be too late to save his family life and career. So he comes to the conclusion that he has to destroy the manuscript. He decides to act in order to destroy the manuscript, and does so.

    The second object inherited by the son is a very valuable vase. During a visit, the son's friend Peter wants to amuse himself by throwing the vase in the air and catching it, and does so (the son does not see him though). He hopes that nothing will happen but he knows that there is a substantial risk that the vase will fall on the floor and get shattered to pieces. And, indeed, this is what happens.

In the cases above, the first actor in every set acts with intent to cause the harm, while the second is reckless. Nevertheless, many would agree, I believe, that in every set the reckless actor is morally more culpable than the one who acts with intent to cause the harm. And we could advance many other examples in which the reckless actor is the more blameworthy one. One may conclude, therefore, that the idea that a person who acts with intent to cause harm is morally more culpable than the person who acts with recklessness with respect to the same harm, is false. And, indeed, if this idea is false then we should not grade offences based on the distinction between intention and recklessness, if this grading is supposed to be based on a moral difference between the two.[18]

2.4   The Key Question: Is There a Difference in Moral Culpability between Intention and Recklessness when the Motive Remains Constant?

It may be argued against the examples advanced above that they fail to refute the argument that a person who acts with intent to cause harm is morally more culpable than the person who acts with recklessness. For in each set of examples there is an important difference between the motives of the actor who acts with intention and the motives of the actor who acts with recklessness. The reason for the judgment that in each set the one who acts with intention is less blameworthy than the one who acts with recklessness is that the motives of the former are either more praiseworthy or more understandable than the motives of the latter. In the first set, the actor's compassion towards his suffering son and his desire to put an end to his agony constitute good motives in themselves, and operate to significantly reduce his moral blameworthiness with respect to the killing. On the other hand, the person who takes a substantial risk that his act will kill his son is motivated by a desire to practice in marksmanship, and taking a substantial risk of killing one's son for this reason is very heinous indeed. In the second set, Sally's motives are much more understandable than those of Sara who acts in order to win a bet. And in the third set, the motives of George who wants to protect his family life and professional career from being destroyed by lies, are much better or much more understandable than the motives of Peter who takes the substantial risk of causing great damage to the property of another just for a little amusement.

The present argument is that the above examples cannot be of assistance in determining whether there is a moral difference between acting with intention and acting with recklessness, because the fact that the motives of the actor do not remain constant in the two cases of each set skews the comparison. Using the examples above in order to prove that acting with intention is not more blameworthy than acting with recklessness is misguided, therefore. Indeed, this is much like the fallacy in the argument designed to prove that acting with intention is not more blameworthy than acting with recklessness, by bringing the example of a person who recklessly causes damage of $100,000 to the property of another and showing that he is more blameworthy than a person who intentionally causes damage of $100 to the property of another.

But directing our attention to the motives of the actor cannot end the discussion. Quite the contrary, it may enable us to counter-attack, and perhaps more clearly, proponents of the distinction between intention and recklessness. Indeed, motives play a very important role in determining the existence and assessing the degree of moral blameworthiness. In proceeding to assess the moral blameworthiness of a person, it is not sufficient to know what she did. It is very important to know why she did it and for what goal. It is important to take notice of her whole complex of motives and purposes.[19] This fact finds expression in various contexts, and one of them is the context of sentencing. It is well accepted that in exercising their discretion in determining the sentence of the offender, judges take (and should take) into account the motives of the offender.[20] They consider the whole array of motives that led the offender to act as she did and the goals that she wanted to achieve. The major rationale for this practice is that the sentence should be proportional to the moral blameworthiness of the offender, and that when assessing the degree of the moral blameworthiness of the offender one should take into account the whole complex of her motives and purposes. But recognising the importance of motives in assessing the degree of moral blameworthiness must lead us to examine now the argument advanced by proponents of the distinction between intention and recklessness. We have to investigate whether they do not make the same mistake described above. We should inquire whether when they want to show that the person who causes a result intentionally is more blameworthy than the person who causes it recklessly they follow the rule that all other factors should remain constant, including the motives of the actor.

When people want to prove that acting with intention is more blameworthy than acting with recklessness, they sometimes advance examples in order to support their argument. But sometimes the sets of examples advanced suffer from the same defect described above. Sometimes the examples on the intention side are examples like killing somebody because his death is needed as an end in itself (i.e. to take pleasure from the death itself, out of sadistic motives) or because the death is needed as a means to a very repugnant end (as when the death is required to inherit from the victim or to facilitate a robbery); while examples on the recklessness side involve people who take risks for acceptable goals even though under the circumstances the taking of the risk is a little unreasonable, as when a doctor, out of enthusiasm to improve the quality of life of a suffering patient, takes an unreasonable risk to his life by giving him some medication. The problem is that in these examples the motives do not remain constant.[21] Of course, the sadistic killer and those who kill for pecuniary gain are more blameworthy than the doctor above, but perhaps the difference in moral blameworthiness stems from the difference in motives rather than from the difference between intention and recklessness.[22] And even if somebody says that acting with intention is more blameworthy than acting with recklessness without giving any examples to prove it, we might suspect that his view was shaped (consciously or unconsciously) by comparing cases which differ in some respect other than the difference between intending the proscribed result and being reckless with respect to it. So we may suggest that if we examine sets of cases in which the only difference between the two cases in each set is the difference between acting with intent to cause the proscribed result and acting with recklessness as to that result – when all other things, *including the motives,* are equal – we will find that there is no moral difference between intention and recklessness. And if this conclusion is correct then it seems that we should not grade offences based on the distinction between intention and recklessness, if this grading is meant to reflect a difference in moral culpability. Thus, we can include all the cases of intention and recklessness within the ambit of the same offence (with the same maximum penalty); or, if we think that this is not desirable because different cases of causing a certain result should be distinguished based on degrees of moral blameworthiness, then we may create separate offences with different penalties, that will be distinguished not by reference to the distinction between intention and recklessness. Rather the basis for the distinction between the two offences would be the degree of the moral blameworthiness of the actor. For example: We can enact two offences of causing a certain result, with a different maximum penalty, and determine that simple recklessness suffices for conviction of the basic offence, while conviction of the aggravated offence would require proof of a very high degree of moral blameworthiness.[23] If we have such offences, then the degree of moral blameworthiness will be determined in every case after taking into consideration all the factors that are relevant to the assessment of the moral blameworthiness of the actor, including the whole complex of his motives and purposes.[24]

But some of the proponents of the distinction between intention and recklessness may not give up so easily; they may say that purposely causing a proscribed result is more blameworthy than causing it recklessly, even when all other things, *including the motives*, are equal.[25] If they are right, then the legislator may be justified in grading offences based on the distinction between intention and recklessness. But are they right? The following two sets of examples are illustrative.

1. John's house is insured. In order to collect money from the insurance company he starts a fire in the house knowing that one person is sleeping there and that there is a substantial risk that he will be burnt to death while sleeping (but he does not have any interest in the death of that person).

   Jack insures the life of a person. In order to collect the money from the insurance company, he starts a fire in his house when that person is sleeping there, with the intention of burning him to death.[26]

2. John is a merchant who sells cooking oil he knows to be poisonous. He does it in order to make money and he knows that there is a substantial risk that some customers will die after using it (but he does not have any interest in their deaths).

Jack is a gravedigger who wants to cause the death of some people in order to create a demand for burial places. To this end, he sells cooking oil he knows to be poisonous with the hope that some customers will die (thereby enabling him to make some money).[27]

In each of the sets of examples advanced above, the ultimate motive of the two actors remains constant (making some money). All of the other variables remain constant as well. The only difference between the two cases in each set is that John is reckless with respect to the death and Jack acts with intent to cause death. The question is whether there is (in each set) a difference between the degree of moral blameworthiness of John and that of Jack. Is Jack more culpable, because he intends the death? Or perhaps there is no moral difference between him and John, as there is no difference in their motives or in any other factor relevant to the culpability assessment. The answer to this question is not simple, and I now turn to deal with it. I will first turn to the discussions in moral philosophy about the double effect theory, in order to see what can be learned from them with regard to our inquiry.

Notes

1   There might be offences in which negligence should suffice but I do not discuss negligence in this book.
2   As explained by Turner (1945) 208: "The main purpose of criminal law, however, is to protect innocent persons from harm caused by others, and this protection is needed no less against those who are reckless or indifferent as to the harm they may cause, than against those (probably a much smaller number) who intend that harm". See also Russell (1964) 42-43.
3   Hart (1968) 21-22; Gordon (1978) 51-52. The idea here is that even if the main purpose of the criminal law is general deterrence, still we should not convict or punish the morally innocent. Of course, the requirement that the actor be morally blameworthy as a condition for punishment is even more natural and basic for those who think that the main purpose of the criminal law is simply to inflict unpleasant consequences upon an offender in response to his offence, because he deserves the punishment.
4   Hart (1968) 21; Card, Cross and Jones (1998) 32; Russell (1964) 40; Kenny's Outlines of Criminal Law (1966) 32-34; Hall (1960) 133-134, 160. Cf. Gordon (1975) 355.
5   See Russell (1964) 42-43.
6   See for example Russell (1964) 42-43 and Turner (1945) 208.
7   See for example clause 20 of the Draft Criminal Code for England and Wales (1989) and section 2.02(3) of the Model Penal Code (1985). For a list of American jurisdictions with similar provisions see Model Penal Code and Commentaries (1985) Part 1, vol. 1, at p. 244.
8   Cf. Silving (1967) 224, 252.
9   See for example Smith and Hogan (1999) 4-6; Ashworth (1989) 344, 354-355; Ashworth (2000) 72-74, 90-131. See also Hart (1963) 34-38. The idea that the amount of punishment should be proportional to the degree of the moral culpability of the offender is naturally held by those who think that retribution is the main goal of the

criminal justice system. But even those who think that the main justification for having a criminal justice system is to prevent harms (for example by way of general deterrence) may say that when a judge exercises his discretion concerning the sentence to be passed on the specific offender before him, his predominant consideration should be that the severity of punishment be proportional to the degree of the offender's moral culpability. Cf. Hart (1963) 34-38; Ashworth (1989) 340-342, 354-355.

10 See Stephen (1883), vol. 3, p. 91; Hart (1968) 234.

11 Clause 70 of the Draft Criminal Code for England and Wales (1989) deals with intentionally causing serious personal harm and clause 71 deals with recklessly causing the same result. The first offence carries a maximum penalty of life imprisonment while the second, when tried on indictment, carries a maximum penalty of five years imprisonment (see Schedule 1). In this draft Code, "intention" includes oblique intention (see supra 1.3.4).

12 See Report on Recodifying Criminal Law (1987) clauses 6(2) and 6(3) at p. 57 (there are also offences of Negligent Homicide and of First Degree Murder in this draft Code). In this draft Code "purpose" includes oblique intention, see supra 1.3.4.

13 See *Homicide* (Working Paper 33), (1984) at p. 68.

14 Model Penal Code (1985).

15 In the Model Penal Code, "purpose" does not include oblique intention (see supra 1.3.4). This means that if a person purposely starts a fire not in order to destroy the building of another, and he is practically certain that his act will bring about the destruction of a building of another, he is guilty only of the lesser offence. But sometimes the Model Penal Code puts oblique intention and direct intention together in the same offence, and draws a distinction between them and recklessness. Thus, Section 220.2(1) provides that a person commits a felony of the second degree when he purposely or knowingly (i.e. with direct intention or with oblique intention) causes a catastrophe (by explosion, fire, flood, etc.), while if he does so recklessly he only commits a felony of the third degree.

16 I will first deal with the question as stated in the text. Later on I will deal with oblique intention.

17 See for example Williams (1983a) 83; *Homicide* (Working Paper 33), (1984) at p. 67. Cf. Smith and Hogan (1983) 58.

18 Kugler (1993) 126-128. Stephen says that the offence of murder should extend not only to cases of acting with intent to kill but also to cases of reckless killing. He says that the idea of grading offences in correspondence with the degree of moral blameworthiness of the actor is well founded, but it cannot justify the distinction between intention and recklessness. The reckless killer should be convicted of murder, rather than manslaughter, because in many cases he is no less blameworthy than the intentional killer. Actually, there are cases in which the reckless killer is even more blameworthy than the intentional killer. See Stephen (1883), vol. 3, pp. 91-93. The examples given by Stephen to show that sometimes the reckless killer is more blameworthy are problematic because more harm is caused in the case of the reckless killer than in the case of the intentional killer. However, other examples may be advanced to make the point, as I have done in the text.
Cross advances the following example: a person selects a pistol from a batch in which, to his knowledge, only one is loaded. He points the pistol at the head of another, pulls the trigger and kills him. If this person hoped that the pistol chosen was loaded, and shot in order to kill the other person, then he acted with direct intention to kill and would obviously be guilty of murder. To which Cross raises the following question:

"Is there any moral difference, and should there be any legal difference, if he had selected the pistol and pointed it at his victim in order to frighten him, to experience the thrill of finding out whether he had chosen the one which was loaded, or in the hope of winning a bet?". Cross sympathises with the view that there is no moral difference between the two cases and that the reckless killer (together with the intentional killer) should be convicted of murder. See Cross (1978) 14-16.

Oberdiek says that sometimes foreseen consequences may deserve as stiff a sentence as intended ones. See Oberdiek (1972) 399-400. He seems to be taking the view that the law should not grade offences based on the distinction between intention and recklessness (see ibid. at 389 and 399-400).

For the possibility that recklessness may be considered a state of mind equal in reprehensibility to intention see Gordon (1975) 373. Cf. Alexander (2000).

19   Cf. Hall (1960) 93; Gordon (1978) 214-217, 227.

20   Smith and Hogan (1999) 79; Williams (1983a) 75; LaFave and Scott (1986) 231; Hall (1960) 101; Gordon (1978) 215-216, 227.

21   See Oberdiek (1972) 399-400; Kugler (1993) 129-130; Gorr (1996) 371. Cf. Thomson (1973) 152-153.

22   It seems that the fallacy described in the text may be found in the example given by Anthony Kenny in order to demonstrate the moral distinction between intention and recklessness and, in turn, the appropriateness of the law's distinction between murder and manslaughter. He advances the example of two nurses, who both have in their possession two pills which are indistinguishable to the eye. One of the pills is a pain-killer and the other contains a poisonous substance. The pills have been mixed up in the medicine cabinet. Nurse A gives a pill to a patient whose money she stands to inherit with the hope (but without the knowledge) that it is the poisonous one. Nurse B gives a pill to a patient who is in great agony with the hope (but without the knowledge) that it is the pain-killer. Neither nurse is blameless, Kenny maintains, though most people would feel that there is an important moral difference between the actions of the two, even if the patient dies. See Kenny (1968) 160. This example seems problematic, however, because there is a significant difference in the ultimate motives of the nurses. The ultimate purpose of nurse A is to inherit money, while the ultimate purpose of nurse B is to relieve the patient of pain. Thus, we might say that the difference in their ultimate purposes, rather than the distinction between intention and recklessness, underlies the variation in blameworthiness. A similar fallacy characterises other examples brought by Kenny to demonstrate a moral difference between intention and mere foresight. This is the case with the examples advanced concerning the moral difference between appointing the most qualified candidate to a position, knowing that this will aggrieve the rival candidate, and making the appointment in order to aggrieve the rival candidate (ibid.); and between sentencing an offender to imprisonment, knowing that this will cause his wife hardship, and imposing imprisonment in order to cause hardship to the wife – against whom the judge has a grudge (Kenny (1978) 90).

23   The idea to list in the context of specific offences all the potential motives for performing the offence, and based on this list to construct a grading scheme, is not realistic because there may be an infinite number of potential motives to commit an offence. Hence, the option suggested in the text. This option has its own disadvantages which I later address (see infra the discussion in chapter 8). Here I will restrict myself to mentioning that an arrangement somewhat similar to that proposed in the text can be found in the law of murder of certain countries. In Scotland, in order to convict of

murder (as opposed to culpable homicide), it must be established that the accused either intended (i.e. wanted) to kill or acted with wicked recklessness. See Gordon (1975) 389-390; Jones and Christie (1996) 208-209; Scottish Law Commission, *Attempted Homicide* (1984) 15-16. In order to establish "wicked recklessness" it is not enough to show that there was simple recklessness, i.e. that the actor knowingly took an unjustified risk that his act would cause death. More is needed (Jones and Christie, ibid.). According to Gordon what is needed is the existence of wickedness and depravity (Gordon (1978) 735). He explains that "to say that 'A is guilty of murder when he kills with wicked recklessness' means only 'A is guilty of murder when he kills with such recklessness that he deserves to be treated as a murderer'" and that this formula may be justified by the claim that when coming to a choice between murder and culpable homicide the result should turn on moral judgments and considerations (Gordon (1978) 737). In some places, Gordon seems to say that we are dealing here with an assessment of the defendant's character, as revealed by the particular action under discussion, that we are inquiring as to whether his action was done out of a wicked disposition and that we are taking his motive into account (which is the clue whereby a man's character can be related to his actions). See Gordon (1978) 214-215, and Gordon (1975) 389. For the role of motive in considering whether the accused acts with "general mens rea" (i.e. out of wickedness) see also Gordon (1978) at 227. The Scottish Law Commission also says that both murder and culpable homicide can result from a reckless act, and that the distinction between a reckless act that constitutes murder and a reckless act that constitutes culpable homicide resides in the degree of wickedness that the particular act is thought to display (Scottish Law Commission, *Attempted Homicide* (1984) 23). The Scottish law of murder takes a similar, though not identical, approach to that mentioned in the text. The difference that is most relevant to our discussion is that under Scottish law, if the accused acts with a direct intention to kill (i.e. he wants to kill) he will be convicted of murder and there is no need to establish that his action reveals wickedness (see for example Gordon (1978) 737). By contrast, if the method suggested in the text is adopted, even actors who acted with direct intention may, in appropriate cases, be exempted from the more serious offence. For the possibility that the Scottish law of murder requires, even in the case of direct intention, that there be an "evil" intention, see Jones and Christie (1996) 208 (though the authors themselves do not accept this view). It should also be noted that Scottish law provides for certain categories of mitigating circumstances (such as the category of provocation), and that a person who acts in circumstances covered by such a category will be convicted of culpable homicide rather than murder, even if he intends to kill. See Jones and Christie (1996) 218-225. (However, it is possible that since 2001 the Scottish law is that even in cases in which there is a direct intention to kill, a conviction of murder is dependent on the existence of wickedness. See infra, chapter 8, at note 7, concerning the decision in *Drury*.)

A similar arrangement to that suggested in the text can also be found in the Model Penal Code (1985). Murder is established if the actor causes the death purposely, knowingly, or recklessly under circumstances manifesting extreme indifference to the value of human life (section 210.2(1)). (An exception to this rule concerns cases of mitigation based on mental or emotional disturbance, but these cases need not be discussed here.) Manslaughter is established when the death is caused recklessly (section 210.3(1)(a)). (Manslaughter is also established where the person, who otherwise should be convicted of murder, acts under extreme mental or emotional disturbance, but this category need not be discussed here.) This means that when the actor acts without direct or oblique intention, but with recklessness, the degree of the offence will turn on whether the accused acts with "extreme indifference to the value of human life". The commentary explains that the definition of murder reflects the judgment that "there is a kind of reckless homicide that cannot fairly be distinguished in grading terms from homicides committed purposely or knowingly". Consequently, the best approach is to leave it to the trier of fact to determine whether the case at hand can be fairly assimilated to cases where the killing is perpetrated with purpose or knowledge. See Model Penal Code and Commentaries (1980) Part 2, vol. 1, pp. 21-22. Fletcher views the Model Penal Code formula as hinging on the moral gravity of the risk-creating act, and seems to suggest that a critical factor in determining whether the actor should be guilty of murder of the "extreme indifference" variety should be whether there was any redeeming social value to his conduct. See Fletcher (1978) 265. In spite of the similarity between the Model Penal Code scheme and the method suggested in the text, an important difference remains: under the Model Penal Code scheme, the moral evaluation of the conduct of the accused is only relevant in cases of recklessness. Upon proof of direct or oblique intention, the actor is guilty of murder and there is no room for moral evaluation. It is also noteworthy that in many American jurisdictions, versions of reckless homicide as murder appear which resemble that of the Model Penal Code, and that they sometimes contain a formula which speaks even more explicitly in terms of moral evaluation of the accused or his acts. Thus, one finds the requirement that the accused act in a way that evinces a "depraved heart regardless of human life" or "a depraved mind regardless of human life" or that he be motivated by "an abandoned and malignant heart" (see Model Penal Code and Commentaries (1980) Part 2, vol. 1, pp. 22 and 26, and Fletcher (1978) 265).

24 Motives relevant in assessing the degree of moral culpability are not only motives described without an express reference to future events (such as compassion, benevolence, jealousy, love, greediness, religious belief, sexual lust, racial hatred, sense of duty, friendship, etc.) but also motives described in terms of a desire to achieve a certain goal. Thus, for example, if John kills his relative in order to receive an inheritance, it is right to say that his motive to kill was the desire to inherit from him. In other cases, the motive behind the killing of a relative may be a desire to relieve him of pain. The motives in the last two examples are no less relevant in assessing the degree of moral culpability than motives described without an express reference to further events. In like manner, when a doctor takes an unjustified risk in giving a patient some medication, the fact that his motive in giving the medication is a desire to substantially improve the patient's quality of life is also relevant in assessing his degree of blameworthiness. In order to emphasise that motives described in terms of a desire to achieve a certain goal are relevant to moral evaluations I have used here and in some other places above the phrase "motives and purposes". But I must emphasise that even in places in this book in which I use the word "motives" and not the words "motives and purposes" I intend for the word to be understood as encompassing also motives described in terms of a desire to achieve a certain goal.

25 Cf. Hall (1960) 134.
26 Cf. Stephen (1883), vol. 3, pp. 92-93.
27 Cf. Foot (1978) 22.

Chapter 3

The Doctrine of the Double Effect

3.1 The Doctrine of the Double Effect and the Counter-Argument

The doctrine of the double effect, originally developed in Catholic theology, is the subject of much dispute among philosophers today. Within Catholic theology we find the view that one should never kill an innocent person with direct intention. This absolute prohibition applies not only to cases in which death is desired by the actor as an end in itself, but also to cases in which death is only needed as a means to a further consequence. In the latter case, the prohibition holds even when the consequences sought by the actor in carrying out the killing are very good. The killing of an innocent person cannot be justified by showing that his death is needed as a means to achieve consequences that outweigh the death of that person, in terms of the goodness involved. Nonetheless, you are allowed to act in order to achieve good results, even if you foresee, when you are acting, that your act will certainly cause the death of an innocent person as a side effect (provided that the results you want to achieve are good enough to outweigh the bad result, namely, the death of the innocent person). This means that even when the ultimate end is the same (achieving a good result which from a utilitarian point of view outweighs the bad result, namely, the death of an innocent person) a distinction still applies: It is forbidden to kill the person with direct intention (i.e. to act in order to kill him as a means to achieve the good result) but it is allowed to act in order to achieve the good result, with the knowledge that the act will certainly cause the death of an innocent person as a side effect. The doctrine that makes this distinction is called the doctrine of the double effect.[1]

Suppose a patient who is terminally ill is administered a drug to relieve the pain, and over time he develops a tolerance for the drug, so that larger and larger doses are required. Eventually the patient reaches the point where the only effective dose is one that is so large in quantity that it will hasten his death. According to a common view in the Catholic tradition, it is permitted in such a case to increase the dosage in order to free him from the pain because the death is not intended as a means, it is only foreseen as a by-product. On the other hand, it is forbidden to shoot him (or to drug him) in order to kill him and thereby stop the pain.[2] Although in the two cases the ultimate end is the same (stopping the pain) and the price is the same (hastening death), there is nonetheless a difference, as only in the second case is there a direct intention to kill. According to the doctrine, this difference is significant enough to permit only the first procedure.

The aforementioned distinction also applies in cases where the life of a pregnant woman can be saved only at the cost of the life of the foetus. According to a common view in the Catholic tradition, it is forbidden to act with direct intention to kill the foetus, even if its death constitutes the only available means to save the life of the mother. Nevertheless, if a woman is found to have cancer in her womb and the womb must be removed otherwise she will die, the surgeon may remove the womb containing the foetus even if it is clear to him that the foetus will later die as a result of the procedure.[3] Here again, in the two cases the ultimate end is the same (saving the life of the mother) and the price is the same (the death of the foetus). From a utilitarian point of view, the two cases seem identical. Nevertheless, the doctrine says that the fact that in the first case there is a direct intention to cause the death of the foetus while in the second there is none (because the death of the foetus is not desired as a means but is only known to follow as a by-product of the womb's removal) suffices for only the second procedure to be permitted.

I now put Catholic theology aside to inquire whether there is a place for the doctrine of the double effect in the framework of a moral philosophy that is not committed to the principles of Catholic theology. Before doing so, however, I would like to clarify that although the doctrine was originally developed within the framework of absolute prohibitions, it can also be embraced by people who deny the very existence of absolute prohibitions. For example, you can say that while it is forbidden to kill one innocent person with direct intention in order to save five other people from death, it is nevertheless permitted to act in order to save five people from death even when you know that your act will certainly cause the death of one other innocent person, as a side effect. At the same time, you may still believe that it is permitted to kill one innocent person with direct intention in order to save, say, a million people. If you share this set of beliefs, then you do not believe that the prohibition against killing an innocent person with direct intention is absolute, but you *do* believe in the doctrine of the double effect. For you think that there are contexts (like when the question is whether to save five people at the price of one person's life) in which causing a certain result with direct intention should be forbidden, but causing the same result knowingly (as a side effect) should be permitted, even though all of the other variables remain constant, including the ultimate end and the price. So for purposes of our discussion, the doctrine of the double effect should be understood as saying that there are circumstances in which it is morally permissible to knowingly bring about as a side effect something which it would be forbidden to bring about purposely as a means, even if the balance of benefit and harm in the consequences remains the same.[4] It should also be clarified that because the doctrine is generally discussed in the context of cases where the side effect (which is not directly intended) is foreseen as certain (and not merely as probable) I will hereinafter deal with it only in this context. Only later will I address cases where the side effect is only seen as probable or possible.

Some authors reject the doctrine of the double effect. For example, after having introduced the Catholic doctrine of the double effect and its applications in cases of euthanasia and abortion, Hart writes:

> Perhaps the most perplexing feature of these cases is that the overriding aim in all of them is the same good result, namely in the first group to save human suffering and in the second

to save the mother's life. The differences between the cases are differences of causal structure leading to the applicability of different verbal distinctions. There seems to be no relevant moral difference between them on any theory of morality. It is perfectly true that those cases that the Catholic doctrine forbids may be correctly described as cases of intentional killing (intentionally killing the dying man to stop his pain, intentionally killing the unborn child to save the mother), whereas the cases which the doctrine allows are naturally described as cases of 'knowingly causing death'. But neither these verbal differences nor the differences in causal structure are correlated with moral factors.[5]

A similar argument is suggested by others who reject the doctrine.[6] The above argument seems very convincing and rational. When confronting a tragic dilemma it seems rational to weigh all of the prospective results against each other and to act following the result of this calculation. The question whether the bad consequence is caused purposely or (merely) knowingly does not seem to bear upon the prospective results. So why should it make a difference on the moral plane?

3.2 The Argument that Moral Intuition Supports the Doctrine of the Double Effect

Despite the argument presented above, there are authors who accept the doctrine.[7] One common line of argument in favour of the doctrine of the double effect is that it provides the sole, or at least the most, reasonable explanation for our moral intuitions concerning certain cases. We are given a pair of cases in which the agent can bring about the same good result at the same price. If we feel that although in both cases the overall results in the world are exactly the same, the actor is only allowed to act in case A and is forbidden to act in case B, then we are left with a puzzle. And if we then find that the difference between the two cases consists in the fact that in case A the actor only foresees the harm as a side effect of his act (an act taken in order to bring about the good result), while in case B the actor acts in order to bring about the harm (because the harm is needed as a means to achieve the good result), then we are inclined to think that this difference in intentions explains the different moral status of the two actions. Thus, the appeal of the doctrine of the double effect lies in its ability to explain our moral intuition concerning pairs of cases.[8]

I will now expose some of the examples presented in the literature to support the doctrine of the double effect. One famous example pertains to the morality of war. Many feel that it is morally forbidden to bomb civilians in order to kill them and thereby to demoralise the enemy country, though it is permitted to bomb a munitions factory in order to reduce the enemy's military strength even though the pilot who drops the bombs knows that several civilians living nearby will be killed as a consequence (provided that the number of the civilians killed is kept in proportion to the military gain achieved by the bombing). This means that even if the extent of military gain and the number of civilians killed are exactly the same in the two cases, it is still forbidden to bomb in the first case whereas in the second it is permissible. Since it seems that there is no difference between the two cases from a utilitarian point of view, because the gains and costs are identical, it seems that the most plausible way to explain our moral intuition in this respect is by means of the double effect theory. In the first case the death of the civilians is desired as a means (to demoralise the enemy country), while in the second case the death of the civilians is not desired (neither as an end nor as a means) but is only foreseen as a certain by-product of the course of action taken. Hence, the different moral status of the two actions.[9]

Other examples deal with cases in which we can save the life of, say, five people at the cost of one innocent person's life. First, I will advance two examples where the action is considered by common intuition to be morally forbidden. Example 1: John is a doctor in a hospital. Five sick people lie in the hospital and they are going to die in half an hour unless they are injected with some substance. This substance can only be found in dead bodies, and the hospital does not have this substance readily handy, nor can it be obtained within half an hour. It then occurs to John that he can kill a person visiting the hospital and extract the substance from his dead body – and use it to save the life of the five sick people. By common moral intuition, he should not be allowed to kill the visitor in these circumstances. Example 2: A terrorist captures 5 hostages. He then comes to Peter and asks him to kill another person. If Peter kills the other person, he says, the five hostages will be released, while if Peter does not kill the other person, the five hostages will be killed. The common moral intuition is that Peter should not be allowed to kill the person he is asked to kill. In these two examples, the protagonist is not allowed to kill one innocent person, even when the act of killing would save the life of five innocent people.

But now consider another case. Sara is a passenger on a tram. The brakes of the tram fail the driver and he faints out of shock. Sara sees that five people are trapped on the track and that the tram is going to hit them and kill them. There is no way to stop the tram before it hits the people and the only way to save them is to swerve the tram onto another track. Unfortunately, one person is trapped on the second track and if Sara swerves the tram on to the second track this person will certainly be killed. Is Sara allowed to swerve the tram? Many people feel that she would be morally permitted to do so (I will not deal here with the question whether she is morally obliged to do so). The reason is, of course, that her action saves the lives of five innocent people and causes the death of only one innocent person. It seems that the world would be better off if she acts, and, therefore, the act is permitted. But then why is it forbidden for John and Peter to kill one innocent person in the first two examples? In these cases, too, five lives would be saved at the price of one innocent person's life. So where does the difference lie? It seems, the argument runs, that the difference lies in the intentions of the actor. In the first example, the death of the visitor is needed as a means to the end of saving the lives of the sick people, because the substance can only be produced by a dead body. So in this case there is a direct intention to kill the visitor. In the second example, the death of the innocent person is needed as a means to the end of saving the lives of five innocent people, as their release is conditioned upon the killing. So in this case as well there is a direct intention to kill. In both cases the actor has to do something *in order* to kill an innocent person. And it is forbidden to kill an innocent person with direct intention, even if this is done in order to save the lives of five innocent people. But in the tram case, Sara swerves the tram in order to save the lives of five innocent people. Though when she swerves the tram she foresees that her act will certainly cause the death of one innocent person, the death is not caused as a means to save the lives of five people. Since Sara does not have a direct intention to kill an innocent person (but only foresees it as certain), her action is permitted. The conclusion that may be drawn, therefore, is that our moral intuition shows that, at least in some contexts, an important moral difference exists between causing a bad result with direct intention and causing the same result with oblique intention, even if all other things are equal in the two cases (including the results in the world and the ultimate motives of the actor).[10]

Now, if we agree with the moral judgments made above in the war example, and in the examples involving the killing of one person which saves five (because our moral intuition suggest that these judgments are right and we do not want to ignore these intuitions) then we have a problem. The problem is that, on the one hand, these judgments seem to uphold the double effect theory; whereas on the other hand, it seems that from a theoretical perspective, the argument against the theory is very strong, as explained in section 3.1. So those who accept the doctrine have to attempt to articulate in theoretical terms a rational basis for the doctrine.

3.3   Utilitarianism and Deontology

I think that in our effort to understand the doctrine of the double effect we should first concentrate on cases of direct intention. We should address the following question: Why is it morally forbidden to cause the death of one innocent person when it is needed as a means to save the lives of five innocent people? If we can kill a person and extract from his dead body a substance that will save the life of five people, why shouldn't we do that? The world will gain four lives if we do that, so why is it forbidden to act in this way? I think that we should first answer this question, because if we have an answer to this basic question, it might help us to better understand the doctrine of the double effect. So, let us put cases of oblique intention aside for a while and concentrate on cases of direct intention.

Utilitarianism as a moral philosophy holds that the moral end to be sought in all we do should be to achieve the greatest possible balance of good over evil. The classic version, called "Act Utilitarianism", holds that the right act in any given situation is the one that will produce the best overall outcome, as judged from an impersonal standpoint. Various systems of utilitarianism may debate the question what should count as the ultimate good (be it pleasure, happiness, welfare, satisfaction of desires, or something else). Yet they all share in common the view that what people should do is to maximise good and minimise evil.[11] One of the main arguments advanced against utilitarianism is that it seems to permit certain courses of action which our intuitions clearly tell us to be forbidden. We have a strong moral intuition that it is forbidden to kill an innocent person in order to save five other sick people by using a substance extracted from his dead body. But utilitarianism seems to imply that such a killing is permitted, because five lives are worth more than one, i.e. the killing would maximise the good in the world.[12] Examples advanced against utilitarianism are not limited to killings; they also deal with other actions like torture. It seems that we are not allowed to torture an innocent person even if torturing him will yield good results that seem to outweigh the pain that he would suffer by the torture.[13]

The examples above seem to suggest that we have to choose between two options. One option is to adopt utilitarianism, because it seems rational, and to insist that we should ignore our moral intuitions concerning the examples above (because they give the wrong answers) and say that we are permitted (or even required) to kill an innocent person in order to save the lives of five people. This option will be rejected by many people.[14] The other option is to adopt the view that there are cases in which people are not allowed to do a certain thing (like killing innocent people) even if doing that thing would produce the best overall outcome. Underlying this view is the belief that morality is not only interested in good states of affairs in the world and in good results. Rather, in certain areas it is heavily interested in the actions of the actor, and in these contexts it sometimes instructs him that he is not allowed to perform a certain act even if it would produce the best overall outcome. This view believes in what is often called "deontological constraints".[15]

Those who believe in "deontological constraints" or "deontological prohibitions" still differ in their views regarding the strength of the prohibitions. The most extreme would think that there can be a totally absolute prohibition against doing a certain thing. For example, they would suggest that it is never permitted to kill an innocent person in order to save the lives of others, even in extreme cases where the death of one person is needed to save, say, millions of people.[16] Others would deny that any prohibition is totally absolute, but would believe in "almost absolute" prohibitions. They would say, for example, that it is forbidden to kill an innocent person in order to save the lives of five people but would admit that in very extreme circumstances (for example where the death is needed as a means to save a nation or millions of people) the prohibition is overridden by the good results, and the action is morally permitted. The adherents of such a view do not state the exact number of saved people needed to justify the killing, but this is not thought to be a serious problem because those cases are imaginary and it is improbable that they would take place in reality. It is important to remember, however, that although this view admits that in very extreme cases the prohibition will be overridden, it still attaches much importance to deontological constraints, in that it says that in other than "very extreme" circumstances, deontological prohibitions remain in force and cannot be overridden by the good results that can be achieved by violating the prohibition.[17]

It seems that not all deontological prohibitions are absolute or almost absolute. Some of them may be overridden not only in very extreme circumstances (like the "almost absolute" prohibitions) but even by "a sufficiently large increment of good". Consider, for instance, the prohibitions against breaking a promise or telling a lie. These prohibitions are perceived by many as "deontological" in nature, meaning that it is not correct to say: "every time telling a lie (or breaking a promise) produces the best overall outcome, it is permissible to take such a course of action". However, these prohibitions are not as stringent as the prohibition against killing an innocent person (as reflected in the judgment that though a certain amount of net good results suffices to override the prohibition against lying, it takes much more to override the prohibition against killing an innocent person). Although prohibitions like "do not lie" are overridden more easily than certain other prohibitions (like "do not kill"), they are still considered by many to form "deontological prohibitions" because (according to them) until the threshold of "a sufficiently large increment of good" is reached – the deontological constraints hold, and do not yield to simple utilitarian calculus.[18]

3.4   Rule Utilitarianism

Act utilitarianism seems to conflict with our moral intuition concerning what is permissible in certain cases. On the other hand, the deontological position, according to which sometimes a person is not allowed to act in the way that yields the best overall outcome, seems paradoxical and puzzling.[19] Some say that the moral philosophy called "rule utilitarianism" provides a way to reconcile our moral intuitions with rationality. According to this viewpoint, we can adopt a utilitarian philosophy and still hold that it is forbidden, for example, to kill one innocent person in order to save the lives of five other people. What is needed in order to justify such a prohibition is to pay attention not only to the immediate results of our actions but also to the consequences produced in the long run. Thus, it is argued in relation to the example above, that a society whose moral code contains an absolute prohibition against killing innocent persons will, in the long run, be in a better situation (in terms of good results, such as the number of people who stay alive) than a society whose moral code contains a rule permitting an innocent person to be killed any time such a course of action yields better consequences, e.g., in order to save the lives of two people. According to rule utilitarianism, a moral system should have rules, and in making decisions about what to do in concrete circumstances the rules should be absolutely binding. The contents of the rules are solely determined by considerations of utility, with a view to promoting the good. But once the rules are set, people have to obey them in concrete cases without inquiring whether obedience in the concrete case promotes utility. While the principle of utility constitutes the sole standard, it is invoked at the rule-making level, not at the level of decision-making in concrete cases.[20] Thus a utilitarian can justify certain absolute rules against doing certain things by relying on the estimation that utility will be promoted in the long run by general obedience to these absolute rules.[21]

The very idea that a moral system should set rules rather than leave it to every person to work out the utilitarian calculation by himself in every concrete case and act accordingly is justified by rule utilitarians by reference to the principle of maximising utility itself. They say that the general good will be most furthered if rules are set in advance, rather than if individuals are permitted to decide in every case what is the best action according to its results. For example, if we permit that an innocent person be killed in every case where such a course of action yields the best results, we create the danger that in certain cases people will err in their calculation pursuant to a lack of factual or moral knowledge. Lack of time may also induce serious mistakes and passion, bias or self-interest may distort the actor's capacity to reason and thus yield the wrong judgement. Also the killing of innocent people, even when done for good ends, tends to vitiate the character of the actor and to undermine his general disposition against killing (the same can be said about other people who see the killing or hear about it). This creates the risk that in other cases he (or the observers) will kill people in cases where the killing cannot be justified. These and other considerations may yield the estimation that, from a utilitarian point of view, it is better for society to have an absolute prohibition against killing an innocent person.[22]

One problem with the foregoing approach is that it relies on estimations and predictions that are very speculative. So if somebody is not sure that these estimations are correct but, at the same time, he is sure that it is forbidden to kill an innocent person in order to save the lives of five other people, then it seems that he cannot accept the above explanation as correct insofar as the aforesaid prohibition is concerned. But even if we assume that the calculations mentioned above are correct, there is still a problem with the suggested explanation, as it does not explain our intuition concerning the reason for the prohibition. We feel that the prohibition against killing an innocent person is categorical, independent of the results of complicated calculations.[23] Even if the results of the calculation would demonstrate that in the long run more lives would be saved if we would permit people to kill an innocent person whenever this saves the lives of at least two people, we would still feel that the prohibition should remain in force. For we feel there is something essentially wrong in the killing of the innocent individual that is not derived from concerns regarding long-term results.[24]

It follows from the discussion above that the intuition regarding the prohibition to kill an innocent person in order to save the lives of five other people cannot be reconciled with utilitarianism.

3.5   Consequentialism

I will now discuss another potential attempt to reconcile our moral intuitions with the idea that morality is only interested in good consequences. Some may suggest that we have to understand that "bad results" are not only related to things like pain, death, etc. When speaking about the bad results of an action, we also have to take into account things that are more abstract in quality, such as the right of a person violated by that action. The argument may be that if we include in the calculation of the results of an action such abstract things (like the right violated) then we can reconcile our moral intuitions with a moral theory requiring that people always act in a way which maximises good results and minimises bad ones. Moral theories that take these abstract results into account are still consequentialist in nature. They only differ from utilitarianism (which is a type of consequentialism) in that they factor in results that are not taken into account by utilitarianism. Thus, it is suggested that we can be consequentialist and still hold, for example, that it is forbidden for a doctor to kill a visitor in a hospital in order to extract from his body a substance that would save the lives of five other people. This is because we would see, after consideration of all the relevant consequences, that it is mistaken to think that in this case the act of killing yields the best overall results. But what are these additional results which need to be taken into account? In the upcoming sections, I will discuss three possible types of such results. In addition, I will address the question whether the suggestion above to reconcile consequentialism with our moral intuitions is acceptable.

3.5.1 *The Victim*

It might be suggested that it is forbidden to kill one innocent person in order to save five other people from dying of a disease because there is a difference between a natural death and being killed by another person. In the example above, the five people are going to die of a disease, so that the harm they suffer if they die is only the death itself. But if the one person is killed, on the other hand, then another bad result follows in addition to his death, namely that his right to life is violated. If we take this additional result into account, then it is wrong to say that killing the innocent person in order to save five people produces the best overall outcome.[25] Another, albeit similar, line of argument is that the additional bad result in the case of a killing (as opposed to a natural death) is the harm caused to the dignity of the victim, in that he is used as a means to the ends of others. In our example the victim, if killed, is used as a means to save the lives of other people; this constitutes a violation of his dignity, an act of disrespect towards him. The harm to his dignity changes the outcome of the calculation so that it is wrong to say that killing one innocent person in order to save five people from dying of a disease yields the best overall results.[26] But the above solution is problematic.

First, it is difficult to accept the idea that the harm done to the dignity of the victim or the injury to his right amounts to a result that is worse than losing the lives of four innocent people. It seems much more reasonable to say that the lives of four innocent people are worth more than the harm to the dignity of one person. So it seems that if we kill one innocent person in order to save five people from dying of a disease, we minimise bad results.[27]

Second, suppose that one person is going to die of a disease and the other is going to be killed by someone and that A can only save one of them. Though many considerations may be taken into account in deciding whom to save, we do not feel that the fact that the second person is going to be killed (rather than die of a disease) constitutes a very important factor. But if the reason for the prohibition of killing one person in order to save five people was that the harm suffered by the victim of killing is much greater than the harm suffered by a person who dies of a disease, then we would feel that there is a decisive reason in the present example to save the one who is going to be killed instead of the one who is going to die of a disease.[28] In fact, we would feel that it is better to save one person from being killed than to save five people from dying of a disease.

Finally, if the reason for not killing one person in order to save five people from dying of a disease was that the harm suffered by the victim of the killing is much greater than the harm suffered by one dying of a disease, then we would be permitted to kill one innocent person in order to save five people from being murdered. For example: If a terrorist orders me to kill one person otherwise he will kill five other people then I should be permitted to kill the one person because when the five are killed by the terrorist (if I do not kill the one) they will also suffer the same additional harm (harm to their dignity, etc.). But our intuition that it is forbidden to kill one person in order to save five equally applies in cases like this one, and this shows that the explanation suggested here is wrong.[29]

3.5.2 *The Value Itself*

Another suggestion might be that in the case of murder, there is an attack on the value of human life, and such an attack does not exist in the case of dying from a disease. In consequentialist terms, we can say that when a person dies of a disease there is only the "material" death itself, but when one murders somebody then there is, in addition to the death itself, the damage to the value of life itself. And this further damage can explain why it is forbidden to kill one innocent person in order to save five other people from dying of a disease. However, arguments similar to those advanced against the previous explanation also apply here.

First, it seems implausible that the damage to the value of life itself constitutes a worse result than the loss of the actual ("material") lives of four innocent people. But this difficulty seems less serious here than in the context of the previous explanation. The previous explanation concerned earthly things like the damage caused to the dignity of the victim, so it was easier to contend that it is not reasonable to view such damages as overly important. But here we are speaking about a damage to a less earthly thing (the value of life itself), and we can be less confident regarding the relative importance of the damage to such a thing. On the other hand, this last point reveals an important weakness in the present explanation. This weakness lies in that the present solution is committed to the belief that there is, in reality, outside our minds and bodies, a non-material transcendent object – the value of life itself (something like the platonic Forms), and that such an object can be damaged by our actions.[30] Or, if we do not want to speak about separate objects (for separate values) but we still want to accept the above explanation, we at least have to believe that our actions may damage the moral structure of the world (in the sense of causing a real damage that is additional to the damage to concrete things like the actual lives of people). Those who do not want to commit themselves to the above metaphysical assumptions cannot accept the present suggested explanation.[31]

Second, if the damage to the value of life is accorded so much weight when we are calculating the outcomes, then in a case when we have to choose between saving one person from dying from a disease and preventing the killing of another person we would feel that there is a decisive reason to choose to prevent the killing. But we do not feel this way.

Third, if the reason for the prohibition against killing one innocent person in order to save five people from dying of a disease was that the harms in the case of murder are greater because of the additional damage caused to the value of life itself, then we would be permitted to kill one innocent person in order to prevent five people from being murdered (because each of the five murders damages the value of life, in addition to taking the concrete life of the victim). But the intuition against killing one person in order to save five people also applies in such cases.

3.5.3 *The Moral Integrity of the Agent*

It might be suggested that when a person murders an innocent person, he harms his own personal moral integrity and purity (he is dirtying his hands, defiling his soul) and that this is a very bad result that should be considered when making the calculation.[32] So the reason for the prohibition against killing an innocent person in order to save five people from dying of a disease is that if they die from the disease the only loss incurred is the loss of their lives, whereas if the agent kills one innocent person in order to save them, then the bad results are the death of the victim coupled with the damage to the moral integrity of the agent, so that the consequences of killing are worse than the consequences of not killing.[33] This may seem like a circular argument. For if the act of killing one innocent person in order to save five from dying of a disease is forbidden based on independent reasons (i.e. not because of the harm done to the moral integrity of the agent) then it is reasonable to say that an agent who kills in these circumstances harms his personal moral integrity (by violating a moral prohibition). But according to the present suggestion there is no such independent reason for the prohibition, and if considerations revolving around the moral integrity of the agent are not taken into account, then the act of killing in the above circumstances would be morally permitted, if not recommended or perhaps even required. So how can an act that is morally right harm the moral integrity of the actor?[34] The answer seems to be that the very act of killing an innocent person "dirties the hands" of the agent (or defiles his soul) and that this phenomenon occurs even when there are morally good reasons for the killing. But even if we are ready to accept the general idea that harm can be caused to the moral integrity of an agent in the above circumstances, the attempt to use this idea in the context of a consequentialist explanation for the prohibition against killing one innocent person in order to save the lives of five innocent people is still problematic.

First, the assumption that the damage caused to the moral integrity of the actor constitutes a worse result than the loss of the lives of four innocent people is problematic. It follows, therefore, that to deny that the killing of one innocent person in order to save five people from dying yields the best overall outcome is problematic as well.[35]

Second, according to the explanation above, the reason for the prohibition lies in the fact that killing yields bad results in addition to the death itself (and these additional results do not exist in the case of dying of a disease). But if this was the reason, then it would be permitted to kill one innocent person in order to prevent five people from being killed by another person: If a terrorist tells me that I should kill one innocent person, otherwise he will kill five other people, I would be permitted to kill the innocent person. When the terrorist kills the five innocent people, the loss caused to the world will not only be the death of five people but also the harm done to his moral integrity. And it seems that from a consequentialist perspective, my moral integrity is no more important to the world (or to morality) than the moral integrity of the terrorist. So when I kill one person, there is the loss of one person's life together with the harm caused to the moral integrity of one person, whereas if the terrorist kills five there is the loss of five lives together with the harm caused to the moral integrity of one person. So it seems that, from a consequentialist perspective, the killing of the one person should be permitted, but this conclusion stands in conflict with the common intuition that the prohibition against killing one innocent person also holds against killing one innocent person in order to prevent the killing of five other people. Hence, the suggested consequentialist explanation cannot explain the common intuition.[36]

In response to the argument above one might suggest that people have a right to act in accordance with their personal projects and life plans, to act in order to fulfil their goals, without always considering the harms that their actions might cause to other people. They do not have to relate to their own interests, plans and lives in a completely neutral way. So a person should be allowed to prefer to preserve his moral integrity over being concerned with the moral integrity of the terrorist. In the same vein, we might even suggest against the first difficulty raised above that a person has the right to prefer his personal moral integrity, which is essential to the quality of his life, over saving the lives of four people, even if from a neutral point of view, four human lives are worth more than his moral integrity. But this line of argument cannot solve our problem, because even if we accept the idea presented above regarding the right of a person to preserve his moral integrity, even at the cost of four human lives (an idea which is not easily justified), we are still left without an explanation for the *prohibition* against killing one innocent person in order to save five from being killed. If from a neutral perspective, the lives of five people are worth more than the life of one person, why is it forbidden to carry out the killing? If the person is ready to waive his right and sacrifice his moral integrity in order to save the lives of several people (or to save the moral integrity of another person) why should there be a prohibition against pursuing such a course of action?[37]

Last, if the harm caused to the moral integrity of an agent is so important (more important than the lives of four people) then we would expect that in having to choose between saving one person from dying of a disease and saving another person from being killed by someone we would feel that the fact that one is going to be killed by a person constitutes a very important factor in deciding whom to save. For in saving the potential murder victim we also prevent the damage to the moral integrity of his potential killer. In fact, we should even feel that we should save one person from being killed even when the alternative is to save five people from dying of a disease. But we do not feel this way.[38]

3.6   The Nature of Deontological Constraints

We can conclude that any attempt to explain absolute (or almost absolute, or deontological) constraints in consequentialist terms must fail, because even if you find some bad result that is engendered by murder but not by death through natural causes, this additional bad result still cannot explain why there is a prohibition against killing one innocent person in order to prevent five *murders*. It doesn't matter what the additional result in the case of murder is, and whether it is connected to the victim or to the agent or to the value itself. There is always the problem that when you murder one person in order to prevent five *murders* your action yields the best overall results. And yet it is still forbidden to kill, so that consequentialism cannot explain the deontological constraints.[39]

This means that those who believe in the existence of deontological prohibitions must be committed to the idea that it is sometimes forbidden to perform a certain act even though the performance of that act produces the best overall outcome.

What emerges is that in the context of deontological constraints, morality consists of norms directed to *each individual,* ordering *him* not to perform certain actions.[40] As Moore puts it:

Such theories view morality as consisting of norms directed to each moral agent, norms whose content says, 'don't *you* torture an innocent child'. Such norms are 'agent relative' in the sense that they do not direct each of us to minimize bad states of affairs, such as murders and tortures. For if that were the content of moral norms, we would be justified in torturing one person ourselves whenever it would prevent the torture of many persons by others. Rather, such norms direct us not to do the forbidden acts, leaving it to others to obey or disobey such norms, as they will.[41]

Morality says to each person "don't *you* kill an innocent person". And this prohibition is absolute (or almost absolute or deontological) and cannot be overruled by a simple consequential calculation. In this context, morality does not say to each individual "see to it that there be fewer deaths in the world", and it even does not say to each individual "see to it that there be fewer killings in the world".[42] Morality in the context of deontological constraints imposes on people a personal responsibility for *their* actions, rather than for the best results in the world or for the actions of other people.

Such a conception of how morality works can accept, and its proponents generally do accept, that there are areas in morality in which the decisive considerations in determining what to do are utilitarian or consequentialist.[43] But it holds that in the context of absolute (or almost absolute) prohibitions, morality issues injunctions that are directed to each and every individual ordering *him* to refrain from performing certain actions. When morality absolutely (or almost absolutely) prohibits the killing of an innocent person, you cannot justify the killing by showing that it saves the lives of several people or prevents five murders. You cannot justify it by pointing towards the good results it produces because the prohibition is absolute (or almost absolute). Nor can you justify it (in the case of preventing five murders) by appealing to the prohibition itself and saying that by killing one person you minimise the number of future violations of this norm (by preventing others from murdering). For the absolute prohibition is directed individually at you and makes you responsible for *your* killing and not for the killings performed by others.[44] It should be emphasised that the point here is not only that in certain contexts morality has a special interest in *actions* (in addition to its general interest in states of affairs). For if this was the whole point, then we would still not be able to understand why it is forbidden to kill one innocent person in order to prevent five *murders*. Rather, deontology has a further feature: it believes in directives directed individually to each person which tell *him* to avoid performing certain actions even when performance of the action will minimise the performance of such actions in the world.[45]

This insight about how morality works in the context of deontological constraints still does not put an end to our quest for the rationale of these constraints. Because even after we understand what morality does in this context, we are still left without an answer to the question why morality "behaves" in this way. Thus, the question remains: if killing is a very bad thing, why does morality forbid killing one person when such a killing will prevent five killings? Why is morality so interested in what *I* do instead of being interested in minimising the amount of bad results or bad actions? It seems that a full answer to this question has yet to be found and that all we have to support these deontological prohibitions is a firm intuition that morality consists of such norms. The fact that we cannot give a logical proof to a moral view, however, does not commit us to reject it. Many think that every moral theory or ideology is based upon one or several basic norms or values that are not deduced logically from other premises but are accepted without such proof as right because they are supported by intuition, perceived as self-evident and so on. According to many, even the basic norm of utilitarianism (to maximise the good) cannot be proven logically and is accepted (by utilitarians) as right without proof. So it seems that in our context what we have to do if we do not want to ignore our moral intuitions concerning deontological constraints is to see the belief that it is forbidden to kill (or torture) an innocent person even in order to prevent several murders (or tortures) as part of our basic moral beliefs which do not derive from other principles but are supported by intuition only.[46] At the same time, the insight that morality orders each person individually not to perform certain actions (even when the actions would yield the best overall results) contributes something to our understanding. Instead of seeing every single deontological prohibition as totally separate and isolated from the other deontological prohibitions, the insight above at least provides an account of the general framework within which deontological prohibitions work and this adds something to our understanding of the phenomenon, although it does not give us the rationale for the very existence of the phenomenon.

Now let us try to make a further move in the direction of understanding more deeply the existence of the deontological prohibitions.

3.7   Understanding Deontological Prohibitions

3.7.1   *Understanding the Prohibitions as Preserving the Moral Integrity of the Actor*

Even if we conclude that the reason for the existence of absolute (or almost absolute) prohibitions cannot be found within a consequentialist framework, we can still connect the existence of such prohibitions to the idea that a person should preserve his moral integrity. Instead of saying that there are several separate and isolated absolute prohibitions like "do not kill an innocent person", "do not torture" and so on, we can view morality as ordering each person: you should preserve your moral integrity and *therefore* you are forbidden to kill an innocent person (even in order to prevent five murders), you should not torture, and so on. In this way we can understand the various absolute (or deontological) prohibitions as being derived from the basic requirement directed towards the agent – to preserve his moral integrity. The difference between this suggestion and the consequentialist explanation discussed earlier is that this suggestion does not try to explain the concern of morality for my moral integrity in a way that reconciles it with the demand to maximise good results in the world. We do not have an answer to the question why morality is more interested in my moral integrity than in the moral integrity of the terrorist who will kill five people if I don't kill one innocent person. The role that the idea of "preserving the moral integrity" plays in the present suggestion is to enable us to understand that the various specific absolute (or deontological) prohibitions are founded on one basic injunction, so that the appeal to intuition as the ultimate justification is done not at the level of the various prohibitions (because they can be derived from a more basic injunction) but only at the level of the justification of the fundamental injunction directed to each person – to preserve his moral integrity. The injunction to preserve one's moral integrity even where obedience to this injunction means that one is required to refrain from maximising good results cannot be justified by derivation from a more basic norm but only by appeal to intuition.

This suggestion is in the vein of what Nagel wrote about the deontological prohibitions. In trying to understand the deontological constraints, Nagel begins with the proposition that when an action is intentionally aimed at a goal (whether the goal is an end in itself or only a means) that action is guided by that goal, and the actor must be prepared to adjust his action to changing circumstances in order to ensure the achievement of the goal. This means that to aim at evil is to have one's action guided by evil.[47] And he continues:

> But the essence of evil is that it should *repel* us. If something is evil, our actions should be guided, if they are guided by it at all, toward its elimination rather than toward its maintenance. That is what evil *means*. So when we aim at evil we are swimming

head-on against the normative current. Our action is guided by the goal at every point in the direction diametrically opposite to that in which the value of that goal points. To put it another way, if we aim at evil we make what we do in the first instance a positive rather than a negative function of it. At every point, the intentional function is simply the normative function reversed, and from the point of view of the agent, this produces an acute sense of moral dislocation.[48]

Nagel is aware of the contrary argument that when you aim at evil as a means to achieve good consequences, you are guided not by evil but by overall good, which includes a balance of goods and evils. Thus, when you twist a child's arm in order to rescue injured persons you are guided by the good aim, and the good of that aim dominates the evil of the child's pain. But, he says, this picture is only correct if we view the act from the outside, from an impersonal viewpoint. But each of us is not only an objective self but also a particular person with a particular perspective, so that "from the internal point of view, the pursuit of evil in twisting the child's arm looms large. The production of pain is the immediate aim, and the fact that from an external perspective you are choosing a balance of good over evil does not cover up the fact that this is the intrinsic character of your action".[49]

Nagel does not expressly speak here of preserving the moral integrity of the agent. However, he does view deontological constraints as based on a concern for the agent and emphasises that in acting in order to cause an evil, the agent swims head-on against the normative current. It is also important to stress that Nagel does not suggest here a consequentialist explanation for deontological constraints. He rejects the idea that deontological constraints can be understood as being based on the idea that a murder constitutes a worse event than a death which occurs by natural causes. Indeed, he is aware of the argument that the prohibition against killing one innocent person in order to prevent five *murders* proves that consequentialism cannot explain the deontological constraints.[50] So there are two things in Nagel's explanation that can support the suggestion made above as to how deontological prohibitions should be understood: his emphasis on what the action does to the *agent*, and the idea that the notion of morality's concern for the agent can be used within the framework of a non-consequentialist understanding of deontological constraints.

Fried also speaks of deontological constraints in terms of concern for the agent. He speaks of the moral integrity of the agent and his refraining from being the agent of the wrong.[51] He says that right and wrong are the foundations of our moral personality, and that they have an overriding status, because they establish our basic position as freely choosing entities. They are, inter alia, expressions of self-respect.[52] He asserts that deontology preserves our position as free moral agents, our status as persons.[53] Thus, Fried suggests an explanation which focuses on the agent and his moral integrity (as well as his self-respect). But this is not a consequentialist explanation. Fried is not a consequentialist,[54] and he is aware of the prohibition against killing one innocent person in order to prevent several *murders*.[55] What we have here, then, is an explanation of the phenomenon of deontological prohibitions that is based on a concern for the agent without being consequentialist in nature. It seems, then, that the explanation presented above regarding the phenomenon of deontological prohibitions finds support in Fried's writings.[56]

3.7.2 *Understanding the Prohibitions as Protecting the Dignity of the Victim*

Another possibility is to understand the deontological constraints by viewing morality as instructing each person: "Don't you harm the dignity of persons by using them as means to an end and therefore don't you kill an innocent person (even to prevent five murders) and don't you torture persons" and so on. Here, too, we are not speaking of a consequentialist explanation that sees the harm to the dignity of the victim as an additional harm that should be taken into account in calculating the consequences. The explanation is still deontological in nature, but instead of viewing the various deontological prohibitions as separate basic norms, we view the injunction directed to each person not to harm the dignity of other people as the basic norm from which the various prohibitions are derived. Also, in this explanation too, we still perceive the basic injunction as being directed to each person individually and as imposing on him a special responsibility for *his* actions, rather than instructing him to minimise all harm caused to the dignity of people in the world (or even to minimise the amount of human actions in the world that harm the dignity of people). Only if the basic norm is understood as imposing a special responsibility on each individual for *his* actions, can it be explained why it is forbidden to kill one innocent person in order to prevent five murders. But the last point reveals a relative weakness in the present explanation, in comparison to the previous one which focused on the agent. For if morality is so interested in what *I* do – in that it orders me not to violate the norm even when the violation would minimise the number of future violations of this norm in the world – it seems more reasonable to assume that this interest in *me* stems from a concern about *my* moral integrity, rather than to assume that it stems from a concern about other people (the victims). When the basic norm is based on a concern for the victims it seems less reasonable to assume that it would not allow preventing five violations by performing one.[57] On the other hand, there is also a relative weakness in the previous explanation when compared to the present one, as we generally tend to understand the norms of morality (not to kill, not to torture) as being primarily based on a concern for the protection of other people, rather than on a concern for the actor.[58] So some may prefer the present explanation to the previous one.

In the previous section, I showed that support may be found in the writings of Nagel and Fried for the idea that the basic norm of deontology is founded on an interest in the moral integrity of the agent. Here I want to add that support for the present explanation can also be found in their writings. As I stressed in the previous section, both of them are aware of the prohibition against killing one person in order to prevent five murders and both reject consequentialist explanations for deontological constraints. Still, they sometimes suggest that deontological constraints be understood in terms of respect for the victim. Fried suggests that deontological norms be viewed as derived from, *inter alia*, the duty to respect other people.[59] Nagel also speaks of the perspective of the victim, that he feels outraged when he is deliberately harmed (even for the greater good of others) because of the assault on his value.[60] Seeing that they reject consequentialist explanations, it seems that they should be understood as suggesting something similar to the present explanation, namely, that the basic norm prohibits acting with disrespect toward the victim, and that this basic norm is not derived from a more basic norm.[61]

3.7.3 *Understanding the Prohibitions as Protecting the Value Itself*

The third possibility is to understand the various deontological constraints as being derived from a norm demanding from each person that he not harm important abstract values by way of *his* actions. Every person is ordered not to harm the value of life itself and, therefore, he should not kill an innocent person (even in order to prevent five murders). The same can be said about torture, and so on. Here, too, we are not faced with a consequentialist explanation (otherwise it would be permitted to act in a way that minimises the harms done to the value of life, for example, by killing an innocent person in order to prevent five murders); rather the abstract values are introduced to suggest that the various deontological constraints are derived from a more basic norm that demands of each individual not to harm the values themselves (or not to harm the moral structure of the world). Like the explanation based on a concern for the victim, this explanation suffers from a weakness when compared with the explanation based on the moral integrity of the agent, as it seems reasonable to assume that if morality is so interested in what *I* do, then this concern is based on a concern for my moral integrity and not on a concern for other objects (like the abstract values). Another problem with the present explanation is that it commits us to believe in the existence of transcendental entities, namely, the values themselves, that can be harmed by our actions (or, at least, in the existence of a moral structure of the world that can be harmed by our actions). Those who do not believe in such entities or such a structure will not embrace the present explanation. On the other hand, there is also a relative weakness in the explanation which focuses on the moral integrity of the agent when compared to the present explanation, as we do not tend to view norms of morality as being primarily based on a concern for the actor.

3.7.4 *Possible Implications of the Different Explanations*

It follows from the discussion above that a consequentialist explanation cannot fully rationalise deontological constraints. They can only be ultimately based on intuition. But we still have four options. One option is to view the various deontological constraints (not to kill, not to torture, and so on) as basic judgments that do not derive from other principles. Alternatively, we can suggest that the various constraints derive from a basic norm. Here three possibilities arise regarding the contents of this basic norm: that it is focused on the moral integrity of the agent, on the idea that we should respect other people and not use them merely as means, or on the values themselves.

There may be implications to the explanation chosen within this context. For example: Assuming that there are moral prohibitions against doing certain things to animals, the question arises whether there are deontological constraints against doing certain things to them. If the deontological constraints are founded on the idea of respect for persons, on the idea that we should not use people as means, then it is very reasonable to conclude that there is no room for deontological constraints with regard to doing certain things to animals, because many of us think that it is permissible to use animals as means, for example by killing them in order to eat them.[62] But if the basic norm is focused on the moral integrity of the agent or on the values themselves then deontological constraints against doing certain things to animals appear more plausible.

The explanation chosen for the existence of deontological constraints may also influence the way in which the distinction made by the doctrine of the double effect is rationalised. The next section will focus on this issue.

3.8   Understanding the Doctrine of the Double Effect

3.8.1   *The General Thrust of the Explanations*

The doctrine of the double effect distinguishes between cases in which a result is desired as a means to another end and cases in which the same result is not desired but is nevertheless foreseen by the actor as a certain result of his course of action. According to this doctrine, there are contexts in which it is forbidden to cause a result when it is desired as a means to an end, though it is permissible to cause the same result when it is not desired as a means, but is foreseen as certain, although all other things are equal in the two cases, including the ultimate good end, i.e. in spite of the fact that the two cases are identical from a utilitarian point of view.

As I pointed out in section 3.1, some authors reject this doctrine. As was explained there, from a utilitarian point of view it is very natural to oppose the doctrine.[63] But from a deontological perspective, maximisation of utility is not the only principle of morality, and hence there is room for distinctions like those made by the doctrine of the double effect. However, not every deontologist must accept the distinction made by the doctrine of the double effect. Indeed, it seems that those who believe in absolute (or deontological) constraints must make some distinctions, otherwise conflicting cases may arise where the same rule demands incompatible courses of action. Take the case in which you can save the lives of five people who are going to die from a disease only by killing an innocent person. If the absolute norm is "Do not cause the death of an innocent person" then regardless of what the agent does he is in violation of the prohibition. If he kills the innocent person in order to save five he violates the prohibition and if he refrains from killing the one person the prohibition is violated just the same because in this case he causes the death of five people. The conflict in such a case can indeed be solved by the doctrine of the double effect.[64] For the killing of the one person is purposeful and hence should be absolutely forbidden, while the death of the five people in the case of not killing the one is only foreseen as a by-product so that the absolute prohibition does not apply. But this is not the only solution available to the problem raised by such a case. The conflict can also be resolved by using another common distinction, namely, the distinction between commission and omission. If the actor kills the innocent person, he kills him by a positive action; but if he refrains from killing him, then he only causes the death of the five people by omission. So we can suggest that the absolute prohibition only applies to killing by positive actions, rather than to killing by omissions (and thereby solve the problem).[65] This means that not every deontologist must accept the doctrine of the double effect. In the literature one finds authors who reject the doctrine of the double effect but make other distinctions in defining the content of deontological constraints.[66] But as I said earlier, some authors accept the validity of the doctrine of the double effect.[67] Needless to say, one may accept the doctrine of the double effect and at the same time accept the validity of other distinctions as well.[68]

Our interest here, however, is the doctrine of the double effect, not other distinctions. I will attempt now to suggest a rationale for the doctrine of the double effect. The question that should be addressed is: Why does the absolute prohibition against killing an innocent person apply to killing with direct intention and not to killing with (mere) foresight of certainty? It seems that the rationale of the doctrine can be related to how the very existence of the absolute prohibition is understood. If we perceive absolute prohibitions as basic norms that are justified only by direct appeal to intuition, then the distinction discussed here can only be justified by direct appeal to intuition. We have to say that as much as our intuition tells us that it is forbidden to kill one innocent person in order to save five people from being murdered, it also tells us that it is permissible to turn a tram in order to save five people from death despite the fact that the actor knows that once the tram is turned, one person will be killed. Thus, moral intuition tells us that it is absolutely (or almost absolutely) forbidden to kill an innocent person with direct intention but that there is no such absolute prohibition against killing a person with (mere) foresight of certainty.[69] And the same holds for several other prohibitions.

But if we base absolute prohibitions on the concern of morality for a certain thing, be it the moral integrity of the actor, the values themselves or the dignity of the victim, then we can connect the rationale of the distinction to that concern.

3.8.2   *Understanding the Distinction in the Context of the Moral Integrity of the*
       Actor

As we saw earlier (in section 3.7.1), Nagel suggests that deontological constraints be understood as being interested in the viewpoint of the agent. He says that the agent is guided by the goal of his action, even in the case where this goal is not his ultimate end but is only needed as a means. Therefore, when an agent twists the arm of a child in order to produce pain, he is guided by evil, and this is manifested by the fact that he must also be prepared to adjust his course of action to ensure the production of the evil (the fact that the ultimate end is good does not change this fact). Nagel observes that "what feels peculiarly wrong about doing evil intentionally even that good may come of it is the headlong striving against value that is internal to one's aim".[70] Nagel also explains in the same context the distinction made by the doctrine of the double effect. He suggests that, when compared with evil side-effects, an intention to cause the evil magnifies the importance of the evil aim from the agent's perspective. This is because when you aim at evil, even as a means, you are guided by the evil goal (you have to be prepared to adjust your course of action to ensure the evil's occurrence) so that you swim head-on against the moral current. Consequently, the action produces an acute sense of moral dislocation from the agent's viewpoint. This is not the case when the actor acts in order to cause a good result and foresees that his action will bring about a bad result as a side-effect, because here the action is not guided by the bad result, so that the agent is not guided by evil.[71]

As we saw earlier (in section 3.7.1), Fried also suggests an understanding of deontological constraints which focuses on the agent. In this context he also explains why absolute prohibitions against causing certain results only apply to causing them with direct intention. He writes that "morality is about the good and the right way of our being in the world *as human beings.* We relate to the world as human beings as we pursue our purposes in the world, as we act intentionally ... The paradigmatic moral judgment is on intentional action as such ...".[72] He also explains that: "[M]eans are part of our plans and thus are invested with our persons in a way that concomitants are not. The means we choose are steps along a way we have mapped out in advance. Concomitants just happen ... The special responsibility we bear for our projects is an appropriate recognition of our special involvement in those projects."[73]

Grisez also focuses on the agent when he explains the distinction, made in the context of absolute prohibitions, between acting with direct intention and acting with mere foresight of certainty. He writes: "A difference of intention can relate identical behavior in quite different ways to our moral attitude, and to the self being created through our moral attitude. If one intends to kill another, he accepts the identity of a killer as an aspect of his moral self".[74]

To conclude: If we view deontological constraints as being derived from the injunction directed to each individual to preserve his moral integrity, then the distinction between direct intention and foresight of certainty can be viewed as being based on an idea connected to the notion of moral integrity, namely, that when a person acts in order to cause a bad result, such as death, his mind (or soul) is guided by and directed towards the evil, and this harms his moral integrity (or his soul). This is so even in a case where the ultimate end is good. On the other hand, when a person acts in order to cause some good result (while foreseeing a bad side effect) his mind is not guided by evil and is not directed towards it, and therefore his moral integrity is not harmed in the same way as it is in the case of direct intention.[75] Because of this, absolute (or deontological) prohibitions apply to causing certain bad results purposely and not to causing them as known side effects.

3.8.3   *Understanding the Distinction in the Context of the Values Themselves*

If we view deontological prohibitions as being based on morality's concern for the values themselves (as was suggested supra in section 3.7.3) we can explain the double effect theory by suggesting that absolute prohibitions only apply to cases of direct intention because it is only when the agent acts with direct intention that there is a direct attack on the value itself. When a person acts in order to kill an innocent person, the destruction of life becomes his goal and target. In this case he puts himself in direct conflict with the value of life itself, in that he attacks that value. Therefore the value (of life) itself is significantly harmed (in spite of the fact that the ultimate end is to save lives). The situation is different, however, when the person acts in order to produce good results, and he only foresees the bad side effects of his action. Here the person concentrates on achieving the good, even though he knows that his action will produce bad side effects. Therefore, in this case, there is no direct attack on the value itself, and therefore the value itself is not harmed in the same way as it is in the case of direct intention. Therefore absolute prohibitions do not apply in cases of side effects.

3.8.4   *Understanding the Distinction in the Context of Concern for the Victim*

It was suggested earlier (in section 3.7.2) that deontological constraints may be viewed as being based on a concern for the victim. I will now turn to suggest an explanation for the doctrine of the double effect that is based on this concern. At first glance, it seems that the distinction between intention and foresight cannot be explained by a concern for the victim, since from his perspective the death he suffers (or the pain he suffers in cases of causing pain) is exactly the same whether it is caused purposely or knowingly. It seems that even speaking of his "right to life" being infringed does not help here because it seems that this right is infringed when there is foresight of certainty to the same extent as it is in cases of direct intention.[76] However, it was also suggested that deontological constraints are based on the prohibition against using the victim as a means to an end. If this is the case, then we can better understand the doctrine of the double effect: The deontological constraints are based on the prohibition against infringing the dignity of the victim by using him as a means to the ends of other people. He is used as a means only when the actor acts with a direct intention to harm him (for example, when his death is needed as a means to save other people). This is not the case, however, where the actor acts in order to promote the good of others and foresees the harm to the victim as a side effect of his action. Therefore, the absolute prohibitions only apply to acting with direct intention to harm.[77]

3.8.5   *Possible Implications of the Different Explanations*

From the discussion above we can conclude that four possibilities exist in attempting to understand the doctrine of the double effect. The doctrine can be explained by a direct appeal to intuition, so that the doctrine is viewed as one of our basic moral beliefs, without further explanation. Or we can understand the doctrine in one of three contexts: The context of the agent, the context of the values themselves or the context of the victim. The explanation chosen may have implications. For example, it was suggested in section 3.7.4 that if deontological constraints are based on the idea that people should not be used as means to the ends of others then it is reasonable to conclude that there will be no deontological constraints with regard to doing certain things to animals. This contention is also relevant to the doctrine of the double effect. If the whole distinction made by the doctrine turns on the idea that people should not be treated as means, then it is reasonable not to use the doctrine of the double effect in the area of prohibitions against doing certain things to animals. But if we base the distinction on explanations connected to the agent or to the values themselves then it is also possible (though not imperative) to invoke the distinction in the area of prohibitions against doing certain things to animals. The question which explanation is adopted may also have implications in the context of voluntary euthanasia. Is it reasonable to apply the distinction made by the doctrine of the double effect to the case of a dying and suffering patient who demands his pain be ended even at the cost of being killed? Is it reasonable to say that we may give him pain-killing drugs in order to stop the pain even when we know that the amount required to stop the pain will also hasten his death, but that we may not act in order to kill him when the death is needed as a means to stop the pain? If we base the doctrine of the double effect on the idea that we should not use people as means to the ends of other people, then it is not reasonable to use the doctrine in the case of voluntary euthanasia, because when we kill the patient in response to his request and in order to help him, we do not use him as a means to the ends of other people.[78] But if we base the doctrine on ideas connected to the values themselves[79] or to the agent, then it is possible (though not imperative) to also apply it in the area of voluntary euthanasia.

Notes

1   On this distinction in Catholic theology, see Rachels (1986) 15-17, 104; Moore (1997) 690-691; Mackie (1977a) 160-161; Nagel (1972) 130; Fried (1976) 184-185; Reeder (1996) 109-110; Quinn (1993) 175-178; Kenny (1995) 77-78; Bennett (1995) 196-197; Foot (1978) 19-20; Hart (1968) 122-125; Finnis (1991a) 67-74. Sometimes one finds interpretations of the Catholic doctrine that differ from the one presented here. I think, however, that the interpretation suggested here is the most common.

2   Mackie (1977a) 161; Rachels (1986) 17, 104; Hart (1968) 122-123; Devine (1974) 47; Frey (1983) 120.

3   Hart (1968) 123-124; Foot (1978) 19-21; Quinn (1993) 177; Sinnott-Armstrong (1988) 90. For an example of a procedure in which the death of the foetus is sought as a means, and thus directly intended, see Hart (1968) 124. It is sometimes said that according to Catholic theology, if the only way to save a mother in labour from death is to crush the head of the foetus (which will kill him immediately), then it is forbidden to perform this procedure because in such a case there is a direct intention to kill. As

against this example it has been argued that in such a case the surgeon does not directly intend the death of the child. Rather, the dimensions of the foetus are such that the mother will die if the surgeon attempts to remove it without changing these dimensions. Though the death of the foetus is inevitable, it is not needed as a means. It is only a by-product of the crushing of its head. See Geddes (1972) 94-95. Cf. Hart (1968) 123. Foot, however, argues that the crushing of the child's head and the death of the child are one and the same event, and that even if we assume that they can be considered as two different events, the two are still much too close to one another to apply the doctrine of the double effect. See Foot (1978) 21-22. Cf. Duff (1973) 17-18 who says that there is a conceptual connection between head crushing and death. But as Foot says (ibid.) difficultiès arise in explaining where the line is to be drawn, and in determining the exact criterion of "closeness" for the purposes of the doctrine. This means that adherents of the distinction may sometimes face borderline cases in which it is not clear whether the death (or another relevant result) is merely foreseen as a by-product or is directly intended. This problem (which can be called the problem of closeness) is not the only problem which complicates the process of putting the distinction into practice. But borderline cases notwithstanding, there are many clear cases of direct intention as well as many clear cases of foresight that a result will certainly follow as a side effect from an action. So from now on I will leave the borderline cases aside and concentrate on the distinction itself and the debate surrounding its moral importance. On the problem of closeness (and other problems in drawing the distinction) see in addition to the sources already mentioned: Fried (1976) 185-186; Fried (1978) 23-24; Devine (1974) 50-55; Grisez (1970) 87-96; Bennett (1995) 204-213; Uniacke (1994) 106-112; Reeder (1996) 147-152; Quinn (1993) 186-187; Simester (1996b) 456-469.

4   See Foot (1978) 22; Foot (1985) 25; Nagel (1972) 130.
5   Hart (1968) 124.
6   Williams (1974) 203, 321-322; Frey (1983) 135-136; Rachels (1986) 92-96, 104-105. Other opponents of the doctrine are for example: Bennett (1981) 95-105, and see also at 106-116; Bennett (1995) 214-224; Kagan (1989) 128-182; Glover (1977) 86-91.
7   See for example Fried (1976) 168-169, 199; Fried (1978) 20-22, 27; Foot (1985) 23, 25; Finnis, Boyle and Grisez (1987) 288-294, 309-316; Walzer (1977) 151-159, 163-164; Cavanaugh (1999). See also Nagel (1986) 179-185 who has shown sympathy for the doctrine. Modified versions of the doctrine are embraced by Quinn (1993) 175-193; Reeder (1996) 130-153. Although I will not enter here into the details of Quinn's and Reeder's versions of the doctrine, arguments or examples raised by these authors will be used in this book insofar as they bear upon the classic definition of the doctrine (as stated in section 3.1).

It should be emphasised that just because one embraces the doctrine, this does not imply that one agrees with its application in all the contexts in which it is applied by others. One may use the doctrine in the context of killing civilians in war or in the context of saving the lives of five people at the price of killing one person, but deny its relevance in the context of abortion, for example, and say that it is always permissible to save the life of the mother at the price of the life of the foetus, even when the procedure taken consists in killing the foetus as a means to save the mother's life (this can be justified for example by the argument that the foetus is not yet a person). One can also deny the relevance of the doctrine in the context of euthanasia if one thinks that the consent of the terminally ill and suffering patient yields a license to end his life, even as a means to end his pain. One who holds such views would still be a proponent of the doctrine, for our purposes, as long as he accepts the idea that there are *some* contexts in which the difference between what a person is allowed to do and not allowed to do turns on the distinction between direct intention and foresight of a side effect.

8　Foot (1978) 22-23; Nagel (1986) 179; Quinn (1993) 176-177; Reeder (1996) 147.

9　For this example see Quinn (1993) 177; Nagel (1972) 130; Fried (1976) 185; Fried (1978) 21; Walzer (1977) 151-164; Reeder (1996) 130, 146-147.

10　The example of extracting a substance from the dead body is based on Foot (1978) 24. A similar example that sometimes appears in the literature concerns the prohibition against dismembering one healthy patient to obtain the organs needed to save five others. See for example Reeder (1996) 120, 130; Fried (1978) 52. This example is not advanced in the text because of the possible counter-argument that in this case the death is not needed as a means. The only thing needed is to sever the organs and put them to use, the death being only a side effect. The answer to this argument will be that the death is too close to the dismemberment so that it has to be considered as being directly intended (see supra note 3). Another option, that will not be discussed here, is to embrace the modified version of the doctrine of the double effect of Reeder or Quinn (see supra note 7). The example of the terrorist is based on Foot (1978) 23. Cf. Thomson (1990) 141. A similar example is that of a person ordered by a tyrant to torture one person – on pain of the tyrant torturing five other people. See Moore (1997) 691. The example of the tram constitutes a modified version of an example which appears in Foot (1978) 23. It can also be found in Reeder (1996) 119-121, 130. Cf. Thomson (1990) 176-178. For a similar example concerning making a breach in a dike cf. Williams (1974) 199-201.

11　See for example Fried (1976) 165-166; Frankena (1973) 34-37; Scheffler (1988a) 1-3.

12　For the example concerning the prohibition to kill one innocent person in order to prevent the deaths of five other people by disease see Scheffler (1982) 108. Cf. Nagel (1986) 178. Another example is furnished by the case of the person ordered by a terrorist to kill one innocent person on pain of the terrorist killing five other people. Here common moral intuition forbids killing the one innocent person in order to prevent the murder of five people. See Foot (1978) 23; Nagel (1986) 179; Fried (1976) 194; Scheffler (1988b) 243.

13　Cf. the examples concerning torturing a little child in order to force his relative to give one information that can save the lives of several people in Scheffler (1988a) 3 and in Nagel (1986) 176. Another example concerns the prohibition to torture one innocent person in order to prevent another person from torturing five other people. See Moore (1997) 691.

14　See Scheffler (1982) 108, 114; Moore (1997) 686, 705.

15　Scheffler (1988a) 3-5; Nagel (1986) 175-180. One might suggest that the prohibition against killing one innocent person in order to save the lives of five other people can be reconciled with utilitarianism by rejecting the idea that the lives of five people are worth more than the life of one person, and insisting that the life of every person has an infinite value. If we accept this idea, we can say that it is better not to intervene and not to kill the one person, since, on balance, the killing does not produce net good consequences. In my view, however, this solution should be rejected. Take the case where a doctor has a limited amount of medication. He can use it all to save the life of one patient or, alternatively, he can use it all to save the lives of five other patients. It seems that we would generally say that he should save the five instead of the one. This suggests that we see the lives of five people as being worth more than the life of one person. If so, the suggestion above fails. Cf. the commentary to the Model Penal Code that says about a case discussed there that "the life of every individual must be taken in such a case to be of equal value" (Model Penal Code and Commentaries (1985) Part 1, vol. 2, p. 15). Moreover, even if we would say that because of the unique status of human life we cannot say that that the lives of five people are worth more than the life of one person, the suggestion above would still not be able to explain why it is forbidden to inflict serious physical suffering upon a single individual in order to prevent the same suffering being inflicted upon five other people. Here it seems very difficult to deny that the state of affairs would be better if only one person is made to suffer.

16   The view that there is an absolute prohibition against directly killing an innocent person is adopted by Grisez (1970) 66, 96. For the view that the norm forbidding the intentional killing of the innocent is absolute cf. Finnis, Boyle and Grisez (1987) 309. See also Thomson (1990) 167-169. Others mention such a view but do not agree with it. See for example Moore (1997) 687-688, 719.

17   Fried, for example, says that a catastrophe may cause the absoluteness of right and wrong to yield, and that in extreme cases such as when killing an innocent person may save a whole nation it is fanatical to maintain the absoluteness of the judgments, to do right even if the heavens will in fact fall. See Fried (1978) 10. He goes on to emphasise, however, that the fact that in extreme circumstances a categorical norm may be overwhelmed, does not mean that it loses its categorical nature, because so long as the consequences fall within a very broad range, the categorical norm holds (ibid. at p. 12). Moore rejects the claim that one should allow a nuclear war or even the destruction of a sizable city by a nuclear device rather than kill or torture an innocent person; to prevent such extraordinary harms, extreme actions seem justified. See Moore (1997) 719 (at 721-722 he says that to justify the torture of one innocent person requires that the torture prevent the destruction of an entire city or, perhaps, a lifeboat or a building full of people). He emphasises, however, that the view allowing for horrendous enough consequences to override norms such as "do not kill an innocent person" does not collapse into a consequentialist morality, because up until the very high threshold of bad consequences – the deontological constraint holds. It is still forbidden to torture one innocent person in order to save two other people from being tortured (ibid. 721-723). And cf. Thomson (1990) 167 who mentions that "where the numbers get very large, however, some people start to feel nervous. Hundreds! Billions! The whole population of Asia!".

18   Nagel says that deontological constraints may be overridden by neutral reasons of sufficient strength. See Nagel (1986) 176, 185. He mentions a number of deontological constraints, such as the prohibition against breaking promises and lying (ibid. 176). (The prohibition against lying is also considered a deontological norm by Fried (1978) 9). Thomson speaks of a "sufficiently large increment of good" which is required to override what I call here "deontological prohibitions". She maintains that although it is forbidden to kick an innocent person in the shin, such a course of action seems to be permissible if it is carried out in order to save the lives of four people, as in this case the increment of good seems to be sufficiently large (Thomson (1990) 149-153). But an increment of good of the same amount is not sufficiently large to make it permissible to kill an innocent person because the prohibition against doing so is more stringent (ibid.). On the possibility that some people probably feel that it is permitted to sacrifice one person if enough people are saved as a consequence cf. Foot (1978) 31.

19   Nagel (1972) 129; Nagel (1986) 178; Scheffler (1988b) 243-244, 252.
20   Brandt (1972) 146-147; Frankena (1973) 39-43. There are various versions of rule
      utilitarianism (see Frankena, ibid.), but the differences between them are without
      importance for the discussion here. See also Hare (1972).
21   Brandt (1972) 147.
22   In this vein, see Hare (1972) especially at 174-178. See also Frankena (1973) 40, and
      Moore (1997) 684-685 (Moore himself rejects rule consequentialism). In certain
      contexts, the argument from long-term consequences may also take another form. For
      example, when asked why a doctor is forbidden to kill a visitor in a hospital in order to
      use his organs to save the lives of five people, utilitarians may answer that in the end,
      others will find out what the doctor has done. Consequently, people will no longer
      come to hospitals for treatment because of their fear that the same will be done to
      them, which will yield many deaths in the long run. Cf. Pettit (1997) 154-155;
      Thomson (1990) 142-143 at note 11 (Thomson herself rejects this answer); Katz
      (1996) 54 (Katz himself rejects this answer).
23   Moore (1997) 685; Nagel (1986) 177-179. The objection raised here also applies to
      the argument made from long-term consequences mentioned supra at note 22 in
      relation to the hospital example. See Thomson (1990) 142-143 at note 11.
24   Scheffler illustrates the point as follows: "Suppose that there was a machine, the
      Infallible Optimizer, which never made mistakes in its judgements about which of the
      actions available to an agent at a time would actually minimize total deaths overall.
      Suppose further that people were causally incapable of killing unless the Infallible
      Optimizer certified that a killing was necessary in order to minimize total deaths".
      Scheffler argues that defenders of deontological constraints would presumably
      continue to claim that the killing is forbidden. See Scheffler (1982) 111. Another
      argument found in the literature is that even in our world we can imagine a case where
      the actor can be sure that killing an innocent person in order to save five will yield the
      best overall results, even after considering all the long-term results. It seems that even
      in this case the actor should not kill, which in turn suggests that the prohibition cannot
      be explained by concerns regarding long-term results. See Moore (1997) 686 for such
      a case. This claim also applies to the argument from long-term consequences
      mentioned supra at note 22 in relation to the hospital example.
25   Cf. Foot (1985) 27; Moore (1997) 679 (they both reject this solution).
26   Cf. Scheffler (1982) 88 (he himself rejects this solution). For the general idea that,
      from the victim's perspective, to be the object of an intentional attack is different from
      being injured by a natural force, even if the actual injury is identical, for in the case of
      an intentional attack there is a denial of respect as the victim is used as a means, cf.
      Fried (1978) 29, 32, 34, 41.
27   Cf. Scheffler (1982) 109; Nagel (1986) 178; Moore (1997) 683.
28   Scheffler (1982) 109; Nagel (1986) 178; Moore (1997) 683.
29   Scheffler (1982) 88-89, 100-101; Foot (1985) 27; Nagel (1972) 131-132; Nagel
      (1986) 179; Moore (1997) 683.
30   Kugler (1993) 143-144. Note that when I refer here to the damage caused to the "value
      of life", I am not referring to the idea that killing an innocent person may weaken the
      respect that the killer (and other people who learn about the killing) have for the value
      of human life, and that this weakening may, in the long run, yield unjustified killings.
      Such a concern belongs to the moral theory of "rule utilitarianism" discussed earlier.
31   Cf. Duff (1976) 75-77.

32 For the idea that absolute (or deontological) prohibitions are concerned with the moral integrity or pureness of the agent cf. Nagel (1972) 132 and Scheffler (1982) 89 (who reject this idea as an answer to our problem) and also Fried (1978) 2 and Moore (1997) 705 (who do not use the idea in the context of a consequentialist explanation). See also Hart (1968) 127 who mentions in another context the feeling that to use a man's death as a means to some further end is a defilement of the agent (Hart, however, does not commit himself to this view).

33 Note that I am not referring here to the claim that the killing will weaken the respect of the actor for the value of human life and that this may induce him to kill in the future, where no justification for the killing obtains. This claim belongs to the moral theory of rule utilitarianism discussed earlier. The idea discussed in the text is that the relevant additional bad result of the killing is the very damage to the moral integrity (or to the soul) of the agent which is considered a very bad result in itself.

34 Nagel (1972) 132-133.

35 Cf. Nagel (1972) 132.

36 Cf. Moore (1997) 705; Scheffler (1982) 89. Actually, you can say that even if we focus only on the harm done to the moral integrity of the actor, the killing of the one person will yield the best results because it seems reasonable to assume that killing five people harms the moral integrity of the killer more than the killing of one person. Alternatively you can imagine a case where five terrorists order you to kill one innocent person, otherwise each one of them will kill one innocent person. Cf. Scheffler (1982) 89. Here it seems more obvious that even if we only focus on the harm done to the moral integrity of the actor, the killing of the innocent person will yield the best overall results.

Against the argument based on the terrorist example one may argue that the soul of the terrorist who decides and intends to kill five innocent people (unless you kill one) is already polluted by that decision, so that his killing five innocent people will not add a significant amount of pollution to his soul, so that, in turn, your killing one innocent person produces results which are worse than if you refrain from killing. But imagine another case in which there is a good and moral person who I predict will decide to kill five people if a certain event happens. In order to prevent that event, I have to kill one innocent person. At the time of the deliberation whether to kill the one person, the idea of perpetrating the killing, let alone the decision to kill, does not yet appear in the mind of the other person, so his soul still remains unpolluted. Still, it seems that I am not allowed to kill the one person.

37 Cf. Scheffler (1982) 94-95; Scheffler (1988b) 258.

38 The potential argument that the moral integrity of the potential killer is already harmed by the decision to kill can be refuted by advancing an example in which the decision is not yet taken, as suggested supra at note 36.

39 Scheffler (1982) 89-90; Nagel (1986) 179; Moore (1997) 683; Foot (1985) 27. The idea that some kind of rule consequentialism (or consideration of long-term results, including those of a more abstract quality) can explain deontological constraints should be rejected for the same reasons raised (in section 3.4) against the solution suggested by rule utilitarianism.

40 Fried (1976) 196; Fried (1978) 11, 16, 25; Foot (1985) 32; Moore (1997) 704; Nozick (1974) 28-29. Cf. Nagel (1986) 177-178; Duff (1976) 74.

41 Moore (1997) 687.

42 Cf. Foot (1985) 32.

43 See for example Fried (1978) 41-42.

44 One might claim that by refraining from killing an innocent person whose death is needed to save five people from dying of a disease, I violate an absolute prohibition against causing the death of innocent people. For my refraining from killing the one person causes the death of five innocent people, so a conflict seems to ensue between two absolute directives. This problem will be addressed later (in section 3.8.1). At this point, it need only be mentioned that a common solution to this problem is to distinguish between actions and omissions and to say that the absolute prohibition applies only to causing death by action and not to causing death by omission. Another solution is to apply here the doctrine of the double effect.

45 See Scheffler (1994) 161-164, who emphasises that deontological restrictions are not only "making-focused" but also "agent-centred".

46 Cf. Scheffler (1982) 112, 114; Moore (1997) 705. See also Katz (1999) 574.

47 Nagel (1986) 181.

48 Nagel (1986) 182.

49 Nagel (1986) 183.

50 Nagel (1986) 178-179.

51 Fried (1978) 2.

52 Fried (1978) 8-9.

53 Fried (1978) 32-34.

54 Fried (1978) 7-9 and passim.

55 Fried (1976) 194.

56 See also Moore (1997) 705 at note 89, where he says that it seems that any explanation for prohibitions like the prohibition to kill one person in order to prevent five murders will have to focus on the moral integrity or well-being of the agent to whom moral prohibitions apply.

57 See Moore ibid., saying that it seems that the explanation for the prohibition against killing one innocent person in order to prevent five murders will have to focus on the moral integrity of the agent to whom moral prohibitions apply and not on the unfairness to the victim or on his rights. Cf. Raz (1986) 285.

58 Cf. Scheffler (1994) 145-147.

59 Fried (1978) 29, 32, 34.

60 Nagel (1986) 184.

61 It seems that Nozick should also be understood in a similar way. He suggests that deontological constraints (he calls them side constraints) be viewed as expressing the inviolability of other persons. Side constraints reflect the underlying Kantian principle that individuals are ends and not merely means. They may not be sacrificed or used to achieve other ends without their consent. See Nozick (1974) 30-33. In the same breath, Nozick emphasises that under a theory which believes in side constraints it is forbidden to violate someone's rights even when doing so minimises the total amount of rights violations in society (ibid. at pp. 28-29). Thus, Nozick cannot be understood as suggesting a consequentialist explanation, and his explanation which is based on a concern for the right of the victim not to be used as a means should be understood in a way similar to the explanation suggested here.

62 Cf. Nozick (1974) 38-39 who discusses the view that there are no side constraints on our treatment of animals, a view he labels "utilitarianism for animals, Kantianism for people". The debate whether animals have rights is also relevant here. See, for example, Nozick (1997) 305-310.

63 But rule utilitarians may adopt the doctrine. Cf. Devine (1974) 57-60.

64   Mackie (1977a) 161-162.
65   See Mackie (1977a) 162. See also Moore (1997) 689-690, 699-700; Katz (1999) 569.
66   For example Foot (1978) first rejected the doctrine of the double effect but accepted the distinction between what one does or causes and what one merely allows. Later, however, she changed her view on the subject. See Foot (1985).
67   Supra section 3.2.
68   This is done by Foot (1985). For a discussion of the various distinctions made in the literature in defining the content of deontological constraints see Moore (1997) 689-703.
69   Hart (1968) 124-125 argues that the distinction made by the doctrine of the double effect (which he opposes) can only be understood "as the result of a legalistic conception of morality as if it were couched in the form of a law in rigid form prohibiting all intentional killing as distinct from knowingly causing death".
70   Nagel (1986) 182.
71   Nagel (1986) 179-183.
72   Fried (1978) 27. See also at 20-22.
73   Fried (1978) 40-41.
74   Grisez (1970) 76. See also at 78. Cf. Finnis (1991a) 72-73; Finnis (1991b) 61-63.
75   Hart says (in another context) concerning the distinction: "The distinction seems to make its appeal to a feeling that to *use* a man's death as a means to some further end is a defilement of the agent: his will is thus identified with an evil aim and it is somehow morally worse than the will of one who in the pursuit of the same further end does something which, as the agent realizes, renders the man's death inevitable as a second effect" (Hart (1968) 127).
76   It may be suggested that the right to life has more strength when it is used against intended killing than when it is used against causing death as a side effect. Even if this suggestion is accepted, it is doubtful whether this statement alone (without further elaboration) has an *explanatory* force (that is whether it adds something to our understanding of the phenomenon that the prohibition against killing intentionally is more stringent than the prohibition against causing death as a side effect, or rather it only says the same thing in other words). Cf. Thomson (1990) 201-202.
77   In this vein see Fried (1978) 29, 32, 41. Cf. Nagel (1986) 184; Quinn (1993) 189-193.
78   Cf. Quinn (1993) 185 at note 17; Kamm (1999) 591. Note also that when Nozick speaks of side constraints he says that individuals may not be sacrificed or used to achieve other ends *without their consent* (Nozick (1974) 31) and that the side constraints prohibit using people for the benefit of others (ibid. at p. 33). Of course those who believe in the idea that a person should not treat himself as a mere means can apply the doctrine to the case of voluntary euthanasia, but many people would reject this idea (which also seems to yield a prohibition against committing suicide). I should also emphasise that I am not dealing here with attempts to justify application of the distinction between direct intention and foresight of side effects to cases of euthanasia which are based on considerations that are non-deontological in nature, but are related to rule utilitarianism, slippery slope arguments, and so on.
79   Cf. Dworkin (1993) 194-195. He says we should distinguish between the idea of autonomy (and of best interests) and the view held by some people that euthanasia is wrong even when the patient desires death or when death is in his best interests – because it violates the intrinsic value and sanctity of life. Those who take the latter view believe that deliberately ending a human life denies its inherent, cosmic value. See also ibid. at 12, 198, 214-215.

Chapter 4

Possible Implications of the Debate about the Doctrine of the Double Effect for the Issue of Degrees of Blameworthiness in the Criminal Law

4.1 Possible Implications of Adopting the Doctrine of the Double Effect

At the end of chapter 2, I raised the question whether causing a proscribed result purposely is more blameworthy than causing it recklessly when all other things, including the motives, are equal. To deal with the question, I first surveyed and elucidated (in chapter 3) the debate about the doctrine of the double effect. Now it is time to see what we can learn from the debate about the double effect theory as concerns the issue of degrees of moral blameworthiness. Given that discussions in moral philosophy about the double effect theory generally take place within the context of the distinction between acting with direct intention and acting with foresight of certainty (without direct intention), I will first inquire as to what can be learned from the debate about the double effect theory with regard to the question whether a difference in the degree of moral blameworthiness exists between acting with direct intention and acting with (merely) foresight of certainty. Only later will I return to the distinction between direct intention and recklessness.

Before trying to draw conclusions from the debate about the double effect theory regarding the issue of degrees of blameworthiness, it should be noted that the philosophical discussion about the double effect doctrine does not deal directly with the issue of degrees of blameworthiness with which this book is interested. The double effect doctrine, it will be recalled, makes a distinction between what an agent is allowed to do and what he is not allowed to do. The debate between proponents and opponents of the doctrine turns on the question whether there are contexts in which it is *permissible* to cause a certain result with (mere) foresight of certainty while it is *forbidden* to cause the same result purposely, even though all other things in the two cases are equal. The question to which we are now seeking an answer, however, is different. It is the question whether acting with direct intention is more blameworthy than acting with (mere) foresight of certainty when all other things are equal and *both* actions are morally forbidden. A related difference is that the double effect doctrine is used in the context of cases in which, from the point of view of utility, the action should be justified because its good results outweigh (from a utilitarian perspective) its bad results. In this context, proponents of the double effect doctrine say that in certain cases there is a prohibition against acting with direct intention to cause the bad result while there is no such prohibition against acting with (mere) foresight of certainty that the same bad result would ensue. But the question regarding degrees of blameworthiness is generally raised in contexts where in both cases (that of acting purposely and that of acting with mere foresight of certainty) the action is forbidden even from a utilitarian perspective, as the bad results outweigh the good results.

In spite of the above mentioned differences between the two contexts I think it reasonable to say that those who believe that the distinction between causing a result purposely and causing it with (mere) foresight of certainty is of significance in deciding what a person is permitted to do (i.e. the proponents of the double effect doctrine) – should also think that this distinction is of significance in assessing degrees of blameworthiness. That is to say, when we have to assess the relative degrees of blameworthiness of two actions that are morally forbidden, assuming that the only difference between them is that in one of them the result is caused purposely and in the other the result is caused with (mere) foresight of certainty, the proponents of the double effect doctrine should say that the moral blameworthiness in the first action is higher than in the other one, even though all other things, including the motives, are identical in both cases and from a utilitarian perspective the two cases are identical.[1] They should say, for example, that a person who kills a person to inherit his fortune is more blameworthy than a person who sets fire to his house to collect the insurance on the house, knowing that someone is sleeping there and that a practical certainty exists that he will be burnt to death. Likewise, they should say that a person who insures the life of a pilot of an aeroplane and causes the destruction of the aeroplane in mid-air to kill the pilot and collect the insurance monies on his life is more blameworthy than a person who insures the plane and causes its destruction in mid-air to collect the insurance monies on the plane, and who knows, when he acts, that a practical certainty exists that his action will also cause the death of the pilot.[2]

Theoretically, one could suggest that the distinction between direct intention and mere foresight of certainty is of importance only in deciding what is permissible to do, and that it loses all importance in comparatively assessing the degree of moral blameworthiness of two actions, both of which are morally forbidden.[3] In my view, however, this view is implausible. For it seems that a doctrine that holds, for example, that it is forbidden to purposely cause the death of one innocent person in order to save five other people while it is permitted to act in order to save five people in spite of the knowledge that the action will certainly cause, as a by-product, the death of an innocent person, must be committed to the idea that it is morally worse (i.e. that it is morally more objectionable) to cause the death of an innocent person purposely than to cause it knowingly, when all other things are equal. Now, if it is morally worse to cause death purposely than to cause it knowingly, when in both cases the performance of the action would bring about the best overall results, then it also seems correct to conclude that it is morally worse to cause death purposely than to cause it knowingly when in both cases the action is morally forbidden even from a utilitarian perspective (such as when both actions are performed in order to collect insurance monies, like in the examples brought above concerning the destruction of the aeroplane). And if we accept that causing death purposely is morally worse than causing it knowingly, then it is reasonable to say that a person who causes death purposely is more blameworthy than a person who causes it knowingly when both actions are morally forbidden (this is similar to the idea that the fact that killing is morally worse than stealing, yields the conclusion that the murderer is more blameworthy than the thief). Some may even say that if the difference between causing a result purposely and causing it knowingly is of sufficient importance to constitute a ground for differentiating between what one is allowed to do and what one is not allowed to do then, *a fortiori,* it can ground a difference in the degrees of blameworthiness between two forbidden actions.

This argument does not depend upon the preferred rationale for the doctrine of the double effect. It doesn't matter whether causing the death purposely is morally worse (i.e. morally more objectionable) than causing it with foresight of certainty because of what it does to the agent or to the value itself or to the victim; nor does it matter if we have no rationale at all and that we only rely upon intuition. What is important is the fact that causing the death purposely is morally worse (i.e. is morally more objectionable), and that on this basis we can conclude that in assessing degrees of blameworthiness as well there is a difference between causing the death purposely and causing it with (mere) foresight of certainty.

Having established that embracing the double effect theory may have implications for the assessment of degrees of blameworthiness, we still have to confront the possible argument that the relevance of that theory to grading offences in the criminal law is very limited, for this theory is only used with regard to absolute (or almost absolute) prohibitions, like those against killing and torturing. There are only a small number of absolute (and almost absolute) prohibitions, and this may suggest, the argument would run, that the concern for the moral integrity of the agent (or for the value itself or for the dignity of the victim) that lies behind both the very existence of the absolute prohibitions and the distinction between purpose and foresight of certainty, is of relevance only to these few absolute (and almost absolute) prohibitions. It would follow, therefore, that the idea that causing a result purposely is more blameworthy than causing it with (mere) foresight of certainty is also applicable only in relation to the most heinous of actions, like causing death, so that the relevance of the doctrine of the double effect to the issue of grading offences in the criminal law is very limited. I suggest two possible responses that may be advanced concerning this argument.

First, although there are only a small number of absolute (and almost absolute) prohibitions, there may be a far greater number of "deontological prohibitions". In section 3.3 I explained that many people believe in the existence of various deontological prohibitions that are not absolute (or almost absolute) which may be overridden by "a sufficiently large increment of good". Such prohibitions, like the prohibitions against lying or breaking a promise, may be overridden more easily than absolute (and almost absolute) prohibitions, but they are still considered "deontological" by many people because (according to them) until the threshold of "a sufficiently large increment of good" is reached – the prohibition holds and does not yield to simple utilitarian calculus.[4] That means that the distinction made by the doctrine of the double effect may be relevant not only to absolute prohibitions but also to the less stringent deontological prohibitions.[5] Consequently, it may also be relevant in assessing degrees of blameworthiness not only within the context of the most heinous of actions (like killings) but also within the context of other moral wrongs (and that means that its relevance to the criminal law is not necessarily limited to the most heinous criminal offences).

Second, even if we assume that the doctrine of the double effect itself is only applicable to a small number of moral wrongs (such as killing and torturing) it may be suggested that it contains a moral lesson of relevance to the assessment of degrees of blameworthiness within the context of numerous other moral wrongs as well. It may be suggested that the doctrine of the double effect instructs us that there is a moral difference between causing a bad result purposely and causing it with (mere) foresight of certainty in that causing a bad result purposely is morally worse than causing it with (mere) foresight of certainty (because, for example, of what causing the result purposely does to the moral integrity of the agent). From this proposition we can conclude that a person who causes a bad result purposely is more culpable than a person who causes the same result with (mere) foresight of certainty, and we can say that this last conclusion is applicable to all (or most) moral wrongs, in spite of the fact that the doctrine of the double effect itself only applies (under the present assumption) to a small number of very heinous actions. The fact that the doctrine itself is limited to the most heinous of actions may be understood as being based on the idea that only in the context of the most heinous of moral wrongs does the fact that the agent directly intends to bring about the harm bear so much importance (because, for example, only in such contexts is the damage to the moral integrity of the agent so great) that it can override the utilitarian considerations and yield a prohibition against promoting the best overall results. In other contexts, the fact that causing harm purposely is more objectionable than causing it with (mere) foresight, is not important enough to overcome the utilitarian calculation. But when proceeding to assess the relative degrees of blameworthiness of two forbidden actions (in the context of every or almost every moral wrong) then we can say that the person who causes the bad result purposely is more culpable than the person who causes the same result with (mere) foresight of certainty. This line of argument enables us to learn from the doctrine of the double effect a general principle about degrees of blameworthiness that is relevant to many criminal offences, even if we assume that the doctrine itself is applicable only to a small number of very heinous actions.[6]

To the above two responses I would add the following observation: even if we assume that the doctrine of the double effect only applies to a small number of very serious moral wrongs (like killing) and that the conclusions which may be inferred from this doctrine to the issue of degrees of moral blameworthiness are also limited in context to the most serious of moral wrongs, the doctrine is still of importance for the purposes of our discussion because the distinction made by the doctrine may be applied in the context of criminal offences that deal with the most serious of moral wrongs (such as killing a person or causing grievous bodily harm to a person).

Thus far, we have shown that if we accept the double effect theory, we should also say that causing a bad result purposely is more blameworthy than causing it with (mere) foresight of certainty, when the two actions are forbidden and all other things are equal (including the motives). From this conclusion we can infer that causing a bad result purposely is more blameworthy than causing it recklessly, when the two actions are forbidden and all other things are equal (including the motives). The reason we say that causing a result purposely is more blameworthy than causing it with (mere) foresight of certainty is that the element of aiming, of acting in order to cause the result, makes an action more blameworthy, and this element is missing when an action is carried out with (mere) foresight of certainty. And since this element is also absent in cases of recklessness, we must conclude that causing a result purposely is more blameworthy than causing it recklessly.

The discussion above leads us to the conclusion that a legislator may legitimately think that causing a bad result with direct intention is more blameworthy than causing it recklessly (when all other things, including the whole complex of motives and purposes, remain constant) because the element of aiming at the bad result is missing in cases of recklessness. This may legitimately lead the legislator to grade offences following the distinction between direct intention and recklessness. For example, the legislator may enact two separate offences, one of causing grievous bodily harm with direct intention and another of causing the same result recklessly, and provide that the maximum penalty for the first offence be higher than the maximum penalty for the second.

What should the legislator in such a case do regarding cases of oblique intention? Should he include such cases within the higher or lesser offence? It seems that there is a good argument for not including such cases within the higher offence. For if the reason for differentiating between direct intention and recklessness is that in cases of direct intention, as opposed to cases of recklessness, the actor acts *in order* to cause the proscribed result (and thereby he harms his moral integrity or the dignity of the victim or the value itself, in a unique way) so that he is more culpable, then the same reason should also lead us to differentiate between direct intention and (mere) foresight of certainty. For the same important element (i.e. that the actor acts *in order* to cause the result, which generates the unique harm to the integrity of the agent or to the dignity of the victim or to the value itself) that is missing in cases of recklessness is also absent in cases of (mere) foresight of certainty. In other words, if recklessness is less blameworthy than direct intention because in cases of recklessness the actor does not act *in order* to cause the result, then oblique intention is also less blameworthy than direct intention (as indeed is implied by the doctrine of the double effect) because in cases of oblique intention, as well, the actor does not act *in order* to cause the result.

To sum up: A reasonable legislator may legitimately think that the fact that a person acts *in order* to cause a bad result is an important factor in assessing the degree of his moral blameworthiness. This means he may legitimately think that causing a bad result purposely is more blameworthy than causing it recklessly, when all other things remain constant (including the motives). A legislator may act upon the above views and grade offences following the distinction between direct intention and recklessness, and if he does so it would also be reasonable for him not to include the case of oblique intention within the higher offence (which would then include only cases of direct intention) but to include it within the lesser offence (which would then include cases of recklessness and foresight of certainty).[7]

4.2   Possible Implications of Rejecting the Doctrine of the Double Effect

4.2.1   *Denying the Importance of Desire*

Those who reject the doctrine of double effect think that the mental difference between acting in order to cause a certain result and acting with (mere) foresight of certainty that the same result will ensue (when all other things, including the motives, are equal) cannot yield a difference between what one is allowed and what one is not allowed to do. It is reasonable to suggest that opponents of the doctrine will also say that there is no difference in the degree of blameworthiness of one who acts with direct intention and one who acts with oblique intention, when both perform actions that are morally forbidden. Generally, opponents of the doctrine of the double effect are utilitarians who think that the only moral guide for action should be utilitarian calculation, so that there is no point in distinguishing between direct and oblique intention in deciding which actions are permissible and which are not. It is reasonable to assume that when those utilitarians come to assess degrees of blameworthiness, they will only take into account utilitarian factors, and factors that do not influence results in the world (such as the question whether the agent directly intends the result or only foresees it as certain) will be ignored. By this approach, therefore, acting with direct intention to cause a certain bad result is not more blameworthy than acting with (mere) foresight of certainty that the same bad result will ensue, when all other things are equal and both actions are morally forbidden.[8]

Put otherwise, opponents of the double effect doctrine actually say that the fact that a person is going to act *in order* to cause the bad result, in itself, should not be considered of importance in deciding how he should behave. This view is generally based on a rejection of the idea that notions like that by his action the agent harms his integrity (or the dignity of the victim or the values themselves) should play a part in our moral decisions. If this is the case, then it seems reasonable to suggest that such considerations should not be taken into account in assessing degrees of moral blameworthiness in the context of forbidden actions.[9]

Now we can take a further step. If the element of desire, of acting in order to cause the result, is not considered to be, in itself, of importance when assessing the degree of blameworthiness of a person who acts with foresight of certainty (because we deny the importance of notions like that of harming the integrity of the agent or the dignity of the victim) then this element will also not be considered of importance in assessing the degree of blameworthiness of a person who acts with foresight of the possibility (as opposed to certainty) that the result will ensue.[10] Take the two following cases:

1. John, a merchant, sells to someone, for cooking, oil he knows to be poisonous. He does so in order to make money and he knows that there is a 50% chance that the buyer will die by using the oil (but he does not have any interest in his death).
2. Jack, a gravedigger, sells the same oil to another person in order for that person to die so that he will receive an order for a grave, and he knows that there is a 50% chance that the buyer will actually die by using the oil.

Is there a difference between the degree of blameworthiness of John and Jack respectively? Following the present line of argument, there is no such difference, because the fact that Jack desires the death of the buyer should not influence the degree of his blameworthiness (because we reject the importance of notions like that of harming the integrity of the agent or the dignity of the victim).[11] If we accept this conclusion, then it seems a reasonable conclusion may be not to grade offences following the distinction between direct intention and (mere) foresight of the result (regardless of whether it is foreseen as certain or as merely possible). For when we have two cases in which all things are equal (including the motives) except for the fact that in one case the agent desires the result to ensue and in the other he only foresees it (as possible or certain), there is no difference in the moral culpability of the agents in the two cases. By this line of reasoning, therefore, a reasonable legislator may legitimately decide not to grade any offences based on the distinction between intention and recklessness.[12]

4.2.2   *Distinguishing between the Context in which the Doctrine of the Double Effect is Discussed and the Context of Degrees of Blameworthiness*

The argument advanced in the previous section was based, inter alia, on the assumption that utilitarians who oppose the doctrine of the double effect would also deny the importance of the distinction between direct and oblique intention in assessing degrees of blameworthiness. Now I would like to point toward the possibility of distinguishing between the two contexts. One may think that in proceeding to decide what one is allowed to do the only appropriate consideration is the promotion of utility. If the utilitarian calculation yields the conclusion that an action is to be permitted then it should be permitted regardless of whether the agent acts with direct or oblique intention. If the act should be permitted when done with oblique intention as to the result, then it should also be permitted when it is done with direct intention (provided that the results of the utilitarian calculation remain constant). But when we are dealing with an action that is forbidden from a utilitarian outlook, then there is a difference between the degree of blameworthiness of a person who acts with direct intention to cause the bad result and that of a person who acts with oblique intention as to same result (when all other things are equal).

Distinguishing between these two contexts is most convincing if we base the distinction between purpose and foresight of certainty on the notion of harming the integrity of the agent. We may say that when proceeding to decide what we are permitted to do we have to make utilitarian calculations, and if the outcome of this calculation is that the action should be done (or should be permitted) then the person who performs this action does not harm his moral integrity at all, because (according to the present argument) only doing what morality forbids can harm the moral integrity of the agent.[13] However, when the utilitarian calculation shows that a certain action of causing death, for example, causes more bad than good, then a prohibition against performing this action is set and, within this context, there may be degrees of blameworthiness. We can say that every action of causing death (when it is prohibited by morality) harms the moral integrity of the agent, but still when the agent acts with direct intention to cause death he is directed and guided by the evil consequence he wants to cause (even if the death is needed to him as a means only) and hence his moral integrity is harmed more than it is harmed in the case of oblique intention.[14] Therefore, the person who acts with direct intention (when all other things are equal) is more blameworthy.

A similar argument can be made if we focus on the values themselves. We can say that when morality requires us to perform (or permits us to perform) a certain action because of utilitarian considerations, no harm is caused to the values themselves (or to the moral structure of the world) because only morally forbidden actions can cause such harm. But when we have two actions of causing death, both of which are morally forbidden, then we can say that only acting with direct intention harms the value of life itself (or, alternatively, we can say that it harms the value more than does acting with oblique intention), and therefore a person who acts with direct intention to cause death is more culpable.

It is less plausible, but still possible, to use this line of argument if we focus on the harm done to the dignity of the victim. The argument here would be that using a person as a means to promote utility (when from a neutral point of view the good results caused by the action outweigh the harm done to the person) does not show disrespect to the victim, because there are justifiable reasons for causing him harm and because morality demands (or permits) that he be harmed,[15] so that using him in this case as a means does not harm his dignity. But when causing harm to the victim is morally prohibited, then the fact that the actor acts in order to harm him, that the victim is used as a means, yields a special harm to his dignity, and hence influences the degree of the agent's culpability.

Suppose a legislator accepts the above line of argument. What are the implications for the issue of grading offences? I think the implications should be the same as those of adopting the double effect theory, described supra in section 4.1. By the approach suggested in the present section, the element of desire, of acting in order to cause a bad result, is important in itself in assessing degrees of blameworthiness. If the element of desire is important in itself, then it should be of importance both in cases where the actor foresees the result as possible and in cases where he foresees the result as certain. It follows, therefore, that a legislator who accepts the line of argument presented in this section may reasonably grade offences following the distinction between direct intention and recklessness, and include cases of oblique intention within the lesser offence.

4.2.3   *Degrees of Causal Contribution*

Another line of argument that may enable us to distinguish between the context of deciding what a person is allowed to do and the context of assessing degrees of blameworthiness can be based on the notion of degrees of causal connection. We can say that a person who acts in order to cause some harm is more causally connected to this harm than a person who only acts with foresight that his action will cause (or may cause) the same result as a by-product. To be sure, in both cases there is a causal connection between the action of the agent and the result, but when the actor wants a certain harm to occur and acts in order to produce it, his causal contribution to that harm can be considered greater than that of a person who acts in order to cause another result but foresees that the same harm will ensue as a by-product of his action. The first person is more causally responsible for the result. Now, when causing a certain result is morally forbidden, we can say that a person who is more causally responsible for causing the result is more culpable than a person who is less causally responsible for the occurrence of the same result (when other things are equal). At the same time, we can be utilitarian in deciding what a person is allowed to do. We can say that when the utilitarian calculation shows that the bad result that one is about to cause is outweighed by the good results his action will produce, then the person is permitted (or sometimes even required) to perform the action. In such a case, there is nothing wrong in being strongly connected to the bad result (that is needed as a means to the achievement of the good result), because in this case causing the bad result is a morally permitted (or even required) action. Only in cases in which causing the result is already forbidden (because of utilitarian considerations) can we say (according to the present argument) that the more a person is causally responsible for the occurrence of the result, the more he is morally culpable for causing it.[16]

The implications of adopting the present argument as regards the issue of grading offences are similar to those of adopting the argument discussed in the previous section. According to the present argument the element of aiming, of acting *in order* to cause a certain result, is important in itself in assessing the moral culpability of a person who causes the result. The element of aiming is missing in the case of recklessness and also in the case of oblique intention. It follows that, according to the present line of argument, causing a result purposely is both more blameworthy than causing the result recklessly and more blameworthy than causing it with oblique intention. Therefore a legislator may reasonably grade offences following the distinction between direct intention and recklessness and include oblique intention within the lesser offence.

Notes

1   Kugler (1993) 156-157. For the view that a person who causes death purposely is morally more culpable than a person who causes death with (mere) foresight of certainty, when all other things (including the ultimate end) are equal and when both actions are morally forbidden, see Moore (1997) 408-410.

2   The example is based on Moore (1997) 451-452.

3   Cf. Foot (1978) 22.

4   For a list of deontological prohibitions see Nagel (1986) 176. See also the references supra, chapter 3, at note 18.

5   Cf. Quinn (1993) 197 who accepts that the doctrine of the double effect has a wide application to a wide range of moral wrongs and is not limited to the realm of absolute prohibitions.

6   But the number of criminal offences for which the conclusions drawn from the double effect theory may be relevant may hinge on the chosen rationale for the theory. For example, in section 3.8.5 I suggested that if we understand the distinction made by the double effect theory as being based on a special prohibition against using persons as a means to the ends of other people, then it is not reasonable to use it in the context of prohibitions against harming animals (whereas if we base the theory on our concern for the values themselves or the agent, we may also apply it to prohibitions against harming animals). Now if we understand the doctrine of the double effect as being based on the special prohibition against using persons as means (and not as being based on our concern for the agent or the values themselves), and if we want to infer from this doctrine that a person who causes a bad result purposely is more blameworthy than a person who causes the same result with (mere) foresight, and to grade criminal offences following this conclusion, then it would be unreasonable to use this kind of grading in the context of offences against animals or against the state (as opposed to the context of offences against the person).

7   Kugler (1993) 160. The Model Penal Code is an example of a code that includes certain offences in which only purpose (direct intention) as to actual or potential results suffices for conviction. See supra section 1.3.4. In the Model Penal Code, direct intention is sometimes required as a prerequisite for criminalisation, i.e. when there is only oblique intention there is no criminal offence at all. However, sometimes the distinction between purpose (direct intention) and knowledge (oblique intention) is used to grade offences. This last context is the one which is relevant to this Part of the book, discussing the issue of grading offences. For an example of the Model Penal Code's use of the distinction in the context of grading offences see supra section 2.2. In Israel, the Supreme Court held that in order to convict of "murder with premeditation" (which is the primary type of murder in Israel, the other three kinds being two variations of felony-murder, and parricide) the prosecution must prove, inter alia, that the defendant actually desired to cause the death. If there was only oblique intention, then the defendant may only be convicted of manslaughter. See Cr.A. 552/68 *Iluz and Elias v. State of Israel*, 23(1) P.D. 377, 390. The question whether this still represents the law in Israel was raised but not resolved recently in Cr. A. 3126/96 *Amir v. State of Israel*, 50(3) P.D. 638, 651.

It seems that Moore understands the distinction made in the Model Penal Code between purpose (direct intention) and knowledge (oblique intention) as being based on the idea that when all other things are equal (including the ultimate ends), acting in order to cause the bad result is more culpable than acting with (mere) foresight of certainty that the same result will ensue. See Moore (1997) 408-410 in conjunction with 417.

The reader must have noticed that in the text I only say that the legislator *may* legitimately and reasonably distinguish between direct intention and oblique intention. I do not say that he *should* take such a course of action. The reason is that various arguments and considerations not yet discussed in this book may lead a legislator not to distinguish between direct and oblique intention (even if he accepts the validity of the doctrine of the double effect). These arguments and considerations will be discussed infra. Thus, what is said in the text should be seen as part of a larger discussion to be pursued throughout the rest of the book. Nonetheless, the conclusion that a reasonable legislator *may* distinguish between direct and oblique intention, and that by doing so he may rely on the doctrine of the double effect, which is accepted by many moral philosophers (i.e. that he is not doing something that is necessarily unreasonable or illogical), is also an important conclusion in itself.

8   Cf. Duff (1989) 87-88.

9   Some deontologists may think that notions like that of harming the integrity of the agent are important when deciding what to do, but that there is no distinction between direct and oblique intention regarding such a harm (while there *is* a difference in this regard, for example, between action and omission). But here also we can say that if the difference between direct and oblique intention is without importance in proceeding to decide what to do, then it is reasonable to think that it is also without importance when proceeding to assess degrees of blameworthiness.

10   Also, if we believe in the importance of notions like that of harming the integrity of the agent or the dignity of the victim, but nevertheless reject the double effect doctrine because we hold the view that the question whether those things are harmed is not influenced by the existence of desire, then the same view should also apply to cases of foresight of possibility.

11   Or because we deny that the element of desire influences the question whether such harms occur.

12   I am not saying here that a reasonable legislator who rejects the doctrine of the double effect *must* refrain from distinguishing between intention and recklessness. For various considerations and arguments may lead even one who rejects the doctrine to distinguish between intention and recklessness. Such considerations and arguments will be discussed infra. The discussion in this section should be viewed, therefore, as part of a larger discussion to be pursued throughout this book. But the argument in this section is also important in its own right because it shows that a reasonable legislator *may* refrain from grading offences following the distinction between intention and recklessness. Another important point that emerges from the discussion here is that a legislator who thinks that cases of oblique intention should not be treated differently from cases of direct intention (in the context of grading offences) on the sole basis that the element of aiming at the result does not in itself matter in assessing degrees of moral blameworthiness, is contradicting himself if, at the same time, he grades offences following the distinction between direct (and oblique) intention and recklessness, and the only explanation he offers for doing so is that the element of aiming at the result (in itself) increases the culpability of actors. A legislator may decide to equate cases of oblique intention with cases of direct intention while differentiating between them and recklessness, but in order to justify such a scheme he must introduce further arguments and considerations. Such possible considerations and arguments will be discussed later in this book.

For sources against the idea of grading offences following the distinction between intention and recklessness, see supra chapter 2 at note 18. For arguments similar to those made in the text see Kugler (1993) 161; Gorr (1996); Simester (1996a).

One may suggest that even if the philosophical truth is that when all other things are equal there is no difference between the moral blameworthiness involved in acting with direct intention and that involved in acting with recklessness, it is possible that the general public thinks (mistakenly) that such a difference *does* exist, and that this constitutes a sufficiently good reason to distinguish between cases of direct intention and cases of recklessness; for sometimes the legislator has to reflect in the criminal law the moral beliefs of the community even if he thinks they are wrong (on this last point see Williams (1983a) 405; Robinson and Darley (1995) 5-7). Now, if a legislator adopts this argument and subsequently grades offences following the distinction between direct intention and recklessness, what should he do concerning cases of oblique intention? It seems he should act following the views of the community regarding cases of oblique intention. Since the grading is based on the beliefs of the general public concerning the moral difference between direct intention and recklessness, the beliefs of the general public concerning oblique intention (i.e. whether it is morally equivalent to direct intention or rather to recklessness) should dictate the law of cases of oblique intention. As for the suggestion above, I don't find it very convincing. I doubt that when faced with cases in which "all other things are equal, including the *motives*" most people will have the firm intuition that the person who acts with direct intention is more culpable than the person who acts with recklessness. Furthermore, since we are dealing here with maximum penalties, I do not think that including intention and recklessness within the same offence subject to the same *maximum* penalty, risks, to a significant extent, detracting from the credibility of the criminal system in the eyes of the general public. Consequently, one of the main reasons for taking community views into account does not seem to be relevant in this context.

13   Cf. Nagel (1972) 132-133; Kagan (1989) 31.

14   Cf. Hart (1968) 127. Hart tries to find some explanation for the distinction sometimes made between cases of direct intention and cases of foresight of certainty and says that the distinction seems to appeal to a feeling that to cause the death of a person with direct intention is a defilement of the agent and that the will of the person who acts with direct intention is identified with an evil aim and is somehow morally worse than the will of one who acts with (mere) foresight of certainty. Hart, however, does not commit himself to this idea.

15   Cf. Kagan (1989) 32, 172-175.

16   Kugler (1993) 162-163. On the idea of degrees in causal responsibility cf. Moore (1997) 700-703. Moore introduces there a number of deontological distinctions and explains some of them (not including the distinction between direct intention and foresight) on the basis of notions such as being less causally responsible, being only a "small cause" and similar ones. The discussion there is pursued with regard to deciding what a person is allowed to do. It seems that in Moore (1997) 409 somewhat similar notions are used in explaining why acting with direct intention is more culpable than acting with mere foresight of the result. He says there: "My own sense is that the differential culpability between intent and foresight has to do with the notion of authorship, or agency. We are the authors of evil when we aim to achieve it in a way we are not if we merely anticipate that evil coming about as a result of our actions". On the general issue of degrees of causal contribution see also Fletcher (1978) 362-372.

Chapter 5

A Common Denominator between Direct and Oblique Intention

5.1   The Absence of Hope that the Forbidden Result Will Not Occur

The discussion in chapter 4 suggested that the idea of grading offences following the distinction between direct intention and recklessness and, at the same time, including cases of oblique intention within the higher offence alongside direct intention, is problematic. The problem is that if the fact that the actor does not aim at the result is morally important (in that it reduces blameworthiness), then it should be considered important not only in cases of recklessness but also in cases of foresight of certainty; and if the fact that he does not aim at the result is not morally important, then we should not distinguish even between direct intention and recklessness.

I will now turn to examine whether there is a way to justify the idea of distinguishing between direct intention and recklessness and, at the same time, including cases of oblique intention within the higher offence together with direct intention. A natural move towards finding such a justification would be to try to find an element that exists both in cases of direct intention and in cases of oblique intention, but does not exist in cases of recklessness. If we find such an element, and if we think that the existence of this element increases moral culpability, then we may explain why both direct and oblique intention can be included in the same offence and distinguished from recklessness. I will now turn to trying to find such an element.

The first candidate I will examine is the absence of hope that the forbidden result will not occur. A person who acts with foresight of certainty that a result will ensue cannot hope that the result will not ensue, hence he does not have a hope that the result will not ensue. This holds not only for cases of complete certainty but also for cases of practical certainty, as defined in chapter 1. There I defined practical certainty as the degree of probability that people treat as absolute certainty. Someone who foresees the result in such a degree of probability by definition cannot hope that the result will not ensue. Similarly, a person who acts in order to cause a certain result does not hope that the result will not ensue; quite the contrary – he positively hopes that the result will ensue (even if the result is needed by him only as a means to another end). But a person who is only reckless as to a result, may hope that the result will not ensue.[1]

We may think that a person who causes a bad result and who, when acting, does not have a hope that the result will not ensue, deserves a higher punishment than a person who causes the same result and that, in acting, positively hopes that the result will not ensue, when all other things (including the motives) are equal. One way to understand this idea is to view it as being related to the character of the agent. We may say that a person who is ready to act without any hope that a certain bad result will not ensue exhibits (or displays) in his action a more wicked character than a person whose action is coupled with a hope that the same result will not ensue (when all other things, including the motives, are equal). When all other things are equal, a person needs to be more wicked to let himself act without any hope that a bad result will not ensue than he needs to be in order to act with the hope that the bad result will not ensue. If we add to this proposition the assumption that the severity of punishment for a crime should be proportional to the gravity of the defect of character displayed by the criminal act,[2] we can understand the above idea that the fact that a person acts without a hope that the result will not ensue increases his deserved punishment. It follows, therefore, that a legislator may grade offences following the distinction between direct intention and recklessness on the basis of the belief that when all other things are equal, a person who acts without a hope that the result will not ensue deserves a higher punishment than a person who acts with the hope that the result will not ensue. And if the legislator does so it is also reasonable for him to include cases of oblique intention within the higher offence, because the same element that exists in cases of direct intention which justifies treating those who act with direct intention more harshly than those who act with recklessness also exists in cases of oblique intention. In other words, the degree of wickedness exhibited in cases of direct intention and in cases of oblique intention is identical. For example: A person who acts in order to kill a person and subsequently collect the insurance monies on the victim displays in his action more wickedness than a person who sets fire to a house in order to collect the insurance monies on the house and foresees the possibility that a person he knows is sleeping in the house will be burnt to death. However, this person displays the same degree of wickedness as a person who sets the fire in order to collect the insurance monies on the house, with the assurance that a person that he knows is sleeping in the house will be burnt to death.

Another way to understand the function of the absence of hope is to view it not as related to the character of the actor but, rather, to the wrongfulness of the action. We may say that acting without hoping that the result will not ensue is doing something that is morally worse (that is more wrongful) than acting while hoping that the result will not ensue (when all other things are equal), so that a person who acts without such a hope is more blameworthy than one who acts with such a hope (because an action that is morally worse generates a higher degree of blameworthiness). The reason why acting without a hope that the result will not ensue is morally worse may be, for example, that acting in such a manner harms the moral integrity of the agent (or the value itself or the dignity of the victim) in a unique way. This line of thinking may lead a legislator who desires to grade offences based on degrees of blameworthiness to distinguish between direct (and oblique) intention, on the one hand, and recklessness, on the other.

A problem arises, however, with this argument. For it ignores the fact that not every person who *can* hope that the result will not ensue *actually* hopes that it will not ensue. Those who foresee the *possibility* that their action will cause a result may be divided into three groups: Those who want the result to ensue, those who hope it will not ensue and those who simply do not care (do not mind) whether it will ensue or not.[3] Cases of actors belonging to the latter category may be called cases of "indifference".[4] In cases of indifference, the actor does not hope that the result will not ensue. In this respect, he resembles the actor who acts with direct intention and the actor who acts with oblique intention. So if we think that the important question when proceeding to grade offences is whether the actor hopes that the result will not ensue then it is not consistent to include within the lesser offence all cases of recklessness, for in some of them the actor does not hope that the result will not ensue. To be consistent, therefore, we should distinguish between cases of direct intention, oblique intention and indifference on the one hand, and cases of hoping that the result will not ensue on the other, by including the former cases within the higher offence and the latter cases within the lesser offence. A legislator may reasonably adopt this view and grade offences following this distinction.[5] But what he cannot do is to distinguish between (direct and oblique) intention and recklessness and justify this distinction solely by saying that in cases of direct intention and oblique intention the actor does not hope that the result will not ensue and that this lack of hope distinguishes between such cases and cases of recklessness. This last argument is valid against both kinds of argument that rely on the element of "lack of hope" (i.e. the one focusing on the character of the agent and the one focusing on the wrongfulness of the action).

In spite of what was said above, perhaps a legislator concerned with practical problems of proof of the relevant mental elements may prefer not to distinguish between "indifference" and "hoping that the result will not ensue", notwithstanding his belief that from a moral perspective they should be treated differently. It may be thought that when we have a case of foresight of the possibility that the result will ensue, and we know that the accused did not have a positive desire that it would ensue (or such a desire is not proven beyond a reasonable doubt) it is very difficult to prove that he did not hope that the result would not ensue but was indifferent towards such a possibility (unless he admits that he was indifferent). Of course, it is sometimes possible to prove this. For example, if there is an easy and inexpensive way to take precautions against the occurrence of the result that do not lessen the probability of achieving the purpose for which the action is taken, and nevertheless the accused does not take them, then we have good evidence that may support the conclusion that the accused was indifferent. However, the legislator may think that, in general, it will be very difficult to prove beyond a reasonable doubt that the accused was indifferent.[6] At the same time the legislator may think that although the task of proving that a person wants a result to ensue is not an easy one, still it is less difficult to fulfil than proving indifference. The presumption of fact that a person intends the natural consequences of his actions is, for example, an efficient tool to prove that the accused acted in order to cause the result. The legislator may further think that to prove that the accused acted with foresight of certainty is an easier task than to prove indifference (in cases of foresight of possibility) because, for example, we can generally assume (unless there is evidence to the contrary) that a result that was practically certain to ensue was also perceived as such by the defendant. So a legislator may think that from a moral perspective the important question is whether the actor hopes that the result will not ensue. From this viewpoint, it is perfectly logical to include within the higher offence not only cases of direct and oblique intention but also cases of indifference. But because of the practical problems of proof described above he may decide not to include indifference within the higher offence but, rather, within the lesser offence, together with cases of hope that the result will not ensue. After deciding to do that it is of course superfluous to mention in the lesser offence the distinction between indifference and hoping that the result would not ensue, and the consequence is that the mental element required for conviction in the lesser offence would be "recklessness". Against the above mentioned practical considerations, one may argue that even assuming that it is substantially more difficult to prove indifference than to prove desire or foresight of certainty, there is still no good reason to include cases of indifference within the lesser offence. After all, some defendants may admit that they were indifferent (or we can sometimes infer such an attitude of indifference from what they said) and in other cases we can sometimes infer indifference from their actions and omissions (for example from the fact that they did not take precautions against causing the result). So we can include indifference within the higher offence and give the prosecution the chance to prove it, and if it fails a conviction of the lesser offence will still be possible. It should also be borne in mind that we are not speaking here about a suggestion to create a new offence just for cases of indifference. The higher offence that will include cases of direct and oblique intention will be enacted anyway and the only question is whether to include cases of indifference within the higher offence or the lesser one. Thus, it may be suggested that not much will be lost if we decide to include cases of indifference within the higher offence. Nevertheless I cannot deny that the above practical consideration may lead a reasonable legislator to include cases of indifference within the lesser offence.[7]

5.2   The Actor Would Have Acted in the Same Way – Had He Known that the Result Would Certainly Ensue

Another attempt to find a common denominator between direct and oblique intention would be to say that in both cases the actor exhibits his readiness to act even when the occurrence of the result is certain. A person who acts with foresight of certainty obviously shows us that he is willing to act even when the result is foreseen as certain. A person who acts with direct intention also shows that he would act in the same manner in a case in which the result would have been foreseen by him as certain. Even if in the present case he only foresees the result as possible, still the fact that he wants the result to ensue reveals that he would take the same course of action (and even more gladly) were he certain that the result would ensue. But a person who is only reckless when he acts only shows that he is prepared to take a risk that the result will ensue; he does not show that he is ready to act in circumstances where the result will certainly ensue.[8]

A person who is prepared to act when there is a certainty that his action will kill a person has a more wicked character (a more morally defective character) than a person who is only prepared to take the risk that his action will kill a person (and is not prepared to act when there is a certainty that his action will kill), when all other things (including the motives) are equal.[9] If we add to this a retributivist assumption that the severity of punishment should be proportional to the gravity of the defect of character displayed by the criminal action, we come to the conclusion that a person who manifests in his action a willingness to act when there is a certainty that death will follow, should be punished more harshly than a person who would not have acted in a case where the result would be certain (but is only prepared to take the risk that the said result would ensue). The conclusion, the argument would run, is that a legislator who wishes to grade offences according to the gravity of the defect of character displayed by the criminal act, may distinguish between cases of direct and oblique intention on the one hand, and cases of recklessness on the other, by setting a higher maximum penalty for acting with direct or oblique intention than for acting recklessly, on the ground that those who act with (direct or oblique) intention are persons who are ready to act even when the result is foreseen by them as certain.[10]

But there is a problem with the above argument. Indeed, some reckless actors would not have proceeded had they been sure that the result would be caused by their action (all other things remaining constant). But this cannot be said of all reckless actors. Those who act with indifference towards the possibility of the result occurring (i.e. who do not care whether the result will follow) would act in the same way even in circumstances in which they know of the certainty that the result will ensue. For if they do not care whether the result will ensue, why should they refrain from acting in a case where they foresee the certainty that the result will ensue? Furthermore, some of the persons who act hoping that the result will not ensue would still proceed even if the result were foreseen by them as certain. The fact that when the result is foreseen by them as a possible by-product of their action they hope that it will not ensue does not guarantee that if on another occasion the only (or most efficient) way to achieve their goal is to take an action the certain by-product of which is the same result, they would refrain from acting. Of course, we can suppose that some of the persons who take a risk of causing the result with the hope that it will not ensue would refrain from acting if they were sure that the result would ensue, but this cannot be said about all of them. So it seems that if we want to grade offences based on whether the actor would have proceeded had he known that the result would certainly ensue, then we should include within the higher offence all persons who would have proceeded in cases of foresight of certainty. It follows, therefore, that the higher offence should include not only those who act with direct or oblique intention but also those who act with indifference, as well as those who hope that the result will not occur but would not have refrained from acting had they known that the result would certainly have been caused by their action. Now, a legislator may decide to embrace such a grading scheme.[11] However, what he cannot do (according to the present argument) is to provide for a scheme which distinguishes between direct and oblique intention on the one hand and recklessness on the other – and to justify this scheme solely by saying that *only* those who act with (direct or oblique) intention, are persons who are ready to act even in cases in which the result is foreseen by them as certain.

One might suggest in response to this last argument that in grading offences according to degrees of defect of character, we only have to take into consideration those characteristics of the defendant that are manifested in the criminal action under discussion.[12] A person who acts with direct or oblique intention exhibits in his action (coupled with the mental state that he has when he acts) that he is ready to act even in cases of foresight of certainty. This readiness is inferred from the conduct of the actor (coupled with his mental state at that time). But a reckless person who hopes the result will not ensue does not exhibit in his action (coupled with his mental state at that time) his readiness to act even in cases of foresight of certainty. Even if he admits that he would have acted in the same way had he known the result would certainly ensue, and even if we accept this admission as true, still this fact about his character cannot be inferred from his action because when he acts he hopes the result will not ensue. Therefore, the response would run, it is justified to distinguish between direct (and oblique) intention and recklessness.

However, it seems that this response should be rejected, because of cases of indifference. For a person who takes a risk that the result will ensue and, when acting, does not care whether the result ensues, exhibits in his action (coupled with the mental state he has when acting) his readiness to act in cases of foresight of certainty. One might suggest, as a response to this last argument, disregarding the mental state of the actor (i.e. his indifference) in inquiring as to which features of his character were exhibited in his action. But this cannot provide an adequate response. For if we disregard the mental state of the actor in cases of indifference, we should do the same in cases of direct intention, so that in cases of direct intention we would also be precluded from saying that the course of action chosen exhibits that the actor would have acted in the same way even in cases of foresight of certainty.[13] In addition, the very idea that when proceeding to see which characteristics of the defendant are exhibited in his criminal action we should disregard his mental state at the time seems odd. The conclusion, therefore, is that if the important factor for grading offences is whether the criminal action (coupled with the mental state of the actor at the time) displays the defendant's readiness to act in the same way even in cases of foresight of certainty, then the legislator should include within the higher offence not only those who act with direct and oblique intention but also those who act with indifference towards the possibility of the result occurring.[14]

Despite what was said above, perhaps a legislator concerned about the practical problems involved in proving the elements required for conviction would take such problems into consideration in grading offences. He may think that although from a purely moral point of view, both persons who act with (direct or oblique) intention and persons who are reckless but would have acted in the same way had they known that the result would certainly occur should be included within the higher offence – still it is better, from a practical perspective, not to include the latter persons within the higher offence because it is very difficult to prove beyond a reasonable doubt that a reckless person would have acted in the same way had he known that the result would certainly follow (unless this person admits that he would have done so).[15] This practical consideration is not decisive, of course, especially given the possible counter-argument that we should give the prosecution the chance to prove the above element and if it fails the defendant can still be convicted of the lesser offence. This counter-argument is especially convincing in this context because the higher offence will be enacted anyway (according to the present line of argument) for cases of intention, so we are not dealing here with the question whether to enact a special offence for the cases under discussion. Nevertheless, a reasonable legislator may think that the practical difficulties of proving the said element warrant including all the cases of recklessness within the lesser offence, and distinguishing between them and cases of (direct or oblique) intention.

The same can be said about a legislator who thinks that the real moral question is whether the person *exhibits* in his criminal action (coupled with his mental state at the time) that he would have acted in the same way had he known the result to be certain to occur. Such a legislator may think that from a purely moral perspective we should include within the higher offence not only cases of (direct or oblique) intention but also cases of indifference, but that because it is difficult to prove that the defendant was indifferent it is better to include all the cases of recklessness within the lesser offence. A similar argument was examined in section 5.1, and the reader is referred thereto.

Our inquiry, thus far, has not yet revealed a common denominator between direct and oblique intention that is missing in all cases of recklessness, which could enable us to justify the distinction between direct and oblique intention, on the one hand, and recklessness on the other, for purposes of grading offences. The discussion in this chapter did, however, yield an approach to understanding a legislator who grades offences based on the distinction between (direct or oblique) intention and recklessness – though such an approach involves admitting that such an arrangement is based not only on moral principles but also on practical considerations related to difficulties in proving certain constituent elements of the offence. I shall now continue my attempt to find a common denominator between cases of direct and oblique intention which is always absent in cases of recklessness.

5.3   The Element of Choice

We can suggest that the relevant mental common denominator between acting with direct intention to kill and acting with (mere) foresight of certainty that one's action will bring about the death of a person is the element of the choice to kill. In both cases the actor chooses to kill and then kills.

A person who takes an action in order to kill somebody, chooses to kill the victim before he takes the action. Consider, for example, a person who sets fire to a house in order to kill a person sleeping there (because, for example, he wants to collect the insurance monies on his life). In this case the action of setting the fire is performed because the actor chooses beforehand to kill the victim. After he chooses to kill him, he searches for a way to kill him and opts for the act of setting a fire. This means that the act of setting the fire is preceded by a choice to kill a person, to cause the death of a person.

In the case of foresight of certainty as well, there is a choice to kill. When an actor intends to set fire to a house in order to collect the insurance monies on the house, and he subsequently learns that a person is sleeping in the house and that he will certainly die if a fire is set to the house, then if he sets the fire despite this information, it means that he chose to kill the person before he acted. So that here, too, the action is preceded by a choice to kill, to cause the death of a person.

In both cases there is a choice to kill. There is a difference between the two cases in the moment at which the choice is first made in the mind of the actor. In cases of direct intention, the actor chooses to kill and then seeks a way to realise his wish. In the second category of cases, the person first chooses to collect the insurance monies by setting a fire; only afterwards does he learn of the person sleeping in the house, at which point he chooses to kill the person. But it may be suggested that this difference is without importance. What is important is that in both cases the action is preceded by a choice to kill.[16]

The mental act of "choosing to kill" present both in cases of direct intention and in cases of oblique intention is not present in cases of recklessness. When a person intends to set fire to a house in order to collect the insurance monies on the house but learns that a person resides therein and that there is a possibility (as opposed to a certainty) that this person will be burnt to death if he sets the fire, and, in spite of this information, sets the fire, we will not say that he chose to kill. We will say that he chose to *risk* the life of that person, that he chose to take the *risk* of killing a person, but not that he chose to kill a person.[17] It is important to stress that what is being said here about cases of recklessness is applicable not only to cases where the actor hopes that the result will not ensue, but also to cases of "indifference", where the actor does not care whether the person in the house will die. For even in this last category of cases we would not say that the person chose to kill.

Now, we may say that when all other things are equal (including the motives), a person whose action is preceded by a choice to cause a certain harm (like death) is morally more blameworthy than a person whose action is not preceded by such a choice.[18] The reason for this may be that the existence of the said choice magnifies the reprehensibility of the action that follows that choice (for example, because when the action is preceded by a choice to cause the bad result the action harms the dignity of the victim in a unique way, or because it harms the integrity of the actor or the value itself in a unique way); or the reason may be that where there is a choice to cause the result, the causal connection between the action and the result is stronger than where the actor merely takes a risk that the result will ensue. At the same time, it may be suggested that the element of desire to cause a result is not important in itself in assessing degrees of moral blameworthiness, so that acting with direct intention is no more blameworthy than acting with oblique intention, when all other things are equal (including the motives).[19]

The conclusion, therefore, is that a reasonable legislator may decide to grade offences following the distinction between direct intention and recklessness, based on the view that when all other things are equal (including the motives) a person whose action is preceded by a choice to cause a bad result is more blameworthy than a person whose action is not preceded by such a choice. If he grades offences on this basis, it will be reasonable for him to include cases of oblique intention within the higher offence based on the view that a choice to cause the result is also present in these cases.

A similar line of argument could take the same form as the argument above but would replace the element of "choice" with that of "decision". The argument would run as follows: In cases of direct intention and in cases of (mere) foresight of certainty there is a decision to cause the bad result,[20] whereas in cases of recklessness there is only a decision to take a *risk* of causing the result.[21]

5.4   Conclusions

The idea of grading offences following the distinction between direct intention and recklessness on the basis of the assumption that one who acts in order to cause a result is morally more blameworthy than one who acts with recklessness with respect to the same result, is a common one. But after further reflection we realise that this idea is questionable: The fact that in many contexts a person who acts with direct intention is more blameworthy than a person who acts with recklessness is not by itself sufficient to justify the generalisation regarding degrees of blameworthiness, as counter-examples may be advanced in which the reckless actor is more blameworthy than one who acts with direct intention. This problem led us to suggest that we should examine whether acting with direct intention is more culpable than acting with recklessness, when all other things (including the whole complex of the motives and purposes of the actor) are equal. The answer to this question is far from simple and reasonable people may answer it differently. The answer given may affect the decision whether to grade offences following the distinction between direct intention and recklessness, and if so – what to do concerning cases of oblique intention. The discussion above yielded the following tentative conclusions: If the legislator thinks that when all other things are equal (including the motives) the person who acts with direct intention is morally more blameworthy than the reckless one because of the intrinsic importance of the element of desire (of acting in order to cause the result) that is present in cases of direct intention, then it would be reasonable for him to grade offences following the distinction between direct intention and recklessness, and not to include cases of oblique intention within the higher offence, because the element of desire is also absent in cases of oblique intention – which means that acting with oblique intention is less blameworthy than acting with direct intention. So the higher offence will include only cases of direct intention.

If a legislator thinks that, when all other things are equal, the person who acts with direct intention is morally more blameworthy than one who acts with recklessness because of the element of choosing to cause the result that exists in cases of direct intention, then it would be reasonable for him to grade offences following the distinction between direct intention and recklessness and to include cases of oblique intention within the higher offence, together with direct intention, on the ground that in cases of oblique intention the actor also chooses to cause the result.[22]

But if the legislator thinks that, when all other things are equal (including the motives), there is no difference in the degree of moral blameworthiness present in cases of direct intention and in cases of recklessness (because elements such as "desire" and "choice" do not influence the actor's degree of moral blameworthiness) then he should not grade offences following the distinction between intention and recklessness at all. In such a case, direct intention, oblique intention and recklessness will all be included within the same offence.

Naturally, the summary given here only covers the discussion conducted thus far. Further arguments and considerations will be discussed and developed in the next chapters, so that the conclusions reached here should be viewed as tentative, not final.

Notes

1   For the possibility that a person who acts with foresight of certainty is more culpable than a person who acts recklessly because only the latter can realistically hope that the result will not ensue, cf. Duff (1989) 88; Duff (1996) 369.

2   See Brandt (1985) 170, who says that some retributivists may take such a view. On the idea that the character of the agent as exhibited (or displayed) in the criminal act plays a role in various contexts of the criminal law see, for example, Gordon (1978) 214-217; Fletcher (1978) 800; Huigens (1995) 1463; Horder (1993) 204-209.

3   See Turner (1945) 206.

4   Williams (1965) 92.

5   Indeed, in Germany some distinguish, for purposes of the criminal law, between cases of direct intention, foresight of certainty and indifference, on the one hand, and cases where there is hope on the part of the actor that the result will not ensue, on the other. See Fletcher (1978) 445-446; Roxin (1996) 67; Bein (1967) 19-20; Mueller (1961) 46-47.

6   For the problem of proving indifference cf. Bein (1967) 27 at note 33; Silving (1967) 228; Mueller (1961) 47.

7   In favour of adopting this scheme one may also add the consideration that it will save the time of the court (which will not have to deal with the question whether the defendant was indifferent or hoped that the result would not ensue). Another consideration that may be suggested is that cases of indifference are rare, as a person who does not positively desire that the result will ensue (i.e. who does not have an interest in causing the result) generally hopes that the result will not ensue. If this is true, then the decision to include cases of indifference within the lesser offence does not entail a significant cost.

8   Cf. Duff (1980b) 411; Duff (1990) 97; Kremnitzer (1987) 281.

9   Brandt (1985) 170-171.

10 Cf. Duff (1980b) 411; Duff (1990) 97; Kremnitzer (1987) 281.

11 Indeed, according to one view taken by some in Germany, persons who act with direct or oblique intention and persons who foresee the result as possible but would have acted in the same way had they known the result to be certain to occur should generally be treated in the same way for purposes of the criminal law, and should be distinguished from those who take the risk that the result will ensue but would not

have acted in the same way had they known the result to be certain to occur. See Silving (1967) 227; Fletcher (1978) 446 at note 27. Cf. Michaels (1998); Mitchell (1996).

12   For the idea that in certain criminal law contexts we are interested in the character of the defendant as exhibited in the criminal action see, for example, Gordon (1978) 214-217; Fletcher (1978) 800; Brandt (1985) 170.

13   Some might retort that in many cases the act itself provides evidence that the actor acted in order to cause the proscribed result and that, in such cases, we can say that the defect of character is displayed by the action itself, but that this is not the case with indifference, where the act itself does not provide evidence that the actor did not care whether the result would ensue. But this answer should be rejected because there are cases in which direct intention is demonstrated not by the action itself but by other evidence (for example when direct intention is proven by the defendant's testimony in court); moreover, there are also cases in which indifference can be proved based on the external conduct of the defendant, such as when he could easily have taken precautions to prevent the occurrence of the result (such precautions as would not have reduced the probability of him achieving the goal of his action) but failed to do so.

14   One might suggest that even when we know that a person who takes the risk that a result will be caused acts with indifference towards the occurrence of the result, we cannot be completely sure that he would have acted in the same way had he known with certainty that the result would ensue. On the other hand, when we are faced with a person who acts with foresight of certainty that the result will ensue, we can be completely sure that this person is prepared to act in cases of foresight of certainty. This can explain why a person who acts with oblique intention should be treated more harshly than a person who acts with indifference. Cf. Kremnitzer (1987) 281, 286. But it seems to me that this argument is problematic. The idea that a person who does not care whether the result will or will not ensue might refrain from acting if he knows that the result will certainly ensue seems to be based on the assumption that although this person says to himself that he does not care at all whether the result will ensue – it might be the case that he unconsciously relies on the fact that there is a chance that the result will not ensue, and that unconsciously he has some hope that the result will not ensue (for if he *consciously* relies on this possibility then he could not say to himself that he does not care whether the result will ensue). But if we are ready to take such unconscious attitudes into consideration, why do we not proceed likewise in cases of direct intention? Take the case in which the defendant desires the result to ensue but there is only a 20% chance that the result will ensue. Here too we can say that it might be the case that he unconsciously relies on the fact that there is an 80% chance that the result will not ensue and that it is possible that he would have refrained from acting had he known that the result would certainly occur. (Cf. Silving (1967) 225, who says that a person who acts with direct intention under conditions in which the probability of success is small indicates an unconscious "withdrawal" or inhibitions and that this should be taken into account in grading offences). So if we take this line of argument seriously we will come up with the idea that in grading offences only cases of foresight of certainty should be included within the higher offence, and that all cases in which the result is only foreseen as possible (as opposed to certain) should be included within the lesser offence (even if the actor wants the result to ensue). One may retort that there is nonetheless a difference in degree here, as the chances that a person who is indifferent towards the result will refrain from acting if he knows the result to be certain to occur are higher than the chances that a person who directly intends the result will refrain from acting in cases of foresight of certainty. But even if we accept

this dubious idea, it seems that such a small difference in degree cannot justify differentiating between direct intention and indifference for the purpose of grading offences.

15   Smith and Hogan say, in another context, that a conclusion to the effect that a defendant would have been indifferent to a risk if he had been aware of it "could usually be drawn only from evidence as to his general character and habits which the law of evidence does not allow" (Smith and Hogan (1999) 68). For a more detailed discussion, see Smith and Hogan (1992) 69.

16   See Duff (1990) 153; Duff (1996) 369; Kremnitzer (1987) 286. Cf. Model Penal Code and Commentaries (1985) Part 1, vol. 2, p. 305; Simester (1996b) 453-454. Some would say that in cases of (mere) foresight of certainty the actor does *not* choose to cause the result. A third possibility is to say that "to choose" may be understood in two senses. In the narrower sense, a person chooses to kill if he acts in order to kill, whereas in the broader sense, a person chooses to kill either if he acts in order to kill or with (mere) foresight of certainty that his action will cause death.

17   See Duff (1990) 108-109, 153; Duff (1996) 369. Cf. Smith and Hogan (1983) 56.

18   Cf. Duff (1990) 109, 153; Duff (1996) 369; Kremnitzer (1987) 286.

19   One who accepts the idea that there is a distinction in the realm of degrees of blameworthiness between direct and oblique intention on the one hand, and taking a risk on the other, is not necessarily committed to the idea that this distinction is important even in deciding what one is morally permitted to do (i.e., he is not necessarily committed to the view that in certain contexts a deontological constraint against causing a certain result will apply only with regard to cases of direct or oblique intention, as opposed to cases where the actor only takes a risk that the result will ensue). Cf. supra sections 4.2.2, 4.2.3. But one *may* adopt the idea that the distinction discussed here also holds true in relation to certain deontological prohibitions, based, for example, on the view that actions performed with direct or oblique intention (as opposed to those performed with recklessness) harm the dignity of the victim in a unique way. Cf. Kadish (1987) 125. Moore views the distinction between foresight of certainty and taking a risk as important in the context of deontological constraints, but he also accepts the validity of the distinction between direct intention and oblique intention, so his view differs in part from the view discussed here. See Moore (1997) 690-692.

20   See *Hyam v. DPP* [1975] AC 55, at 74; Smith and Hogan (1983) 49-51; Williams (1983a) 409 at note 6. Some would say that in cases of (mere) foresight of certainty there is no decision to cause the result. Cf. Duff (1980a) 157-158; Cross and Jones (1984) 30-31. A third possibility is that there are two senses to the term "decide" as suggested supra at note 16 concerning the term "choose". There is a fourth possibility as well. One may suggest that the contention that in cases of oblique intention there is a decision (or a choice) to bring about the bad result is correct, but only if the awareness of the actor that his action will certainly bring about the result causes him to think and deliberate about whether to perform the action. If there is a deliberation that culminates in taking the action then we should say that the actor has decided (or chosen) to bring about the result. But if the information that the action will certainly cause the side effect does not trigger any process of deliberation (as in a case of acting spontaneously out of passion or out of fear) then although the actor knows that his action will cause the result, we would not say that he decides (or chooses) to cause it (cf. Mackie (1977b) at p. 181). If we accept this view (and, in addition, think that in cases of direct intention there is a decision, or choice, even in cases of spontaneous actions) then we can suggest that the higher offence will include cases of direct

intention, together with cases of (mere) foresight of certainty where the action is preceded by a deliberation. The other view, which does not make the present distinction, would say that even in cases of oblique intention that are not preceded by deliberation there is a decision (or choice) to cause the result, or, alternatively, that in every case of oblique intention (in the context of causing bad results that are relevant to criminal law) there is a deliberation whether to act, although sometimes it is extremely brief.

21   For the idea that in recklessness there is a decision to take a risk see Hall (1960) 115.

22   One may suggest that there are three degrees of moral blameworthiness. Acting with a desire to cause the result is the worst; this is followed by acting when choosing to cause the result; the least blameworthy is acting recklessly. If we accept this idea then we can divide offences into three sub-categories, so that causing a result with direct intention will carry the highest punishment, causing it with oblique intention will carry a lesser punishment, and causing it with recklessness will carry the lowest punishment. I will return in the next chapter (in section 6.3) to the idea of viewing cases of oblique intention as forming an intermediate category situated between direct intention and recklessness.

Two further options were discussed in the present chapter. The first one is that the element which makes direct intention highly blameworthy is that of acting without a hope that the result will not ensue. The adoption of this view should lead us to include within the higher offence, together with direct intention, not only cases of oblique intention but also cases of indifference (unless we accept the argument that practical problems in proving indifference may justify not including cases of indifference within the higher offence). The second option is that the element which justifies viewing the person who acts with direct intention as deserving a higher punishment is that he shows us that he would have acted in the same way even if he had known that the result would certainly ensue from his action. Adopting this view should lead us to include within the higher offence, together with direct intention, not only cases of oblique intention but also cases of recklessness in which the actor who takes the risk of causing the result would have acted in the same way even if he had known that the result would certainly ensue, or at least, those cases of recklessness in which the actor manifests in his action that he would have acted in the same way in such circumstances (unless we accept the argument that practical problems of proof may justify that only direct and oblique intention be included within the higher offence).

Chapter 6

Degrees of Probability

6.1 An Argument Based on Degrees of Probability

It is common to say that the degree of moral blameworthiness of an actor increases in proportion to the degree of probability in which he foresees the occurrence of the bad result. That is to say, when all other things are equal (including the motives and the amount of harm that might occur) a person who takes an unjustifiable risk of causing a certain harm knowing that there is, say, a 40% chance that the harm will ensue, is more blameworthy than a person who takes an unjustifiable risk that the same amount of harm will ensue knowing there is only a 20% chance that the harm will ensue. Within this scale, the maximum amount of blameworthiness exists when the actor foresees that the harm will certainly ensue. When all other things are equal, the person who is practically certain that his act will cause the bad result is more blameworthy than the person who takes, say, a risk of 80% that the result will ensue. Note that the point made here is not that there is a qualitative difference between the two last mentioned cases. The possibility that there is a qualitative difference between them was discussed in the previous chapter, dealing with ideas like the one that in cases of foresight of certainty, as opposed to cases of foresight of a high probability, there is a decision to cause the result. Here I am speaking of a quantitative difference, about a difference in degree of probability (which generates a difference in degree of blameworthiness) between foresight of certainty and foresight of, say, 80% that the result will ensue.

Now, one might suggest that the above mentioned quantitative difference may legitimately lead a legislator to include cases of oblique intention together with cases of direct intention within the same offence and to distinguish them from cases of recklessness. The argument would run as follows: one who acts with a desire that the result ensue is more blameworthy than one who acts without such a desire, so that offences should be graded following the distinction between direct intention and recklessness. But one who acts with foresight of the practical certainty that the result will ensue is more blameworthy than one who acts with foresight of the result in degrees of probability that fall short of certainty. Now, the offence of causing the result with direct intention encompasses all cases in which the actor desires the result to ensue, including when there is only a little chance that the result will ensue (for example, when the degree of probability that the result will ensue is only 10%). That means that an X amount of blameworthiness which is constituted by the combination of desire and foresight of a 10% chance of harm, suffices for inclusion within the higher offence. Now, in cases of mere foresight of certainty, the element of desire is absent; but on the other hand, the probability in which the result is foreseen is very high, thereby yielding a very high degree of blameworthiness, which is identical to X. And since such a degree of blameworthiness is sufficient to justify the inclusion of the cases of direct intention (in which the probability that the result will ensue is low) within the higher offence, it should also suffice to justify the inclusion of cases of oblique intention within the same offence. Put otherwise, the fact that in cases of oblique intention the result is foreseen in such a high degree of probability makes up for the lack of desire, with the result that the degree of moral blameworthiness present in those cases is identical to the degree of moral blameworthiness present in those cases of desire in which the actor knows that the degree of probability that the result will ensue is low.[1] This justification for equating the law of cases of oblique intention to that of cases of direct intention differs from the justifications discussed in the previous chapter. For the justifications discussed in the previous chapter were based on finding some mental common denominator between cases of direct intention and cases of oblique intention. The present justification, however, is not based on such a common mental element, but rather on the argument that two different states of mind yield the same amount of blameworthiness. Another difference is that, in order to succeed, the justifications discussed in the previous chapter had to reject the idea that the element of desire is intrinsically important and that it, in itself, increases the degree of blameworthiness. The present argument, on the other hand, accepts this idea.

6.2   Degrees of Probability and Degrees of Blameworthiness

The above argument is based on the assumption that the degree of blameworthiness increases in proportion to the degree of probability that the result will ensue.[2] The question I would like to raise now is whether this assumption is only correct in cases of recklessness (i.e. in cases in which the result is not desired by the actor) or also in cases in which the result is desired by him. The idea that a person who does not act in order to cause a certain harm but takes an unjustifiable risk that his action will cause this harm as a side effect, where there is a risk of 40% that the harm will ensue, is more blameworthy than a person who takes an unjustified risk of 20% that the harm will ensue, when all other things are equal (including his purpose or motive in the action, the amount of harm that would be caused if the risk would be realised and so on) sounds very convincing. But is it also true that a person who acts *in order* to cause a certain harm and takes an action that has only a 20% chance of succeeding in causing the harm is less blameworthy than a person who acts in order to cause the same result and takes an action that has a 40% chance of succeeding (when all others things are equal, including the motives)? I think that whereas the first mentioned assumption (concerning cases of recklessness) fits easily with common intuition, whether the second assumption is equally correct is far from clear.[3] This may explain why the general practice of the criminal law is to distinguish between degrees of probability only in the context of cases in which the result is not desired by the actor, and not to distinguish within the category of direct intention between different degrees of probability.[4]

A possible explanation for the idea that the blameworthiness of the actor increases in proportion to the degree of probability of the result being caused concerns the character of the actor as manifested in the action. Let us focus first on cases in which the actor hopes that the result will not ensue. Take two persons who act for the same purpose and take an unjustifiable risk that their action will cause a certain amount of harm, both of them hoping that the harm will not ensue. Assume that the only difference between them is that A takes a 40% risk that the harm will ensue while B takes a 20% risk that the harm will ensue. A shows by his action that he is a person who is willing to take a 40% risk that the said harm will ensue. But B does not manifest in his action that he is a person who is willing to take a 40% risk that the same result will ensue (when all other things, including the purpose, remain constant). B takes a risk of only 20% that the result will ensue and hopes that it will not ensue, so it is possible that had the risk been 40% he would not have taken the action. The character of a person who is willing to take a risk of 40% that a bad result will ensue is morally more defective (is morally worse) than the character of a person who is only willing to take a risk of 20% that the same result will ensue (when all other things are equal). So if we accept the retributive idea that the severity of the punishment should be proportional to the gravity of the defect of character displayed in the act, we can understand the idea that A deserves a higher punishment than B.[5] But if this is the explanation for the idea that the degree of culpability varies according to the magnitude of the risk, then it seems that the picture changes when we come to consider cases of direct intention. For if a person who wants a result to ensue, who acts in order to achieve the result, takes a course of action that produces a 20% risk that the result will ensue, we cannot say that he might have refrained from acting had the chances of achieving the result been 40% (all other things being equal). Since he wants the result to ensue, he will welcome the opportunity to take an action which generates a greater chance that the result will be caused. Actually, we can assume that if he knew of a course of action that would certainly cause the same result (when all other things remain equal), he would take it. This means that a person who takes a course of action *in order* to cause a certain bad result when the chance of causing the result are 20%, and a person who (when all other things are equal) takes a course of action in order to achieve the same result when he is practically certain that his act will bring about the same result, both display in their actions (coupled with their states of mind) the same degree of defect of character.[6] The upshot is that (according to the present explanation) the idea that the degree of moral culpability varies in accordance with the degree of probability is not applicable with respect to direct intention.[7]

If we accept the idea that within the category of direct intention the degree of culpability does not vary in accordance with the degree of probability that the result will ensue, then we should reject the argument suggested in section 6.1, for it seems to be committed to the assumption that acting with direct intention when the result is foreseen as practically certain is more blameworthy than acting with direct intention when the probability of causing the result is low, because of the difference in the degree of probability.

To clarify this point, it should be recalled that the argument suggested in section 6.1 assumes that the existence of desire increases moral culpability. It relies on this assumption in explaining why direct intention should be distinguished from recklessness for grading purposes. It assumes, then, that when we speak of two cases in which the degree of probability that the bad result will ensue is, say, 20%, the culpability in cases of direct intention is higher than the culpability in cases of recklessness (when all other things are equal) because of the element of desire, which exists only in cases of direct intention. Now, if the element of desire in itself increases the actor's culpability, then it seems that it should do the same when the degree of probability that the result will ensue is high. This means that when the probability that the result will ensue is 80%, a person acting with direct intention is more culpable than one acting with (mere) foresight of the result. And the same holds in cases of practical certainty.[8] Now, if in cases of practical certainty, one who acts in order to cause the result is more culpable than one who (merely) foresees it, how can the argument suggested in section 6.1 succeed? Only by comparing cases of foresight of practical certainty (without desire) with cases of direct intention that is coupled with foresight of a *low* degree of probability that the result will ensue. And indeed the argument made in section 6.1 was based on this analogy: That since the amount of culpability present in cases of direct intention coupled with foresight of the result in a low degree of probability suffices for inclusion within the higher offence, the same amount of culpability which (according to the argument) exists in cases of (mere) foresight of practical certainty should also suffice to justify the inclusion of cases of (mere) foresight of practical certainty within the higher offence.[9]

The above analysis shows that the argument suggested in section 6.1 is committed to two assumptions:
(1) That when there is foresight of practical certainty, the actor who desires the result to ensue (case A) is more culpable than one who does not (case B).
(2) That the amount of culpability in cases of (mere) foresight of practical certainty (case B) is identical to that which exists in cases where desire is coupled with foresight of low probability that the result will ensue (case C).

Now, if the amount of culpability in case A is higher than that in case B, and the amount of culpability in case B is identical to that in case C, then the conclusion must be that the degree of culpability in case A is higher than that in case C. This means that the argument suggested in section 6.1 must be committed to the idea that the degree of culpability in cases of practical certainty is higher than that in cases of low probability, even when in both cases the actor acts in order to cause the result. And this lies in conflict with the conclusion of the discussion above, that within the category of direct intention, the degree of blameworthiness does not vary in accordance with degrees of probability. So if we accept the conclusion reached above, we should reject the argument suggested in section 6.1.

But perhaps we can find another explanation to the idea that the degree of blameworthiness varies in accordance with the probability that the result will ensue; an explanation that will enable us to accept the relevance of this idea even within the category of direct intention. Perhaps we can say that taking a course of action when the probability of causing the harm is 80% amounts to *doing* something that is morally worse, that is more wrongful, than taking a course of action when the probability of causing the harm is 60% (when all other things are equal), and therefore a person who takes the first course of action is more culpable; and perhaps it can also be said that this holds even within the category of direct intention. But then the following question arises: Why is it the case that the degree of moral wrongfulness of an act varies in accordance with the degree of probability? One possibility is to speak of degrees of harm to the dignity of the victim. Take two people who, for the same reason, take an unjustified risk that their action will cause a harm to another person and both of them cause the harm. Both hope that the result will not ensue, and the only difference between them is that A takes a risk of 80% that the result will ensue, whereas B takes a risk of 60%. One may suggest that since both of them take an unjustifiable risk, both of them harm the dignity of the victim to a certain degree, and that the degree of this harm (and, consequently, the degree of the moral wrongfulness of the action) varies in accordance with the degree of probability. Although the material bad result (for example, the bodily harm) is identical in both cases, an additional factor should be considered – the harm to the dignity of the victim, the extent of which varies in proportion with the degree of probability. But is this idea applicable to cases of direct intention? Does a person who takes a course of action intending a bad result to ensue with only a 60% chance to bring about the bad result harm the dignity of the victim to a lesser degree than a person who, intending the same bad result to ensue, takes a course of action with an 80% chance to bring about the result? The first actor takes a course of action that has only a 60% chance of success, not because he respects the victim more than the second person does, but because he does not have the opportunity (or money or time, etc.) to take an action which has a better chance of succeeding. So it seems implausible to say that he harms the dignity of the victim to a lesser degree than the second person does. In the same vein, if we focus on the harm to the moral integrity of the actor, we arrive, I think, at similar conclusions. Even if we would be ready to say that when a person takes an unjustified risk that his act will cause a bad result while hoping that the result will not ensue, the harm to his moral integrity varies in accordance with the degree of probability that the result will ensue, it seems implausible to apply the same idea in cases of direct intention. In cases of direct intention the actor acts in order to cause the result, he wants it to ensue, he commits himself to achieving it, and if he could, he would change his plans and take a course of action with a better chance of succeeding. In so acting, he puts himself in full conflict with the protected value, and it seems that the harm to his moral integrity does not vary in accordance with the degree of probability. As for the possibility of focussing on the harm caused to the "value itself", one might suggest that the harm caused to the value itself varies in accordance with the degree of probability that the result will ensue, and that this holds even within the category of direct intention. Since the very idea of causing harm to the "value itself" pertains to a realm which is less familiar to us, which is more remote from our everyday thinking, it is more difficult to evaluate the argument and, hence, to criticise it. However, it should be recalled that this remoteness constitutes a major drawback of the very concept of "harm to the value itself".

Another possible line of argument may focus on degrees of causal connection. I have already discussed the idea that one who causes a result purposely is more causally connected to it than one who causes it recklessly or knowingly and, therefore, is more blameworthy.[10] The strength of the causal contribution may be influenced by various factors (such as the intervention of an action of another person, spatial and temporal remoteness and so on).[11] One may suggest a further factor: The degree of probability,[12] that is, when two people take a risk that a certain harm will ensue from their action and both of them hope that it will not ensue, then if the harm nevertheless occurs, the one who takes the higher risk is more causally connected to the harm, and, hence, is morally more blameworthy.[13] Taking this line of argument further, one may say that this difference in the degree of causal contribution holds even within the category of direct intention. The idea that the intervention of another person or the remoteness in time of the result influences the degree of causal contribution even *within* the category of direct intention is not implausible, so that one may suggest that the same can be said about degrees of probability (although, all things considered, it seems that application of this idea within the context of degrees of probability produces less plausible results, as there is some feeling that the fact that the actor acts *in order* to achieve the result somehow renders degrees of probability devoid of importance).

Another possibility is to understand the role of degrees of probability in determining degrees of blameworthiness as being connected to the notion of "expected harm". In proceeding to determine, from a utilitarian perspective, whether to take a certain course of action in order to achieve some good result, the actor has to take into consideration the bad side effects that his action may produce. And in doing so, he should take into consideration not only the amount of the harm that his action might produce but also the degree of probability that the harm will occur. Take for example a case in which it is certain that the action will immediately produce some good result (which is the end for which the action is taken), a result that should be balanced against some harm which may be brought about as a side effect later on. Let us assume that (from a utilitarian point of view) the harm that may be caused outweighs the good result. This means that if the actor is sure that his action will cause the bad result, he should refrain from taking the action. But since there is only a *risk* that the bad result will occur, we are faced with a different situation, and the question whether the action is permitted depends upon the degree of probability that the bad result will occur. For example, it may be the case that if the degree of probability that the bad result will occur is less than 20% then the action will be morally permitted, but if it is more than 20% then it will not. The degree of probability affects the "expected harm" and, as such, constitutes an important factor in deciding whether the action should be permitted. Now consider the cases in which the action is forbidden, i.e. when the probability that the harm will ensue is higher than 20%. Assuming that all others things remain constant, is there a moral difference between acting when the probability that the harm will ensue is 80% and acting when the probability of the harm occurring is 60%? We may suggest that there is such a difference. We may say that when all other things are equal (including the good result achieved by the action), taking a risk of 80% that the result will occur is doing something that is morally worse, that is more wrongful, than taking a risk of 60% that the same result will ensue, and, therefore, a person who takes the first action is more culpable than one who takes the second one. It is well accepted that a person who recklessly takes a risk of 50% that some harm will occur is more blameworthy than one who recklessly takes a risk of 50% that less harm will occur (when all other things are equal). So one may say that the same holds when the amount of the potential harm is constant and only the degree of probability varies. In the example introduced above, the "expected harm" in the case of 80% is higher than that in the case of 60%, and therefore taking action in the case of 80% is doing something that is morally worse than taking the 60% risk, and that, in turn, makes the first actor, i.e. the person who *chooses* to take the first action, more culpable than the second one (who only chooses to take a less wrongful action).[14] This analysis seems convincing in cases in which the harm does not materialise. In these cases, we cannot blame the actors for causing the result but only for choosing to act, and the first actor chooses to take an action that is morally worse than the action chosen by the second actor. But does this difference in culpability remain important even in cases in which the harm materialises? Some may feel that if the harm materialises, the fact that the harm does occur eliminates or at least significantly reduces the importance of the degree of probability. They may feel that once the harm has occurred, the main complaint against the actor is that he recklessly caused the harm, so that the question of the degree of probability somehow appears of less importance (since the bad result *did* occur). But even if we intuitively sympathise with the above emotion, it seems that if we accept that when a result does not occur, the degree of blameworthiness varies in accordance with the degree of probability, then we cannot accept that this difference in blameworthiness loses all importance where the result materialises.[15]

What are the implications of this explanation with regard to cases of direct intention? Does moral culpability vary in accordance with degrees of probability even within the context of direct intention? One may say that, in the present explanation, the whole idea is that choosing to take a risk of 60% is doing something that is morally worse than choosing to take a risk of, say, 40%, but that in cases of direct intention the actor chooses to *cause* the result (as opposed to choosing only to take a *risk* that his act will cause the result) and this fact is not contingent upon the degree of probability that his act will cause the result.[16] There are no degrees in choosing to kill, the argument would run, and therefore two cases of acting in order to kill that only differ in the degree of probability that the death will be achieved cannot be described as differing in the "degree of choice of the actor" or some similar notion. Therefore, the idea that the degree of culpability varies in accordance with the degree of probability is not applicable within the context of direct intention. But perhaps we can say that, all things considered, there is something to be said for the importance of degrees of probability, even in the context of direct intention. After all, from society's viewpoint, a person who acts in order to cause a result where the chances of success in achieving the result are only 20% acts less dangerously than a person who acts with direct intention to cause the same result where the chances of success in achieving the result are 40%. So from society's viewpoint, the actor in the case of 40% does something worse than the actor in the case of 20%. The fact that the actor in the 20% case would be glad to take a course of action in which the degree of probability is higher than 20% if he had the opportunity to do so, does not change the fact that in the present case he takes an action the chances of success of which are only 20%. So we can say that from an "objective" point of view, this actor actually does something that is less dangerous, and hence less wrongful, than the actor who acts with 40% chances of success. The actor's situation in the 20% case can be considered as somewhat similar to that of a thief who only steals $100, but who would have stolen $10,000 had he found such an amount. If we think that in this case the thief's degree of culpability is lower than that of a thief that actually stole $10,000, then perhaps we can say something similar to that about the actor who only acts with a 20% chance of success. The idea here is that taking an action which is more dangerous (from society's viewpoint) is morally worse than taking an action which is less dangerous, and that this holds even within the context of direct intention. Therefore, the person who acts in order to cause a certain bad result and, to this end, takes an course of action with only a 20% chance of succeeding is less blameworthy than one who, in order to cause the same result, takes an act with a 40% chance of success (when all other things, including the motives, are equal).

The upshot of our discussion concerning the relevance of degrees of probability to degrees of blameworthiness is that although the idea that within the category of recklessness the degree of culpability varies in accordance with the degree of probability is very plausible, the idea that the same holds in cases of direct intention is problematic. Some of the explanations suggested above for the idea that the degree of culpability varies in accordance with degrees of probability lead to the conclusion that this idea is not applicable to cases of direct intention. Other explanations suggested above might lead to the conclusion that the said idea is relevant even to cases of direct intention, though strong arguments may be raised from within these explanations themselves in favour of the position that the said idea is *not* applicable to cases of direct intention.

Since the argument suggested in section 6.1 is dependent on the idea that the degree of blameworthiness varies in accordance with the degree of probability even in cases of direct intention, and since this idea is problematic, we can conclude that the argument suggested in section 6.1 is problematic.

But even if the idea that the degree of moral culpability varies in accordance with the degree of probability is applicable even in cases of direct intention there is still another problem with the argument suggested in section 6.1. Since this argument accepts that in cases of direct intention in which the result is foreseen as certain there is more culpability than in cases of (mere) foresight of certainty, the argument must rely on an equation of cases of (mere) foresight of certainty with cases of direct intention in which the result is foreseen in a low probability. The argument is that if a fixed amount of blameworthiness, X, present in cases of direct intention in which the result is foreseen in a low probability, suffices to include such cases within the higher offence, then the same amount of culpability present in cases of (mere) foresight of certainty, should also justify the inclusion of such cases within the higher offence. The problem with this kind of argument, however, is that it violates the principle of "all other things being equal". Many factors influence the degree of blameworthiness of offenders, even within the same actus reus. One factor is the amount of the damage caused to the protected interest, should the harmful result occur. Within the offence of causing grievous bodily harm to a person, blameworthiness varies in accordance with the amount of the harm caused to the victim (as foreseen by the actor). The same holds, for example, in relation to offences of causing bodily harm to a person and causing damage to the property of another. This yields the result that in certain cases of recklessness (in which the prospective harm is very large) the degree of the culpability of the actor is higher than in certain cases of direct intention (in which the prospective harm is minor), even within the boundaries of the same actus reus. Other factors that influence the degree of moral culpability are, for example, the motives and purposes of the actor, and whether his action (be it in cases of intention or of recklessness) is planned in advance and taken after deliberation or, rather, was impulsively performed on the spur of the moment. These factors can yield the result that in certain cases an actor who recklessly causes a certain harm will be considered more blameworthy than an actor who causes the same result purposely.[17] If this is the case, then a legislator who distinguishes between causing bodily harm purposely and causing bodily harm recklessly should not be viewed as positing that in all cases of direct intention the culpability of the actor is higher than in all cases of recklessness, but rather as saying that when all other things are equal (including the motives, the amount of the prospective harm, etc.), one who acts with direct intention is more culpable than one who acts with recklessness.[18] Now, the argument suggested in section 6.1 accepts that the degree of probability that the result will ensue is one of the factors which influence the degree of culpability and that this factor is important both in cases of recklessness and in cases of direct intention. It follows, therefore, that comparing cases of mere foresight in which the degree of probability is very high with cases of direct intention in which the degree of probability is very low violates the principle of "all other things being equal" on which the grading is based. I think that this point weakens further the argument made in section 6.1.[19]

Another relative weakness of the argument suggested in section 6.1 is that it is not based on an argument that there is a qualitative difference between cases of foresight of certainty and cases of recklessness. According to the argument, it will be recalled, in the realm of recklessness, a higher degree of probability yields a higher degree of culpability, until the degree of probability reaches a point which is so elevated that it yields a sufficiently high degree of culpability to ground the equation of the culpability present with that present in cases of direct intention when the probability of the result occurring is low. This point is that of practical certainty. According to the argument, this point of practical certainty is no different in quality from lesser degrees of probability, and the difference is only one of degree. Actually, the same argument could justify the inclusion of cases in which the probability is of 80% (or 60%, etc.) within the higher offence if we were of the view that the amount of culpability in these cases is identical to that present in cases of direct intention when the probability of the result occurring is low. The justification for only including cases of foresight of practical certainty within the higher offence resides, according to the argument, simply in the assessment that only when the degree of probability is so high is the amount of culpability equal to that present in cases of direct intention when the probability of the result occurring is low. Since we are speaking here of degrees and assessments, the argument suffers from some degree of arbitrariness and this adds to its relative weakness.[20]

The cumulative force of the above problems leads, I think, to the conclusion that a legislator should not act upon the argument suggested in section 6.1.

6.3   Foresight of Certainty as an Intermediate Case

Even if one denies the argument suggested in section 6.1, and even if one holds that the degree of moral blameworthiness in cases of direct intention does not vary in accordance with the degree of probability, one may still suggest an argument for including foresight of certainty together with direct intention within the same offence and differentiating this offence from a lower offence of recklessness, based on the importance of degrees of probability within the context of recklessness. As was said in section 6.2, the idea that within recklessness the degree of culpability varies in accordance with the degree of probability that the result will ensue is convincing and, in this respect, several possible explanations were suggested. If this is the case, we can view foresight of certainty as intermediately situated between cases of direct intention and cases of recklessness. We can start by saying that the element of desire is important in itself and that an actor who acts with direct intention is more blameworthy than an actor who acts with (mere) foresight of the result, when all other things are equal (including the motives). The amount of blameworthiness within direct intention does not vary in accordance with the degrees of probability, and the degree of culpability in all cases of direct intention (including cases in which the probability that the result will be caused is low) is identical, and by the same token, higher than the culpability in all cases of mere foresight, including where there is foresight of certainty (when all other things, including the motives, are equal). But when we turn to cases of recklessness we see that within this category we have numerous degrees of culpability, as every increase in the degree of probability yields an increase in culpability (when all other things remain constant). This, in turn, enables us to view the category of foresight of certainty (i.e. the category which comprises those cases of foresight in which the culpability of the actor is at its highest) as constituting an intermediate case between direct intention and recklessness. The upshot is that we can speak of three degrees of moral culpability: direct intention, foresight of certainty (that is not coupled with a desire that the result will ensue), and recklessness. This can lead a legislator to create three degrees of causing, say, grievous bodily harm: causing it with direct intention, causing it with oblique intention, and causing it recklessly. But a legislator is not obliged to create a separate offence for every degree of culpability. Otherwise, he would have to create numerous offences of recklessly causing grievous bodily harm, when every increase of, say, 5% in the probability that the result will ensue would provide the basis for a higher offence. The legislator must gather under the same offence various cases with different degrees of culpability, and leave it to the sentencer to determine the "exact" degree of culpability in the case before him. Therefore, even if the legislator accepts that the case of oblique intention is an intermediate one, he may legitimately decide to create only two levels of causing a certain result. In such a case, cases of direct intention will be included within the higher offence and cases of recklessness will be included within the lesser offence, and an additional decision will be required concerning cases of oblique intention: whether to include them within the higher offence or within the lesser offence (this decision may, in turn, influence the decision regarding the appropriate maximum penalty for the lesser offence). If the legislator thinks that the degree of culpability in cases of foresight of certainty is closer to that present in cases of direct intention than it is to that present in most cases of recklessness (when all other things are equal), then this is a good reason to include oblique intention within the higher offence.[21] On the other hand, the assessment that the degree of culpability present in cases of (mere) foresight of certainty is closer to that present in cases of recklessness than to that present in cases of direct intention, yields the conclusion that it is more reasonable to include cases of foresight of certainty within the lesser offence. If the legislator cannot reach a decision as to where foresight of certainty should be situated on the continuum between direct intention and recklessness or if he thinks that foresight of certainty lies "right in the middle", the decision will be somewhat arbitrary. The upshot is that a reasonable legislator may think that the element of desire is important in itself in assessing the actor's degree of culpability, and therefore may grade offences based on the distinction between direct intention and recklessness. At the same time he may include cases of oblique intention (which are viewed by him as an intermediate set of cases) within the higher offence, as explained above.[22] But he may take a different approach: To include this intermediate set of cases within the lesser offence, or to create a separate offence for cases of oblique intention that will carry a higher punishment than that prescribed for the recklessness offence and a lower punishment than that prescribed for the direct intention offence.

The argument suggested here, that a reasonable legislator may decide to include cases of foresight of practical certainty within the higher offence together with cases of direct intention because cases of foresight of certainty form an intermediate case, seems to suffer from a relative weakness, as it does not suggest that there is a qualitative difference between cases of (mere) practical certainty and cases of recklessness. It only says that the higher the risk, the higher the culpability; and although within this range the maximum culpability is reached in cases of foresight of certainty, there is only a difference in degree between such cases and cases of foresight of, say, 90% or 80% that the result will ensue. This means that there is some arbitrariness involved in deciding that only cases of foresight of certainty should be included within the higher offence.[23] This drawback is less important in the present context than in the context of the argument suggested in section 6.1. In that context, it will be recalled, the argument was that the degree of culpability in cases of foresight of certainty is *identical* to the degree of culpability present in cases of direct intention (when the probability of the result occurring is low). But if the only difference between the degree of culpability in cases of foresight of certainty and that present in cases of foresight of high degrees of probability is one of degree, it does not seem very convincing to say that exactly at this point (namely, that of practical certainty) the amount of culpability reaches the degree present in cases of direct intention (in circumstances of low probability that the result will ensue). In the present context, however, we are speaking, from the outset, only about an intermediate case, and about similarities and proximity, so the fact that some arbitrariness is involved in deciding where to draw the line is less problematic.

Those who view the problem of "arbitrariness" as important might prefer to include cases of oblique intention within the lesser offence, together with cases of recklessness. But there is still another option: To follow a line of argument that can enable us to view cases of foresight of certainty as intermediate cases which are different in quality from cases of recklessness. According to this argument, cases of foresight of practical certainty are different in quality from cases of recklessness in that in cases of foresight of certainty, the actor chooses to cause the result, whereas in cases of recklessness he only chooses to take a risk that the result will ensue.[24] This is a qualitative difference which renders the actor in cases of foresight of certainty more culpable than the actor in cases of recklessness (when all other things are equal). At the same time, the argument would run, an actor who acts with direct intention (regardless of the probability that the result will ensue) does not only choose to cause the result but also wants it to ensue and, therefore, there is a qualitative difference between him and the reckless actor, on the one hand, and the actor who acts with (mere) foresight of certainty, on the other. Since the one who acts with direct intention is more culpable than the one who acts with (mere) foresight of certainty, we end up with three degrees of culpability, each one different from the other in quality. A legislator who accepts this picture may reasonably decide to create three degrees of the offence he is dealing with.[25] But he may also decide to only create two degrees, one for direct intention and the other for recklessness. In this case, he has to make another decision, namely, whether to include the intermediate case of foresight of certainty within the higher offence or within the lower one.

6.4   Conclusions

In section 5.4 I summarised the conclusions that can be derived from the discussion conducted until that point. What should be added to this summary in light of the discussion in this chapter is that even a legislator who thinks that the desire to cause the bad result is in itself an important factor which increases the degree of culpability, and decides to distinguish between direct intention and recklessness on this basis, may reasonably include cases of oblique intention within the higher offence together with direct intention, based on the view that the case of oblique intention constitutes an intermediate case (insofar as the degree of blameworthiness is concerned) between direct intention and recklessness. On the other hand, since we are speaking here of a view that the case of oblique intention constitutes an intermediate case, it is also reasonable for the legislator to make a different decision, namely, to include cases of oblique intention within the lesser offence together with recklessness or, alternatively, to create a separate (intermediate) offence for cases of oblique intention.

Notes

1   In this vein see Feller (1970) 359-360. I understand his argument to be that the blameworthiness present in cases of oblique intention is identical to that present in cases of desire (which is coupled with foresight of a low probability that the result will ensue), and the discussion that will immediately follow assumes such understanding of the claim. The possibility that in cases of oblique intention there is a higher degree of blameworthiness than in cases of recklessness but a lower one than in cases of direct intention will be discussed later, in section 6.3.

2   It should be emphasised that the determining element in this respect is the degree of probability actually foreseen by the actor, not the "objective" probability. So when I hereinafter speak of degrees of probability, it should be understood as referring to the degree of probability perceived by the actor.

3   Ashworth, for example, in discussing cases of recklessness, says that the degree of culpability surely varies in accordance with the magnitude of the anticipated risk. He does not make the same point concerning direct intention. See Ashworth (2000) 124.

4   For example: The Model Penal Code provides that a person acts purposely with respect to a result if it is his conscious object to cause such a result. Within this category there is no differentiation based on degrees of probability. But when the result is not desired by the actor, the Code distinguishes between two categories, namely, that of acting "knowingly" with respect to a result, which is defined in terms of foresight of practical certainty, and that of acting "recklessly", in which the actor takes a substantial risk that the result will ensue. See Model Penal Code (1985), section 2.02.

5   Cf. Michael and Wechsler (1937) 1277 who say: "... the less dangerous to life he believed his act to be, the less is the depreciation of the value of human life which his act indicates and, hence, the less grave the moral weakness which it manifests ..." (but note that the interest of these authors in degrees of moral weakness is not related to retribution and deserved punishments but to the dangerousness of the actor, a factor which bears upon the appropriate punishment from a utilitarian perspective). See also Simons (1992) 497.

6   A different view was introduced by Silving. She says that "action under conditions in which the probability of success is small ... indicates an unconscious 'withdrawal' or inhibitions bearing on intent and thus on the degree of guilt" and that therefore a criminal code should distinguish between different degrees of probability even within the category of intention. See Silving (1967) 225. But I do not find this speculation regarding unconscious inhibitions convincing. Generally, we can assume that the fact that the person who acts in order to cause the result takes a course of action with a relatively low chance to produce the result is attributable to a lack of opportunity (or money or time, etc.) to take a course of action which carries a higher chance of success. There might be exceptional cases in which further evidence may prove he had unconscious inhibitions which preclude the inference that he would have acted in the same way even if he had known the result was certain to ensue. But without such evidence the inference is reliable.

7 Cf. Michael and Wechsler (1937) 1277 who say that in assessing the actor's character, it is of favourable import that he believed death to be a less rather than a more probable result of his act, *unless he intended to kill*. See also the discussion supra in section 5.2. Actually, as was explained in section 5.2, the idea that a person who only takes a risk might not have acted in the same way had he known of the practical certainty that the result would ensue is also inapplicable to cases in which the actor simply does not mind whether the result will ensue (as opposed to cases in which he hopes that it will not ensue). So, the idea that the degree of blameworthiness varies in accordance with the magnitude of the risk (if it is based upon the present explanation) is also inapplicable to cases of "indifference", as opposed to cases in which the actor hopes that the result will not ensue. As to the further possible argument that this idea is also inapplicable to some cases in which the actor hopes that the result will not ensue, namely, cases concerning which we estimate (based on further evidence) that the actor would not have refrained from acting even if he had known, for example, that the result would certainly ensue, we may reply that in such cases (as opposed to cases of intention and indifference) the actor does not exhibit in the criminal action (coupled with the mental state he has when he acts) that with foresight of certainty he would have acted similarly. See supra section 5.2.

8 One might reject this conclusion by saying that the element of desire is of importance only when the actor is not sure that the result will ensue. In cases of certainty, however, the element of desire, of acting in order to cause the result, loses all importance and adds nothing to the actor's blameworthiness. But to advance such an argument is to say that the reason why in cases where the result is foreseen to a degree of 50%, for example, one who acts with direct intention is more blameworthy than one who acts with recklessness is that only the former actor *chooses (or decides)* to cause the result and that, therefore, in cases of foresight of certainty the difference between direct intention and oblique intention collapses, for the element of foresight of certainty, by itself, suffices to establish the actor's choice to cause the result (so that, in such cases, the further element of desire adds nothing to the actor's blameworthiness). This argument was already discussed in the previous chapter: That the element of choice to cause the result constitutes the determining factor in assessing degrees of culpability and that this element is present to the same extent in cases of direct intention and cases of (mere) foresight of certainty. Of course, the element of desire is relevant in the context of this argument, as the existence of desire in cases where the result is not certain is what makes the actor's foresight of a 50% chance that the result will ensue a *choice* to cause the result. But in this case, the desire is not the intrinsically important factor for assessing moral culpability. Rather its importance lies in the fact that it generates a choice on the part of the actor to cause the result. The argument suggested in section 6.1, on the other hand, is of a different nature. It assumes that the element of desire, in itself, rather than the element of choice, constitutes the determining factor in assessing degrees of blameworthiness because of the direct attack constituted by it. Consequently, the element of desire should continue to be viewed as important even in cases of foresight of certainty, as was explained supra in chapter 4.

9 Cf. Feller (1970) 359-360.

10 See supra section 4.2.3.

11 Cf. Moore (1997) 703.

12 Cf. Gross (1979) 87-88.

13 I should remind the reader that when, throughout this chapter, I speak of degrees of probability influencing degrees of culpability, I am only referring to cases in which the

actor is aware of the relevant degree of probability. This proviso also applies in the context of the present argument. One might argue that degrees of causal contribution are generally determined by objective factors, independent of considerations related to the actor's awareness, so that in the present argument we have to focus on "objective" probability. In response, we may say that in the context of degrees of probability the situation is different, as the degree of causal contribution *is* dependent upon the awareness of the actor; or, alternatively, that even assuming that the degree of causal contribution is determined independently of the awareness of the actor, the fact that there is a higher degree of causal contribution on the actor's part does not increase his *culpability* unless he is aware that he is going to make such a high contribution (for example, that he takes a risk of 80% rather than 60%).

14   Cf. Moore (1997) 410-411.

15   If we think, like many authors, that the fact that the result materialises does not affect at all the amount of the deserved punishment, then we should say that the importance of degrees of probability is not diminished by the fact that the result materialises. But even if we think that the occurrence of the result increases the actor's deserved punishment, the fact that he *chooses* to take the risk constitutes an important factor in blaming him. And if we accept that at the moment the actor acts, in the 80% case, a certain amount of blameworthiness immediately crystallises, and that less blameworthiness crystallises in the 60% case – then the fact that the harm materialises afterwards, although it may possibly increase, by the same amount, the deserved punishment in both cases, cannot eliminate altogether the difference in blameworthiness between the two actors which was present before the result occurred (although if we believe that the increase in punishment deserved by reason of the result's occurrence is very substantial, we might accept that the difference in degrees of probability assumes less importance in determining the deserved punishment).

16   The fact that the argument suggested in section 6.1 views the element of desire that exists in cases of direct intention as an important factor in itself for moral purposes does not mean that it denies the fact that in cases of direct intention there is also an element of choice to cause the result.

17   See Ashworth (2000) 124, who says that "it is possible that some of the more calculated forms of recklessness might be adjudged more serious than impulsive forms of intention".

18   A different understanding of the practice of grading will be suggested in chapter 9. The discussion here takes place in the context of the explanation for grading offences suggested in chapter 2, whereby the grading is based on the idea that when all other things are equal (including the motives), the actor who causes the result purposely is more culpable than the reckless actor.

19   It should be noted that the justification suggested in chapter 5 for the inclusion of cases of oblique intention within the higher offence together with cases of direct intention does not suffer from the difficulty presented here. For according to the explanation suggested in chapter 5, the important element by virtue of which cases of direct intention may be distinguished from cases of recklessness is not the element of desire, in itself, but rather the element of choice (or decision) to cause the result. According to that argument, the element of choice is invariably present in both cases of direct intention (irrespective of the probability that the result will ensue) and cases of oblique intention. This argument is based, therefore, on the idea that there is something in common between *all* cases of direct intention and *all* cases of oblique intention, and on the view that this common denominator is the factor that increases the degree of culpability and not the element of desire in itself. It follows, therefore, that this

argument does not confine itself to comparing cases of oblique intention with ca~~s~~ direct intention in which the probability that the result will ensue is low.

20 The argument presented in chapter 5 for justifying the inclusion of cases of foresight of certainty within the higher offence does not suffer from this weakness, for it is based on the idea that there is a qualitative difference between recklessness and foresight of certainty, in that only in cases of foresight of certainty does the actor choose to cause the result.

As for the charge of arbitrariness made in the text, one may respond that practical considerations may justify that the line be drawn at the point of practical certainty even if we believe that the "required" amount of culpability is possibly reached at some lower point on the scale of probability. I will refer to such considerations later at note 23.

21 Ashworth maintains that "there is a strong argument that someone who takes a risk of death that amounts to a virtual certainty comes very close to the person who chooses someone's death as the means to an end". See Ashworth (1999) 179. And cf. Moore (1997) 411, who considers that "the differences in culpability between belief states undoubtedly exceeds the difference in culpability between the most culpable belief (of certain wrongdoing) and the yet more culpable states of intention or desire".

22 If the legislator adopts this approach, what should he do concerning cases of "indifference" (i.e., the cases in which the reckless actor does not positively hope that the result will not ensue but simply does not mind that it will)? The question here is whether the idea that within cases of recklessness the culpability of the actor varies in accordance with the degree of probability is only applicable to cases of "hoping that the result will not ensue" or whether it is equally applicable to cases of indifference. It seems that the answer will depend upon the explanation adopted for the phenomenon that the degree of an actor's culpability varies in accordance with the degree of probability that the result will ensue. For example: If we think that the reason why a reckless person who takes a 40% risk that he will cause a certain result is considered more culpable than a person who takes a 20% risk of causing the same result is that the former displays in his action (coupled with his state of mind) a character that is more morally defective, given that the latter might have refrained from acting had he known that the probability of causing the result was 40%, then the conclusion should be that within cases of "indifference" the degree of culpability does not vary in accordance with the degree of probability. For a person who takes a 20% risk that the result will ensue and does not mind whether it will ensue displays in his action (coupled with his state of mind) that he would have acted just the same had he known that the probability was higher than 20%, and therefore he does not display in his act a less morally defective character than that displayed by an indifferent actor, who is sure that he would cause the result (and see supra at note 7). This means that if the legislator acts upon this explanation, he should view all cases of indifference (irrespective of the degree of probability of causing the result) as equivalent in their degree of culpability to cases of oblique intention, and he should include not only cases of direct and oblique intention within the higher offence but cases of indifference as well. By this approach, the lesser offence would only include cases in which the actor hopes that the result will not ensue (unless the legislator is of the view that practical difficulties in proving "indifference" justify the inclusion of cases of "indifference" within the lesser offence, despite the fact that from a theoretical point of view they should be included within the higher offence. See supra section 5.1).

But if the explanation for the phenomenon that the degree of culpability varies in accordance with the degree of probability is, for example, that a reckless actor who takes a 40% risk that the result will ensue chooses to take a morally worse action than a reckless actor who takes a 20% risk, then this idea should apply not only to cases in which the actor hopes that the result will not ensue but also to cases in which the actor is indifferent (even if we believe that this idea is inapplicable to cases of direct intention, because in such cases the actor chooses to cause the result, rather than to take a risk). So if the legislator adopts this explanation as to the significance of degrees of probability, he can reasonably include all cases of recklessness (including cases of indifference) within the lesser offence.

23   Indeed, it seems that in the past (before 1985) the English law held that in certain "crimes of intention" the defendant could be convicted (when he did not act with direct intention) even if the degree of probability in which he foresaw the result was lower than that of practical certainty (but higher than mere possibility). According to the 5th edition of Smith and Hogan's *Criminal Law* (published in 1983), "intention" had four different legal meanings. According to the first one, only direct intention constitutes intention. According to the other three, foresight of a certain degree of probability (that is higher than mere possibility) that the result will ensue suffices for conviction of "crimes of intention" in cases where there is no direct intention. The last three legal meanings differ one from another, however, in the degree of probability that suffices for conviction. The three degrees are: Foresight that it is certain the result will ensue, foresight that it is highly probable the result will ensue, and foresight that it is probable the result will ensue. Smith and Hogan explained that the courts had to decide for every "crime of intention" which of the above four definitions would apply. See Smith and Hogan (1983) 47-51. Buzzard held that the law was (and should remain) that, in general, "intention" should be interpreted as being satisfied (in cases in which there is no direct intention) by foresight of probability that the result will ensue. See Buzzard (1978).

One argument against the extension of "intention" to cases of foresight of probability was that the notion of probability is too vague (Williams (1983a) 83-84) and that the meaning of "probable" is very uncertain (Smith (1978) 19-20). It seems that the notion of "high probability" is also vague. This vagueness may provide something of a defence against the charge of arbitrariness, made in the text. For it may be argued that although there is no qualitative difference in the degree of blameworthiness between foresight of practical certainty and foresight of high degrees of probability, there is a reason for distinguishing between them and including within the higher offence (together with direct intention) only cases of practical certainty, namely, that the notion of "high probability" suffers from considerable vagueness. Although it can be argued that the notion of practical (or moral or virtual or human) certainty also suffers from vagueness, I think that the notion of practical certainty as defined in chapter 1, is far less vague than the notion of "high probability". One might respond by suggesting that the problem of vagueness can be resolved by defining oblique intention as, for example, foresight of the result to a probability of 80%. But it could be counter-argued that this will create another problem. Except for rare and specific contexts (like those of "Russian roulette"), people who take risks do not define in exact terms the probability that the result will ensue, so it is not realistic to expect of the trier of fact to decide whether the defendant foresaw that there was a 80% risk, for example, that the result would ensue (and even if some persons sometimes think about risks in such terms the trier of fact will not generally – except for rare and specific cases – be able to decide whether the defendant before him thought about the risk in these terms). Though the task of determining whether the defendant was practically certain that the result would ensue is not an easy one, it is nonetheless less difficult than deciding whether he foresaw that there was a risk of 80% that the result would ensue.

One might suggest that if there is no qualitative difference in the degree of culpability between practical certainty and lesser degrees of probability then perhaps we should prefer to draw the line at another level. It seems that taking a risk of 51% that the result will ensue is doing something that is different in quality from taking a risk of 49% that the result will ensue. It might be suggested that in the first case a rational person would believe that the result would ensue, whereas in the second case a rational person would believe that the result would not ensue. Thus, the culpability of the first person is different in quality (and not only in degree) from that of the second (cf. Duff (1990) 96-97). Consequently, the argument runs, the legislator should include within the higher offence (together with direct intention) all cases in which the actor foresees that it is more probable than not that the result will ensue. However, the argument above to the effect that it is not practical to expect of the trier of fact to determine whether the defendant foresaw that there was an 80% chance that the result would ensue also holds for determinations whether defendants foresaw the result in the probability of 51% (cf. Gillies (1997) 633). So even if we would be prepared to say that from a moral point of view, cases of 51% could be included within the higher offence, the practical difficulty may justify limiting the extension of the higher offence only to cases of foresight of certainty. Of course, if the legislator thinks that the degree of culpability that exists in cases of 51% is too low to be included within the higher offence, then he has a more principled reason for rejecting the idea that such cases should be included within the higher offence. A further possible argument against the suggestion to include cases of 51% within the higher offence runs as follows: Although it may seem rational that the point of 50% divide people who believe that the result will ensue from people who believe that the result will not ensue, the reality might be that people do not think in such terms; whether they take a risk of 40% or 60% they view themselves as taking risks and they do not feel obliged to answer to themselves in a "yes or no" manner whether the result will happen (or whether they believe it will happen). If this is indeed the reality, then the difference between foresight of 51% and foresight of 49% that the result will ensue is not a qualitative difference, in terms of degrees of culpability.

24 See supra section 5.3.

25 This option was already mentioned supra in chapter 5, note 22. And cf. Kugler (1993) 203-204; Robinson (1997) 200, 235, 237.

Chapter 7

Reconsidering the Idea of Grading Offences Based on the Distinction between Intention and Recklessness

7.1 Reconsidering Grading Offences Based on the Distinction between Intention and Recklessness

7.1.1 Many Factors Affect the Actual Punishment Imposed on the Offender

In chapter 2 I challenged the idea of grading offences following the distinction between intention and recklessness by pointing out that there are cases in which a reckless actor is more blameworthy than an actor who acts with intent to cause the result. Then I suggested that we should ask whether, when all other things are equal, *including the motives of the actor,* acting with intent to cause the result is more blameworthy than acting recklessly with respect to that result. This suggestion was based on two related claims. First, that if we think that, when all other things are equal, there is no difference in moral blameworthiness between causing a result purposely and causing the same result recklessly, then we are not able to justify the idea of grading offences following the distinction between intention and recklessness by relying on the argument regarding degrees of moral blameworthiness. Second, that if we think that, when all other things are equal (including the motives), there is a difference in culpability between causing a result purposely and causing it recklessly, then we have a reasonable justification for grading offences based on the distinction between intention and recklessness. Thus far our discussion has assumed the validity of the mentioned claims. What I would like to do in this chapter is to subject the second claim to critical scrutiny.

The fact that a legislator believes that, when all other things (including the purposes and motives of the actor) are equal, causing a result purposely is more blameworthy than causing it recklessly, does not necessarily dictate that he should think it desirable to grade offences following this distinction. Taking the view that *when all other things are equal, including the motives,* there is a difference in culpability between intention and recklessness, may be of great significance for philosophical purposes, but *in reality,* people differ in the motives for their actions, so that even one who accepts such a view should nonetheless concede the possibility that in many cases the reckless actor is more blameworthy (because his motives are significantly worse) than the actor who acts with intent to cause the result. Thus, the question arises whether there is a point to a grading scheme which is based on comparing in the abstract pairs of cases in which the motives remain constant. The following hypothetical is illustrative. Suppose a legislator has to enact offences relating to causing grievous bodily harm, and before him lies a proposal to enact two separate offences: One of causing grievous bodily harm purposely, which carries a maximum penalty of 20 years imprisonment, and one of causing grievous bodily harm recklessly, which carries a maximum penalty of 10 years imprisonment. There seems to be a valuable argument against adopting such a proposal, even granting that when all other things are equal, including the motives, causing a result purposely is more culpable than causing it recklessly. The argument is that since in reality there may be many cases in which the reckless actor is more blameworthy than certain actors who cause the result purposely, there may be many cases in which the reckless actor deserves a higher punishment than certain purposeful actors. Hence, it seems there is a strong case against adopting the mentioned proposal. Consequently, it may be argued that it is better to enact only one offence of causing the forbidden result to cover both cases of intention and recklessness. Actually the argument against the mentioned proposal is even stronger, as the degree of blameworthiness of an actor is also determined by reference to many factors which vary from case to case and which are extraneous to his intentions, motives and purposes. Accordingly, there may be many cases of recklessly causing grievous bodily harm in which the degree of blameworthiness of the actor is higher than that present in certain cases of purposely causing grievous bodily harm. This casts a heavy doubt on the desirability of adopting the mentioned proposal. It may be argued, then, that it is better to enact only one offence of causing grievous bodily harm to cover both cases of intention and recklessness, and to leave it to the sentencer to determine the appropriate punishment for the offender before him, in consideration of all the factors that bear upon the degree of his moral blameworthiness. More to the point, the fundamental question which arises at this juncture is: If many factors bear upon the degree of blameworthiness, is there a point in isolating one of them (that of intention versus recklessness) and using it as a basis for grading offences?

It is commonly said that in using their discretion in sentencing specific offenders, judges should (and actually do) take into consideration the degree of moral blameworthiness of the offender, given the principle that the severity of the punishment should be proportional to the degree of the offender's moral culpability.[1]

It follows, therefore, that in principle every factor which bears on the degree of the offender's moral blameworthiness should be considered in the determination of sentence. One of the most important factors bearing on the degree of the offender's blameworthiness is the motive for his action;[2] hence the well accepted view that in exercising their discretion in sentencing, judges should (and actually do) take into account the motives of the offender.[3]

In addition to the general rule that motives are of importance at the sentencing stage, specific categories of mitigation based on the motives of the offender bear emphasising. One set of cases in which motives are relevant is composed of those cases which contain an element of duress, necessity or self-defence, but do not quite fall within the narrow confines of these defences against criminal responsibility. Since some requirements of these defences remain unfulfilled, the defendant cannot be completely exempted from liability, but the fact that he acted under circumstances tied in with elements of those defences can operate to reduce the punishment.[4] Another specific category of mitigation based on motive is provocation.[5]

Thus far, I have focused on motives as a factor of relevance to the degree of moral blameworthiness. But there are other factors as well that affect the degree of moral blameworthiness, which are (and should be) taken into account in determining sentence.

First, there is the amount of harm or damage foreseen and caused by the offender.[6] Within an offence of causing damage to the property of another, the culpability of the offender will vary in accordance with the magnitude of the damage suffered. The higher the damage caused and foreseen by the actor, the higher his culpability, assuming all other things are equal.[7] Thus, causing a minimal amount of damage purposely may sometimes be less culpable then causing a significant amount of damage recklessly. The same can be said about other offences, such as causing bodily harm, causing grievous bodily harm and others.

Another factor which bears upon the degree of culpability is the existence and the degree of planning and deliberation that preceded the action. As Ashworth observes, cases of intention comprise "a whole range of mental states, from planning, through deliberation, to a hastily conceived intent, a 'spur of the moment' decision and an impulsive response to a situation". He adds that "there are degrees of culpability within the concept of intention, running from the careful plan down to the sudden impulse". He also remarks that a similar scale exists within recklessness "running from a carefully calculated risk, through to a deliberate risk, and a sudden risk, to impulsive risk taking". And he contends that it is possible "that some of the more calculated forms of recklessness might be adjudged more serious than impulsive forms of intention".[8]

Many other factors bear on the offender's degree of blameworthiness. Factors considered to mitigate the culpability of the offender which, as such, should be taken into account in sentencing, include: That the offender is fairly young;[9] that he is fairly old;[10] that he suffers from mental impairment;[11] the minor role of the offender;[12] the fact that the offence was committed by omission;[13] mistake of law;[14] lack of experience.[15] Factors considered to aggravate the culpability of the offender include: That the crime is performed against a vulnerable victim[16] or that the crime involves an abuse of trust.[17]

Thus far, I have focused on factors that bear upon the degree of culpability of the offender, as manifested in his criminal act. I did not endeavour to provide an exhaustive list of such factors but only to show the vast array of factors that need to be taken into account when proceeding to evaluate moral culpability.

This, however, is only part of the story of sentencing. Even if we confine ourselves to factors that have to do with "just deserts" and proportionality concerns, we may take into account additional factors that are not directly connected to the blameworthiness manifested in the criminal action. Take the following two examples. First, the criminal record of the offender. The idea that the offender's prior history should be taken into account in sentencing is widely accepted. It is viewed by many as being based on considerations of incapacitation, individual deterrence and rehabilitation. Some, however, take the view that consideration of an offender's criminal record may be connected to the principle of "just deserts" by basing this consideration on the idea that a sentence reduction may be appropriate for a first offender as his commission of the offence may be viewed as a lapse. This viewpoint proceeds on the assumption that ordinary people can sometimes lose their self-discipline for a moment, and the system should show understanding for human frailty by reducing the punishment of first offenders. But if the offender, after his first conviction, commits other offences, then he should not receive a punishment discount as his later offences are less and less susceptible to characterisation as a lapse.[18] Second, there is the practice of occasionally reducing the punishment of an offender who throughout his life has shown himself to be a good person, even though this character assessment is based on actions of his which are totally extraneous to the criminal action for which he is being sentenced.[19]

In addition to factors connected to proportionality and just deserts concerns, numerous other factors are generally taken into account in sentencing. Many of them are based on considerations of general deterrence, individual deterrence, incapacitation and rehabilitation. Other considerations taken into account in sentencing include the desire to provide defendants with an incentive to plead guilty so as to reduce case processing times, and the desire to encourage defendants to compensate victims or to testify against others. I will not exhaustively list here the considerations which are taken into account in sentencing.[20]

The question may be put as follows: Since so many factors are taken into account at the sentencing stage and, as such, affect the punishment imposed on the offender, is there any point in isolating from all the various factors which bear upon the appropriate punishment the factor of intention versus recklessness, and using it as a basis for grading offences?

7.1.2 *Since So Many Factors are Taken into Account in the Sentencing Stage – Is there a Justification for Grading Offences Based on the Distinction between Intention and Recklessness?*

Since so many factors should be taken into consideration at the sentencing stage, it is well accepted that sentencers should have discretion in determining the amount of punishment to be imposed in the concrete case before them.[21] Giving all robbers the same punishment would ignore important differences between specific cases. The same obviously holds true for other offences as well. Hence, the common practice that offences do not generally carry mandatory sentences, discretion as to the appropriate punishment to be imposed under the circumstances being left to the sentencer. In many countries, like England, for example, the general practice is to only provide for maximum penalties. Since I believe this is the preferred practice, the discussion to follow will proceed on the assumption that the legislative context only provides for maximum sentences.[22]

Theoretically, the legislator could take every offence and divide it into hundreds or even thousands of sub-categories, each dealing with a case that is slightly different from the others in the combination of relevant concrete circumstances, and determine what the punishment should be for every sub-category, and in this way not leave any discretion to the sentencer, all the while avoiding the problem of treating unlike cases alike. But the legislator cannot envisage in advance all of the potential combinations of circumstances, and even if he could, the division of every offence into hundreds or thousands of categories is far from desirable.[23]

The advantages of granting discretion to judges in sentencing thus are clear. But there are disadvantages as well. There is the problem of disparity in sentences. Judges differ in their philosophies, beliefs and characters, and this may yield the result that similar cases are treated differently by different judges.[24] This result is unjust in itself and also risks detracting from the respect of the public for the legal system.[25] Another problem is discrimination. Leaving discretion within the hands of sentencers creates the danger of conscious or subconscious discrimination, particularly insofar as concerns offenders who come from a deprived social background or who belong to specific races.[26] Such discrimination is unjust in itself and, in addition, risks reducing the public's faith in the system, especially that of communities which generally suffer from discrimination. There is also the idea that in a democratic society, important decisions should be taken by the legislator.[27]

One way to partially attenuate the problems created by broad judicial discretion in sentencing is to provide for more guidance in sentencing. This can be done, for example, by specifying by way of statute (or by way of precedent-setting decisions of high courts) the appropriate purposes of sentencing, the considerations to be taken into account in sentencing, together with an open list of aggravating and mitigating factors.[28] However, the question we are dealing with here lies in another realm. The specific question is whether the legislator should distinguish between causing a certain result purposely and causing it recklessly by creating two separate offences with different maximum penalties. This is related to a broader question, namely, which factors bearing upon the appropriate punishment should find expression in the legislative definition of the offence (by way of creating different degrees of, say, robbery, with different maximum penalties), and which factors should not appear in the legislative definition of the offence, but should be left for consideration at the sentencing stage.

It seems that many differences exist between various codes on the question whether the existence of a certain factor establishes a separate offence or whether the said factor is left for consideration at the sentencing stage. Much depends on tradition, actual cases that prompted legislative responses, political pressures, luck, and so on.[29] It seems that the criminal law of England has tended towards broadly defined offences, leaving many issues for determination at the sentencing stage.[30] This seems to be the situation in other countries as well.[31] This fact heightens the importance of the question whether there is a point in grading offences following the distinction between intention and recklessness. As we saw in this chapter, the motives of the actor are taken into account at the sentencing stage. And it seems that by reason of the great importance of motives in assessing moral culpability, many cases may arise in which a person who causes a certain result recklessly will be considered more culpable than a certain person who causes the same result purposely, simply by reason of the difference in their motives.[32] It follows, therefore, that even assuming that when all other things are equal, including the motives, the actor who causes the result purposely is more culpable than the reckless one, when the motives are not the same the situation may totally change. And in reality, cases do differ from each other insofar as the motives of the actor are concerned. The same holds true for specific categories of motives like those of "partial duress", "partial necessity", "partial self-defence" and provocation. The existence of such mitigating factors in cases of intention may reduce the moral culpability of the actor to a point beneath the culpability of an actor who acts recklessly under ordinary circumstances.

The amount of harm caused and foreseen by the actor also constitutes an important factor in assessing moral culpability. It seems that many cases may arise in which intentionally causing a small amount of harm will be considered less culpable than recklessly causing a greater amount of harm, even where the same offence is involved (like that of causing damage to property). The fact that when the respective harms are identical the actor who acts with intent to cause the harm is more culpable, should not prevent us from recognising that the reckless actor may be considered more culpable in cases where the harms differ from one another.

The same can be said about planning and deliberating. It seems that in certain cases impulsively responding to a situation and causing the result intentionally entails a lower degree of culpability than where the actor takes a carefully calculated risk (when all other things are equal).[33]

The same can be said about many other factors that are relevant to assessing the degree of moral culpability and, in turn, to the deserved punishment (see supra section 7.1.1). It seems, then, that even assuming that when all other things are equal, a difference in the degree of blameworthiness exists between causing a result purposely and causing it recklessly – in many cases it will be sufficient for *one* factor not to remain constant for the reckless actor to be considered more culpable and, hence, deserving of a harsher punishment. Of course, if more than one factor does not remain constant, the chances that the reckless actor will deserve a harsher punishment than the one who caused the result purposely will increase. Since in reality cases differ from one another in many respects, it seems questionable whether there is any point in grading offences on the basis of the distinction between intention and recklessness, if all that can be said in support of this distinction is that in the "abstract" case in which all other things are equal the actor who causes the result purposely is more culpable than the reckless actor.

The discussion in this section thus far focused only on factors that bear upon the deserved punishment. The reality, however, is that many other considerations not related to the deserved punishment, are taken into account in sentencing, as was explained above.[34] This fact enlarges the range of potential cases in which the appropriate punishment in certain cases of recklessness will be harsher than in certain cases of intention, with the result that the argument against grading offences based on the distinction between intention and recklessness is even stronger.

7.1.3   *The Appeal of the Distinction between Intention and Recklessness as a Criterion for Grading Offences*

In the previous section I referred to the question of which factors should be left to the sentencing stage and which factors should find expression in the definition of offences by creating sub-degrees of offences. I will not try here to formulate a comprehensive theory on this issue. Rather, I will attempt to suggest a number of considerations that perhaps can explain why certain factors generally tend not to be included in legislative definitions of offences but to be left for consideration at the sentencing stage – and to examine what the implications of these considerations are insofar as the distinction between intention and recklessness is concerned. My objective is not to provide a detailed justification for the reliance on these considerations as a basis for leaving certain issues to the sentencing stage. Rather my purpose is twofold: First, to suggest that these considerations actually motivate certain legislators' decisions; second, to suggest that these considerations are (at least intuitively) *prima facie* appealing.

1.   The factor concerned with the amount of harm or damage caused (and foreseen) by the actor in the concrete case is not a question that can be answered in a yes or no fashion. For there is a continuum here. The higher the damage, the higher the degree of moral culpability. In an offence of causing damage to property, for instance, the continuum starts with a minimal amount of damage and progressively increases. This constitutes an impediment to differentiating offences based on the amount of damage caused. Where should one put the line? At $1000 or at $20,000? Any point would be arbitrary. Hence, the natural tendency to leave such factors, and others which similarly involve a continuum, to the sentencing stage. In contrast, the distinction between intention and recklessness does not involve such a continuum, and can be positively answered in a yes or no fashion.

2.   If we wanted to grade offences based on the motives of the actor, we would be confronted with a problem. The number of possible reasons that can motivate a person to commit a certain offence is extremely large. Since it is not practical to list, for every offence, the whole range of potential motives for committing the offence and to enact sub-categories in accordance therewith, there is a tendency to leave the issue of the motives and purposes of the defendant for consideration at the sentencing stage.[35] Grading an offence based on whether the actor intended to cause the result (which is part of the actus reus), on the other hand, does not entail assembling an endless list.

3.   If listing all the potential motives for a certain offence is not practical, perhaps we could grade offences based on whether the motives were "very wicked" or on some other similar basis. We could, for example, provide for an aggravated form of causing bodily harm, established by the presence of "very wicked motives". But the problem with this approach is that it accords moral discretion to the decision-maker. To decide whether to convict of the aggravated offence in such a case, a value judgment is needed. As such a judgment is influenced by personal beliefs, it tends to be subjective. There is a

tendency to try to free, as much as possible, the decision on the offence of conviction from the need to make value judgments, and to leave issues that involve such judgments for consideration at the sentencing stage. This is why it is not common to find offences which are graded based on such formulae as "very wicked motives". In contrast, whether the actor intended to cause the result is generally not dependent on value judgments.

4.   It may be claimed that only factors which bear upon the blameworthiness of the actor as manifested in the act under discussion should be used in grading offences. Therefore, all factors that pertain to such interests as general and individual deterrence, incapacitation, rehabilitation, etc., and factors such as the defendant's assistance to the police, should be left for consideration at the sentencing stage. In contrast, the distinction between intention and recklessness is related to degrees of blameworthiness and as such can serve as a basis for grading offences.

5.   There seems to be a tendency not to include within the definition of offences, concepts that suffer from considerable vagueness, because of the danger that their application in concrete cases will involve a significant amount of subjective appreciation. This can explain why it is not popular to grade offences based on whether the act was preceded by provocation. The factor of loss of self-control varies in degree, and any attempt to define a turning point for grading purposes will suffer from considerable vagueness.[36] This can also explain why we do not tend to grade offence like causing damage to property based on whether the amount of damage caused was "great". In contrast, the line between causing a result purposely and causing it recklessly is, despite some borderline cases, relatively clear.

6.   There seems to be a tendency to try to keep the trial focused on the criminal action and its circumstances and to leave factors that directly touch upon the offender's personality, abilities and character to the sentencing stage.[37] This can explain why considerations such as the offender's old or young age, his mental impairment, his lack of experience, and his past contributions to society, are generally left for consideration at the sentencing stage. In contrast, intention is something that accompanies the act under consideration, and therefore can form a basis for grading offences.

7.   Some questions are not dealt with during the trial because their consideration may unduly bear upon the decision as to whether the defendant committed the crime of which he is accused, thereby creating a bias against him. This is why, for instance, the defendant's criminal record is not discussed during the trial. No such problem arises with respect to the issue of intention.

8.   Factors that are only relevant in rare cases tend, by the nature of things, to be left for consideration at the sentencing stage. This, for example, seems to be the case with such factors as "partial self-defence" and "partial duress".[38] This consideration, however, does not apply to the element of intention.

9.   It may be suggested that with regard to certain questions it is better for the judge, rather than the jury, to make the decision, as he is more professional and more experienced. For example, even those who would not have a philosophical or principled objection to offences being graded based on

considerations of general deterrence, dangerousness of the actor, etc., might prefer that decisions on these issues be left to the sentencing stage because they will be better handled by judges than juries. This consideration is not relevant to the issue of intention.

10. There seems to be a tendency to leave the treatment of facts the existence of which is significantly difficult to ascertain for the sentencing stage. This may explain why the element of "provocation" is usually not used in grading offences, for it is difficult to ascertain whether the defendant lost his self-control. It may also explain why offences of recklessness are not divided into several sub-categories based on the degree of probability of the risk foreseen by the defendant. As for the issue of intention, though it must be conceded that the decision whether the result was desired by the defendant is not always an easy one, nonetheless the presumption of fact that a person intends the natural consequences of his actions does provide a helpful tool to prove intention.

The above survey, which did not endeavour to provide an exhaustive list of the relevant considerations, shows, I think, why the idea of grading offences following the distinction between intention and recklessness holds much appeal. Put simply, the distinction does not suffer from many of the drawbacks which characterise the other candidates for determining elements in grading offences. Indeed, the question whether the actor intends the result to occur can be answered in a yes or no fashion, the concept of intention is relatively not vague, and establishing the existence of intention does not generally involve a value judgment. The distinction between intention and recklessness can be used in grading offences without having to devise numerous sub-categories for every offence; and it can be used in trials without frustrating the goal of keeping the decision regarding the offence of conviction as objective as possible by keeping it (as much as possible) free of value judgments, of decisions as to facts the existence of which is very difficult to ascertain and of decisions that can only be articulated in terms of "more or less" rather than "yes or no".[39]

7.1.4   *How Large Is the Difference in Culpability between Intention and Recklessness?*

The discussion above explained why the idea of grading offences based on the distinction between intention and recklessness is attractive and popular, but it did not fully address the objections raised in sections 7.1.1 and 7.1.2 against grading offences in such a manner. Now, if we think that when all other things, including the motives, are equal, no difference in culpability obtains between acting with intent to cause a result and acting recklessly, then there will be no point in grading offences based on this distinction. But the discussion in this chapter assumes that there *is* a difference in moral culpability between causing a result purposely and causing it recklessly when all other things, including the motives, are equal. However, even if we take this assumption to be correct, the question remains: Since so many factors which bear upon the appropriate punishment are left for consideration at the sentencing stage, is there any point in dealing with the distinction between intention and recklessness at the trial stage? One may suggest that only factors relevant to the degree of moral culpability should be dealt with at the trial stage, and that considerations not bearing upon moral culpability should only be dealt with at the sentencing stage. But as we saw earlier in this chapter, numerous factors that are relevant to the degree of culpability of the offender are considered at the sentencing stage. The question, therefore, still stands. For, as was explained in section 7.1.2, even a difference in one factor (like the motive of the actor or the amount of damage caused) may yield the conclusion that a reckless person is more culpable than one who causes the result purposely. A combination of such variations may even substantiate such a conclusion more easily. So what is the point in grading offences based on the mentioned distinction, if courts may frequently face cases in which the culpability of the reckless actor exceeds the culpability of certain people who purposely cause the result?

It seems that in order to properly reflect upon whether there is a point in using the above mentioned grading scheme we should raise the following question: How large is the difference in moral culpability between acting with intent to cause the result and causing it recklessly? For even if we accept that when all other things are equal, including the motives, causing the result purposely is more culpable than causing it recklessly, the question remains: By how much is it more culpable? We cannot answer such a question with numbers, but we can try to assess whether this difference is minimal, significant or vast; and we can also try to assess the *relative* weight of this difference in comparison to other factors that affect the degree of culpability (like motives, etc.). If the difference in culpability between intention and recklessness is sufficiently large, there may be a point in grading offences based on the distinction between the two. For if, relative to other factors which bear upon the degree of culpability, the presence or absence of intention influences to a large extent the degree of the actor's culpability, then the number of cases in which the final conclusion is that one who acts with intention is more culpable than one who acts with recklessness will be relatively high. And if this is the case, then it makes sense to grade offences based on the distinction between intention and recklessness. But if, relative to other factors that affect the degree of moral culpability, this distinction does not carry much weight, then the number of cases in which the final conclusion is that the actor who acts with intention is more culpable than the one who acts with recklessness will be relatively low. And if this is the case then, first, there is little point in using such a grading scheme, for there is not much point in addressing during the trial the question whether the accused acted with intent to cause the result, as at the end of the day it will not carry much weight in the determination of sentence; and second, isolating the factor of intention versus recklessness from the whole range of factors that affect the degree of culpability to be used in grading offences involves an inconsistency. Another problem may arise as well, namely, the risk that the fact that the legislator opted to grade the offence under discussion based on the mentioned distinction will create in judges the wrong impression that the moral importance of the question of intention is great, which in turn may influence them in the wrong direction, i.e. it may move them, in deliberating about the appropriate sentence, to accord more weight than they should to the question of intention.

The question of the weight (or relative importance) of the difference in the degree of culpability between cases of intention and cases of recklessness (when all other things, including the motives, are equal) is not one that can be answered scientifically or logically. It is, rather, a matter of moral intuition. My feeling is that this difference (assuming that there is such a difference) does not carry much weight; and that, relative to other factors that affect moral culpability (like motives), this difference is not sufficiently large to justify its use for the purpose of grading offences.[40]

Therefore I would suggest that even a legislator who thinks that when all other things are equal (including the motives) one who acts with intent to cause the result is more blameworthy than one who acts with recklessness, should not grade offences based on the distinction between intention and recklessness[41] (if the only justification for the said grading is that when all other things are equal, intention is more culpable than recklessness).[42]

But it may be the case that a legislator decides to grade offences based on this distinction, because he thinks there is a large difference in culpability between intention and recklessness, when all other things are equal (or because he thinks that even a small difference in culpability justifies such grading). If he takes this course of action,[43] then he will have to decide what to do concerning cases of oblique intention. In this case I would recommend that he consult the discussion in chapters 3-6 of this book, as it may be of assistance in his deliberation concerning cases of oblique intention.[44] Needless to say, as was explained in previous chapters, if the legislator thinks that when all other things are equal there is *no* difference in the degree of culpability between causing the result purposely and causing it recklessly, then there is no justification for grading offences based on the distinction between intention and recklessness, if this grading scheme is meant to reflect degrees of moral culpability.[45]

7.2   Mandatory Sentences and Homicide

The suggestion in section 7.1.4 not to grade offences based on the distinction between intention and recklessness appears problematic when applied to offences that carry mandatory or mandatory minimum sentences. For the consequence would be that the mandatory (or mandatory minimum) penalty would apply even to cases of recklessness. However, I am of the view that there should be no mandatory or mandatory minimum sentences in the criminal law system. Andrew Ashworth summarises the four main arguments raised against the enactment of such sentences,[46] the most important of which is, to my mind, that such sentences carry considerable potential for injustice.[47] They force the judge to impose the mandatory or minimum mandatory sentence even where the offender before him does not deserve such a punishment. In my view, this, by itself, amounts to a sufficient reason to reject mandatory and mandatory minimum sentences. So if we have a system that only provides for maximum sentences, then the suggestion not to grade offences based on the mentioned distinction will be relevant to all offences.

But what about murder? In many countries this offence carries a mandatory sentence of life imprisonment. What should be done concerning this offence? My answer is that murder too should *not* carry a mandatory sentence, but only a maximum sentence (at most life imprisonment).[48] The risk that an offender will receive a higher punishment than he deserves also exists in murder cases, so that murder should not carry a mandatory sentence.[49] Hence, the suggestion to include within the same offence both cases of intention and cases of recklessness may also be applied to homicide.[50]

7.3   The Possibility of a Variable Treatment

As I said in section 7.1.4, if the legislator thinks that when all other things are equal (including the motives) there is a difference in the degree of culpability between causing the result purposely and causing it recklessly, and if he thinks that this difference is sufficiently large, he may reasonably grade offences based on the distinction between intention and recklessness. The question arises whether, to be consistent, such a legislator is logically bound to distinguish between intention and recklessness in the context of *all* crimes dealing with (actual or potential) results.

In my view, it may be legitimate not to treat all result crimes in the same manner in this respect. I will give here several possible reasons that may legitimately lead a legislator not to adopt for all result crimes a uniform approach on the question of grading based on the distinction between intention and recklessness.

First, a legislator may think that the reason why, when all other things are equal, causing a result purposely is more culpable than causing it recklessly, is that when the actor acts in order to cause the result he uses the victim as a means to satisfy the needs of others and in this manner harms his dignity. If this is the reason behind the aforementioned difference in culpability, then it is very reasonable to assume that it applies in the context of offences against the person and not, for example, in the context of offences against animals or against the state. It would be perfectly consistent, therefore, for such a legislator not to grade offences dealing with causing pain to animals (or giving away information to the enemy with foresight that such a course of action may possibly lead to harm being caused to the security of the state) following the distinction between intention and recklessness.[51]

Second, a legislator may think that notions such as harm to the dignity of the person, or to the moral integrity of the actor, or to the value itself, only take on meaning in the context of the most serious of moral wrongs (and not in the context of the less serious ones), so that only with regard to such wrongs does the distinction in culpability between causing the result purposely and doing so recklessly hold true. If he adopts this viewpoint, he may legitimately decide to confine the practice of grading offences following the distinction between intention and recklessness to the most serious of moral wrongs within the criminal law (such as causing death or causing grievous bodily harm).[52]

Third, even a legislator who thinks that the difference in the degree of moral blameworthiness between intention and recklessness exists in the context of all (or most) moral offences, may legitimately want to refrain, for practical reasons, from grading *every* result crime based on the mentioned distinction. If the legislator thinks it desirable that the criminal code be as concise, clear and simple as possible, and free of numerous sub-categories of offences, and if he also thinks that it is desirable to refrain as much as possible from overburdening and confusing juries, then he may want to avoid dividing offences into sub-categories, when this can be done without incurring a substantial loss. In our context, it may lead him to limit the practice of grading offences following the mentioned distinction to offences that carry the harshest penalties. In the context of an offence in which causing the forbidden result purposely should be exposed to a maximum punishment of, say, 20 years imprisonment, there is a point in creating a different category for reckless offenders, that carries, say, a maximum penalty of 10 years imprisonment. But in the context of an offence with a minor maximum penalty even for cases of intention, the need to create a separate offence for recklessness, with a lower penalty, is much less urgent.[53] Hence, there is more to be said, in this context, for the inclusion of recklessness and intention within the same crime, subject to the same maximum penalty.[54]

Another issue is whether a reasonable legislator may legitimately provide for variable treatment of cases of oblique intention. Suppose that a legislator decides to grade some result crimes following the distinction between intention and recklessness. The next step is to decide what should be done concerning cases of oblique intention. To be logically consistent, must this legislator uniformly treat cases of oblique intention in the context of all the result crimes under discussion? Or may he, perhaps, legitimately decide that cases of oblique intention will not be uniformly treated in all contexts? I think that a reasonable legislator may (but not must) provide for variable treatment of cases of oblique intention. Throughout the book I have raised various possible reasons for grading offences following the distinction between direct intention and recklessness, and maintained that the treatment of cases of oblique intention should depend on the legislator's preferred justification for distinguishing between direct intention and recklessness. Now a legislator may think there is more than one reason to distinguish between intention and recklessness, and he may think further that the reasons do not indiscriminately apply in all contexts. This may yield the result that the treatment given to cases of oblique intention will vary according to the context, depending on the reason or reasons that lie at the basis of the grading *in the specific context.*

For illustrative purposes, suppose that a legislator thinks that a person who acts with intent to cause a certain bad result manifests in his action a more wicked character than a person who acts with recklessness with regard to the same result (when all other things are equal) because he shows that he is ready to act even when his act is not accompanied by a hope that the result will not ensue, so that he deserves a higher punishment. This may lead the legislator to grade certain offences following the distinction between intention and recklessness.[55] Now, in the context of these offences it is logical to include cases of oblique intention within the higher offence together with cases of direct intention, as in cases of oblique intention there can be no hope that the result will not ensue, so that in such cases the offender also manifests his readiness to proceed even when his act is not accompanied by a hope that the result will not ensue.[56]

The justification mentioned here for distinguishing between (direct and oblique) intention and recklessness, if accepted, seems to apply in principle to most (or all) result crimes. Of course, practical considerations like those mentioned above in this section may lead the legislator to refrain from grading *every* result crime following the distinction between intention and recklessness, hence we may suppose that in crimes with low sentences, for example, no distinction between intention and recklessness will be provided for; but such a legislator may, based on the above mentioned justification, still follow this distinction in many offences and in various contexts (even those not connected to the protection of human beings).

The same legislator may further think, for example, that in the limited area of serious offences against the person there is an additional justification for distinguishing between direct intention and recklessness, namely, that the person who acts with the intention of harming another person uses him as a means, and therefore is more culpable than one who acts with recklessness. This justification strengthens the case for distinguishing between direct intention and recklessness in the context of such offences. However, this justification may, just the same, support the conclusion that there is good reason to also distinguish in such offences between direct intention and oblique intention, as the element of using the other person as a means is absent in cases of oblique intention. This may legitimately lead the legislator to create three sub-categories in the context of serious offences against the person (one for direct intention, the second for oblique intention, and the third for recklessness) and, at the same time, to divide some other result crimes into only two sub-categories (one for direct and oblique intention, and one for recklessness).

The above discussion illustrates how the discussion in the previous chapters may be used to provide a justification for a variable treatment of cases of oblique intention.[57] In addition, we should always be sensitive to practical considerations, which in this context may legitimately lead the legislator to limit the application of certain distinctions to certain contexts, such as the context of offences with harsh maximum penalties, even if from a theoretical and moral point of view the same distinctions could also apply to other contexts, such as those involving offences with low penalties.

The discussion in this section assumed a legislator who decides to grade offences following the distinction between intention and recklessness, and who does so based on the view that when all other things are equal (including the motives) there is a sufficiently large difference in the degree of blameworthiness between causing a forbidden result purposely and doing so recklessly, to justify enacting such a grading scheme. But, as I explained in section 7.1.4, my own inclination is that even if we assume that when all other things are equal there is a difference in the degree of culpability between intention and recklessness, the difference is not large enough to justify the mentioned grading scheme. Therefore, if no other justification for the grading scheme can be advanced, I would tend to recommend that the legislator not grade any offence following the mentioned distinction. However, in chapter 9 I will examine another possible justification for grading offences following the distinction between intention and recklessness. This justification will still relate to degrees of culpability but will be different in nature from the justifications discussed thus far. Before turning to this possible justification, I will examine (in chapter 8) the possibility of grading offences by using a moral formula.

Notes

1   See Smith and Hogan (1999) 4-6; Ashworth (1989) 344, 354-355; Ashworth (2000) 72-74, 90-131. On the importance of the degree of culpability in the Swedish law of sentencing, see von Hirsch (1998c) 243-245.
2   Cf. Hall (1960) 93; Gordon (1978) 214-217, 227.
3   Hall (1960) 101. In Sweden the legislator provided that the motives of the actor should be taken into account in sentencing. See von Hirsch and Jareborg (1998) 248-250. For good motives as a factor which reduces the punishment see Smith and Hogan (1999) 79; Williams (1983a) 75; LaFave and Scott (1986) 231; Gordon (1978) 215-216, 227. For the idea that in the context of fraud relating to social security, a person motivated by desperate poverty and a need to obtain money for the necessities of life exhibits low culpability and should benefit from mitigation in sentence see Ashworth (2000) 139. In Sweden, the legislator provided that when strong human compassion leads to the commission of the crime, it shall operate as a mitigating factor. See von Hirsch and Jareborg (1998) 250. A good motive can reduce the punishment even to the point of an absolute discharge. See Wasik (1983) 455; Wasik (1985a) 219, 227. For a proposal in Israel that the legislator provide that the sentencer may take into account the actor's motive in committing the offence when by itself it is commendable, see Ohana (1998) 639. For bad motives as increasing the punishment see LaFave and Scott (1986) 231. Racial motives constitute an aggravating factor in sentencing. See Ashworth (1995b) 130; Ashworth (2000) 135. In the Netherlands, motives like jealousy and hate operate to increase the punishment. See Tak (1997) 199.
4   For such cases see Ashworth (2000) 124-127, 140; Wasik (1983) 455-456. See also Husak (1998). Husak distinguishes between "partial excuses" which reduce the blameworthiness of agents, and "partial justifications" which reduce the wrongfulness of acts. As an example of the first category he advances a case that contains elements of duress (ibid. 183-184), and as an example of the second category he advances a case that contains elements of self-defence (ibid. 184-185).
     Coercion and threats constitute a mitigating factor under Finnish statutory law. See Tornudd (1997) 192. See also Sentencing Reform: A Canadian Approach (1987) 320 (acting under duress), and Ohana (1998) 638 (for a proposal in Israel to provide by statute that a mitigating factor obtain where the offender deviates from the reasonableness standard in cases of duress, necessity and self-defence). The Model Penal Code provides that when deciding whether to withhold a sentence of imprisonment the court should accord weight to the fact that "there were substantial grounds tending to excuse or justify the defendant's criminal conduct, though failing to establish a defense". See Model Penal Code (1985), section 7.01(2)(d). This section covers, inter alia, the cases discussed here.

5   The issue of provocation is frequently discussed in the context of homicide, where it operates as a distinguishing factor between murder and manslaughter. However, provocation is important in the context of other offences as well, for it can be taken into account at the sentencing stage as a factor which reduces the punishment. See Ashworth (2000) 125; Sentencing Reform: A Canadian Approach (1987) 320; Model Penal Code (1985), section 7.01(2)(c); Ohana (1998) 638 (for a proposal made in Israel). In Sweden, the legislator provided that the fact that the crime was elicited by another's grossly offensive behaviour diminishes the "penal value" (of the criminal action). See von Hirsch and Jareborg (1998) 250.

6   I am speaking here of the rather simple case in which the same amount of damage foreseen by the actor was actually caused. I will not address here those cases in which the amount of harm foreseen differs from the amount of harm actually caused.

7   For the idea that the degree of culpability varies in accordance with the magnitude of the harm to which the mental element is related, see Ashworth (2000) 97. For the principle that a small amount of damage constitutes a mitigating factor see ibid. at 139, Husak (1998) 171, and Model Penal Code (1985), sections 7.01(2)(a) and 7.01(2)(b). The Swedish legislator provided that the "penal value" (of the criminal action) is to be determined with special regard to "the harm, offence, or risk which the conduct involved, what the accused realized or should have realized about it ...". See von Hirsch and Jareborg (1998) 249-250. The reference to harm is meant, inter alia, to instruct the judge to differentiate in the determination of sentence between offenders convicted of the same offence by the degree of the (actual or potential) harm. See von Hirsch (1998c) 244.

8   Ashworth (2000) 124. See also ibid. at 136: "A person who plans or organises a crime is generally more culpable, because the offence is premeditated and the offender is therefore more fully confirmed in his anti-social motivation than someone who acts on impulse". For the role of premeditation in increasing the blameworthiness of the actor see also Kremnitzer (1998) 641. In Finland, the legislator provided that the sentencer should take into consideration the degree to which the criminal activity was planned. See Tornudd (1997) 192.

9   Ashworth (2000) 139-140. Husak views youth as an example of a "partial excuse". He suggests two explanations for the importance of youth as a mitigating factor. The first is based on the idea that youth is one of the factors that can lead choice to deviate from the paradigm of full voluntariness, whereas the second proceeds on the basis that "the normal inference to traits of character that would be drawn in the case of mature defendants becomes problematic" in the case of a very young offender (Husak (1998) 182-183). See also Sentencing Reform: A Canadian Approach (1987) 320; Ohana (1998) 628.

10   Ashworth asserts that when the offender is fairly old this may be treated as a mitigating factor. He explains that it might be assumed that "elderly people sometimes become less rational in their behaviour" (Ashworth (2000) 139-140). See also Sentencing Reform: A Canadian Approach (1987) 320.

11   Ashworth relates to cases in which the defendant falls just short of the legal requirements of the insanity defence (Ashworth (2000) 140). For the idea that a low I.Q. constitutes a "partial excuse" see Husak (1998) 171. In Sweden one of the circumstances which diminish the "penal value" (of the criminal action) is that the accused, because of a mental abnormality, suffers from a reduced capacity to control his behaviour. See von Hirsch and Jareborg (1998) 250. See also Sentencing Reform: A Canadian Approach (1987) 320.

12   Ashworth (2000) 139; Husak (1998) 174; Sentencing Reform: A Canadian Approach (1987) 320; Ohana (1998) 628 (a legislation proposal in Israel).
13   Ashworth (2000) 139 (in relation to social security frauds).
14   Ashworth (2000) 140; Wasik (1983) 455.
15   In Sweden the "penal value" (of the criminal action) is diminished when the defendant's conduct was connected with a manifest lack of development, experience, or capacity for judgement on his part. See von Hirsch and Jareborg (1998) 250. Some would suggest adding to the list of mitigating factors based on diminished culpability the disadvantaged background of the offender. See Hudson (1998). See also the discussion in Ashworth (2000) 125-127 and von Hirsch (1998a) 177, whether a disadvantaged background should be recognised as a mitigating factor.
16   See Ashworth (2000) 134 who mentions that it is widely accepted for the commission of an offence against an elderly or young victim to be an aggravating factor. He explains (ibid. 135) that "there is a widely shared view that it is worse to take advantage of a relatively helpless person, and so the offender is more culpable if aware that the victim is specially vulnerable (eg old, very young, disabled etc.)". See also von Hirsch and Jareborg (1998) 250 on the Swedish law; Sentencing Reform: A Canadian Approach (1987) 320.
17   Abuse of trust is considered an aggravating factor in English sentencing practice. See Ashworth (2000) 134-137. Ashworth offers as a justification for this practice the idea that an additional harm occurs where there is a breach of trust, but I think it can also be understood as being based on the idea that the abuse of trust increases the culpability of the offender. See also von Hirsch and Jareborg (1998) 250 on the Swedish law.
18   See von Hirsch (1998b) 191-197; Ashworth (2000) 165-167.
19   See Ashworth (2000) 150-151. Ashworth views this practice as implying "that passing sentence is a form of social accounting, and that courts should draw up a kind of balance sheet when sentencing". He thinks the practice is not easily justified, and appears to think that it cannot be based on the ideas of "just deserts" or retribution. However, the idea that, in certain contexts, the criminal law is interested in the character of the accused as manifested in his criminal action (such as in excuses and in criminal negligence) and the idea that the quantum of the punishment should be proportional to the gravity of the defect in the character of the accused (as manifested in the criminal action) are accepted by many scholars. These ideas are related to concepts of blameworthiness and just deserts, and the mentioned practice can be viewed as somewhat of an extension of these ideas. If we say that a person deserves a harsh punishment because he has shown in his criminal act that he is a very bad person, it might be said that if his whole life story reveals that he is a good person, then we should not treat him as a very bad person. Note that we are only speaking here of considering the general good character of the offender as a mitigating factor, and not on taking his "general bad character" as an aggravating factor.
     In Israel, it was proposed to include within a list of mitigating factors to be considered by the courts in the determination of sentence, the good behaviour of the accused towards others and his commendable way of life prior to the commission of the offence. See Ohana (1998) 638.
20   For a discussion of the various factors taken into account in sentencing and their possible justifications see Ashworth (2000). For lists and discussions of factors see also: von Hirsch and Jareborg (1998) (on Swedish law); Tornudd (1997) (on Finland); Tak (1997) (on the Netherlands); Ohana (1998) (on proposals in Israel); Sentencing Reform: A Canadian Approach (1987) (especially at 320); Wasik (1983); Model Penal Code (1985), section 7.01.

21 See Weigend (1991) 630 who says that a rigid statutory sentencing system yields manifest injustice "for it lacks the ability to capture the universe of criteria potentially relevant to determination of just punishment, regardless even of the offender's rehabilitative needs". Ashworth (2000) 34 refers to the primary argument in favour of discretion in sentencing, namely, that "there are so many, often conflicting points to be taken into account" and that "different combinations of facts present themselves, and rules may prove too rigid and too crude to yield sensible decisions. Without discretion, unfairness results from treating alike cases which are unalike". Even in a discussion that is confined to mitigating factors Husak asserts that the number and variation of possible mitigating circumstances seem endless (Husak (1998) 174-175, 187).

22 I will return later to the subject of minimum sentences and I will also refer to the issue of mandatory punishment for murder. See infra section 7.2.

23 Tom Hadden asserts that empirical studies of murder and violence "provide an almost unlimited range of factors which might be used in the classification of offences" (Hadden (1968) 534), but adds that it is important to avoid undue complexity in the law (ibid. 536). Wasik contends that it is clear that there will always be matters deferred to the sentencer's discretion, one of the reasons being "the need to keep within reasonable bounds the number of contentious issues which a jury has to deal with in any particular case" (Wasik (1983) 464). On the danger that the jury will be confused or overburdened by too many issues see also Wasik (1985b) 187. Weigend (1991) 630 accepts that "legislatures are unable to divide offence descriptions into as many degrees or subcategories as there are relevant sentencing factors and combinations of factors". See also Husak (1998) 176, at note 47, who says that "as a practical matter, there is surely some upper limit to the complexity that should be allowed in a criminal code. No legislator should strive to create thousands of offences to correspond to the many varieties of mitigating circumstances that should affect sentencing". It seems that one of the considerations against extreme complexity in legislation is that it substantially detracts from the willingness of citizens to read the criminal code.

24 See Ashworth (2000) 34; Ashworth (1998) 229; Ohana (1998) 595.

25 Ashworth (1998) 236.

26 See the discussion in Ashworth (2000) 199-212.

27 Weigend (1991) 628-629; Ohana (1998) 595. See also Kremnitzer (1991) 678-679.

28 Various methods of structuring the sentencing process are discussed in Ashworth (1998). I will not discuss the various methods here; rather, I will confine myself to stating my position against mandatory and mandatory minimum sentences as well as numerical guidelines. The most preferable method, I think, combines legislative maximum penalties together with (judicial or statutory) sentencing principles, guidelines and open lists of aggravating and mitigating factors (with no statutory numerical guidelines).

29 Ashworth mentions that one legal system may have separate offences of robbery and armed robbery while another, like England and Wales, may have a single offence of robbery, leaving it to the sentencer to take account of the question whether the robber was armed. He also gives another example and concludes that "It may therefore be a matter of legislative tradition whether such factors are part of the definition of the crime or are left to sentencing". See Ashworth (2000) 133-134. See also Husak (1998) 175-176.

30 Ashworth (2000) 311. See also ibid. at p. 307; Wasik (1983) 450; Wasik (1985b) 189.

31 See Tonry (1982) 626-627; Weigend (1991) 633-634.

32 Examples were given in chapter 2.

33 See Ashworth (2000) 124.
34 See supra the text accompanying note 20.
35 This does not mean that legislators never grade offences on the basis of a specific motive, for example by creating aggravated forms of offences against the person for racially motivated attacks. See Ashworth (2000) 135.
36 The common practice to legislatively create a "partial defence" for provocation in the context of murder is generally connected to the fact that murder carries a mandatory sentence.
37 Unless they can form a complete defence, as in the case of insanity.
38 The fact that in certain countries excessive self-defence constitutes a formal defence to murder is generally connected to the fact that there is a mandatory sentence for murder.
39 It seems that the desire for decisions about convictions (not only those about whether the accused will be convicted at all, but even those as to whether he will be convicted of a certain offence or of an aggravated form thereof) to be as objective as possible lies behind many of the considerations in favour of leaving certain issues to the sentencing stage. Since the process of sentencing should take into account numerous considerations (some of which stand in conflict with each other), and since there is no choice but to consider at this stage factors that cannot be answered in a yes or no manner (like the amount of harm), we are less reluctant to increase the number of factors for consideration at this stage, including factors that involve subjective judgments and assessments. The final result will in any case depend on balances and estimations, so that the addition of more factors which cannot be "objectively" determined will not generate strong rejection. Another point is that when the issue in question is, for example, how many months the offender should spend in prison, we know from the outset that there is no exact number of months that forms the "correct" answer. Everybody knows that there are several reasonable answers to this question (10 months, 11 months, 12 months etc.). And if nobody expects to get "exactly the right answer", then there is much more willingness to ask questions which cannot be answered by "objective yes/no answers", when such questions are important to determining the appropriate punishment for the concrete offender. The situation is different, however, in dealing with the question whether the accused should be convicted, and of what offence.
40 The reader may use the two sets of examples given towards the end of chapter 2 to test his intuitions concerning the degree of the difference in culpability. And cf. Quinn (1993) 195; Quinn (1993) 151-152.
41 For sources against the grading of offences following the mentioned distinction, see supra chapter 2 at note 18.
42 The condition in the brackets is added for two reasons. First, in chapter 9, I will consider a justification for the mentioned grading that is related to degrees of blameworthiness but is not based on the assumption that when all other things are equal, intention is more culpable than recklessness. Second, one might suggest that the mentioned grading be justified by arguments which are not related to degrees of blameworthiness (but, for example, to utilitarian considerations). Such potential justifications, however, are not discussed in this book.
43 It should be noted that even a legislator who thinks there is a large difference in culpability between intention and recklessness when all other things are equal, is not logically obliged to grade offences following this distinction. Since, after all, there will still be cases in which reckless actors, despite the importance of the mentioned difference in culpability, will be more culpable than some of those who act purposely,

the legislator may decide to leave the issue of intention to the sentencing stage (in section 9.3 I will return to this point).

44 See the summaries in sections 5.4 and 6.4.

45 This conclusion is based on the discussion conducted thus far (and see supra section 4.2.1). In chapter 9 I will reconsider this conclusion.

46 Ashworth (1998) 234-235.

47 Ibid. 235.

48 I am against the death penalty.

49 A Select Committee of the House of Lords recommended that the mandatory life sentence for murder be abolished. See: House of Lords, *Report of the Select Committee on Murder and Life Imprisonment* (Session 1988-89, H.L. Paper 78), paras 118 and 201. Ashworth welcomed this recommendation (Ashworth (1990) 83). He remarks, inter alia, that "even murders vary in their gravity and may be less serious than some manslaughter" (ibid. at 77). A subsequent Select Committee issued the following recommendation: "We strongly endorse the recommendation of a previous Select Committee that the mandatory life sentence should be abolished. This would enable the judicial process to take proper account of the circumstances of a case and the motives of the accused ..." (House of Lords, *Report of the Select Committee on Medical Ethics,* Session 1993-94, H.L. Paper 21, vol. 1, pp. 53-54. See also pp. 29-31). The Law Reform Commission of Canada recommended in a working paper that the proposed crime of "intentional homicide", which would require an intention to kill, not carry a fixed or a minimum penalty. The Working Paper explains that "murders are by no means all of the same kind: they vary enormously one from another in various ways and in particular as to their moral culpability ... the law should surely take account in this context of the circumstances of each case and in particular of the offender's motive. This, after all, is what is done throughout the rest of criminal law. ... We believe the same approach should be taken with murder ... the punishment ... could be left to be determined by the judge, who after all is in the best position to take account of all the individual circumstances of each particular crime. In short, this kind of homicide could, like all other offences, be made to carry merely a maximum penalty" (Law Reform Commission of Canada, *Homicide* (1984) 68-69). The commission stated that removal of the minimum penalty would obviate the need for special rules on excess force in self-defence, provocation and infanticide, and added that such a result should be welcomed since instead of burdening the judge and jury with technical and complex rules of law, these matters will be taken into account flexibly in sentencing as is done in the context of other offences (ibid. 70). However, the commission also recommended the enactment of a crime of first degree intentional homicide which would carry a minimum penalty and which would include specific cases of intentional homicide (ibid. 78-83).

In New Zealand, the New Zealand Criminal Law Reform Committee in its *Report on Culpable Homicide* (1976) pp. 3-4, recommended that there be no mandatory penalty for killing.

In Australia, in the jurisdictions of New South Wales and Victoria, the courts possess discretion in sentencing for murder and may, if they find it suitable, impose a lesser sentence than life imprisonment. See Gillies (1997) 644. Gillies explains that "The legislatures, in giving the courts a discretion have recognised that murders do vary in gravity" (ibid. at 613).

50 In *Hyam v. DPP* [1975] AC 55, Lord Kilbrandon stated (at 98): "Since no homicides are now punishable with death, these many hours and days have been occupied in trying to adjust a definition of that which has no content. There does not appear to be

any good reason why the crimes of murder and manslaughter should not both be abolished and the single crime of unlawful homicide substituted; one case will differ from another in gravity, and that can be taken care of by variation of sentences downwards from life imprisonment. It is no longer true, if it was ever true, to say that murder as we now define it is necessarily the most heinous example of unlawful homicide. The present case could form an excellent example exhibiting as it does, assuming it to be capable of classification as manslaughter, a degree of cold-blooded cruelty exceeding that to be found in many an impulsive crime which could never, on our present law, be so classified". Lord Cross of Chelsea stated : "I agree with my noble and learned friend, Lord Kilbrandon, that now that murder no longer attracts the death penalty it would be logical to replace the two crimes of murder and manslaughter by a single offence of unlawful homicide ..." (ibid. at 96). For a similar proposal in New Zealand see Criminal Law Reform Committee, *Report on Culpable Homicide* (1976) pp. 3-4.

Gillies asserts that the division of homicide into murder and manslaughter is not a wholly logical one, given that homicides can vary greatly in circumstances. He adds: "It has then often been asked – is there any point in persisting with this broad and primitive dichotomy? It would be possible to have a single global offence of homicide. The argument for this is the more compelling because of the trend in Australia ... to vest in the court a general discretion in sentencing for murder (as the court has always had for manslaughter). The court can in such a case discriminate between homicides with precision at the level of sentencing, having regard to the circumstances of the killing" (Gillies (1997) 614). At p. 615 he also says that "no doubt if a criminal code was being drawn up afresh, there would be much to be said for a global offence of unlawful killing".

The present law in Australia, however, retains the distinction between murder and manslaughter. Nonetheless, the present law in several Australian jurisdictions is similar to the suggestion made in the text. As Gillies's survey of the law (ibid. at 629-642) indicates, in Victoria, South Australia and New South Wales, murder is established by either intention or recklessness (there is also constructive murder which will not be dealt with here). This means that the same offence covers both intention and recklessness, similar to the suggestion made in the text. Gillies explains (ibid. at 631) that the justification for including recklessness in the crime of murder is that a person who foresees that his action is likely to cause death and nevertheless takes the risk is sufficiently culpable to warrant being convicted of murder, alongside the person who acts with the intention of causing death. And he inquires: "Is there, for example, any substantive difference between the person who throws a brick from a tall building into a crowded city street, intending to kill or cause serious bodily harm, and the person who does this act knowing that one or both of these two events is probably going to happen, even as he or she does not act specifically with the purpose of causing either?" (ibid. 631-632). However, the law in the Australian jurisdictions mentioned above differs in some respects from the suggestion in the text, notably in that recklessness in the context of murder is not established there by foresight of the mere *possibility* that the result would ensue; rather what must be established is that the accused knew that the result was "likely" or "probable" to happen (but note that (according to Gillies) it is not required that the accused foresaw that the result was more likely than not to happen; what is needed is only that the prospect of the causation of the result constituted a more than merely possible outcome of the act, i.e. that the act created a real or substantial risk of the result occurring). See ibid. at 632-

633. And cf. the sources brought supra (chapter 2, at note 18) on the desirability of the inclusion of recklessness in murder.

Against the idea of having one offence of unlawful killing for both cases of intention and cases of recklessness one might argue that it is important to retain the distinction between murder and manslaughter for symbolic and expressive reasons. The argument would be that it is desirable that those who perform the most heinous of killings, who manifest in the killing a great amount of wickedness, be convicted of a special offence, i.e. murder, that is different from the offence of which other people who culpably cause death are convicted (i.e. manslaughter). Society should express a special and extreme denunciation of the most heinous of killings by labelling them as murders, and should stigmatise the most heinous of killers by imposing upon them the worst stigma – that of murderers. Therefore we should have a special offence reserved for the most heinous of killings.

My answer to this argument runs as follows: Assuming that the idea of grading homicide offences to express a special form of denunciation towards the most heinous of killers is accepted, we still have to determine the criterion for such a grading scheme. Surely it would be the degree of blameworthiness of the accused. The most culpable killers should be labelled as murderers. But according to the argument advanced in section 7.1.4, the distinction between people who intend to kill and people who are reckless with regard to the death, simply does *not* succeed in separating the more culpable actors from the less culpable ones, for in reality a considerable number of the actors who cause death purposely are less culpable than a considerable number of those who do so recklessly. If all that can be said is that when all other things are equal, the person who kills purposely is more culpable than the person who kills recklessly, and if this difference in culpability is not large enough to yield a significant difference between the degree of moral culpability of most of the actual actors who intend to kill on the one hand, and that of most of the actual reckless actors on the other, then what is the justification for distinguishing between those who cause death purposely and those who cause death recklessly, by stigmatising only the former, and not the latter, as murderers? If we would find another criterion that would adequately distinguish between actors who are more culpable and actors who are less culpable, then we might want to grade homicide offences based on that criterion. But if we accept the argument suggested in section 7.1.4 to the effect that the distinction between intention and recklessness does not adequately differentiate the more culpable actors from the less culpable ones, then the interest in labelling certain people as "murderers" cannot justify grading homicide offences along the lines drawn by the distinction between intention and recklessness. Furthermore, if the moral assumptions made in section 7.1.4 are accepted, then such a grading scheme would send the public the wrong message, namely, that there is a crucial and significant moral difference between killing purposely and killing recklessly. I will return to the subject of the expressive function of the law of murder in chapters 8 and 9.

51 See supra chapter 4, note 6.
52 See chapter 4, text following note 6.
53 By less urgent I mean that even if refraining from grading would create some danger that once in a while a reckless offender will get a higher punishment than he deserves, still the overall amount of possible "extra undeserved months in prison" in the context of less serious offences (with their low penalties) would not be as high as the possible "extra undeserved months in prison" in the context of the more serious offences (given their high maximum penalties).
54 I will return to the subject of variable schemes in section 9.1.3.

55   See supra section 5.1. As explained there, the legislator may decide not to include cases of "indifference" within the higher offence because of the practical problems involved in proving indifference.

56   See supra section 5.1.

57   I will return to the issue of variable treatment of cases of oblique intention in section 9.2.

Chapter 8

Grading Offences by Using a Moral Formula

8.1   The Idea of Grading Offences by Using a Moral Formula

The discussion in the previous chapters suggested that if it is true that when all other things are equal, including the motives, there is no difference in the degree of culpability present in causing the result purposely and that present in causing it recklessly then there is no justification for grading offences based on the distinction between intention and recklessness (if the grading is supposed to reflect differences in degrees of culpability). In chapter 7 I added the claim that even if we assume that when all other things are equal there is such a difference, it does not seem to be large enough to justify adopting such a grading scheme. This led me to suggest that both causing the result purposely and causing it recklessly be included within the same offence, with the same maximum penalty. But it may be claimed that sub-dividing offences based on the distinction between intention and recklessness on the one hand and not sub-dividing them at all, on the other, do not constitute the only possible alternatives. Another option is available, namely, to grade offences by using a moral formula, i.e. by saying, for example, that causing grievous bodily harm (recklessly or intentionally) carries a maximum penalty of 10 years imprisonment, and that causing the same result (recklessly or intentionally) carries a maximum penalty of 20 years imprisonment when it is done in circumstances manifesting a (very) high degree of culpability.[1] If this formulation is used, then there will be a perfect fit between the purpose for which the grading was undertaken (namely, to differentiate between various degrees of culpability) and the legal rule adopted to achieve it.

Actually something similar to this is found in the Scottish law of murder. In Scotland, liability for murder (as opposed to culpable homicide) is established where the accused either intended (i.e. wanted) to kill or acted with wicked recklessness.[2] To establish "wicked recklessness", it is not sufficient to show simple recklessness (i.e. that the actor knowingly took an unjustified risk that his act would cause death). Rather, the existence of wickedness and depravity on the part of the actor must be established.[3] Gordon explains that "to say that 'A is guilty of murder when he kills with wicked recklessness' means only 'A is guilty of murder when he kills with such recklessness that he deserves to be treated as a murderer'" and that this formula may be justified by the claim that in choosing between murder and culpable homicide the result should turn on moral judgments and considerations.[4] The Scottish Law Commission also says that both murder and culpable homicide can follow from a reckless act, and that the only distinction between them (in a case of recklessness) is the degree of wickedness that the particular act is thought to display.[5]

The Scottish law of murder is similar, though not identical, to my suggestion above for a moral formula in grading offences. The most relevant difference for our discussion is that under Scottish law, the moral evaluation of the actor's conduct (as to whether it manifests wickedness) is relevant only in cases of recklessness; if the actor causes the death purposely he is guilty of murder and there is no room for moral evaluation.[6] By contrast, under the suggestion made here, the legislator would not distinguish between intention and recklessness, which means that in appropriate cases even actors who act with direct intention may be acquitted from the more serious offence.[7] It should also be noted that in Scotland murder carries a fixed sentence of life imprisonment.[8]

A somewhat similar scheme to that suggested above can also be found in the murder provisions of the Model Penal Code. Under the Code a person is subject to a murder conviction if he causes the death purposely, knowingly, or recklessly under circumstances manifesting extreme indifference to the value of human life.[9] Manslaughter is established when the death is caused recklessly.[10] This means that when the actor acts without direct or oblique intention, but with recklessness, the seriousness of the offence will turn on whether he acts with "extreme indifference to the value of human life". The commentary explains that the murder definition reflects the judgment that there is a kind of reckless homicide that cannot be fairly distinguished in grading terms from homicides committed purposely or knowingly. Consequently, the best approach is to leave it to the trier of fact to determine whether the case at hand can be fairly assimilated to cases where the killing is perpetrated with purpose or knowledge.[11] In spite of the similarity between the Model Penal Code scheme and the suggestion made above, an important difference remains: Under the Model Penal Code scheme, the moral evaluation is only relevant in cases of recklessness; if the actor causes the result purposely or with oblique intention, the actor is guilty of murder and there is no room for moral evaluation. By contrast, under the suggestion above the legislator would not distinguish between cases of intention and cases of recklessness, so that in appropriate cases even one who acts with intention to cause the result may be acquitted from the more serious offence.

8.2   Evaluation of the Idea of Grading Offences by Using a Moral Formula

8.2.1   *The Arguments for Using a Moral Formula*

Suppose a legislator who has to prepare legislation prohibiting the act of causing grievous bodily harm has to choose between two alternatives. First, to enact two separate offences of causing grievous bodily harm, one to cover cases of recklessly or purposely causing grievous bodily harm that would carry a maximum penalty of 10 years imprisonment, and one to cover cases of recklessly or purposely causing the same result in which the circumstances manifest a very high degree of culpability, that would carry a maximum penalty of 20 years imprisonment. The second alternative is to only enact one offence of (recklessly or purposely) causing grievous bodily harm that would carry a maximum penalty of 20 years imprisonment. What should the legislator do?

At first glance, the second alternative seems the better one since the first seems to yield a considerable waste of time and energy. For adopting the first alternative entails setting two separate stages in which all the factors relevant to the degree of culpability of the actor will be considered and assessed: first, at the trial stage, where all the factors that affect the degree of culpability of the actor will need to be taken into account, and the trier of fact will have to reach a clear-cut decision as to whether the degree of culpability of the actor was very high or not; then, after conviction, at the sentencing stage, the judge, in deliberating about the appropriate punishment, will have to consider again all the factors that affect the degree of culpability in order to assess the deserved punishment and, after taking into account further factors that bear upon the appropriate punishment (factors relevant to general and individual deterrence, incapacitation and rehabilitation concerns, and factors like the offender's criminal record, his assistance to the police, etc.), he will have to decide about the actual punishment that should be inflicted on the offender before him. Thus, the following question arises: What is the point of considering the same factors twice?

It seems that the main argument in support of the first alternative may be that the jury should play an important role in the decision regarding the degree of culpability of the defendant. The argument would be that the degree of culpability of the defendant is a moral question which should be decided according to the values of the community. The value judgment of the community can best be expressed by the jury, and hence the jury should have an important part in determining the defendant's degree of culpability. Therefore, there *is* a point to adopting the first alternative, as it would mean that the jury gets to decide whether the degree of culpability of the defendant is very high or not, and accordingly to decide on what offence to convict and thereby to determine the maximum penalty liable to be imposed on the defendant by the judge.[12]

Now, even if the first alternative is adopted, the jury would not get to determine the exact sentence to be imposed on the offender. The judge will still have broad discretion in sentencing the offender. In deliberating about the appropriate punishment, he will have to assess the degree of moral culpability of the offender and, in turn, the deserved punishment. He will also have to take into account many factors that were not taken into account by the jury (such as factors related to general and individual deterrence, incapacitation and rehabilitation concerns, the criminal record of the offender, his assistance to the police, and many others). Nonetheless, it might be said that there is a point in the first alternative. For if the jury decides to convict of the lesser offence because it thinks that the degree of culpability is not very high, it sets a limit to the sentencing discretion of the judge. In our example, conviction of the lesser offence means that the maximum penalty liable to be imposed is 10 years imprisonment. In this way the jury protects the offender from an excessively harsh punishment to which he might have been subjected had there only been one offence with a maximum penalty of 20 years imprisonment. When the jury convicts of the lesser offence it guarantees that even if the judge thinks (wrongly, according to the jury) that the offender deserves a higher punishment than 10 years imprisonment, the judge would not be able to act following his (wrong) belief and impose a punishment of, say, 15 years imprisonment, because he is confined by the earlier decision of the jury concerning the degree of culpability and the maximum penalty.[13] A conviction of the lesser offence also guarantees that a judge who is overly concerned with the protection of the public will not be able to impose on an offender who was *not* highly culpable a harsher punishment than 10 years of imprisonment, for purposes of deterrence and incapacitation.[14] The first alternative, then, provides offenders with more protection against excessively harsh sentences than the second one.[15]

If, under the first alternative, the jury decides to convict of the more serious offence because it thinks the offender was very culpable, the judge's discretion is still vast and he is free to impose a very lenient punishment, since the more serious offence only sets a maximum penalty. But even in a case of conviction of the more serious offence the jury can affect the sentence to a larger extent than merely enabling the judge to impose a penalty that is higher than 10 years imprisonment. For in deliberating about the sentence that should be imposed on the offender before him, the judge has, inter alia, to assess the degree of culpability of the offender, and here the fact that the jury, as the representative of the community, thinks that the offender is *highly* culpable, will probably affect the decision of the judge as to the deserved punishment, and this in turn will influence the actual punishment imposed on the offender. The present line of argument rests on the assumption that such an influence should be welcomed; it would not exist if the second alternative (that of having only one offence with a maximum punishment of 20 years imprisonment) is adopted.

8.2.2   *The Arguments Against Using a Moral Formula*

The discussion in section 8.2.1 suggested that there is a point to grading offences by using a moral formula. But the fact that there is some point in grading offences in this way does not necessarily mean that the legislator should embrace this scheme, for its advantages may be outweighed by its disadvantages.

Several arguments may be advanced against the idea of grading offences by using a moral formula as described above.

First, there is the issue of efficiency already mentioned above. To consider twice the factors that determine the degree of blameworthiness is very time and energy consuming.

Second, there is the need not to overburden and confuse juries, which may be the case if the jury has to take into account and assess all the factors relevant to the degree of blameworthiness.[16]

Third, adopting the said alternative may also be problematic because the jury will have to make a value judgment and use its moral discretion in order to decide whether the actor was highly culpable.[17] This entails a danger of disparity, as different juries may have different moral beliefs, which may result in like cases being judged differently by different juries. If such disparity appears it will constitute an injustice, and in addition it may detract from public confidence in the criminal justice system. Against this argument it might be claimed that insofar as the need to make a value judgment is concerned, the second alternative is no less problematic. For if the second alternative is adopted (i.e. a single offence with a maximum penalty of 20 years imprisonment) the need to make a value judgment will still remain. As at the sentencing stage, the *judge* will still have to make a value judgment concerning the offender's degree of culpability, in deliberating about the penalty to be imposed on the offender. Thus, even if the second alternative is adopted, the danger of disparity in assessing the degree of culpability will still remain. However, it may be claimed that a difference between the two alternatives subsists. If the first alternative is adopted, then the value judgment will be made with a view to answering in a yes/no manner as to whether the accused should be convicted of the higher or lower offence. And because the afore-mentioned question is meant to be answered in a yes/no manner and to be decided at the trial stage, public expectations arise that the criteria for the decision be objective and not open to considerable subjective discretion in their application. This expectation seems more rational when the question to be decided is whether the accused should be convicted of a certain offence or not convicted at all, than in our context in which only the appropriate offence of conviction is in question (a decision which is only taken for purposes of setting the maximum penalty). But it seems that, in reality, expectations as to the use of objective criteria exist even when the decision to be taken only concerns the appropriate offence of conviction. By contrast, the decision taken at the sentencing stage is not of the yes/no sort but rather concerns the question "how much will the accused get?", and numerous, often conflicting, considerations are expected to be taken into account. Everybody knows and accepts that at this stage there is much room for discretion, value judgments and some unavoidable disparity. Therefore the second alternative fits in more easily with general practice and expectations. In contrast, adopting the first alternative brings into the trial stage an element which we generally seek to exclude from this stage – a direct value judgment. One may argue that the expectation that even where only the appropriate offence of conviction is in question the decision should be "objective", is not rational (especially in a regime of maximum penalties). Perhaps so. But if in a certain society such an expectation exists, then before a decision to ignore such an expectation is taken, the danger of detracting from public confidence in the criminal justice system should also be taken into account. Another argument against the claim that even adopting the second alternative does not eliminate the need for value judgments might emphasise the continuity in judicial personnel, which may result in more consistent decision-making and less disparity than when juries are involved.[18]

Fourth, there is the danger of discrimination. The fact that under the first alternative the jury has to make a value judgment, creates the danger of discrimination against certain groups.[19] If such discrimination appears it will constitute an injustice, and in addition it may detract from public confidence in the criminal justice system. Here again it might be argued that even if the second alternative is adopted moral discretion at the sentencing stage would subsist, so that the danger of discrimination would remain.

It seems that the answer to the question of discrimination is country dependent. First, the question whether there is a real danger of discrimination and the extent of its influence depends on the country under discussion. Second, when there is a real danger of discrimination, the further question which arises as to whether this danger is larger in the context of decisions made by juries than in the context of decisions made by judges is, again, country dependent. So whether the problem of discrimination constitutes an argument against adopting the first alternative is country dependent.

The four arguments introduced here against adopting the first alternative should be weighed against the argument introduced in section 8.2.1 in favour of adopting the first alternative.[20] The answer need not be the same for all countries, since the importance assigned to the requirement that significant value judgments should be made, as much as possible, by the jury (and not by the judge) is in itself culture dependent.[21]

I tend toward recommending that the legislator not grade offences based on a moral formula,[22] but the final decision is country dependent, as said above.[23] I would also add that even in a country in which the legislator would embrace the idea of grading offences by using a moral formula, it seems that it should be limited to offences that carry high maximum penalties. The need to protect offenders from excessively harsh punishments seems the most important reason to adopt the first alternative; this need is most pressing in the context of offences that carry high maximum penalties. It seems that considerations of efficiency, and perhaps other considerations raised above against the first alternative as well, suggest that if the idea of grading offences by using a moral formula is adopted at all, it should be limited to the most serious of offences, which carry the highest maximum penalties (such as offences dealing with causing grievous bodily harm or homicide).

8.2.3 *Homicide*

In section 8.2.2 I expressed an inclination to prefer the alternative of enacting one offence for both intentionally and recklessly causing the proscribed result over the alternative of grading result crimes by using a moral formula. But it is possible to assert that even if the said inclination is generally justified, the case of homicide is different and that in this context it may be justified to embrace the idea of grading offences by using a moral formula. It may be suggested that it is important to distinguish between murder and manslaughter for symbolic and expressive reasons, even if there is no significant difference between the maximum penalties of these offences (or even if both of them carry the same maximum penalty of, for example, life imprisonment). The argument would run as follows: It is important that those who perform the most heinous of killings, those who manifest in the killing a great amount of wickedness, should be convicted of a special offence (i.e. murder) which is distinct from the offence of which other people who culpably cause death are convicted (i.e. manslaughter). Society should express a special and extreme denunciation of the most heinous of killings by labelling them as murders, and it should stigmatise the most heinous of killers by imposing on them the most excessive stigma – that of murderers.[24] Labelling the action as murder and stigmatising the killer as a murderer may be perceived as an end in itself (akin to retribution) and/or as being done for educational purposes (i.e. to reinforce the extreme importance of the value of human life and thereby influence the conduct of citizens).[25]

The idea then is that the distinction between murder and manslaughter should be retained, and that it should be made in such a manner that the most heinous of killings be included within the crime of murder. Assuming that the distinction between intention and recklessness cannot do the work of distinguishing between the most heinous of killings and the other killings (as explained in chapter 7), the only reasonable way to distinguish between murder and manslaughter seems to be to use a moral formula. This means that the legislator would have to provide that intended and reckless killings which are performed in circumstances manifesting a (very) high degree of culpability should be included within the crime of murder, whereas all other intended and reckless killings should be included within the crime of manslaughter. The argument, then, is that even if in other contexts the disadvantages of using a moral formula outweigh the advantages of using it, the situation in the context of murder is different, and in this context it is better to use this formula than to collapse the distinction between murder and manslaughter.[26]

One possible response to the above argument would recognise the great significance of labelling the most heinous of killings as murders but would also say that nonetheless, the disadvantages of using a moral formula outweigh the advantages of the said act of labelling, so that it is better to have one offence of unlawful killing.[27] Another possible response would be to deny the importance of labelling the most heinous of killings as murders or to deny that the criminal law should be used for expressive goals. Still another response would be to claim that even if the formal distinction between murder and manslaughter is eradicated the public will continue to distinguish between "murderers" and other killers based on the circumstances of the killing and perhaps also based on the punishment actually inflicted.[28]

All in all, therefore, the argument in favour of distinguishing between murder and manslaughter by using a moral formula is not conclusive, and there is much to be said for having only one offence for all intentional and reckless killings,[29] though I must admit that the case for grading offences by using a moral formula is much stronger in the context of homicide than in other contexts.[30]

It should be noted that if the idea of using a moral formula in the context of homicide is adopted, the legislator may decide to provide by statute that in certain specified circumstances the accused will not be convicted of murder. If the legislator identifies in advance certain cases of causing death that should not be labelled as "murders" it would be perfectly reasonable for him to provide by legislation that those who cause death under such circumstances should not be convicted of murder. In this way, he will ensure that people who cause death under such circumstances will not be wrongly and mistakenly branded as murderers, and will to some small extent alleviate the problem of disparity and discrimination. He can do this, for example, with regard to cases of causing death by reckless driving.[31]

It should also be added that if the distinction between murder and manslaughter is made by using a moral formula, the case against a mandatory sentence for murder loses in persuasiveness. To my mind, the main argument against a mandatory life sentence for murder is that not all the people who purposely kill another person deserve to be subjected to a penalty of life imprisonment (even if they do not fall under such formal defences to murder as provocation). But if the legislator provides that all murderers should receive a sentence of life imprisonment and that only those who kill under circumstances manifesting a very high degree of culpability should be convicted of murder, then we can expect that only those who deserve a sentence of life imprisonment will be classified by the jury as murderers, so that the main argument against mandatory sentences loses its persuasive power. Of course, this does not mean that the legislator should provide for such a sentence. For it is incumbent on supporters of a mandatory sentence for murder to adduce a persuasive reason *in favour* of such a mandatory sentence. One such reason might perhaps refer to the expressive and educational function of a murder conviction. It might be said that for a murder conviction to adequately deliver the message of extreme denunciation and stigmatisation, it must be accompanied by an automatic imposition of the highest available punishment – that of life imprisonment.[32]

Of course, if the legislator decides to provide for murder to carry a mandatory sentence, then the idea of listing in the legislation certain circumstances in which causing death should *not* entail a murder conviction (such as causing death by reckless driving) will appear even more appealing than if the penalty for murder is not a mandatory one.

Notes

1   One might suggest that since the actor's motives constitute a highly important factor in evaluating his degree of culpability, we may have a further option, namely, to grade offences based on the motives of the actor. But in the context of many offences the number of the actors' potential motives seems to be infinite, so it is not practical to list all the possible motives and grade offences according to them. One may retort that we can still stay in the realm of motives by using a "moral formula" as to the motives of the actor, without having to list all the possible motives. For example, we can predicate the aggravated offence upon proof that the motives of the actor were "very bad" or "very wicked". But it seems that if we are ready to embrace a "moral formula", which entails that the appropriate offence of conviction will depend on direct moral evaluation, then it seems more reasonable to provide that all factors which bear upon the degree of moral culpability (and not only the motives) should be taken into account in determining the appropriate offence of conviction. Hence the suggestion in the text. For a list of factors that bear upon the degree of culpability see supra section 7.1.1.

2   See Gordon (1975) 389-390; Jones and Christie (1996) 208-209; Scottish Law Commission, *Attempted Homicide* (1984) 15-16.

3   Gordon (1978) 735.

4   Gordon (1978) 737. For further references to Gordon see supra chapter 2 at note 23.

5   Scottish Law Commission, *Attempted Homicide* (1984) 23.

6   Gordon (1978) 737. But see infra at note 7 concerning the decision in *Drury*.

7   For the possibility that the Scottish law of murder requires, even in the case of direct
       intention, that there be an "evil" intention, see Jones and Christie (1996) 208 (though
       the authors themselves do not accept this view). It should also be noted that Scottish
       law provides for certain categories of mitigating circumstances (such as the category of
       provocation), and that a person who acts in circumstances covered by one of these
       categories will be convicted of culpable homicide rather than murder, even if he
       intends to kill. See Jones and Christie (1996) 218-225. However, in 2001 the High
       Court decided that the mens rea for murder is not "either an intention to kill or wicked
       recklessness" but is "either a *wicked* intention to kill or wicked recklessness". See
       Drury v. H.M. Advocate 2001 S.L.T. 1013. The High Court also explained that the
       categories of provocation and diminished responsibility should not be viewed as
       forming exceptions to a rule which says that "an intention to kill" is sufficient for
       conviction of murder, but rather they should be understood as applications of the
       correct rule which is that the mens rea for murder is "either a *wicked* intention to kill or
       wicked recklessness". One interpretation for the decision in *Drury* is that it establishes
       that even in cases in which the accused intended to kill, the jury has broad moral
       discretion to decide between murder and culpable homicide, and that when
       deliberating on this question the jury is generally entitled to take into account every
       factor that is relevant to determining the accused's degree of moral blameworthiness. If
       this is the correct interpretation of *Drury*, then the practical implications of the
       decision for the mens rea for murder are very important. However, it is doubtful that
       this is the correct interpretation. It is possible that the Court only wanted to declare that
       cases of provocation and of diminished responsibility should be viewed as cases in
       which the mens rea for murder ia absent (and not as cases which form partial excuses
       or as cases in which murder is reduced to culpable homicide, as they were sometimes
       viewed); but it did not intend to give the jury moral discretion to decide between
       murder and culpable homicide (according to the accused's degree of moral
       blameworthiness), even in cases of "intention to kill" that are *not* covered by the
       traditional "partial defences to murder" (as they were sometimes called) such as
       provocation. If this is the correct interpretation of *Drury*, then the practical
       implications of the decision, for the mens rea for murder, are limited in scope.

8   Jones and Christie (1996) 206.

9   Model Penal Code (1985), section 210.2(1). An exception to this rule concerns cases
       of mitigation based on mental or emotional disturbance.

10   Section 210.3(1)(a). Manslaughter is also established where the accused, who
       otherwise should be convicted of murder, acts under extreme mental or emotional
       disturbance.

11   See Model Penal Code and Commentaries (1980) Part 2, vol. 1, pp. 21-22. Fletcher
       views the Model Penal Code formula as hinging on the moral gravity of the risk
       taking. See Fletcher (1978) 265. In many American jurisdictions, versions of reckless
       murder appear which resemble that of the Model Penal Code. Thus one finds the
       requirement that the accused acted in a way that evinced a "depraved heart regardless
       of human life" or "a depraved mind regardless of human life" or that he was motivated
       by "an abandoned and malignant heart". See Model Penal Code and Commentaries
       (1980) Part 2, vol. 1, pp. 22 and 26, and Fletcher (1978) 265.

12   Cf. Gordon (1975) 388, 390; Model Penal Code and Commentaries (1980) Part 2, vol.
       1, p. 144. There may also be practical arguments for empowering the jury to influence
       the sentence. First, if there is only one offence with a very high maximum penalty (in
       our example, 20 years imprisonment) the jury, in certain cases in which the accused
       (who should be convicted) deserves only a relatively low punishment, will prefer to

acquit him because of a fear that the judge will act harshly in passing the sentence. Cf. Model Penal Code, ibid. Second, in cases in which the offender deserves only a relatively low punishment, a lenient sentence imposed by the judge may be more accepted by the community if it follows a decision of the jury (i.e. the representative of the community) to the effect that the degree of blameworthiness was not very high. Cf. New South Wales Law Reform Commission, *Partial Defences to Murder: Provocation and Infanticide* (1997) 24.

13   We have to remember that the present argument proceeds on the assumption that in cases of disagreement between the judge and the jury concerning the degree of culpability, the opinion of the jury, acting as the representative of the community, should be considered the right one.

14   Of course, if the legislator thinks that in the context of the offence under discussion judges *should* have the discretion to impose a higher punishment than the one deserved because of utilitarian considerations such as deterrence or incapacitation, and that such punishment (in the context under discussion) should sometimes exceed 10 years imprisonment, he would not see the point mentioned in the text as an advantage. But the assumption in the text is that considerations of utility cannot justify imposing upon an offender a higher punishment than he deserves or, alternatively, that in the context of the offence under discussion utilitarian considerations cannot justify imposing a penalty that is higher than 10 years imprisonment, or that even if in the said context there might be some cases in which utilitarian considerations might justify imposing a punishment that is higher than 10 years imprisonment the danger that judges who are overly concerned with the protection of the public would impose excessively high punishments in inappropriate cases justifies limiting the discretion of the judge by setting the maximum penalty at 10 years imprisonment (for cases in which the degree of culpability was not very high).

15   Cf. Williams (1983a) 100.

16   Cf. Wasik (1983) 464; Wasik (1985b) 187.

17   For the problem of vagueness which would arise if the evaluation of motives were to be required for decisions about convictions cf. Hall (1960) 95, 99. For the disadvantages of using ethical standards in criminal law because they are vague and unstable cf. *Russell on Crime* (1964) 31-32. And cf. Ashworth (1990) 80-81.

18   Cf. Model Penal Code and Commentaries (1980) Part 2, vol. 1, p. 143.

19   Cf. Ashworth (1990) 81; Ashworth (1999) 272.

20   One might suggest a further argument against the first alternative. One of the most important factors in assessing the degree of culpability of the defendant is his motives. To assess the degree of culpability we have, inter alia, to determine what were the motives and purposes of the defendant, and to form a moral judgment concerning them. One might claim that it is very difficult to determine the whole complex of the motives and purposes of the defendant in his action (cf. Hall (1960) 99), so that the question of motives should not be dealt with at the trial stage but should rather be left to the sentencing stage. And if the question of motives is not be dealt with at the trial stage, then the whole idea of assessing the degree of moral culpability at the trial stage should be abandoned. I do not find this argument strong. First, if ascertaining the motives of the defendant is so problematic, why is it legitimate to take them into account at the sentencing stage? Second, I do not find the difficulties involved in ascertaining the motives of the defendant much greater than those involved in determining whether the accused acted with a direct intention to cause the proscribed result. Although the decision whether the accused wanted to cause the proscribed result is not always a very easy one, it is currently made by triers of fact at the trial stage

(sometimes with the help of the presumption of fact that a person intends the natural consequences of his action) in the context of certain offences, and the determination of the whole complex of the defendant's motives and purposes, while it may amount to somewhat of a more difficult task, does not appear to be much more difficult. See Wasik (1979) 547-548.

Another argument against the first alternative might be that judges have professional knowledge and experience that juries lack and therefore they are better trained to deal with questions related to the amount of punishment (cf. Model Penal Code and Commentaries (1985) Part 1, vol. 3, p. 49). But it seems that this consideration is relevant only to issues related to deterrence, incapacitation, rehabilitation and so on, and not to the moral evaluation of the degree of moral culpability of the actor. Hence this point cannot establish an argument against giving the jury an important part in evaluating the degree of culpability.

21   Another question that is country dependent concerns the extent of the danger that judges will impose excessively harsh punishments on offenders. As was explained in section 8.2.1, the main point in assigning to the jury the role of determining the offence of conviction is to protect the offender from excessively harsh sentencers. A further question that is country dependent concerns discrimination, as was claimed in this section.

22   The case of homicide might constitute an exception. See infra section 8.2.3.

23   In countries without juries (like Israel) where the same judge (or panel of judges) which passes judgment as to the conviction also (pursuant to additional proceedings) imposes the sentence, the case for the first alternative is much weaker than in countries with a jury system, since the whole idea of involving the jury in the moral evaluation of the offence is simply not relevant. However, one might suggest that there may still be a point for such countries to adopt the first alternative. If we adopt the principle that (in all offences or, at least, in certain offences) punishment should not be visited upon offenders beyond their just deserts even when considerations of utility would have required a higher punishment, then in order to reduce the risk that judges will violate the afore-mentioned principle of just deserts, we might want them to divide their deliberation in the determination of sentence into two stages: First, to consider only the degree of culpability of the offender with a view to setting the upper limits of the penalty, and second, to consider all the factors relevant to the appropriate punishment and to determine the punishment to impose on the offender before them. One way to ensure that judges will divide their deliberation into the mentioned two stages is to divide offences into two sub-categories by using the moral formula suggested in the text. But it seems to me that even if we wish to assign such an important function (namely, to set the upper limits of the sentence) to the deserved punishment, this can still be achieved by regulating the sentencing process, i.e. by directing judges that in deliberating about punishments they should assign to the degree of culpability of the offender the above mentioned important function. Although the division of offences into two sub-categories might provide more assurance that judges will in fact give the element of culpability such a highly important role, it seems that, at the end of the day, the case for such a division in countries without a jury system is very weak. The case of homicide might form an exception to this conclusion. See infra at note 26.

24   For the importance of retaining the distinction between murder and manslaughter for declaratory and symbolic reasons see Ashworth (1990) 76, 78. See also Ashworth (1999) 273, 297; Gordon (1975) 388-389.

25   Cf. Griffiths and Verdun-Jones (1994) 417-419, on the two aspects of the "declaratory function".

26   Supra at note 23 I claimed that in countries without juries the case for grading offences by using a moral formula is much weaker than in countries with a jury system, because the whole idea of involving the jury in the moral evaluation of the offence is simply not relevant in the former countries. However, the argument made here for using a moral formula in the special context of homicide, for expressive purposes, *can* apply even to countries without juries. For if in such countries there is only one offence for all intentional and reckless killings, then the judge will be left without a means to impose a special stigma on the most heinous of killers.

27   It might even be suggested that some of the arguments raised against using a moral formula are especially significant in the present context, for if the stigma of a "murderer" is so important a matter, then the fact that the moral formula creates a risk of disparity and discrimination might be considered even more of a drawback in the present context.

28   Cf. Criminal Law Reform Committee, New Zealand, *Report on Culpable Homicide* (1976) p. 4; Wells (1978) 671.

29   See supra, chapter 7, at note 50.

30   On the merits of using a moral formula in the context of homicide cf. Gordon (1975) 389-390; Gordon (1978) 737.

31   Other examples are the categories of provocation, mental impairment (that is not sufficient to establish a complete defence of insanity) and excessive self-defence. But note that since many borderline cases arise in the context of these categories, and since the jury, according to the present suggestion of using a moral formula, will in any case possess a vast amount of moral discretion, it might be said that there is not much point in including these categories in the list of circumstances in which the jury must acquit of murder. The situation is different concerning, for example, killing by reckless driving, because we may want to provide that in *all* killings by reckless driving the actor will be acquitted of murder, in which case no real problem of borderline cases will arise.

It should be noted that the legislator may also list certain circumstances in which the defendant must be convicted of murder. For example he might say that a sadistic killer should be convicted of murder. Cf. Pillsbury (1998) chapter 7.

It should also be added that the idea of determining by legislation that certain specified cases should be treated more leniently than others may be adopted even if the idea of having only one offence of unlawful killing is adopted. Assuming that the penalty for such an offence would be a maximum penalty of life imprisonment, the legislator might want to provide, for example, that a person convicted of the said offence because he caused death by reckless driving should not receive a punishment in excess of 10 years imprisonment. In this way, the legislator who, following the assumption made here, is of the view that no reckless driver should receive a harsher sentence than 10 years imprisonment, protects reckless drivers from being punished too sternly by tough sentencers. The reason why the group of "reckless drivers" is a good candidate for being specifically mentioned by the legislator is not that all other killers are more culpable than all reckless drivers who cause death (of course there are many killers who are less culpable than many reckless drivers and should not get more than ten years imprisonment). Rather, the reason is that this group is large enough to warrant special reference in the code, and that the decision whether the culpable killer falls under the rubric of "reckless driver" or whether he belongs to other categories of culpable killers does not involve real problems of proof, borderline cases, vagueness, continuum, etc. The question whether the accused belongs to this category (or to other categories of culpable killers) can generally be answered immediately with a simple yes/no answer. The technique mentioned here may also apply to the context of other offences.

32   Cf. Ashworth (1999) 265. Another possible argument for the mandatory sentence of life imprisonment might be that society wants to guarantee that the most heinous of killers be sentenced to life imprisonment and it thinks that the jury, rather than the judge, is the appropriate authority to represent the community ethic in identifying the most heinous of killers. If the penalty for murder is not mandatory then a risk may arise that judges will (wrongly) impose excessively lenient punishments for some very heinous killers. It seems that the question whether there is such a real risk is country dependent.

Chapter 9

An Alternative Justification for Grading Offences Based on the Distinction between Intention and Recklessness

9.1   An Alternative Justification for Distinguishing between Intention and Recklessness

9.1.1   A Correlation between Intention and Higher Degrees of Culpability

In chapter 2, I challenged the idea of grading offences based on the distinction between intention and recklessness by referring to the fact that there are cases in which a reckless actor is more blameworthy than an actor who acts with direct intention. Then I suggested that we should ask whether, when all other things are equal, including the motives of the actor, acting with intention to cause the result is more blameworthy than acting recklessly with regard thereto. This suggestion was based, inter alia, on the assumption that if it is true that when all other things (including the motives) are equal, there is no difference in moral blameworthiness between causing a result purposely and causing it recklessly, then there is no way to justify grading offences based on the distinction between intention and recklessness (if this is supposed to be based on considerations related to degrees of blameworthiness). I will now reconsider this assumption.

It might be the case that the distinction between direct intention and recklessness has no intrinsic moral significance, but that in the context of certain offences this distinction is empirically correlated with different degrees of moral blameworthiness. That is to say, that in the context of certain offences, those who cause the result purposely are *generally* (but not always) more blameworthy than those who cause it recklessly. And if this empirical correlation, between causing the result purposely and acting with a higher degree of culpability, exists in a certain context, then there may be a justification in this context to enact two separate offences, with different maximum penalties, one for causing the result purposely and one for causing it recklessly. The idea here is that in spite of the fact that when all other things are equal, including the motives, there is *no* difference in culpability between causing the result purposely and causing it recklessly, still, in reality, cases differ in certain factors that affect the degree of moral culpability of the actor (i.e., in reality things do *not* remain equal). Therefore it is possible that in reality an empirical correlation exists (in the context of certain offences) between causing the result purposely and acting with a higher degree of culpability. Under this justification, the element of direct intention does not, in itself, constitute the factor of importance which generates an increase in the degree of blameworthiness; rather, it is only used in the grading scheme because it gives an *approximation* of the important factor – which is a high degree of culpability. If in a certain context, the legislator decides to grade offences based on the above justification, then the fact that there are some examples of cases of recklessness in which the degree of culpability is higher than in certain cases of intention, cannot yield a counter-argument, because the legislator does not base the grading on the assumption that in the context under discussion *all* the actors who act with direct intention are more culpable than *all* the reckless ones. He only assumes that this is generally the case.

Now, if intention in itself does not increase the degree of culpability, the fact that in the context of certain offences there is a correlation between intention and higher degrees of culpability should be understood as resulting from an empirical correlation between intention and some other factor that in itself increases the degree of culpability. What is this factor? It may be suggested that in the context of certain offences the explanation may be connected to the motives of the actor. Sometimes when a person takes a risk that a certain result will ensue, the motive for the action is good in itself, and in some of these cases the actor's good motive renders the taking of the risk justified. In these last mentioned cases there is no recklessness and no conviction will ensue. In other cases, although the motive is good in itself, it cannot justify taking the risk, and therefore the actor who takes the risk is reckless. In other cases of recklessness, the motives of the actor are in themselves neutral or even bad. In the context of cases of intention, when the motives are good in themselves they may give rise to a defence (like the defence of necessity or that of the lesser evil) but in cases in which the good motives do not give rise to a defence, a conviction will follow. And here too, cases will arise in which the motives of the actor are in themselves neutral or bad. Now, it might be the case that in the context of a certain offence the reality is, for example, that the cases of acting with bad motives are much more frequent where the actor intends to cause the result than where the actor behaves recklessly with respect to the same result (and perhaps there is an additional fact – that even when reckless actions are performed from bad motives, the motives are generally less reprehensible than those of people who act with intent to cause the same result). Or, in the same vein, perhaps in the context of a certain offence the actions of reckless people are almost always performed from good motives, whereas many cases arise in which the result is caused purposely from bad motives. Now, if we are faced with such data with regard to a certain offence, then it is logical to suppose that in this context a correlation will exist between intention and higher degrees of culpability, for the motives of the actor are one of the most important factors that affect the degree of moral culpability.[1]

To illustrate, suppose that a legislator has to enact legislation relative to causing grievous bodily harm. Suppose further that this legislator is of the view that when all other things are equal (including the motives) there is no difference in the degree of culpability between causing a result purposely and causing it recklessly. Suppose further that when this legislator contemplates the vast array of cases in which grievous bodily harm is caused in reality, he finds a correlation between causing the result recklessly and acting with relatively low degrees of culpability. Specifically, he estimates that (taking into account the various factors that affect the degree of culpability) most of the actors who cause the result recklessly do not deserve more than 10 years imprisonment, and that only in rare cases will the reckless actor merit incarceration for a longer period of time. He also estimates that (taking into account the various factors that affect the degree of culpability) there are many (or significantly) more cases of causing the result purposely in which the actor deserves a harsher punishment than 10 years imprisonment, though no more than 20 years imprisonment (although there are also actors who cause the result purposely who deserve a lower penalty than 10 years imprisonment). If this is the case, it seems that such a legislator may have a reason to enact two offences: One of causing the said result with direct intention (that would carry a maximum penalty of 20 years imprisonment) and another one of causing the same result recklessly (that would carry a maximum penalty of 10 years imprisonment).[2]

9.1.2   *The Pros and Cons of the Justification*

The fact that the legislator has the above mentioned beliefs and estimations does not, of course, mean that he *should* adopt the above mentioned legislative scheme. What is demonstrated here is only that if he does have the said set of beliefs and estimations, adopting such a legislative scheme represents a reasonable option. But we still have to consider whether even such a legislator might have good reasons not to adopt such a scheme. In this respect, it is useful to weigh the above mentioned option against the possible alternatives. In relation to the example above, one alternative is to have only one offence of causing the said result (purposely or recklessly), with a maximum penalty of 20 years imprisonment. Another alternative is to grade the offence by using a moral formula. I will first assume that the idea of grading offences by using a moral formula is rejected (for reasons similar to those advanced in chapter 8) and that the legislator must choose between two options: To have only one offence of causing the mentioned result (purposely or recklessly) with a maximum penalty of 20 years imprisonment, or to enact two separate offences – one of causing the result with direct intention (with a maximum penalty of 20 years imprisonment) and one of causing the same result recklessly (with a maximum penalty of 10 years imprisonment).[3]

The justification suggested in section 9.1.1 is not based on there being an intrinsic difference between intention and recklessness. Rather, it is contingent upon the existence of an empirical correlation. The empirical data may vary from offence to offence, hence it is completely possible that the correlation between intention and higher degrees of culpability will exist in the context of certain offences, but not in the context of others. This may happen for various reasons, one of the most important being that the motives that typically induce people to engage in the conduct of a certain offence may be different from the motives that typically induce people to engage in the conduct of another offence. So our discussion is limited to offences with regard to which the legislator estimates that the mentioned correlation exists. Of course, it may be that there is no offence in the context of which the mentioned correlation exists, and if this is so then the legislator should not rely on the justification discussed here. But our discussion assumes a legislator who estimates that the said correlation exists in the context of certain offences, and the discussion will proceed on this assumption. Returning to the example given above in the context of causing grievous bodily harm, the following question should be addressed: Assuming that the mentioned correlation exists in the context of this crime, is it better to divide the offence into two categories based on the distinction between intention and recklessness, or is it better to have only one offence with a maximum penalty of 20 years imprisonment?

At first glance, the idea of only having one offence seems much better. If we have only one offence, with a maximum penalty of 20 years imprisonment, the judge will have the discretion to determine the appropriate punishment for every case, after taking into account all the relevant factors (the most important of which will be related to the degree of blameworthiness of the offender). On the other hand, dividing the offence into two categories entails a cost, as the grading scheme is only based on an approximation. For in spite of the empirical correlation, there *are* cases in which the reckless actor is more culpable than certain actors who act with intent to cause the result. Grading the offence in such a manner, therefore, carries the price that in certain exceptional cases, the judge will not be able to impose the deserved punishment on the offender. But is this price high enough to merit serious consideration? It seems that the price is paid in the context of recklessness and not in the context of intention. Since we are only speaking of maximum penalties (because mandatory and minimum sentences should be rejected) there is no real price to be paid in the context of intention, for even a person convicted of the intention-offence, the maximum penalty for which is 20 years imprisonment, may receive a very lenient punishment. So if the judge thinks that the offender only deserves a very lenient punishment, the law does not prevent him from passing such a sentence upon him. The price is paid, then, in the realm of recklessness. The assumption in our discussion is that there *are* reckless actors who deserve a harsher punishment than 10 years imprisonment, but that the number of such actors is significantly smaller relative to the number of actors who cause the result purposely and deserve such a punishment. Since there *are* reckless actors who deserve a harsher punishment than 10 years imprisonment, adopting a scheme by which the maximum penalty for recklessly causing the result is 10 years imprisonment entails the cost that certain reckless actors will not receive the punishment they deserve (because the judge cannot impose on an offender a punishment in excess of the maximum penalty provided by the legislator). So adopting the grading scheme does entail certain costs. Should we be ready to accept these costs to gain the advantage provided by adopting the above mentioned grading scheme? First of all, we have to specify exactly what this advantage is. I think the main potential reason for not having one offence for both recklessly and purposely causing the result, with a maximum penalty of 20 years imprisonment, has to do with the desire to protect offenders from excessively harsh sentencers. If we think that most reckless actors, in the context of the offence under discussion, do not deserve more than 10 years imprisonment, and that therefore they should not be sentenced to more than 10 years imprisonment, we might want to protect them from excessively harsh sentencers who might impose on them punishments in excess of 10 years imprisonment because of those sentencers' (wrong) estimation of the degree of punishment that the offender before them deserves, or because of their concern for public safety. And the safest way to protect them from such sentencers is to provide for a maximum penalty for reckless actors of 10 years imprisonment.[4] The advantage then lies in the protection afforded to reckless offenders from excessively harsh punishments, and the cost is that several reckless people who deserve a punishment in excess of 10 years imprisonment will not receive the harsh punishment they should get. As for offenders who act with intent to cause the result, although many of them might deserve a milder punishment than 10 years imprisonment, the number of those who act with direct intention (in the context under discussion) who deserve a punishment in excess of 10 years imprisonment may be so high as to make it unacceptable to provide that the maximum penalty for purposely causing the result would also only be 10 years imprisonment. Hence, the maximum penalty for these offenders will be 20 years imprisonment.

The mentioned cost and benefit should be weighed one against the other. Of course, the higher the number of recklessness cases that deserve a punishment in excess of 10 years imprisonment, the stronger the case for only having one offence. And the higher the risk that judges will be too tough, the stronger the case for dividing the offence into two sub-categories. It should also be noted that the question whether there is a real risk that judges will be too tough is country dependent. Another noteworthy point is that the number of reckless people who deserve harsh punishments may vary from offence to offence, even within the category of offences in which the correlation discussed in this chapter exists. That means that the process of weighing the mentioned cost and benefit against one another should be performed for every offence separately, based on the empirical data relevant to that offence.

The discussion above suggests that there is a potential way to justify the grading of offences based on the distinction between intention and recklessness, even if we assume that when all other things (including the motives) are equal there is no difference in the degree of culpability between intention and recklessness. By characterising this line of justification as only potential, I mean that it can only justifiably lead to an actual grading scheme if certain empirical data (relevant to the offence under discussion) exist, and only after, based on the data, the cost and benefit of grading the offence are weighed against one another in the context of the said offence. This means that it is possible that the suggested potential justification will not actually lead to a grading scheme in any offence. This may be so for various potential reasons: It might be that there is no offence in the context of which a correlation exists between intention and higher degrees of culpability; it might be that although such a correlation does exist in the context of certain offences, it is not significant enough;[5] it might be that in every offence in which the correlation exists, the number of cases of recklessness in which the offender deserves the harsher punishment (e.g. more than 10 years imprisonment) is too considerable to be ignored; it might be that in certain countries the legislator will not be ready to disregard even a small number of cases of reckless actors who should receive the harsher punishment; and it may also be the case that in a certain country the risk that judges will be too tough does not exist or is negligible. So it might be that the potential justification will not lead to actual grading in any offence. But it may also be the case that in certain countries it will lead to a legitimate grading scheme based on the distinction between intention and recklessness.

The cost and benefit mentioned above constitute the main factors that should be considered in deliberating whether to grade an offence based on the justification suggested in this chapter. But before leaving the assessment of the suggested justification, I would like to add other considerations, albeit of less importance (in this context), that might be taken into account in deliberating about whether to base a grading scheme on the present justification. One consideration for having only one offence is that of efficiency. If the grading scheme is adopted, the question whether the defendant intended to cause the result or was only reckless with respect thereto will be of importance at the trial, and perhaps much time will be devoted to its determination. By contrast, if only one offence is enacted then the said question will not be so important at the conviction stage and much time can sometimes be saved. However, other considerations might support adopting a grading scheme. First, if the grading scheme is adopted, then the legislator will be more "involved" in the actual sentence imposed on the offender than if only one offence is adopted. Although this added involvement is modest, one might nevertheless welcome it as contributing to the rule of law and the separation of powers. Second, if the grading scheme is adopted, then the maximum penalty for *recklessly* causing the result will be considerably lower than the maximum punishment for causing the same result recklessly under a unitary offence. This means that if the grading scheme is adopted, the scope of the penalties available for reckless actors will be narrower than if a unitary offence is adopted. And the fact that the scope is narrower can contribute to some extent to alleviate the problems of disparity and discrimination in sentencing (in the context of the offence under discussion).[6]

9.1.3 *The Possibility of a Variable Treatment*

From the discussion in the previous section it is clear that the decision whether to divide a certain result crime into two sub-categories based on the distinction between intention and recklessness on the basis of the present justification, depends upon the empirical data relevant to the offence under discussion. The relevant data (for example, the motives that typically motivate people to engage in the relevant conduct) vary from offence to offence, so that granting the validity in principle of the present justification for grading offences, does not necessarily entail that a legislator should grade all result crimes based on the distinction between intention and recklessness. A rational legislator may decide to grade some offences following the present justification, and opt not to distinguish between intention and recklessness in the context of other offences. And the reason for this variable treatment of intention may simply be that the relevant empirical data vary from offence to offence.

Furthermore, even within the group of offences in the context of which a significant correlation exists between intention and higher degrees of culpability, the legislator may still distinguish between those offences in which the grading scheme is more needed and those in which it is less needed. He may decide, for example, that the grading scheme will be established only for offences that carry high maximum penalties. The need to protect offenders from excessively harsh sentencers will be more pressing if the result of having only one offence is that reckless actors are subject to a maximum penalty of 20 years imprisonment, than if the result is that reckless actors are exposed to a maximum penalty of, say, only 2 years imprisonment. Therefore, considerations of efficiency and the desire not to confuse and overburden the jury (and perhaps also the desire to have a clear and concise code) may yield the conclusion that the method of grading offences based on the distinction between intention and recklessness should generally be adopted only in the realm of serious offences.[7]

9.2   Oblique Intention

If the legislator decides to distinguish between direct intention and recklessness in the context of a certain offence on the basis of the present justification, then he will also have to decide what to do concerning cases of oblique intention. Since according to the present justification, the rationale for the distinction between intention and recklessness is that there is an empirical correlation between intention and higher degrees of culpability, the question concerning oblique intention should be whether a similar correlation exists between oblique intention and higher degrees of culpability. If the answer to the latter question is positive, then it is logical to equate (for purposes of the offence under discussion) the law of cases of oblique intention to the law of cases of direct intention (i.e. to include the cases of oblique intention within the higher offence together with the cases of direct intention). If, on the other hand, there is no correlation between oblique intention and higher degrees of culpability in the context of the offence under discussion but the degrees of culpability in cases of oblique intention are generally similar to those present in cases of recklessness, then it is logical to equate (in the context of the offence under discussion) the law of cases of oblique intention to that of cases of recklessness, and to include cases of oblique intention within the lesser offence, alongside cases of recklessness.[8] Now, it may be that in the context of a certain offence, the answer to the above question will be that cases of oblique intention form an intermediate set of cases between cases of direct intention and cases of recklessness.[9] If this is so in the context of a certain offence, then the legislator should decide whether to include oblique intention within the higher offence (with direct intention) or within the lower offence (together with recklessness). He may also decide to divide the offence under discussion into three sub-categories, so that the intermediate sub-category will include cases of oblique intention (but of course considerations of efficiency should be taken into account before adopting such a three sub-category scheme).

Since under the present justification for distinguishing between intention and recklessness the decision about oblique intention hinges to a significant extent on empirical data which vary from offence to offence, it may be the case that in the context of certain offences oblique intention should be included within the higher offence (with direct intention) and in the context of other offences it should be included within the lower offence (with recklessness). The conclusion, then, is that a legislator who decides to distinguish in the context of certain offences between intention and recklessness on the basis of the present justification, may legitimately decide that the law of cases of oblique intention need not be uniform for all "intention crimes", that it will vary from one "crime of intention" to another.[10]

It should also be noted that since the present justification is based on an empirical correlation between certain mental states and degrees of culpability, it may be the case that in the context of a certain offence the empirical data will lead to the conclusion that there is a correlation between, say, foresight of the result as "highly probable" (or as more likely than not to occur) and higher degrees of culpability, and that this correlation is similar to the correlation that exists between intention and such degrees of culpability. This means that a justification exists for such an offence, at least in principle, to include not only cases of foresight of certainty within the higher offence but also cases of, say, foresight of the result as being highly probable. The discussion in this book is generally confined to cases of foresight of certainty, but it is important to understand the point made here which stems from the fact that, insofar as the present justification is concerned, the line between foresight of certainty and foresight of lesser degrees of probability in many contexts does not mark a qualitative moral difference but only a difference in degree. However, we also have to remember that even if there exists, in a certain context, a justification in principle to include even cases of foresight of the result as "highly probable" within the higher offence, it may be the case that practical considerations (like the desire to avoid using vague concepts and to diminish potential difficulties in proving the elements of offences) will justify the decision *not* to include in the higher offence cases of foresight of "high probability", but only cases of foresight of certainty (alongside cases of direct intention).[11]

9.3   The Present Justification in Comparison with its Predecessor

In this chapter I assumed that when all other things are equal, including the motives, there is no difference in culpability between intention and recklessness, and I suggested a possible justification for grading certain offences based on the distinction between intention and recklessness that would be valid despite the above mentioned assumption.

The suggested justification may also be of importance to those who embrace the position that when all other things, including the motives, are equal, there *is* a difference in the degree of culpability between those who act with direct intention and those who act with recklessness, but that this difference is not large. In section 7.1.4, I suggested that if we embrace the position that the said difference is not large, then there is no justification for grading offences based on the distinction between intention and recklessness, if all that can be said in support of this distinction is that when all other things (including the motives) are equal, causing a result purposely is more culpable than causing it recklessly. But of course those who embrace the above position may still like to grade certain offences on the basis of the justification suggested in the present chapter. The justification suggested in the present chapter is not dependent on any intrinsic difference between intention and recklessness: It may justify grading even assuming there is no intrinsic difference between intention and recklessness; and it can a fortiori justify grading assuming that there is such an intrinsic difference, albeit a small one. Actually it might be the case that in the context of a certain offence this small difference may carry some weight in justifying the grading scheme. For if we view the justification suggested in the present chapter as valid in principle, then it may be the case that the correlation between intention and other factors that increase moral culpability present within the context of a certain offence is not significant enough to justify the grading scheme – but the fact that a small intrinsic difference exists between intention and recklessness may slightly increase the degree of culpability present in cases of intention, and in this way engender the result that, in the final analysis, the correlation between intention and higher degrees of culpability is sufficiently significant to justify the grading scheme.

As stated in section 7.1.4, if the legislator embraces the view that the difference in culpability between intention and recklessness (when all other things, including the motives, are equal) is large, it is legitimate for him to grade offences based on the distinction between intention and recklessness. But it is important to understand that embracing the mentioned view does not necessarily logically dictate that he take such a course of action. The fact that, when all other things are equal, one who causes grievous bodily harm purposely is significantly more culpable than one who causes the same result recklessly does not, of course, yield the conclusion that all those who cause the said result purposely are more culpable than all those who cause it recklessly. In reality, there are cases of recklessly causing the result in which the actor is more culpable than in certain cases of causing the same result purposely. So if embracing the said view leads one to undertake a division of the offence of causing grievous bodily harm into two sub-categories, one of recklessly causing the result (with a maximum penalty of 10 years imprisonment) and the other of causing the result purposely (with a maximum penalty of 20 years imprisonment), it does so only on the basis of the belief that the difference in culpability between intention and recklessness (when all other things are equal) yields the effect that in reality people who act with intent to cause the result are *generally* more culpable than reckless actors. And if we assume that (albeit few) cases of recklessness will nonetheless arise that deserve a harsher punishment than 10 years imprisonment, it follows that the argument that the said offence should be divided into two sub-categories is not a conclusive one. The legislator should weigh the benefit gained by protecting reckless people from excessively harsh sentencers against the cost entailed by the fact that some reckless people will not receive the harsh punishment they should get. In the final analysis, what emerges is that the justification discussed in chapters 3-7 is similar in one respect to the justification discussed in this chapter. Both of them ultimately rely on the fact that, in reality, a higher degree of culpability is *generally* present in cases of intention than in cases of recklessness. The difference between them lies first of all in the fact that according to the justification discussed in chapters 3-7, this discrepancy stems from an intrinsic difference between intention and recklessness (i.e., from the fact that when all other things are equal, including the motives, intention is more culpable than recklessness), whereas under the justification presented in this chapter, it stems from an empirical correlation between intention and a factor (or group of factors) that increases the degree of culpability. Of course, the said difference between the two justifications yields many other differences, like the one that since the justification discussed in chapters 3-7 is based on general theoretical assumptions it may apply, at least in principle, to all of the result crimes (or at least to a big number of them) and is not dependent (unlike the justification presented in the present chapter) upon contingent empirical data that vary from offence to offence. Another difference is related, for example, to the law of cases of oblique intention. The question whether the grading scheme is based on the justification discussed in chapters 3-7 or on the justification suggested in the present chapter, influences the decision concerning cases of oblique intention because, as has been explained, such a decision is influenced by the rationale given for distinguishing between direct intention and recklessness.

It should also be noted that a certain legislator may accept both the justification discussed in chapters 3-7 and the justification suggested in the present chapter. He may think, for example, that when all other things (including the motives) are equal, causing grievous bodily harm to another person purposely is significantly more culpable than causing the same result recklessly, because of the element, in the former case, of using the other person as a means, and he may therefore distinguish between purposely causing the result and causing it recklessly. At the same time, in the context of some other offence (for example, in the context of causing pain to animals) he may think that although the just mentioned justification does not apply, nevertheless the justification suggested in the present chapter does apply, so that in this offence as well he will distinguish between causing the result purposely and causing it recklessly (though for a different reason). The fact that the rationale given for the distinction in the two contexts is different may also yield the result that the law of cases of oblique intention will not be the same in the two contexts.

Another point worth mentioning concerns the possibility that in the context of a certain offence both justifications (the one discussed in chapters 3-7 and the one suggested in the present chapter) will apply. For it is possible that the legislator thinks, for example, that the two following propositions are correct in the context of a certain offence: First, that when all other things are equal (including the motives) causing the result purposely is significantly more culpable than causing it recklessly; and second, that the motives of the actor in cases of direct intention are generally worse than those present in cases of recklessness. In this case, the fact that causing the result purposely is generally more culpable than causing it recklessly stems from two separate causes, and this may lead one to the conclusion that in the context of such an offence the cumulative force of the two causes will yield a larger difference in culpability between intention and recklessness than in other contexts, so that the case for adopting a grading scheme in this context will be stronger than in others.

9.4   Homicide

The discussion in this chapter suggests that even if we assume that there is no difference in culpability between intention and recklessness when all other things (including the motives) are equal (or that such a difference exists, but it is not large), we can still justify grading certain offences based on the distinction between intention and recklessness, if in the context of those offences there is a significant empirical correlation between intention and higher degrees of culpability. But the discussion also suggests that even in the context of such offences a reasonable legislator may decide not to grade the offences, but to include intention and recklessness within the same offence.

This analysis is also valid in the context of homicide. As I said earlier, to my mind, even in the context of homicide there should be no mandatory sentences.[12] Hence, the analysis above also holds within this context, which means that if the legislator thinks that in the context of homicide there is a significant empirical correlation between intention and higher degrees of culpability, he may reasonably distinguish between causing death purposely and causing it recklessly, and provide that causing death purposely will carry a maximum penalty that is higher than the maximum penalty for causing death recklessly. Here too, the legislator may reasonably decide that in spite of the mentioned correlation, he will not distinguish between intention and recklessness, and will include both mental states within the same offence of causing death.[13]

However it might be argued that, when deliberating what to do concerning homicide, we should also take into account the special stigma which is commonly thought to attach to a murder conviction, so that perhaps the analysis conducted in this chapter should not apply to homicide in the same way it applies to other offences. I will now consider this argument.

Let us assume that in the context of homicide there is a significant empirical correlation between intention and higher degrees of culpability, on the one hand, and between recklessness and lower degrees of culpability, on the other. Let us assume now that in the context of other offences in which such significant correlation exists, the legislator, for the reasons set forth in section 9.1.2, decides that this correlation does not justify adopting the grading scheme. One might argue that despite this decision, there is a special reason to distinguish between murder (that would be defined in terms of purposely causing death) and manslaughter (that would be defined in terms of recklessly causing death). The reason is that a murder conviction carries a special stigma, which brands the offender as an extremely heinous killer. Now, since most reckless killers, following the present assumption, are not very heinous, we must conclude that most reckless killers do not deserve the stigma of "murderer", so that including reckless killers within the offence of murder would impose upon many people a stigma that they do not deserve. Thus a special reason emanates for distinguishing between intention and recklessness in the context of homicide.

The argument as it was introduced here is not based on the proposition that society *should,* for expressive and declaratory reasons, impose a special stigma on the most heinous of killers; rather, it only assumes that a by-product of a murder conviction is such a severe stigmatisation of the convicted offender. I will first address the argument in this form. Three arguments may be advanced in response to this argument. First, it may be argued that people do not necessarily view all offenders convicted of murder as the most heinous of killers; rather, people are also influenced by the details of the specific story and perhaps by the sentence imposed.[14] Second, even if we assume that in a country in which the offence of murder is confined to causing death purposely a murder conviction always entails the stigma of "a very heinous killer", the situation would probably differ in a country in which the crime of "murder" includes reckless killings, for if most reckless killers are not very heinous (and this is the assumption in the present discussion), the inclusion of them within the offence will change its image.

The most important argument, however, is that if indeed the word "murder" connotes a very heinous killing, the difficulties entailed by this connotation may be side-stepped by simply dropping the term from the criminal code. We can enact an offence called "causing death" or "unlawful killing", that would include both reckless and intentional killings.[15]

Another form of the argument from the stigma issue is that the criminal law *should* distinguish between the most heinous of killings and less heinous ones for expressive reasons,[16] so that even if in other areas the legislator decides not to grade offences based on the distinction between intention and recklessness, in the case of homicide he should grade the offence based on this distinction, for it affords an approximation of the distinction between the most heinous of killers and less heinous ones. According to the present form of the argument, including reckless and intentional killings within the same offence would defeat the expressive role of the law of homicide.

One possible response to this argument would be to recognise the importance of labelling the most heinous of killings as murders but to say that nonetheless the disadvantages of dividing the offence into two sub-categories (mainly, the fact that very culpable reckless killers will not receive the punishment they deserve) outweigh society's interest in such labelling, so that the offence should not be divided.[17] Another possible response is to deny the importance of labelling the most heinous killers as murderers or to deny that the criminal law should be used for expressive goals. Still another response may be that even if the criminal law does not formally distinguish between "murderers" and other killers, the public will still distinguish between "murderers" and other killers in light of the circumstances of the killing and perhaps of the punishment actually imposed.[18]

But I think that the most significant point against the above argument for distinguishing between intention and recklessness in the context of homicide is that if we think that stigmatising the offender as a very heinous killer is a very serious matter, and if we think that every murder conviction imposes on the offender such a stigma, then a problem of over-inclusiveness arises, since cases arise in which intended killings are not "very heinous" (and that do not fall within the confines of the traditional defences to murder). A conviction of murder in such cases is not just, as it imposes on the offenders a stigma which they do not deserve. If this stigma was not a very serious matter, then its imposition upon some undeserving people would perhaps not present a very serious problem. But the whole point of the present argument is that this stigma *is* a very serious matter.[19] Unless we want to sacrifice some killers (by imposing upon them a stigma that they do not deserve) or to rely on the discretion of prosecutors, we have to conclude, so it seems, that if the mentioned stigma is a very serious matter we should deny the idea of defining murder in terms of "intended killing".[20]

It seems, then, that if we think that in the context of offences other than homicide even the existence of a significant empirical correlation between intention and higher degrees of culpability does not justify adopting a grading scheme following the distinction between intention and recklessness, then the same view can be held in the context of homicide.

Actually the point made above (concerning the problem of over-inclusiveness) may even be used to formulate an argument against grading homicide offences based on the distinction between intention and recklessness, even assuming that in other contexts we *should* grade offences based on this distinction. Assuming that in the context of a certain offence, like that of causing grievous bodily harm, there is an empirical correlation between intention and higher degrees of culpability, on the one hand, and between recklessness and lower degrees of culpability, on the other – the legislator may reasonably distinguish in this context between purposely and recklessly causing the result, by providing, for example, that the maximum penalty for causing the result purposely would carry a maximum penalty of 20 years imprisonment, and causing it recklessly a maximum penalty of 10 years imprisonment. The fact that in some cases the actor who acts with intent to cause the result does not deserve a high punishment does not give rise to a serious problem, because in those cases the judge can impose a lenient punishment on the offender. But in the context of homicide, *if* indeed *every* conviction of the higher offence imposes on the offender the stigma of a very heinous killer, then the result would be that such a stigma would also be imposed in cases in which the actor (who caused the result purposely) does not deserve it. And *if* indeed being stigmatised in such a manner is a very serious matter, then we have an argument here against grading homicide based on the said distinction, even if we think that in other contexts we should use this distinction in grading offences.[21]

In section 9.3 I explained that the justification suggested in the present chapter for distinguishing between intention and recklessness is similar in one respect to the justification given for distinguishing between intention and recklessness that is based on the assumption that when all other things are equal (including the motives) there is a large difference in culpability between causing a bad result purposely and causing it recklessly. And I added that by reason of this similarity, the discussion in section 9.1.2 is also relevant to a discussion conducted on the basis of the latter justification. What I should add here is that the discussion in the present section as well is also relevant to a discussion conducted on the basis of the latter justification.

9.5 The Option of Using a Moral Formula

9.5.1 *Using a Moral Formula versus Distinguishing between Intention and Recklessness*

In section 9.1.2, I said that even if the legislator finds that in a certain context there is a significant correlation between intention and higher degrees of culpability, it does not logically dictate that he should distinguish in this context between intention and recklessness. The decision whether to make such a distinction depends on how one weighs the option of distinguishing between them against the other alternatives, namely, to have only one offence for both intention and recklessness or to use a moral formula. In the discussion conducted thus far in this chapter, I assumed that the option of using a moral formula was closed and I only weighed the option of distinguishing between intention and recklessness against the option of having one offence for intention and recklessness. I will now turn to weighing the option of distinguishing between intention and recklessness against the option of using a moral formula.[22]

The assumption here is that in a certain context there is a significant correlation between intention and higher degrees of culpability, on the one hand, and between recklessness and lower degrees of culpability, on the other. Assuming that the option of having only one offence for all the cases of intention and recklessness is rejected in this context (mainly because adopting such an option does not provide offenders with sufficient protection against excessively harsh sentencers), the question arises as to whether a distinction should be made in the said context between intention and recklessness or whether a moral formula should be used. For example: Let us assume that in the context of causing grievous bodily harm to a person, we are faced with the data that only rarely does an offender in cases of recklessness deserve a harsher punishment than 10 years imprisonment; however, many cases arise in which people who act with intent to cause the said result deserve a harsher punishment than 10 years imprisonment. One option is to enact one offence of causing the said result purposely, which would carry a maximum penalty of 20 years imprisonment, and a second offence of causing it recklessly, which would carry a maximum penalty of 10 years imprisonment. The other option is not to distinguish between intention and recklessness but to enact one offence for cases in which the degree of culpability is very high, which would carry a maximum penalty of 20 years imprisonment, and a second offence for cases in which the degree of culpability is not so high, which would carry a maximum penalty of 10 years imprisonment.

In section 8.2.2, I expressed my inclination to reject the idea of using a moral formula in favour of enacting a single offence for all cases of intention and recklessness (the option of distinguishing between intention and recklessness was rejected at that point of the discussion based on the view that it does not adequately distinguish between different degrees of culpability). This inclination meant, *inter alia*, that although using a moral formula would provide offenders with some protection from excessively harsh sentencers, the disadvantages of using a moral formula (mainly, that it makes the specific crime of conviction subject to the moral discretion of the jury) outweigh the importance of this protection. Since the assumption in the present section is that in the context of the offence under discussion the option of grading based on the distinction between intention and recklessness is preferable to the option of only having one offence for all cases of recklessness and intention, the conclusion is that one who identifies with my inclination (as formulated in section 8.2.2) would also incline, in our context, to prefer the option of distinguishing between intention and recklessness to the option of using a moral formula.

But suppose that a person disagrees with my inclination in section 8.2.2 and thinks that where the choice is between either having a single offence for all cases of recklessness and intention or using a moral formula, we should, at least in the context of serious offences, use a moral formula (mainly in order to protect offenders from excessively harsh sentencers). Suppose further that he accepts that in the context of causing grievous bodily harm a correlation exists between intention and higher degrees of culpability. In this case, he should weigh the option of grading the offence based on the distinction between intention and recklessness against that of using a moral formula. I will now discuss the main arguments that should be considered in deliberating about this matter.

The first point that should be noted is that both methods protect offenders from excessively harsh sentencers to a higher degree than where we only have one offence for all cases of intention and recklessness. But each of the two methods works in a different way. The method of distinguishing between intention and recklessness (hereinafter, the first method) protects offenders by providing, in our example, that reckless actors are liable to a maximum penalty of only 10 years imprisonment. The method of using a moral formula (hereinafter, the second method), on the other hand, protects offenders by providing, in our example, that those who are not very culpable are liable to a maximum penalty of only 10 years imprisonment.

Insofar as ensuring that justice be done in each specific case, the second method seems preferable, for if the first method is adopted, reckless actors who deserve more than 10 years imprisonment will not get the penalty they deserve. This price is not paid under the second method, as the jury can decide to convict certain reckless actors of the higher offence based on their high culpability. Another point, albeit a less important one, is that if the first method is adopted, all actors who cause the result purposely will be held liable to a maximum penalty of 20 years imprisonment, including those whose degree of culpability is very low, whereas if the second method is adopted, the jury will be left free to decide that a certain actor who caused the result purposely was not very culpable, and to convict him of the lower offence, thereby protecting him from an excessively harsh sentencer.

On the other hand, the second method suffers from the drawback that the decision as to the specific crime of conviction is subject to the moral discretion of the jury, which may give rise to disparity and discrimination, as was explained in section 8.2.2. The first method does not present such difficulties because the question whether the accused intended to cause the result is a factual question. So we have here another example of the known conflict which appears in many areas of the law between the desire to have rules and the desire to arrive at the just result under the specific circumstances of the case. This conflict is the main issue here, and I tend to think that the first method is the better one.[23]

There are several additional points that support using the first method. In section 8.2.2 I mentioned that using the second method entails to some extent a waste of resources, because the same question (the degree of culpability) is addressed twice. This problem does not arise in the same manner within the first method, as the question dealt with at the trial stage does not concern the degree of culpability of the accused (by taking into account all the relevant factors), but only whether he intended to cause the result or not. In the same section I also referred to the desire not to overburden the jury as one of the considerations which may warrant eschewing the use of a moral formula. This point is also relevant to the present discussion, as it seems that the burden to consider all the factors relevant to the degree of culpability of the accused and make a value judgment is generally more substantial than the burden of determining whether the accused intended to cause the result. I would also add that under the first method the legislator is somewhat more involved in the decision regarding the determination of sentence than where a moral formula is used (for in the latter case he leaves the moral discretion to the jury), a fact that some might find to contribute to the rule of law.[24]

9.5.2 Homicide

The analysis carried out in the previous section may in principle equally apply in the context of homicide. But the analysis may differ if we view the issue of stigma as an important factor in the context of homicide. If we think that in the context of homicide we should separate between different degrees of homicide not only in order to separate between different degrees of maximum penalties, but also in order to impose a special stigma on the most heinous of killers, then it may be suggested that the preferable method is to use a moral formula. For if we define murder in terms of causing death purposely, then the stigma of "murderer" will be imposed on every person who causes death purposely. But cases arise where those who cause death purposely do not deserve such a stigma.[25] If we are not ready to "sacrifice" those killers (by imposing upon them a stigma they do not deserve) or to rely on the discretion of the prosecution, then we will have a good argument, in this context, for preferring the use of a moral formula over the method of distinguishing between intention and recklessness. The use of a moral formula assures us that the stigma of "murderer" will only be branded upon those people who (following the opinion of the jury, the representative of society) deserve it.[26] The conclusion, then, is that even if in the context of other offences we should not use a moral formula, there is more to be said for its use in the area of homicide.[27] But of course, even in this area the argument for using a moral formula is not conclusive.[28]

In deliberating about the method to be adopted one should also keep in mind that the use of a moral formula may be preferred over the method of distinguishing between intention and recklessness not only because it enables the jury to refrain from imposing a special stigma upon people who do not deserve it, but also because it enables the jury to impose such a stigma on reckless people who deserve it, by convicting them of the higher offence. One might suggest that even if in the context of other offences the legislator would be ready to accept that several reckless people will not receive the sentence they deserve, he may nonetheless be reluctant to accept that some reckless killers who are very heinous will not receive the stigma they deserve.

It should also be noted that the legislator may combine elements from each of the two methods discussed in this section. Suppose that in the context of homicide most of those who cause death purposely deserve the special stigma of "murderer" whereas most reckless killers do not. A legislator may think that the method of using a moral formula is problematic given the broad moral discretion it imparts to juries and, therefore, he may be ready to provide that *all* reckless killers should be convicted of the lesser offence, in spite of the fact that in exceptional cases a reckless killer deserves the stigma of "murderer". In other words, he may be ready to pay the price that in certain exceptional cases a reckless killer will not receive the stigma he deserves, in order to confine the moral discretion of the jury. The legislator may also think that since in some (albeit exceptional) cases an actor who causes death purposely does not deserve the stigma of "murderer", and since no offender should be stigmatised beyond his just deserts, it is unacceptable to provide that *all* those who cause death purposely will be convicted of murder.[29] He may, therefore, come to the conclusion that although granting the jury moral discretion is problematic, no better option than to use a moral formula is available with regard to cases of direct intention. He may also think that since (in his view) only in exceptional cases will a real possibility arise that one who causes death purposely does not deserve the stigma of "murderer", the number of cases in which the jury will have to seriously deliberate on the moral issue will be minimal. Hence, this legislator may provide that murder is established where the actor intends to cause death, unless the killing is performed under circumstances which do not manifest a (very) high degree of culpability, and that the lesser offence is established where the actor is reckless with regard to the death, or where he intends to cause death but does not manifest in his action a (very) high degree of culpability.[30] A similar formula would be to provide that murder is only established where the actor intends the death *and* manifests in his action a (very) high degree of culpability.[31]

Notes

1   Kugler (1993) 187. One might reject the inference made here as to the existence of a correlation between intention and higher degrees of culpability from the correlation between intention and worse motives, by pointing to the fact that there are many other factors, in addition to motives, that affect the degree of culpability, so that even assuming that there is a correlation between intention and worse motives we should not come to the conclusion mentioned in the text. For it might also be the case that there is a correlation between recklessness and some other factor that increases the degree of culpability to the same level as that produced by the existence of worse motives. But the answer to this argument is that, in a certain context, it may be that the legislator only sees a correlation between intention and worse motives, and sees no

correlation (or no significant correlation) between intention or recklessness and other factors that affect the degree of culpability, so that the correlation between intention and worse motives can justify, in this context, the conclusion as to there being a correlation between intention and higher degrees of culpability. One might then ask: If the only reason for concluding that in cases of intention the degree of culpability is generally high is connected to the motives, why not directly grade the offence based on the motives? The answer is that there is such a vast array of potential motives for acting in a way that may cause a certain result that it is not practical to list in the code all the potential motives and set the punishment accordingly. As for the alternative suggestion that offences be graded based on the question whether the motives were "very bad" or not – this suggestion brings us back to the idea of using a moral formula and the assumption in the discussion here is that the idea of using a moral formula should be rejected, for similar reasons to those given in the previous chapter. I will return later, in section 9.5, to the idea of using a moral formula.

I would also add that it may be that in the context of certain offences the legislator may see, in addition to the correlation between intention and worse motives, a correlation between intention and another factor that increases the degree of moral culpability, so that in this context the conclusion regarding the correlation between intention and higher degrees of culpability will be based on the combined effect of two factors. Of course, there may be more than two relevant correlations in a given context.

Cf. Duff (1976) 73-74 on the possibility that the distinction between intention and recklessness has no intrinsic moral significance, but that there may be a correlation between this distinction and other factors which are morally important. And cf. Pillsbury (1998) 100, that the moral force of the doctrine of premeditation in the law of murder "comes from the way that premeditation often serves as a proxy for the worst motives to kill".

2   The idea of enacting two offences on the basis of the correlation suggested here is only reasonable if the correlation yields a result that is sufficiently significant. If the estimation is that the number of cases of intention in which the degree of culpability is high is only slightly greater than the number of cases of recklessness in which the same degree of culpability exists (or, alternatively, if the number of cases in which the degree of culpability in cases of intention is higher than in cases of recklessness is significantly greater but the difference in the degree of culpability between the cases that belong to these two groups is not significant), then there would be no point in enacting separate offences on the basis of the mentioned correlation.

3   If the legislator decides to enact two offences, he will also have to decide regarding cases of oblique intention. I will deal with this issue in section 9.2.

4   For the idea of protecting offenders against excessively harsh sentencers, see also supra section 8.2.1. Note also that the discussion at note 14 in that section is also relevant to the text here.

5   See supra note 2.

6   One might add a further argument. The fact that recklessly causing certain results establishes criminal liability has some chilling effect on taking risks. Some people may be deterred from taking justifiable risks because of the fear that a risk perceived by them as being justified will be considered unjustified by the court. Now, in the context under discussion, the legislator decided to criminalise actions which recklessly cause the relevant result, so that chilling effect concerns did not prevent him from establishing criminal liability for recklessness. But there may still be degrees in chilling effect, and it may be argued that the degree of this effect increases in proportion with the potential punishment for reckless offenders. Therefore, if in the

context of a certain offence cases rarely arise in which reckless people deserve a higher punishment than 10 years imprisonment, it might be wise to provide by statute that in the context of this offence no reckless actor will receive a sentence in excess of 10 years imprisonment, for if we provide that reckless actors (like actors who intend to cause the result) will be held liable to a maximum penalty of 20 years imprisonment, this will increase the chilling effect. But one may respond that this is a weak argument, because if the *amount* of potential punishments has any influence on taking risks, this influence is caused by the actual punishments generally imposed and not by exceptionally high punishments which are imposed in rare cases (or by the maximum penalty provided for in the book of statutes).

7   The treatment of the offences of causing personal harm in the Draft Criminal Code for England and Wales (1989) may serve as an illustration. The draft code distinguishes between intentionally causing serious personal harm (clause 70) and recklessly causing serious personal harm (clause 71). The first offence carries a maximum penalty of life imprisonment while the second, when tried on indictment, carries a maximum penalty of five years imprisonment (see Schedule 1). At the same time, in the context of causing "personal harm", the draft code does not distinguish between cases of intention and cases of recklessness, and both of them are included within the same offence (clause 72) which carries, when tried on indictment, a maximum penalty of 3 years imprisonment. It should also be noted that the principle mentioned here in the text was discussed earlier in this book in another context. See supra, chapter 7, text following note 52.

8   The answer to the question concerning the degree of culpability present in cases of oblique intention may depend, for example, on the empirical data concerning the typical motives of those who act, in the context of the offence under discussion, in circumstances of foresight of certainty.

9   The conclusion that cases of oblique intention form an intermediate set of cases in the context of a certain offence may be reached in two different situations. The first situation is when the degree of culpability in most cases of oblique intention is higher than in most cases of recklessness and lower than in most cases of direct intention. The second situation is when the number of actors who deserve a harsher punishment than, for example, 10 years imprisonment, is greater among those who act with oblique intention than among reckless actors, but lower than among those who act with direct intention. Of course it may also be the case that in a certain context oblique intention will form an intermediate category in terms of the two situations described here.

10   He may also decide, as was explained, to divide some offences into three sub-categories.

11   For a similar point in another context see supra, chapter 6, at note 23.

12   See supra section 7.2. Only if we define murder by using a moral formula may it be appropriate to consider setting a mandatory sentence for this offence (see supra section 8.2.3).

13   See supra, chapter 7, at note 50. It should also be noted that if the legislator decides to only have one offence for both reckless and intentional killings, he may still provide that the maximum penalty for certain defined categories of killing (for example, for killing by reckless driving) will be lower than the regular maximum penalty for causing death. See supra, chapter 8, at note 31. As was said there, the same technique may also apply in the context of other offences.

Of course the technique of providing by statute that in certain defined cases the maximum penalty will be lower than in other cases may also be adopted if the legislator decides to grade some offences based on the distinction between intention and recklessness. For example, in the context of homicide, the legislator may provide that the maximum penalty for causing death purposely will be life imprisonment and the maximum penalty for reckless killing will be, say, 15 years imprisonment. And he may also provide that in cases of, for example, provocation or excessive self-defence, the actor who kills purposely will be convicted of the lesser offence. Of course since we are speaking here of maximum penalties, and since the boundaries of the categories of provocation or excessive self-defence are vague, much can be said for refraining from enacting such "specific defences" and for leaving it to the sentencer to take the mitigating circumstances of provocation or excessive self-defence into account in the sentencing process. See the recommendations made in Law Reform Commission of Canada, Working Paper 33, *Homicide* (1984). The Commission recommends distinguishing between an offence of "intentional homicide" and an offence of "reckless homicide" and providing for a higher maximum penalty for the former than for the latter. The Commission also recommends that if this scheme is adopted there be no specific defences of provocation and excessive self-defence. It explains that the removal of the minimum penalty from intentional homicide "would obviate the need for special rules on excess force in self-defence, provocation and infanticide. Instead of burdening the judge and jury with technical, complex rules of law, because of the fixed penalty for murder, we would allow the judge to take account of all such matters flexibly in sentencing ..." (ibid., pp. 69-70). But note that the Commission also recommends enactment of a crime of first degree intentional homicide that will carry a minimum penalty. See ibid., pp. 78-83.

The main argument for enacting defences for persons who act in circumstances such as provocation or excessive self-defence, in the context of crimes which carry maximum penalties, seems to be that the defences will protect them from excessively harsh sentencers. Since the boundaries of defences like provocation and excessive self-defence are vague and their application to concrete cases involves, in many cases, the exercise of moral evaluation and discretion, this argument is more convincing in the context of countries with a jury system. For it may be said that in countries with a jury system, the legislator may want the jury to decide about the moral issues raised in cases of provocation and excessive self-defence; and in appropriate cases to limit the discretion of the judge by convicting the defendant of the lesser offence (thereby protecting him). See the view adopted in a report of the New South Wales Law Reform Commission according to which, in spite of the abolition of the mandatory penalty for murder in New South Wales, there is no room to abolish the defence of provocation. The report says, inter alia, that the defence of provocation "remains necessary as a means of involving the community, as represented by the jury, in the process of determining the degree of an accused's culpability according to his or her loss of self-control in response to provocation". See: New South Wales Law Reform Commission, Report 83, *Partial Defences to Murder: Provocation and Infanticide* (1997) 28.

14   Recall that the discussion in the text proceeds on the assumption that there is no mandatory penalty for murder.

15   See supra, chapter 7, note 50.

16   See supra section 8.2.3.

17   Against the argument regarding the cost entailed with regard to very heinous reckless killers who will not receive the punishment they deserve, one may suggest that both offences of murder (intended killing) and manslaughter (reckless killing) carry the same maximum penalty (e.g., life imprisonment), so that the distinction between the two will only reside on the expressive plane. Cf. Ashworth (1990) 78.

18 Cf. Criminal Law Reform Committee, New Zealand *Report on Culpable Homicide* (1976) p. 4; Wells (1978) 671.
19 A possible answer to this argument may be that if we do not have two separate offences, we will not be able to impose a special stigma on anybody. Since the same offence will include both intentional and reckless killings, the result will be that in *many* cases people convicted of this offence will not be particularly heinous. Therefore, a conviction of this offence will no longer carry a special stigma. But if we have a separate offence for intended killings, then most of the actors convicted of this offence will be very heinous (because of the correlation assumed here), so that a conviction of this offence will impose a special stigma on the offender. But the public will still recognise those exceptional cases of intended killings in which the actor does not deserve the special stigma and will consequently refrain from branding them with this stigma. If this is the case, the problem of imposing a stigma on an offender who does not deserve it is solved.
20 It seems that if we think that stigma is a very serious matter and if we think that the criminal law should perform the expressive role mentioned in the text, the preferred way will be to adopt a moral formula. See supra section 8.2.3 and infra section 9.5.2.
21 The assumption here is that including both intention and recklessness within the same offence of unlawful killing will not give rise to a situation in which all those who cause death (purposely or recklessly) will receive the stigma "very heinous killer". This is a very reasonable assumption, as was explained above in this section. It should also be added that if the legislator wants to distinguish, within the law of homicide, between intention and recklessness for reasons related to the maximum penalties (and not to the stigma), but he is concerned about the problem of stigma discussed here, and if he thinks that the special stigma depends on using the term "murder" as the label of the higher offence, he may solve the problem by dropping the word "murder" from the code, and using another name for the higher offence. For example, he may distinguish between the crime of "intentional killing" and "reckless killing". Cf. Law Reform Commission of Canada, Working Paper 33, *Homicide* (1984) 74.
22 The discussion in chapter 8 assumed that the distinction between intention and recklessness cannot reflect a distinction between different degrees of culpability, and it weighed the option of using a moral formula against that of having one offence for all cases of intention and recklessness. The discussion that will take place here weighs the option of the moral formula against that of distinguishing between intention and recklessness, and it assumes that this last mentioned option has merit because there is a correlation, in actual cases, between intention and higher degrees of culpability, on the one hand, and between recklessness and lower degrees of culpability, on the other. (For purposes of the present discussion it will not matter whether the correlation is based on a significant intrinsic difference between intention and recklessness or on an empirical correlation between intention and factors that increase the degree of moral culpability of the actor, like bad motives.)
23 This conclusion is even more justified in countries without a jury system. See supra, chapter 8, note 23.
24 One might raise the point made supra at note 6 about the chilling effect as a further point in favour of the first method since under the second method a reckless actor may be convicted of the higher offence.
25 Even if there are some defences to murder (like provocation) there will still be actors who cause death purposely in circumstances which do not fall within the confined boundaries of such defences but who nonetheless do not deserve the stigma of "murderer".

26 The argument here was articulated on the assumption that the legislator sees particular importance in imposing a special stigma on the most heinous of killers. If this is not the case, we may still argue for the moral formula by saying that even if our only purpose in grading homicide is to distinguish between different maximum penalties, still a by-product of the grading is that a special stigma will be imposed on every offender convicted of the higher offence, hence we should prefer using a moral formula over distinguishing between intention and recklessness. But if this is the suggested basis for using a moral formula, we may respond by suggesting that the label of "murder" be removed and that the higher offence be called "intentional killing". (This response proceeds on the assumption that the special stigma is connected to the word "murder" and that it will not attach to a new offence of "intentional killing". See supra note 21.) Another option is, of course, to prefer having only one offence in the area of homicide for all reckless and intentional killings (see supra the text accompanying note 21), but this entails the drawback that reckless killers will be left without protection from excessively harsh sentencers. In any case, the argument for using a moral formula is stronger if we assume that the legislator has an interest in imposing a special stigma upon the most heinous of killers.

27 A similar point was made supra in section 8.2.3, where I suggested that, even if we prefer, within the context of other offences, to include all cases of intention and recklessness within the same offence, it may be argued that in the context of homicide we should distinguish between different degrees of homicide (by using the moral formula) because of the desire to impose a special stigma on the most heinous of killers. It should also be noted that even if the moral formula is adopted the legislator may still provide that people who act in certain defined circumstances will not be convicted of the higher offence but only of the lesser one. See supra section 8.2.3. And see there also the point that if the legislator adopts the idea of using a moral formula in the context of homicide, then the argument against having a mandatory sentence for murder is weakened.

28 First, even if one accepts the importance of stigma, we may think that the arguments mentioned in section 9.5.1 against using a moral formula outweigh the advantages of adopting this method (see also chapter 8, at note 27). Second, one may deny the importance of stigma or deny that the criminal law should be used for expressive goals (as for the problem that grading offences based on the distinction between intention and recklessness will, as a by-product, stigmatise all offenders convicted of the higher offence as very heinous killers, a possible solution is to define the offences without using the word "murder". See supra note 21). Third, one may deny that stigma is totally dependent on the offence of which the accused is convicted but claim that the public judges the accused based on the details of the case and perhaps also on the sentence imposed on him, so that even if we define "murder" as including all cases of intended killings, the public will nonetheless refrain from relating to every person convicted of this offence as it relates to typical actors who cause death purposely who indeed deserve the stigma of a "very heinous killer" (see supra note 19).

29 One might suggest that the problem can be solved by enacting specific defences like provocation. But it is not possible to comprehensively define, in terms which do not involve a value judgment in their application, the cases in which the actor will not deserve the stigma of "murderer".

30 If the legislator adopts such a scheme he will also have to decide whether to enact specific defences for actors who cause death purposely but do not deserve the stigma of a "murderer" (like the defence of provocation), or to refrain from enacting such

defences, given that the jury will still have the discretion not to pass a murder conviction in appropriate cases. And see supra note 27, and supra chapter 8 at note 31.

31 Cf. Pillsbury (1998) chapter 7.

Chapter 10

Conclusions

In Part One of this book I have discussed the question whether the legislator should grade offences based on the distinction between intention and recklessness. A further question that was dealt with was: What should a legislator who grades offences based on the mentioned distinction do concerning cases of oblique intention? In this chapter I would like to summarise briefly the main conclusions of the discussion.

10.1

10.1.1

The idea of grading offences based on the distinction between intention and recklessness is a common one, and it is generally justified by the claim that a person who causes a bad result purposely is more blameworthy than one who causes the same result recklessly, and hence he deserves a higher punishment. In chapter 2, I challenged this justification by showing that there are cases in which a person who causes a bad result recklessly is more blameworthy than one who causes the same result purposely. Then I suggested that an inquiry be undertaken as to whether when all other things, *including the motives,* are equal, causing a result purposely is more blameworthy then causing it recklessly. This suggestion was based on the assumption that only if we believe that when all other things (including the motives) are equal, the actor who causes the result purposely is more blameworthy than the reckless actor, will we have a justification for grading offences based on the distinction between intention and recklessness.[1]

The suggested inquiry, and discussions about its implications for the issue of oblique intention, were carried out in chapters 3-6. The discussion in these chapters showed that the answer to the question whether when all other things (including the motives) are equal, the actor who causes the result purposely is more blameworthy than the reckless actor, is not simple, and that reasonable people may disagree about it. I claimed that if the legislator thinks that in such a case there is no difference in culpability, then he should not grade any offence based on the distinction between intention and recklessness but include both intention and recklessness in the same offence. In this case, the question what to do concerning cases of oblique intention will simply not arise.

But what should the legislator do if he thinks that when all other things (including the motives) are equal, the actor who causes the result purposely is more blameworthy than the reckless actor? In chapters 3-6 I assumed that in this case he has a good reason to grade offences based on the distinction between intention and recklessness. But then in chapter 7 I challenged this assumption, pointing out that many factors determine the degree of culpability of an actor (like his motives, the degree of the harm he caused, etc.) and that these factors (together with some other factors not related to the actor's degree of blameworthiness) are all taken into account at the sentencing stage. In reality, cases differ from one another in various aspects, and this raises the question whether there is a justification for isolating the factor of intention versus recklessness from all the factors that affect the appropriate punishment and using it as a basis for grading offences. My answer to this question was that only if the difference in culpability between the actor who causes the result purposely and the reckless actor (when all other things, including the motives, are equal) is sufficiently large (relative to the other factors that determine the degree of blameworthiness) – will we have a reasonable basis for grading offences based on the distinction between intention and recklessness. The answer to the question whether this difference (assuming that such a difference exists) is relatively large is not simple, and reasonable people may disagree about it. My own feeling is that even if there is a difference, it is not large enough to justify grading offences based on the mentioned distinction. A legislator who feels the same way would not grade any offence based on the distinction between intention and recklessness, but would rather include both of them within the same offence (see section 7.1.4).[2] This also means that the question what to do concerning cases of oblique intention will simply not arise.[3]

The conclusion reached here applies also in the context of homicide, so that, according to this line of argument, reckless and intended killings should be included within the same offence of "unlawful killing", that will only carry a maximum penalty (see section 7.2).

10.1.2

If the distinction between intention and recklessness cannot do the work of distinguishing between different degrees of culpability, then the possibility arises that the legislator should prefer the option of grading offences by using a moral formula over that of having only one offence for all cases of intention and recklessness. This question was discussed in chapter 8. There I discussed the arguments for and against using a moral formula, and showed that it is not easy to choose between the two mentioned options. I also pointed to the possibility that the decision should be country dependent. That said, however, I expressed my inclination against using a moral formula, and in favour of enacting one offence for all cases of intention and recklessness (see sections 8.2.1 and 8.2.2).[4] However, the case of homicide might form an exception to this inclination. It may be argued that society should impose a special stigma upon the most heinous of killers by convicting them of a specific offence reserved for such killers. Therefore, we might want to distinguish between "murder" and "manslaughter" by using a moral formula. I discussed this argument in section 8.2.3 and said that after all there is much to be said against using a moral formula (and preferring it over the option of enacting only one offence) even in this context, but I added that the case for using a moral formula is much stronger in the context of homicide than in other contexts.

10.1.3

Until chapter 9 the discussion assumed that if we think that when all other things (including the motives) are equal, there is no difference in culpability between intention and recklessness, then there is no justification for grading any offence based on the distinction between these two states of mind. But in chapter 9 I suggested that even assuming that there is no difference in culpability between intention and recklessness when all other things (including the motives) are equal (or that there is only a small difference between them), there may still be a potential justification for grading *certain* offences based on the distinction between intention and recklessness. The suggested potential justification is based on the possibility that in the context of a certain offence a correlation will exist between intention and higher degrees of culpability, on the one hand, and recklessness and lower degrees of culpability, on the other. This correlation may exist in the context of a certain offence for various reasons. For example, it may be the case that in the context of a certain offence, the motives of those who cause the result purposely are generally worse than the motives of those who cause the same result recklessly, and therefore those who cause the result purposely are *generally* more culpable than the reckless ones. And if such a correlation exists in the context of a certain offence, and if it is significant enough, then we will have a good reason for distinguishing in the context of this offence between intention and recklessness, and providing for a higher maximum penalty for causing the result purposely than for causing it recklessly.

Now, even in the context of an offence in which the said correlation exists and is significant, arguments may still be adduced against adopting a grading scheme instead of enacting one offence for all cases of intention and recklessness. The arguments for and against grading (in the context of an offence in which a significant correlation exists) were discussed in section 9.1.2, and it seems that in such a context it may be reasonable to distinguish between intention and recklessness. The final decision concerning any specific offence under discussion will depend on the data relevant to this offence, and may be country dependent (see ibid.). However, it should be emphasised that the mentioned justification is only a "potential" one, as it might be the case that in no offence will the above correlation exist or be significant enough, and because even in the context of an offence in which the correlation exists and is significant, the arguments against grading might outweigh the arguments in favour thereof (see ibid.).[5]

The decision whether to divide a specific result crime into two sub-categories based on the distinction between intention and recklessness on the basis of the mentioned justification depends upon the empirical data relevant to the specific offence under discussion. The relevant data (for example, the typical motives that motivate people to act) vary from offence to offence. Therefore a rational legislator may legitimately decide to grade some offences based on the distinction between intention and recklessness (on the basis of the mentioned justification) and at the same time not to distinguish, in the context of other offences, between intention and recklessness (see section 9.1.3). In addition, the legislator may reasonably decide that the mentioned correlation will not lead to the adoption of a grading scheme in the context of offences that do not carry high maximum penalties (see ibid.).

10.1.4

If the legislator decides to distinguish between intention and recklessness in the context of a certain offence on the basis of the mentioned justification, he will have to decide what to do concerning cases of oblique intention. The decision should depend on whether the empirical correlation that exists in the context of the specific offence between direct intention and higher degrees of culpability also exists between oblique intention and higher degrees of culpability, or whether oblique intention, like recklessness, correlates with lower degrees of culpability. The result of this assessment will dictate whether oblique intention should be included within the higher offence or within the lower offence (see section 9.2). It may also be the case that cases of oblique intention will form an intermediate case between direct intention and recklessness insofar as the correlation with degrees of culpability is concerned. If this is the case in the context of a certain offence, then the legislator will have to decide whether to include cases of oblique intention within the higher offence or within the lower one. He may also decide, in such a case, to divide the offence into three sub-categories (see ibid.).

It is also possible that the law of cases of oblique intention should not be the same for all intention crimes, but should vary from one intention crime to another. For under the mentioned justification for distinguishing between intention and recklessness, the decision regarding cases of oblique intention depends to a large extent on empirical data that may vary from one offence to another. Therefore, it may be the case that in the context of certain offences oblique intention should be included within the higher offence, whereas in the context of other offences it should be included within the lower offence (and it may also be the case that in the context of some other offences oblique intention will form an intermediate case). See section 9.2.

10.1.5

If the legislator thinks that in the context of homicide a significant correlation exists between intention and higher degrees of culpability, on the one hand, and between recklessness and lower degrees of culpability, on the other, then he should decide whether to distinguish in the context of homicide between intention and recklessness and to provide for a higher maximum penalty for causing death purposely than for causing it recklessly or whether (in spite of the mentioned correlation) to only have one offence for both categories of causing death. As was mentioned in section 10.1.3, the two methods are reasonable (in the context of other offences in which the correlation exists), and the same can basically be said concerning homicide.

But one might suggest that dividing an offence into sub-categories is more important in the context of homicide, because of the stigma, than in other contexts, so that even a legislator who decides not to grade offences based on the distinction between intention and recklessness (even when the mentioned correlation exists) should distinguish between intention and recklessness in the context of homicide. This argument was discussed in section 9.4 and the discussion shows that this argument is not a conclusive one and that a reasonable legislator may prefer not to distinguish between intention and recklessness even in the context of homicide.[6]

However, in the context of homicide, the legislator should also consider the option of using a moral formula. One may claim that the legislator should distinguish between the most heinous of killers and other killers by imposing a special stigma on the former, and that even if in the context of homicide a correlation exists between intention and higher degrees of culpability, on the one hand, and between recklessness and lower degrees of culpability, on the other, still the best way to ensure that all (and only) the most heinous of killers be the object of the special stigma reserved for the most heinous of killers is to use a moral formula.[7] This argument was discussed in section 9.5.2. The discussion showed that this argument is not a conclusive one, but recognised that the case for using a moral formula is much stronger in the context of homicide than in other contexts.[8]

10.2

10.2.1

As I mentioned in section 10.1.1 my own feeling is that even if a difference in culpability exists between intention and recklessness when all other things (including the motives) are equal, this difference is not large enough to justify grading offences based on the distinction between intention and recklessness.[9]

But a reasonable legislator may be of the view that there *is* a large difference in culpability between intention and recklessness, when all other things (including the motives) are equal, and such a view may reasonably lead him to grade offences based on the distinction between intention and recklessness.

It should be noted that even a legislator who believes that when all other things are equal there is a *large* difference in culpability between intention and recklessness may legitimately decide *not* to grade any offence based on the mentioned distinction. After all, in reality, cases differ from one another in many aspects that affect the actor's degree of moral culpability, so that in reality there are cases of causing a result recklessly in which the degree of culpability of the actor is higher than in some cases of causing the same result purposely. Therefore, even those who embrace the view that there is a large difference in culpability between intention and recklessness should admit that sometimes a reckless actor deserves a higher punishment than certain actors who cause the result purposely. Hence, a reasonable legislator may decide not to grade any offence based on the mentioned distinction, even if he believes that the difference in culpability between intention and recklessness is large (see section 9.3). However, a reasonable legislator may think that the above mentioned large difference in culpability justifies grading offences based on the distinction between intention and recklessness (see section 9.3).

10.2.2

If a legislator decides to grade some offences based on the distinction between intention and recklessness on the basis of the justification mentioned in section 10.2.1, what should he do concerning cases of oblique intention? I suggested that such a legislator should articulate to himself why, in his view, there is a difference in culpability between direct intention and recklessness and, in the light of his answer to this question, decide what to do concerning cases of oblique intention. If the legislator thinks that an actor who acts with direct intention is more culpable than the reckless one because of the intrinsic importance of the desire to cause the result (of acting in order to cause the result) then it will be reasonable for him to include oblique intention within the lower offence (with recklessness), as the element of desire is also absent in cases of oblique intention. If, on the other hand, the legislator thinks that an actor who acts with direct intention is more culpable than the reckless one because the former, unlike the reckless actor, chooses to cause the proscribed result, then it will be reasonable for such a legislator to include cases of oblique intention within the higher offence (with direct intention) because in the case of oblique intention (as in the case of direct intention) the actor chooses to cause the proscribed result.[10] See section 5.4.

In chapter 6, I added that even a legislator who is of the view that the element of desire increases the actor's degree of culpability (and consequently should think that causing a result with direct intention is more culpable than causing it with oblique intention) may still think that cases of oblique intention form an intermediate case between direct intention and recklessness (see section 6.3).[11] If he adopts this position, he may reasonably decide to include this intermediate case within the higher offence, but he may also reasonably decide to include it within the lower offence, or to divide certain offences into three sub-categories: one for direct intention, the second for oblique intention and the third for recklessness (ibid.).

10.2.3

The justification discussed here for grading offences based on the distinction between intention and recklessness is not based on the specific factual data of certain offences. Rather, it is theoretical in nature. This means that, in principle, it can apply to all result crimes. Actually, at first glance it may be thought that a legislator who grades some result crimes on the basis of the present justification, and at the same time decides, in the context of some other result crimes, not to distinguish between intention and recklessness, is doing something illogical. But this is not necessarily the case. As I explained in section 7.3, a reasonable legislator may (but not must) think that the present justification for grading offences based on the distinction between intention and recklessness applies (from a theoretical point of view) only in the context of certain kinds of offences: for example, only to offences that deal with the most serious of moral wrongs; or, only to offences against the person. In addition, it was explained there that even a legislator who thinks that from a theoretical point of view the present justification for grading offences may apply to all (or most) result crimes, may have good practical reasons to confine the grading scheme based on the present justification to the context of offences that carry high penalties.[12]

10.2.4

A legislator who accepts the validity of the present justification for grading offences may, in addition, accept the validity of the justification for grading offences that was developed in chapter 9. This may lead him to grade some offences by distinguishing between intention and recklessness on the basis of the present justification, and to grade others in the same manner on the basis of the justification developed in chapter 9 (see section 9.3). This may (but not must) lead him to treat cases of oblique intention, in the context of the first group of offences, differently than in the context of the second group of offences (ibid.).

In addition, a legislator who accepts the validity of both justifications may think that both justifications apply in the context of a certain offence, so that in such a context the case for grading will be stronger than in other contexts (ibid.).

10.2.5

As stated above, a legislator who thinks that when all other things are equal a person who causes a result purposely is much more culpable than a person who causes the same result recklessly, may reasonably grade offences based on the distinction between intention and recklessness, but he may also reasonably decide not to grade offences based on this distinction, in spite of the mentioned difference in culpability. The same basically holds for homicide. As for the questions whether even a legislator who prefers not to grade offences based on the above distinction should do so in the context of homicide because of the special issue of stigma and whether a legislator who decides to grade some offences based on the mentioned distinction should prefer in the context of homicide to grade the offence by using a moral formula (because of the special issue of stigma) – what was said concerning these questions in the context of the justification developed in chapter 9 can also apply in the context of the present justification (see sections 10.1.5, 9.4 and 9.5.2).

Notes

1   The discussion in this book is confined to the idea of distinguishing between intention and recklessness on the basis of justifications related to degrees of blameworthiness. It does not deal with other potential justifications for distinguishing between them.

2   The conclusion here is based on the discussion concerning the potential theoretical justification for grading offences conducted in chapters 3-7, which did not depend on specific factual data regarding any specific offence. But in chapter 9, I discussed an

alternative justification for grading offences based on the distinction between intention and recklessness, a justification that does depend on factual data of certain offences. This justification is summarised below in section 10.1.3.

3   However, I am aware of the possibility that a reasonable legislator will think that there *is* a relatively large difference in culpability between causing a result purposely and causing the same result recklessly (when all other things, including the motives, are equal), and I would like to summarise my thoughts about how such a legislator should deal with the issue of intention. This summary will not take place here but infra in section 10.2, so as not to interrupt the present summary, which is based on the assumption that the mentioned difference (if such a difference exists at all) is not large enough.

4   I also added (in section 8.2.2) that if a legislator decides to grade some offences by using a moral formula, I think that he should limit the use of this method to the context of offences that carry high maximum penalties.

5   In section 9.5.1 I weighed the option of grading offences on the basis of the mentioned justification (in the context of offences to which this justification applies) against the option of using a moral formula. My inclination was to prefer the first option.

6   Actually there is even a possible (but not conclusive) argument according to which concerns regarding the issue of stigma may reasonably lead to a decision not to distinguish between intention and recklessness in the homicide context, even if we are ready to distinguish between them in the context of other offences. See section 9.4.

7   In the context of other offences I incline to suggest that the legislator not use a moral formula. See section 9.5.1.

8   I also raised (in section 9.5.2) the possibility of providing that murder be established only where the actor intends to cause death *and* manifests in the action a (very) high degree of culpability.

9   Hereinafter, the discussion in this chapter will not refer to the potential justification for distinguishing between intention and recklessness in certain offences developed in chapter 9 (except for in sections 10.2.4 and 10.2.5).

10   If the legislator thinks that what makes an actor who acts with direct intention more culpable than the reckless one is that the action of the former is not accompanied by a hope that the result will not ensue, then he should include oblique intention within the higher offence. But to be consistent such a legislator should also include within the higher offence those reckless actors who acted with indifference with respect to the proscribed result (unless we accept the argument that practical problems involved in proving indifference may justify removing indifference from the higher offence). See chapter 5, at note 22 (and see there for a further option).

11   As was explained there, the view that cases of oblique intention form an intermediate case may be justified in two alternative ways: One is to rely on the idea that within cases of recklessness the degree of culpability varies in accordance with the degree of probability, and the other is to rely on the idea that in cases of oblique intention the actor chooses to cause the result.

12   For the possibility that a legislator who decides to grade some offences following the present justification may decide not to treat oblique intention in the same way in the context of all of these offences, see section 7.3.

PART TWO

Chapter 11

A Possible Justification for Enacting Basic Crimes of Intention: The Threshold of Culpability Requirement

11.1   Introduction

In chapter 2 I claimed that the idea of grading offences based on the distinction between intention and recklessness seems more understandable than that of enacting "basic crimes of intention". The discussion in Part One of this book was confined to the idea of grading offences based on the mentioned distinction. In Part Two, I will discuss the idea of enacting basic crimes of intention.

In chapter 2 I explained that even if we assume that intention is more culpable than recklessness, the idea of enacting "basic crimes of intention" still seems highly problematic, because in the context of those crimes acting recklessly (with regard to the actual or potential result) does not establish criminal responsibility at all.[1] As was explained in the aforementioned chapter, assuming that the main purpose of the criminal law is to protect against harms by general deterrence, it seems that recklessness should suffice for conviction of "basic crimes", for the legislator should not only deter people who are going to cause harm purposely but also people who are going to take unjustified risks of causing harm. If, for example, in a certain country there is no offence of causing bodily harm recklessly (but only an offence of causing such a harm intentionally) then the criminal law of that country does not act as a deterrent against acting recklessly as to causing bodily harm, and consequently the protection afforded to bodily integrity is deficient. The same seems to hold, at least at first glance, for other offences which contain an element of actual or potential result. Of course, even if the main purpose of the criminal law is general deterrence, justice and fairness require that we not convict and punish morally innocent people, even if doing so would contribute in some way to an increase in general deterrence; but it seems that the reckless actor, who knowingly takes an unjustified risk that the result will ensue, is sufficiently morally blameworthy to permit conviction and punishment for the purpose of general deterrence.

The idea of having basic crimes of intention is highly problematic, then, even assuming that intention is more culpable than recklessness, and it is perfectly reasonable to have a criminal code with no basic crimes of intention at all.[2]

In Part Two of this book I will raise and examine possible justifications for enacting basic crimes of intention. These justifications will be based on the assumption that "intention is more culpable than recklessness" and will endeavour to explain why in certain contexts this difference in culpability may, in spite of the above argument, justify the enactment of basic crimes of intention. Of course, if we take the view that there is no difference in culpability between intention and recklessness, then there can be no justification (based on degrees of blameworthiness) for enacting basic crimes of intention (just as there can be no such justification, under the mentioned view, for grading offences based on the distinction between intention and recklessness).[3] Hereinafter, the discussion will proceed on the assumption that "intention is more culpable than recklessness".

The discussion of the first justification will begin without analysing and elaborating upon the exact meaning of the proposition that "intention is more culpable than recklessness". Although the discussion in Part One of the book suggested that this proposition can be understood in different ways, an analysis thereof for purposes of the suggested justification will be left until later (section 11.5).

It should also be noted that, as in Part One, the discussion in Part Two will be confined to considerations directly related to degrees of blameworthiness. Possible justifications for enacting basic crimes of intention that are not directly related to degrees of blameworthiness will not be discussed in this book.

11.2   The Principle of a Threshold of Culpability

In sections 2.1 and 11.1, I mentioned the common idea that even if the main purpose of the criminal law is general deterrence, justice and fairness require that we not convict and punish morally innocent people (even if doing so would contribute to an increase in general deterrence). The idea is that even if the justification of punishment lies in the desire to prevent and diminish crime, there is also a limiting condition: that only culpable people may be convicted. This idea may explain, for example, the requirement that the actor act with a culpable state of mind as a condition for criminal liability.

But should any amount of culpability suffice to permit the imposition of criminal liability? Perhaps not. Certain doctrines of the criminal law seem to be based on the idea that a minimal amount of blameworthiness is required to permit the imposition of criminal liability. The idea is that a threshold of blameworthiness must be met to permit the imposition of criminal liability, and that people who are culpable to a degree that lies below this threshold should not be convicted and punished. We can call this idea "the principle of a threshold of culpability".

It seems that the existence or the scope of some criminal law excuses can be explained by this principle. The duress defence, for example, seems to encompass not only cases in which the actor is not culpable at all, but also cases in which the degree of his culpability is too low to permit conviction and punishment.[4]

The mentioned principle may also explain the Model Penal Code's definition of recklessness. The Model Penal Code provides that when the culpability sufficient to establish a material element of an offence is not prescribed by law, such an element is established if a person acts purposely, knowingly or recklessly with respect thereto.[5] This provision is based on the assumption that in most of the criminal offences in the Code, recklessness should be required and sufficient for conviction. Recklessness is defined in section 2.02(2)(c) of the Code, which provides: "A person acts recklessly with respect to a material element of an offense when he consciously disregards a substantial and unjustifiable risk that the material element exists or will result from his conduct. The risk must be of such a nature and degree that, considering the nature and purpose of the actor's conduct and the circumstances known to him, its disregard involves a gross deviation from the standard of conduct that a law-abiding person would observe in the actor's situation". According to this definition, the fact that a person knowingly takes a substantial and unjustifiable risk that, for example, a proscribed result will ensue, does not suffice to establish recklessness with regard to that result. In order to establish recklessness, the prosecution must also show a *gross* deviation, in the case at hand, from the standard of conduct of a law-abiding person. Since many of the "basic offences" in the Code cannot be established unless at least recklessness (as opposed to negligence) is proven, the requirement of a *gross* deviation from the standard of conduct of a law-abiding person (as part of the definition of recklessness) is relevant for many "basic offences" in the Code.[6] It seems, then, that this requirement stems from the view that (in those offences) even the conscious taking of a substantial and unjustifiable risk is not *sufficiently* culpable to permit the imposition of criminal liability, unless it is done in circumstances constitutive of a *gross* deviation from the standard of conduct of a law-abiding person.[7] Such a view seems to reflect an acceptance of "the principle of a threshold of culpability" mentioned above. However, it should be noted that in many countries the definition of recklessness does not contain an element of "gross deviation". In England, for example, recklessness with regard to a consequence exists when the actor foresees that there is a risk that the consequence may possibly result from his act, and it is unreasonable for him to take the risk of it occurring.[8] This means that any conscious taking of an unjustified risk suffices to establish recklessness.[9]

The principle of a threshold of culpability may also explain one of the alternative grounds for the *de minimis* defence found in the Model Penal Code. According to section 2.12(2) of the Code, the court shall dismiss a prosecution if it finds that the conduct of the defendant did not cause or threaten the harm or evil sought to be prevented by the law defining the offence or "did so only to an extent too trivial to warrant the condemnation of conviction". The rule that a person who causes a harm which is "too trivial to warrant the condemnation of conviction" should not be convicted may be understood as being based on the idea that although this person is culpable, he is not *sufficiently* culpable to warrant a conviction.

Finally, certain types of actions that constitute moral wrongs (including some that cause harm or hurt to others) do not constitute criminal offences in many countries. This is the case, for example, concerning such acts as telling lies, breaking promises, breaching contracts, insulting people, hurting the feelings of people, and taking something from another person (without his permission) for several hours.[10] A possible explanation of this phenomenon is that certain moral wrongs are not *sufficiently* wrongful or serious, and therefore those who perform the actions that constitute those wrongs are not *sufficiently* culpable to warrant a criminal conviction.[11]

The above discussion shows that the principle of a threshold of culpability finds expression in certain contexts of the criminal law. That said, I am not suggesting that current criminal law is always consistent with this principle.[12] For our discussion, suffice it to say that in certain contexts in the criminal law, this principle does find expression.

What is the rationale for the requirement of a threshold of culpability? Why does *any* amount of moral culpability not suffice for the imposition of criminal liability? A possible answer would be that people who are only slightly culpable do not deserve the harsh penalties that are sometimes imposed on criminal offenders. But this answer seems problematic where the criminal law provides for only maximum penalties for all (or most) criminal offences, as the judge is given discretion concerning the type and quantum of the punishment to be imposed, and if the offender is only slightly culpable, and hence only deserves a lenient punishment, the judge may actually impose a lenient punishment which is proportional to his degree of culpability, such as a very low fine, for example. Therefore, it is more convincing to base an argument in favour of "the principle of a threshold of culpability" by referring to the condemnatory aspect of a criminal conviction. The argument may be based on the claim that a criminal conviction does not only constitute a necessary stage before a punishment can be imposed but that it also operates as a form of public censure and condemnation of the accused and his action, and of imposing on him the stigma of a criminal offender, in conjunction with the view that a person who is only slightly culpable does not deserve this condemnation and stigma. This justification need not deny that there are degrees in condemnation and stigma; but it does assume that every (or almost every) conviction carries with it a basic minimal amount of condemnation and stigma, and that even this amount of condemnation and stigma is not deserved by those who are only slightly culpable. The fact that a lenient punishment may be imposed, therefore, cannot address the problem presented by a case in which a person is condemned and stigmatised to a degree that he does not deserve.[13]

It may be added further that a conviction may have various adverse consequences, aside from the punishment which follows – even if the punishment is lenient. As Wasik says, " ... it is now very well accepted that there are numerous adverse consequences of a defendant's criminal conviction which fall outside the official legal sanction imposed by the court ... the registering of a conviction may bring with it certain disqualifications or prohibitions such as the holding of licenses under betting or gaming laws, holding public office, or keeping foster children. In particular, it will be more difficult to obtain or hold down employment".[14] These adverse consequences add weight to the argument that a slight amount of culpability should not suffice to establish criminal liability.

We should also remember the stress, shame and embarrassment suffered by the accused (and his innocent family) by the investigation and questioning, the prosecution, and the trial itself (and sometimes by media coverage as well).[15] This distress is not redressed by the fact that at the conclusion of the trial a lenient sentence is imposed, and it can be strongly argued that a person who is only slightly culpable does not deserve to undergo such grief. If this is the case, an effort should be made to draft legal rules in such a way that reduces the chances that people who are only slightly culpable will be questioned, prosecuted and tried.[16]

Finally, in spite of what is said above against basing "the principle of a threshold of culpability" on the harshness of the penalties available in the criminal law, it seems that this factor may nevertheless, in certain contexts, add weight to the arguments in favour of the mentioned principle. For the argument made above, to the effect that if the accused is only slightly culpable, the judge will only impose the lenient punishment he deserves, would be convincing if we could guarantee that an offender who is only slightly culpable will not get a harsher penalty than that which he deserves. But since judges have discretion in sentencing, we cannot be so sure. Therefore, if we draft legal rules in such a way that renders it possible for people who are only slightly culpable to be convicted of offences with serious maximum penalties, we expose some people who are only slightly culpable to the risk that they will receive a much harsher penalty than they deserve. Although this risk will always remain to a certain degree, it may be reduced in certain contexts by drafting certain rules governing criminal responsibility in such a way that persons who are only slightly culpable will not be convicted (or prosecuted) at all. Therefore, a legislator who attaches importance to protecting defendants from excessively harsh sentencers may wish, for example, to delimit the scope of some excuses in such a way that cases of "low culpability", and not only cases with "no culpability", will give rise to a defence, or to adopt a definition of recklessness similar to that which appears in the Model Penal Code.

11.3 Acting with Recklessness in Certain Contexts is not Sufficiently Culpable

Assuming that "intention is more culpable than recklessness", the principle of a threshold of culpability may justify the enactment of certain "basic crimes of intention", based on the view that in some contexts only causing the proscribed result purposely (as opposed to recklessly) establishes the degree of blameworthiness required to permit the imposition of criminal liability.

The degree of culpability of an agent is determined by various factors. One of the most important factors is the degree of harm caused (and anticipated) by the agent. Actions can cause harm or damage to various interests. Some of these interests are considered by society to be of more importance than others, and consequently harming them is generally considered more wrongful and serious, and hence more culpable, than harming others. For example, causing harm to the body of another person is generally more serious than causing damage to the property of another, and therefore a person who causes bodily harm to another is generally considered more morally culpable than a person who causes damage to the property of another. Another factor that affects the degree of moral culpability is the mental state of the agent at the time he acts. In this respect, the present discussion proceeds on the assumption that "intention is more culpable than recklessness", so that causing a certain harm purposely is more culpable than causing it recklessly.[17]

Many interests are so important that even a person who harms them recklessly is so culpable that he deserves to be prosecuted, convicted and punished. In other words, and in terms of the "principle of a threshold of culpability", the degree of culpability established by harming these interests recklessly, reaches the threshold of culpability required for the imposition of criminal liability. This is the case, for example, with the offences of causing death or causing bodily harm. A criminal code should certainly criminalise causing death (and causing bodily harm) recklessly.

A legislator who embraces "the principle of a threshold of culpability" may think that there are some interests the relative importance of which is so low that even harming them purposely does not establish the degree of culpability required for imposing criminal liability. This may be a possible explanation why in many countries even purposely hurting the feelings of another person, for example, or purposely insulting him, does not constitute a criminal offence.

But there may be a third (and intermediate) category of interests as well. It may be the case that a legislator who accepts "the principle of a threshold of culpability" and who also thinks that "intention is more culpable than recklessness", thinks that the degree of importance of some interests does not warrant the conclusion that harming them recklessly establishes the degree of culpability required for the imposition of criminal liability, but does warrant the conclusion that harming them purposely does. Consequently, such a legislator may decide to impose criminal liability only in cases of purposely (as opposed to recklessly) causing harm to those interests. In other words, such a legislator may enact "basic crimes of intention".[18]

The above discussion suggests a possible justification for enacting certain basic crimes of intention. The justification is described in general terms; in order to enable a proper evaluation, further elaboration and analysis is required. But before I proceed in this direction, I would like to present, in the next section, some examples of "basic crimes of intention" that may be understood in light of the present suggested justification for requiring intention as a condition for criminalisation.[19]

11.4   Some Basic Crimes of Intention that May Be Explained by the Present Justification

(A) The first example is from the proposed Canadian draft Criminal Code of 1987.[20] Chapter 7 of the code deals with crimes against bodily integrity. Clause 7(2) deals with assault by harming. It provides that everyone commits a crime who harms another person purposely, recklessly or negligently. To "Harm" is defined in clause 1(2) as "to impair the body or its functions permanently or temporarily". Clause 7(1) deals with assault by touching or hurting. It provides that everyone commits a crime who touches or hurts another person without that person's consent. To "Hurt" is defined in clause 1(2) as "to inflict physical pain". No mental element is mentioned in clause 7(1). Clause 2(4)(d) of the code provides that "where the definition of a crime does not explicitly specify the requisite level of culpability, it shall be interpreted as requiring purpose". Accordingly, the offence under clause 7(1) can only be committed purposely (as opposed to recklessly).[21] Thus, only in cases of causing *harm* to the other person, does recklessness (or even negligence) suffice for criminal liability, but where there is only physical contact or force (or even physical pain), recklessness does not suffice for a conviction. Clause 7(1) is, then, a "basic crime of intention". The situation in England is different. According to current English law even recklessness as to whether force might be applied suffices to convict of battery.[22] In the same manner, according to the Draft Criminal Code for England and Wales of 1989, a person is guilty of assault if he intentionally or *recklessly* applies force to or causes an impact on the body of another without his consent.[23] The Canadian Law Reform Commission was aware of the legal situation in England,[24] but decided to require a mental state of purpose. What is the rationale for the commission's decision? A reasonable explanation may be that it believed that with regard to mere contact or hurt (as opposed to harm), the actor who is merely reckless is not sufficiently culpable to meet the "threshold of culpability" required for the imposition of criminal liability. Therefore, purpose is required. In contrast, in the case of harming another the injury is more serious, and therefore even one who acts with recklessness (or even negligence) is sufficiently culpable to be prosecuted, convicted and punished. Thus, clause 7(1) of the proposed Canadian draft Criminal Code can serve as an illustration of a "basic crime of intention" that may be explained by the present suggested justification.[25]

(B) Clause 20(1) of the proposed Canadian draft Criminal Code deals with cruelty to animals. It provides that "everyone commits a crime who unnecessarily causes injury or serious physical pain to an animal". No mental element is mentioned in the clause, which means that "purpose" is required, so that recklessness with respect to the injury or serious pain does not suffice for conviction.[26] So we have here another example of a "basic crime of intention". In contrast to the proposed Canadian offence, the Model Penal Code's offence of cruelty to animals can be established even by recklessness.[27] The Canadian commission's approach of requiring purpose may be understood as being based on the idea that the relative importance of the interest that animals not suffer injury or pain is not high, and therefore those who recklessly (as opposed to purposely) cause injury or pain to them do not reach the threshold of culpability required to permit the imposition of criminal liability.[28] If this is the explanation, then we have here another example of a "basic crime of intention" that is based on the present suggested justification.[29]

(C) Section 250.4 of the Model Penal Code deals with various types of actions which may harass another person. Subsections (1) through (5) define various actions that are criminal. According to the opening of section 250.4, engaging in any of these actions does not establish the offence unless the conduct is performed "with purpose to harass another". I will focus here on subsections (1) and (3). According to section 250.4(1), a person commits a petty misdemeanor if, with purpose to harass another, he makes a telephone call without purpose of legitimate communication. And according to section 250.4(3), a person commits a petty misdemeanor if, with purpose to harass another, he makes repeated communications anonymously or at extremely inconvenient hours, or in offensively coarse language. One may ask why the actions described at these subsections should not establish criminal liability when the agent performing them is reckless with respect to the possibility that his conduct will harass another person. A possible explanation is that the harassment caused by the mentioned actions was not considered by the drafters of the code to be a considerably serious harm,[30] and therefore they thought that one who commits such actions with only recklessness as to whether harassment will ensue from his conduct, is not sufficiently culpable to be prosecuted, convicted and punished. If this is the explanation for the purpose requirement, then this is another example of a "basic crime of intention" that is based on the present suggested justification.[31]

Before proceeding to analyse and evaluate the present suggested justification for requiring intention, I would like to point out an interesting feature of this justification. According to this justification, the rationale for removing cases of recklessness from the reach of the offences under discussion is not that in the context of these offences it is always morally (and socially) right or permissible to take conscious risks that the proscribed result will ensue. Quite the contrary: There *are* cases in which the conscious taking of the risk is unjustifiable. But despite this, the legislator decides to remove the cases of taking an unjustifiable risk from the reach of these offences, because those who take these risks are not *sufficiently* culpable, and therefore it is not appropriate to prosecute, convict and punish them. Thus, for example, taking an unjustified risk of applying force to another person (without his consent), or of causing injury or serious physical pain to animals, is morally (and socially) wrongful. Nonetheless, the Canadian proposed draft does not include such cases in the offences under discussion because (according to the present explanation) a person who engages in such actions is not considered to be *sufficiently* culpable. The same point can be made with regard to the exclusion of reckless harassment from the Model Penal Code's offences mentioned above. In this respect, there is some similarity between the present rationale for enacting "basic crimes of intention" and that which lies behind excuse defences (as opposed to justification defences). For unlike justification defences, the rationale behind excuse defences is not that the actions exempted from criminal responsibility are morally and socially right or permissible, but that in spite of the fact that those actions are morally (and socially) wrongful, there is no room for a criminal conviction due to the absence of culpability or the absence of a sufficient degree of culpability to warrant a criminal conviction.[32]

11.5   Evaluation of the Suggested Justification

The present suggested justification is based on "the principle of a threshold of culpability" and one who rejects this principle based on the view that any amount of culpability should suffice to permit the imposition of criminal liability will also reject the present justification. Thus, one may refer to the fact that many actions that are only minor wrongs are criminalised under current criminal law, simply because criminalisation is considered an efficient tool to deter people from performing these actions.[33] On this basis, one may argue that since current law ignores the principle of a threshold of culpability in some contexts, it is inconsistent to rely on this principle in other contexts. One may also argue against one of the rationales suggested above for the mentioned principle by saying, for example, that when a person is convicted, public opinion regarding him is influenced by the details of the case and by the punishment imposed, so that if in reality his culpability is low, the degree of the stigma suffered will be low as well. I will not pursue any further the discussion concerning the mentioned principle, but will assume that this principle has (and should have) a role in the criminal law and proceed in the discussion based on this assumption.

Another assumption underlying the present justification is that "intention is more culpable than recklessness". In chapter 2 I challenged the idea that causing a bad result purposely is more culpable than causing it recklessly, by bringing counter-examples in which causing a result recklessly seems to be more culpable than causing it purposely. I then suggested inquiring whether when all other things, *including the motives,* are equal, causing a result purposely is more culpable than causing it recklessly. The discussion in chapters 3-6 showed that the answer to this question is not simple and that reasonable people may disagree about it. If the legislator thinks that when all other things are equal (including the motives) there is no difference in culpability between causing a result purposely and causing it recklessly, then he should reject the present justification for enacting "basic crimes of intention" (if in the context of this justification the statement that "intention is more culpable than recklessness" only means that when all other things are equal, intention is more culpable).[34] But what about a legislator who believes that "when all other things (including the motives) are equal, causing a result purposely is more culpable than causing it recklessly"? This belief, by itself, does not justify the enactment of *basic* crimes of intention. For if the reality is that in the context of a certain offence, in many (or in a sufficient number of) cases of recklessness the degree of culpability of the actor (considering all the relevant factors that affect it) suffices for the imposition of criminal liability, then it is not justified to exempt all the reckless actors from criminal liability (in spite of the fact that when all other things are equal, those who cause the result purposely are *more* culpable than those who cause the result recklessly). So it seems that the justification suggested in this chapter for enacting "basic crimes of intention" is worth considering only with regard to offences in the context of which the reality is that (taking into account all the factors relevant to the degree of culpability) a great majority of the agents who act with recklessness with respect to the proscribed result do not reach the threshold of culpability required for the imposition of criminal liability, while many (or a sufficient number) of those who act with direct intention with respect to the result do reach this threshold.

Now, what can generate such a reality? In chapter 7, I explained that many factors determine the degree of culpability of an actor (including his motives, the specific degree of harm caused by his action, etc.) and that in reality cases differ from one another in various respects that affect the actor's degree of culpability. Given this fact, it seems to me unreasonable to assume that the reality described above – namely, that a great majority of the agents who act with recklessness with respect to the proscribed result do not reach the threshold of culpability required for the imposition of criminal liability, while many (or a sufficient number) of those who act with direct intention with respect to the result do reach this threshold – will be generated merely by the fact that when all other things are equal, "purpose is more culpable than recklessness". As I said earlier (in section 7.1.4), my own feeling is that this last mentioned difference in culpability (if it exists at all) is not relatively large. And if this is the case, it is unreasonable that it would yield by itself the result that in the context of a certain offence the reality described above will exist. But in chapter 9 I suggested that even assuming that there is no difference in culpability between intention and recklessness when all other things are equal (or that there is only a small difference between them), it may still be the case that in the context of a certain offence there will be a significant empirical correlation between intention and high degrees of culpability on the one hand, and recklessness and lower degrees of culpability, on the other. I suggested there that this correlation may exist for various reasons. For example, it may be that in the context of a certain offence, the motives of those who cause the result purposely are generally worse than the motives of those who cause the result recklessly. The discussion in chapter 9 dealt with grading offences, but a similar line of thinking to that developed there may be suggested in the present context. If in the context of a certain offence there is an empirical correlation between recklessness and low degrees of culpability, on the one hand, and between intention and higher degrees of culpability, on the other; and if in the context of this offence the correlation yields the reality that (considering all the factors relevant to the degree of culpability) in a great majority of the cases of recklessness the degree of culpability does not suffice to permit the imposition of criminal liability, while in many (or in a sufficient number of) cases of intention the degree of culpability suffices to permit such an imposition, then we have a prima facie argument for deciding that in this context all the reckless actors will be exempted from criminal liability, i.e. for enacting a "basic crime of intention".[35]

Now, the question whether the reality and correlation described above exist in the context of a certain offence depends, inter alia, on the empirical data relevant to that offence (for example, the typical motives of the actors). It follows, therefore, that it is perfectly possible for a legislator to reach the conclusion that the reality described above does not exist in any offence (either because there is no offence in the context of which there is a significant difference in culpability between cases of intention and cases of recklessness, or because although there are offences in the context of which such a difference exists, nonetheless in the context of all of these latter offences there are many cases of recklessness in which the culpability of the actor suffices for the imposition of criminal liability). In this event, the present justification, even if it is accepted as valid in theory and principle, will not lead to the actual enactment of any basic crime of intention. But I will now assume that a legislator finds that the above described reality does exist in the context of certain offences, and proceed to examine the present justification for enacting basic crimes of intention in the context of these offences.

Suppose that a legislator thinks that in the context of a certain offence most of the actors who act recklessly (i.e., who consciously take an unjustified risk that the proscribed result will ensue) are not sufficiently culpable to permit the imposition of criminal liability. Although even those reckless actors (who constitute the majority) perform actions that are morally and socially wrongful and that the legislator would like to prevent, the fact that they are not sufficiently culpable to permit the imposition of criminal liability constitutes a good reason not to subject those actors to the offence under discussion. The technique suggested in the above discussion to ensure that those reckless actors who should not be convicted (and who constitute a majority of the reckless actors) will not be prosecuted, convicted and punished was to exclude *all* reckless actors from the scope of the offence, by enacting a basic crime of intention. However, using the mentioned technique carries a price, because it yields the result that even those reckless actors (who constitute a minority of the reckless actors) who are sufficiently culpable (and perhaps sometimes even very culpable), and who should be convicted and punished, will be excluded from the scope of the offence. The price is not only that wicked people will not get what they deserve, but also that in the context of the offence under discussion, no case of reckless risk-taking that the proscribed result will ensue will be subject to the deterrent effect of the criminal law, even when this risk-taking is sufficiently or highly culpable.[36] Because of this price, alternative options should be considered before deciding to enact a basic crime of intention on the basis of the present justification. One alternative option is to include all cases of recklessness within the definition of the offence (alongside the cases of intention) but to rely on the prosecution authorities not to prosecute in cases of recklessness unless the agent is sufficiently culpable (i.e., to rely on the hope that in most cases of recklessness no prosecution will be brought). Another alternative option is to use a moral formula by including within the definition of the offence a requirement such as that the actor, in cases of recklessness, is "sufficiently culpable".

I will begin by discussing the first alternative option, assuming for a moment that the second is rejected. Prosecutors have the discretion not to prosecute when the prosecution is not in the public interest. This discretionary power not to prosecute is used, inter alia, in cases in which although the agent can be convicted (because in his case all the elements of the relevant offence can be proved and no criminal defence is available), the circumstances of the case are such that he is not sufficiently morally culpable. The first alternative option mentioned above is then, to rely, in our context, on this discretion. But this option has its own disadvantages. When we enact a serious offence we intend that in most cases people who can be convicted of the offence will be prosecuted. The power of the prosecution authorities not to prosecute for lack of public interest is meant to be used rarely in this context. But the idea of enacting an offence that is defined in broad terms, while intending that only rarely will a prosecution for this offence be brought, is problematic. For example, it might be the case that in certain extreme circumstances a person who breaks a promise is so culpable that he should be convicted and punished. Even so, is it appropriate to enact an offence that criminalises all promise-breakings and to rely on the prosecution authorities that they will only prosecute in those rare cases in which the actor is sufficiently culpable? Several problems arise when we enact an offence that is meant to be rarely enforced. First, there is the risk that the prosecution authorities will be more eager to prosecute than they should be, so that in many cases in which the actor is not sufficiently culpable he will nevertheless be prosecuted and convicted. Second, because the discretion of the prosecution authorities in the context of such an offence is very wide, the risk that this discretion will be used in a discriminatory way and the risk that like cases will be treated differently are considerably higher than in the context of offences concerning which the ordinary decision should be to prosecute. Third, in such a context, the legislator delegates the power and responsibility to decide who should be convicted to another authority to such a degree that it may seem to violate the principles of the rule of law and separation of powers. Now, it is true that our context (i.e., the context of deliberating whether to include all reckless actors in a criminal offence in spite of the fact that only a minority of them should be prosecuted) differs somewhat from the context of deliberating whether, for example, to enact an offence that criminalises all promise-breakings, for in our context the assumption is that the offence under discussion will be enacted anyway (for cases of intention) and the question is only whether to include cases of recklessness within this offence, or to exclude them. But, still, the three problems mentioned above arise in our context as well (though perhaps to a lesser degree), so that including cases of recklessness within the offences under discussion and relying on the prosecution authorities (to prosecute reckless actors only in rare cases) presents its own disadvantages. It should be noted, however, that in spite of the three problems mentioned here, the reality is that there *are* offences that are only rarely prosecuted[37] and that there are contexts in which legislators define a crime in broad terms, even though they hold the view that in many cases that fall under the definition of the crime there should be no prosecution, as they rely on the prosecution authorities prosecuting only in appropriate cases.[38] But the fact that in certain contexts legislators heavily rely on prosecutorial discretion does not mean that this technique is unproblematic. It is problematic, and therefore it should be adopted, if at all, only after considering the available alternatives.

So when a legislator thinks that in a certain context most of the reckless actors are not sufficiently culpable to permit the imposition of criminal liability (but that many of those who act with intent to cause the proscribed result are sufficiently culpable) he has to choose between two options: to enact a basic crime of intention or to include both recklessness and intention within the offence and rely on the prosecution authorities that only in rare cases will a reckless actor be prosecuted.[39] Each of these options is problematic, as was explained above, and therefore the legislator should weigh one against the other. I do not think that either one of them is clearly better than the other, and I believe that reasonable people may disagree as to which option should be preferred. Furthermore, much depends on the data relevant to the specific offence under discussion. For even within a group of offences that belong to a category of offences in the context of which most of the reckless actors (as opposed to those who act with intent to cause the result) are not sufficiently culpable, differences may be found between the various offences with regard to such questions as: In how many cases of recklessness *is* the actor sufficiently culpable? What generally is the degree of culpability in *those* cases, is it high or not? Will the fact that the criminal law would not supply any deterrence against reckless actions yield an intolerably large amount of harm? These questions, and others, should be taken into account in weighing the two options, and therefore it is perfectly reasonable to decide that even within the category of offences with which we are dealing, the chosen solution will vary from offence to offence.

Another point that should be mentioned is that the decision as to which of the two above mentioned options is to be preferred may be country dependent. This can be so not only because the answers to the questions just mentioned may vary from country to country, but also because answers to questions concerning the prosecution authorities (like the extent of the risk that the prosecution will be too eager to prosecute, or that it will use its discretion in a discriminatory way) may also vary from country to country.[40]

It is not my goal to decide here what should be done concerning a certain offence. My purpose is only to examine whether a reasonable legislator may legitimately decide in a certain context to enact a basic crime of intention. The discussion thus far shows, I think, that *if* in the context of a certain offence the empirical data are such that (taking into account all the factors that are relevant to the degree of culpability of the actor) a great majority of the reckless actors (as opposed to those who act with intent to cause the proscribed result) are not sufficiently culpable to permit the imposition of criminal liability, then a reasonable legislator may (but not must) decide to enact in such a context a "basic crime of intention".

However, before concluding that the enactment of basic crimes of intention in the described context is reasonable, we have to consider the further alternative mentioned above, namely, that of using a moral formula. With this option, when we find in the context of a certain offence that most of the reckless actors (as opposed to those who act with intent to cause the proscribed result) are not sufficiently culpable to permit the imposition of criminal liability, and we want to ensure that only those who should be convicted will in fact be convicted, we can simply include within the definition of the offence under discussion an explicit requirement of a sufficient degree of culpability to warrant a criminal conviction. The offence will be defined in such terms as that in order to be convicted, the agent must either intend that the result will ensue or act "with recklessness (with regard to the result) in circumstances manifesting a degree of culpability that is sufficient to permit conviction". The decision whether the required degree of culpability obtains in the specific case of recklessness at hand is meant to be made, following the present suggestion, after taking into account all the factors that are relevant to the assessment of the agent's moral culpability. One may suggest that this alternative should be preferred over that of enacting a basic crime of intention, because it enables us to convict those reckless actors who *should* be convicted (and also enables us to deter against the commission of some reckless actions), while at the same time ensuring that those reckless actors who should not be convicted because they are not sufficiently culpable will be exempted from criminal liability. But the alternative of using a moral formula has its own disadvantages when compared to that of enacting a basic crime of intention. Including the element of "sufficient moral culpability" within the definition of the offence entails that in every case of recklessness the court or jury will have to make a moral judgment in order to decide whether the actor is (taking into account all the factors that affect the degree of moral culpability) sufficiently morally culpable to permit a conviction. This means that a highly critical question (namely whether the defendant will be convicted) will depend on the moral judgment of the specific court or jury before which the actor is tried. This is problematic for several reasons. First, there is a risk that people will be treated differently depending on the court or jury before which they are tried. The personal moral beliefs of judges and juries may vary and may affect their decisions as to whether the accused is "sufficiently culpable". This may yield the result that one person will be convicted while another person who acted under similar circumstances but was tried before another court or jury will be acquitted. This is unjust, and it may also reduce the faith of society in the criminal justice system. Second, the fact that the court or jury has to make a value judgment creates the danger of discrimination against certain groups. If such discrimination appears it will, by itself, constitute an injustice, and in addition it may detract from public confidence in the criminal justice system.[41] Third, a convicted defendant who knows that the court or jury possessed a considerable amount of moral discretion whether to convict him may be less ready to accept his conviction as just and correct. Fourth, it may be claimed that empowering judges and juries with a vast amount of moral discretion in this context violates the principles of the rule of law and separation of powers according to which important moral decisions (such as which types of conduct should lead to conviction) should be made by the legislator.

Several other possible problems should be taken into account. If the legislator thinks that in a certain context a reckless actor is only rarely sufficiently culpable to permit the imposition of criminal liability, he should be aware of the risk that if he does not exclude all reckless actors from the scope of the offence, but leaves it to the court or jury to decide whether the reckless actor is sufficiently culpable, some judges and juries perhaps will be too harsh and will find that a "sufficient degree of moral culpability" is present in many cases in which they should not, and thus will convict many people that should not be convicted. Another problem is that defining offences in a way that renders the determination as to the crystallisation of the elements of the offence dependent to a large extent on a moral judgment, gives a vast amount of discretion to the prosecution authorities. Another, perhaps less important, problem is that the need to take into account all the relevant factors and to assess whether the accused is sufficiently culpable may overburden juries.

The discussion above shows that the option of using a moral formula has its own disadvantages. It is not clear, then, that it should be preferred over the option of enacting a basic crime of intention.[42]

So a legislator who thinks that in a certain context most of the reckless actors are not sufficiently culpable to permit the imposition of criminal liability (and who rejects the option of including all cases of recklessness in the offence under discussion and relying on the proper use of prosecutorial discretion) has to choose between the option of enacting a basic crime of intention and that of using a moral formula described above. Each of these options is problematic and reasonable people may disagree about which one should be preferred. Furthermore, much depends upon the data relevant to the specific offence under discussion. For even within the group of offences that belong to the category of offences in the context of which most of the reckless actors are not sufficiently culpable, specific offences may vary with regard to such questions as: In how many cases of recklessness *is* the actor sufficiently culpable? What generally is the agent's degree of culpability in *those* cases? Will the fact that the criminal law would not supply any deterrence against reckless actions yield an intolerably large amount of harm in the context under discussion? Therefore, it is perfectly reasonable to decide that even within the category of offences with which we are dealing, the solution chosen will vary from offence to offence. Another point worth mentioning is that the decision may be country dependent for various reasons, including the fact that the answers to such questions as how high the risk is that the court or jury will be too harsh, or that they will discriminate between various groups, may vary from country to country.

The discussion above regarding the alternative of using a moral formula shows, I think, that this alternative (like that of relying heavily on prosecutorial discretion, discussed earlier in this chapter) is not clearly better than that of enacting a basic crime of intention. Therefore we can conclude that *if* in the context of a certain offence the factual data are such that (taking into account all the factors that are relevant to the degree of culpability of the actor) a great majority of the reckless actors (as opposed to those who act with intent to cause the proscribed result) are not sufficiently culpable to permit the imposition of criminal culpability, then a reasonable legislator may (but not must) decide to enact in such a context "a basic crime of intention". The other two options are to use a moral formula or to include cases of recklessness within the offence and to rely heavily on prosecutorial discretion.[43]

11.6 Oblique Intention

The discussion in the previous section showed that a reasonable legislator may legitimately decide to enact, in certain contexts, basic crimes of intention. Assuming that in a certain context the legislator actually decides to enact a basic crime of intention on the basis of the present justification, what should he do concerning cases of oblique intention? As I explained in section 11.5, the present justification for enacting basic crimes of intention is not based on a general claim about an intrinsic moral difference between intention and recklessness, i.e., on the claim that when all other things (including the motives) are equal, causing a bad result purposely is more blameworthy than causing it recklessly. Rather, this justification is context dependent, it depends on the empirical data relevant to the specific offence under consideration. It says that in contexts in which the empirical data are such that (taking into account all the factors relevant to the degree of moral culpability) most of the reckless actors (as opposed to those who act with intent to cause the proscribed result) are not sufficiently culpable to permit the imposition of criminal liability, there is a reasonable basis to enact a basic crime of intention. Now, since the justification for requiring intention in a certain offence lies in the empirical data relevant to that offence, the decision what to do concerning cases of oblique intention should also depend on such data. In other words, the question should be whether (taking into account all the data relevant to the degree of moral culpability) in a great majority of the cases of oblique intention, the degree of moral culpability is too low to permit the imposition of criminal liability, so that excluding all cases of foresight of certainty from the scope of the offence is justified. If, for example, in 90% of the cases of oblique intention the "threshold of culpability" is not reached and this is also the case in the context of recklessness, then it is reasonable to treat cases of "oblique intention" in the same way we treat cases of recklessness (i.e., to remove them from the scope of the offence). If, on the other hand, in 50% of the cases of oblique intention the "threshold of culpability" is reached and this is also the case in the context of direct intention, then it is reasonable to treat cases of oblique intention in the same way we treat cases of direct intention (i.e., to include them within the offence).[44]

Of course, because the law governing cases of oblique intention should depend on empirical data that may vary from offence to offence (such as the data concerning the typical motives out of which people engage in the conduct under discussion when there is foresight of certainty that the result under discussion will ensue), it is perfectly possible that the law of cases of oblique intention will have to vary from one offence to another. This means that the fact that in the context of two different basic crimes of intention the requirement of intention is based on the present justification, does not exclude the possibility that in the one offence cases of oblique intention will have to be penalised, while in the other they will have to be exempted from criminal liability.[45]

We should also be aware of the possibility that in the context of a certain offence, oblique intention will form an "intermediate case" (between direct intention and recklessness), as concerns the percentage of the whole body of cases of oblique intention in which the "threshold of culpability" is reached. In this case, the legislator will have to decide, in the said context, whether to exempt all cases of oblique intention from criminal liability or to include them in the offence alongside cases of direct intention.[46]

It should also be noted that in the context of a certain offence the empirical data may justify the conclusion that in many cases (or in a sufficient number of cases) of (mere) foresight of *high probability*, the degree of culpability (taking into account all the factors relevant to the degree of moral culpability) suffices for the imposition of criminal liability, whereas the number of cases in which the result is foreseen as merely possible or probable (as opposed to highly probable) in which the threshold of culpability is reached, is very low. In this case, there is, at least in principle, a justification for including within the offence under discussion, together with the cases of direct intention, not only cases of (mere) foresight of certainty but also cases of (mere) foresight of high probability. This justification stems from the fact that in terms of the present justification for enacting basic crimes of intention, the line between foresight of certainty and foresight of lower degrees of probability does not mark a qualitative principled moral difference between the two. However, even if in the context of a certain offence there is in principle a justification for extending it even to cases of foresight of "high probability", it is possible that practical considerations (such as the desire to avoid the using of vague terms and to diminish potential difficulties in proving the elements of the offence) will justify the conclusion that it is better to include within the offence, alongside cases of direct intention, only cases of foresight of certainty (as opposed to cases of foresight of high probability).[47]

Before leaving the issue of oblique intention it should be emphasised that the discussion in this section was based on the analysis of the present justification for enacting basic crimes of intention, that was conducted in section 11.5. It was explained there why I think that if in a certain context the culpability of the actor does not reach the "threshold of culpability" in most cases of recklessness (as opposed to cases of intention), this state of things does not stem from an *intrinsic* difference between intention and recklessness. However, as I suggested there (at note 35), if a legislator believes that there is a large intrinsic difference between intention and recklessness, then he may come to the conclusion that in the context of a certain offence this difference can produce the reality that a great majority of the reckless actors (as opposed to those who act with intent to cause the proscribed result) are not sufficiently culpable to permit the imposition of criminal liability. If, in such a context and on the basis of the said intrinsic difference, he decides to enact a basic crime of intention, then the decision what to do concerning cases of oblique intention should be influenced by the reason underlying the legislator's decision to distinguish between intention and recklessness (by removing cases of recklessness from the scope of the offence under discussion). In section 10.2.2, in dealing with the issue of grading offences, I summarised how a legislator who grades offences based on the distinction between intention and recklessness, and who bases this grading scheme on the belief in a significant intrinsic difference between intention and recklessness, should deal with the issue of oblique intention. What I said there can basically apply here with necessary modifications, such as that when I suggest there that cases of oblique intention should be included within the lower offence, this should be read in the present context as a suggestion for excluding oblique intention from the scope of the basic crime of intention; and that when I suggest there to include cases oblique intention within the higher offence, this should be read in the present context as a suggestion to include cases of oblique intention within the basic crime of intention.

Notes

1   See supra section 2.1.
2   Cf. Silving (1967) 224, 252.

3   Cf. Stephen (1883), vol. 2, pp. 359-360 (discussing basic crimes of intention); Stephen
       (1883), vol. 3, pp. 91-93 (discussing grading offences. This discussion was referred to
       supra in chapter 2, note 18).

4   See Kugler (1997) 393-394; Smith A.T.H. (1978) 99, 106; Perkins and Boyce (1982)
       1073. Husak too accepts that excuses sometimes cover cases in which blame is not
       completely negated, but only reduced to a sufficient degree to preclude liability (Husak
       (1998) 172). He adds: "In concluding that a defendant is completely excused, no one
       need suppose that his degree of blame must be zero. A child who is completely
       excused from criminal liability, for example, might well bear *some* degree of blame for
       his conduct. One need only suppose that his degree of blame is below whatever
       threshold is required to justify the imposition of criminal liability. Of course,
       reasonable minds will differ about where this threshold is to be located. Clearly,
       however, this threshold should be placed well above the point at which an agent bears
       no degree of blame at all" (ibid. at 173).

5   Model Penal Code (1985), section 2.02(3).

6   The definition of negligence in the Model Penal Code also contains a requirement of
       "gross deviation". See Model Penal Code (1985), section 2.02(2)(d).

7   This explanation of the requirement finds support in the commentary to the Model
       Penal Code, that explains the requirement in the following terms: "Some standard is
       needed for determining *how* substantial and *how* unjustifiable the risk must be in order
       to warrant a finding of culpability. There is no way to state this value judgment that
       does not beg the question in the last analysis; the point is that the jury must evaluate
       the actor's conduct and determine whether it should be condemned. The Code
       proposes, therefore, that this difficulty be accepted frankly ... the jury is to make the
       culpability judgment in terms of whether the defendant's conscious disregard of the
       risk justifies condemnation" (Model Penal Code and Commentaries (1985) Part 1, vol.
       1, pp. 237-238).
       The definition of negligence in the Model Penal Code also contains a requirement of
       gross deviation. Negligence is established only if the actor's failure to perceive the risk
       involves a *gross* deviation from the standard of care that a reasonable person would
       observe in the actor's situation. See Model Penal Code (1985), section 2.02(2)(d). This
       requirement may also be linked with "the principle of a threshold of culpability".

8   See supra at the beginning of section 1.1 and see chapter 1, notes 1-2. I do not discuss
       in this book the Caldwell-type of recklessness mentioned ibid. at note 1.

9   The assumption in the text is that the requirement that it be unreasonable to take the
       risk is identical to the requirement that the taking of the risk be unjustified. And indeed
       this is the common view. See Ashworth (1999) 184 (who speaks of an unjustified risk).
       See also Smith and Hogan (1999) 60 (who speak of an unjustifiable risk). There is a
       further aspect in which the definitions of recklessness found in English law and the
       Model Penal Code differ. Under English law, any risk, however slight, may suffice to
       constitute recklessness (provided that the actor is aware of the risk and that it is
       unjustified to take it). See Ashworth (1999) 184; Smith and Hogan (1999) 61. In
       contrast, under the Model Penal Code recklessness cannot be established unless the
       actor consciously takes a risk that is both unjustifiable and *substantial.* The
       requirement of the Model Penal Code that the risk be substantial may also be linked
       with "the principle of a threshold of culpability" mentioned in the text.

10   Some of the actions mentioned here may constitute criminal offences if they are
       performed in certain special circumstances, or directed against special categories of
       victims or performed in certain specified places, etc. Still, they do not constitute
       criminal offences (in many countries) unless those further elements are present.

11   The Commentary to the Model Penal Code states: "The criminal law cannot be simply a code of right behavior. It must be, rather, a specification of behavior so far below common standards that it identifies the actor as a dangerous and reprehensible person..." (Model Penal Code and Commentaries (1980) Part 2, vol. 3, p. 483). See also Perkins and Boyce (1982) 1073 ("The criminal law was never intended to be a complete moral code. Only when conduct falls far below proper moral behavior, is punishment deemed appropriate") and Ashworth (1999) 32-37 (according to the minimalist approach the criminal law should be used for the most reprehensible types of wrongdoing, for the most serious invasions of interests, and it should not be used for minor wrongs).

12   See Ashworth (1999) 37, 50-51; Husak (1998) 173 at note 31.

13   It is common to refer to the element of condemnation and stigma in dealing with the idea of "a threshold of culpability" or with doctrines in which the mentioned idea finds expression. See Smith A.T.H. (1978) 106; Kugler (1997) 394; Ashworth (1999) 34-37, 50; Model Penal Code and Commentaries (1985) Part 1, vol. 1, pp. 237-238; Model Penal Code (1985), section 2.12(2); Robinson (1984), vol.1, p. 324.

14   Wasik (1985a) 215. See also Ashworth (1999) 18 who refers to the fact that many convictions make it difficult or impossible to obtain certain jobs or enter a profession. A criminal record may also influence the sentence in subsequent proceedings.

15   See Wasik (1985a) 215; Ashworth (2000) 67-68.

16   The fact that some defendants are acquitted at the conclusion of their trial, and that their acquittal does not redress the stress, shame and embarrassment suffered throughout the proceedings adds further weight to the argument in the text.

17   As I said in section 11.1, I have put off the detailed analysis of the proposition "intention is more culpable than recklessness" to section 11.5.

18   It is possible to make an analogy between the present suggested justification and a possible explanation for the treatment of negligence in certain jurisdictions. Some codes, while providing that negligence does not suffice to establish liability in most criminal offences, nevertheless provide that certain exceptional offences *can* be established by negligence. Some of these exceptional offences protect very important interests, like that of life. A case in point may be found in the Model Penal Code, where negligence is generally not sufficient for criminal liability (see Model Penal Code (1985), section 2.02(3)), but causing the death of another human being negligently constitutes a criminal offence (see section 210.4). A possible explanation is that causing harm negligently is considered to be significantly less culpable than doing so recklessly, and that causing most harms negligently does not establish the degree of moral culpability required to permit the imposition of criminal liability. But when the harm is very serious, like in the case of causing death, even causing the harm negligently is sufficiently culpable to permit the imposition of criminal liability. Since I am not dealing in this book with negligence I will not take the discussion on this point any further.

19   The offences to be brought in section 11.4 are basic crimes that are not established where the actor is only reckless with respect to the (actual or potential) result, but are so where he acts with direct intention. Since I will not deal (in this chapter) with oblique intention until section 11.6, I will relate to the question whether the offences brought in section 11.4 are established in cases of oblique intention only infra at note 45.

20   Report on Recodifying Criminal Law (1987).

21   As is explicitly clarified by the comment to clause 7(1). See ibid. at p. 62.

22   Smith and Hogan (1999) 407. As for the actus reus of battery, even the slightest degree
      of force, including mere touching, suffices: Smith and Hogan (1999) 405; Ashworth
      (1999) 326-328.
23   See clause 75(a).
24   Report on Recodifying Criminal Law (1987) p. 61.
25   That said, I am obviously not committing myself to the Canadian commission's
      position concerning the specific offence under discussion. Even those who would, in
      principle, accept the validity of the present suggested justification for requiring
      intention in certain basic crimes, may possibly think that the commission's position is
      wrong concerning assault (especially in relation to cases of hurting, i.e., of causing
      physical pain).
26   This is so by virtue of clause 2(4)(d) which was referred to in the discussion of
      example A above. Indeed the comment to clause 20(1) makes it clear that the
      culpability requirement for the offence defined in this clause is one of purpose. See
      ibid. at p. 98.
27   According to section 250.11(1) of the Model Penal Code (1985) a person commits a
      misdemeanor if he purposely or *recklessly* subjects any animal to cruel mistreatment.
28   What is said supra at note 25 is relevant here, too.
29   The explanation suggested here for clause 20(1) may also apply to clause 20(4) of the
      proposed Canadian draft Criminal Code which provides that "everyone commits a
      crime who fails to take reasonable steps to provide necessaries of life to an animal
      under his care and unable to provide itself with necessaries and thereby causes it injury
      or serious physical pain". Here too purpose with regard to the injury or pain is required
      (see ibid. at p. 99). The Model Penal Code's treatment of this issue is different.
      According to section 250.11(2), a person commits a misdemeanor if he purposely or
      recklessly subjects any animal in his custody to cruel neglect.
30   The fact that the actions described in section 250.4 only establish a petty misdemeanor
      lends support to the assumption that the drafters of the Model Penal Code did not view
      the harassment caused by these actions as a considerably serious harm.
31   The present suggested explanation may also apply to section 250.4(4) which deals with
      a person who subjects another to offensive touching, with the purpose of harassing him
      (recklessness with respect to possible harassment is not sufficient). I should add here
      that the Model Penal Code does not criminalise as an assault the mere reckless (or
      even the intended) application of force to another person without his consent (that does
      not involve either the actual infliction or prospect of physical injury). See Model Penal
      Code and Commentaries (1980) Part 2, vol. 1, at p. 185. The English law differs, as
      was mentioned in discussing example A above.
      Other "basic crimes of intention" that might be explained by the present explanation
      are, for example, the offence of "desecration of venerated objects" under section 250.9
      of the Model Penal Code (1985) which requires that the agent *purposely* desecrate the
      object, and defamatory libel (in those jurisdictions in which it requires an intent to
      injure the reputation of the victim. See infra, chapter 12, at note 43).
32   See Kugler (1997) 391-395.
33   For this phenomenon see Smith and Hogan (1999) 17; Ashworth (1999) 37; Lacey and
      Wells (1998) 6.
34   A different meaning for this statement will be suggested later in this section.
35   If we think that there *is* a small *intrinsic* difference between intention and recklessness,
      it might also be the case that in the context of a certain offence this difference will add
      some weight to the amount of culpability present in cases of intention, and will thus

contribute towards the decision to criminalise the actions performed with intent to cause the result. For a similar idea see supra section 9.3.

I should add here that if, contrary to my view, the legislator thinks there is a *large intrinsic* difference in culpability between intention and recklessness, then he may come to the conclusion that in the context of a certain offence this difference alone *can* explain why a great majority of the reckless actors are not sufficiently culpable to be convicted, whereas many actors who act with intent to cause the result are sufficiently culpable to be convicted. However it should be recalled that following one line of thought the intrinsic difference between intention and recklessness only exists in the context of the most heinous of moral wrongs (see supra section 7.3), whereas the present suggested justification for basic crimes of intention is confined, from the outset, to causing harms that are not highly serious. Another point worth mentioning here is that *if* the existence of an intrinsic difference is understood in terms of the importance assigned to not harming the dignity of people by using them as a means to an end, then this difference will not exist in the context of offences against animals (see supra section 7.3), and therefore we will not be able to explain the requirement of purpose in the offence which prohibits causing suffering to animals (which appears in the proposed Canadian draft Criminal Code and was brought above in section 11.4) on the basis of the mentioned intrinsic difference.

36   Of course, if in the context of a certain offence *no* reckless actor is sufficiently culpable to permit the imposition of criminal liability, then the price mentioned in the text will not be paid.

37   An example is criminal libel, see: Smith and Hogan (1999) 717; Williams (1983a) 25.

38   As Ashworth says: "English law sometimes defines an offence very broadly in order to catch a small group of perpetrators: there is an offence of unlawful sexual intercourse with a girl under 16, but it is widely accepted that no prosecution should be brought where the girl is 15 and the boy is only slightly older. Proposals to narrow the offence by exempting cases in which the age difference is, say, only two years have been rejected on the grounds of undue technicality. We therefore tolerate an offence which has what the Americans call 'overbreath', in the belief that prosecutorial discretion is a more reliable means of identifying truly criminal incidents than legal definition. This flies in the face of maximum certainty" (Ashworth (1999) 78). See also ibid. at 364 where Ashworth says, concerning the above mentioned offence, that the law is framed widely in the expectation that it will be enforced selectively.

Concerning the law of impossible attempts Williams wrote that "it has proved to be impracticable to devise a rule limiting the kinds of impossible attempts that are to be punishable. The only solution is reliance upon the good sense of prosecutors and sentencers; and it is not extending our confidence in them too largely to allow prosecution in theory for reckless impossible attempts" (Williams (1983b) 375).

39   The assumption in the discussion here is that the alternative of using a moral formula (which was briefly mentioned above) is rejected. I will return to this alternative later in this section. Needless to say, another assumption of our discussion is that in the context of the offences under discussion there is no available distinction which can be articulated in factual terms (i.e., a distinction the application of which does not involve moral judgment) and that can perform the task of separating those who are sufficiently culpable from those who are not, better than the distinction between intention and recklessness. It should also be added that if a decision is made to criminalise reckless actors, a further decision will have to be made as to whether to grade the offence under discussion, following the distinction between intention and recklessness. This question should be addressed in light of the discussion in Part One of the book.

40   It should also be noted that even two legislators who both accept "the principle of a threshold of culpability" may disagree as to how high this threshold should be. This possible disagreement provides one of the potential explanations for why one legislator may think that in most cases of, say, recklessly causing pain to animals, the actor is not sufficiently culpable to permit the imposition of criminal liability, whereas another may think that in most of them he is. Also, even if two legislators agree that in the context of causing pain to animals most of the reckless actors are not sufficiently culpable to permit the imposition of criminal liability, a disagreement about the height of the threshold that should be required may yield a disagreement as to the number of cases in which reckless actors *are* sufficiently culpable, and this, in turn, may yield a disagreement as to whether in the context of an offence dealing with causing pain to animals the preferred approach should be to enact a basic crime of intention or to rely on the discretion of the prosecution authorities. On the possibility that reasonable people may differ about where the threshold of culpability should be located, see Husak (1998) 173.

41   The first two problems referred to here were also raised when I discussed the possibility of using a moral formula in order to grade offences. One may suggest that these problems are even more acute in the present context because in many cases the question whether a person will be convicted or not is more critical (to him, to his family and to society) than the precise quantum of the punishment that will be imposed on him.

42   According to the suggestion of using a moral formula examined here, the element of "sufficient moral culpability" would be required only in cases of recklessness, not in cases of intention. Another option would be to require an element of "sufficient moral culpability" both in cases of intention and recklessness. In this case, the offence would not distinguish at all between intention and recklessness. But assuming that we are dealing with a context in which most of the actors who act with intent to cause the result are sufficiently culpable, there is not much point in this suggestion. In the context of every offence, there are rare cases in which the actor should not be prosecuted. Hence, the law provides that prosecutors may decide not to prosecute when there is a lack of public interest in the prosecution. Thus, in our context as well, we may rely on the proper exercise of prosecutorial discretion, that in those rare cases of intention in which the actor is not sufficiently culpable, there will be no prosecution. In addition, if the element of sufficient moral culpability will be required even in cases of intention, the scope of the moral discretion given to the court or jury will be larger than if the suggestion examined in the text is adopted, and hence the problems that stem from the existence of moral discretion will be exacerbated. Therefore, I think that if we decide to use a moral formula we should require "sufficient moral culpability" only in cases of recklessness.

43   As was explained in section 1.1, according to the English law, the conscious taking of an unjustified risk that a result will ensue constitutes recklessness with respect to this result. When I refer to the concept of recklessness throughout this book, including the discussion in the present chapter, it is in the mentioned English sense. In section 11.2, however, I mentioned the Model Penal Code's definition of recklessness. According to this definition, a person is reckless with respect to a result only if his conscious taking of the substantial and unjustifiable risk that the result will ensue constitutes a *gross* deviation from the standard of conduct of a law-abiding person. The explanation given in the commentary for the requirement of a gross deviation indicates that the jury is required to make a value judgment in order to decide whether the conduct of the actor warrants condemnation (see supra at note 7). One may suggest that a legislator who

defines recklessness in this manner actually guarantees that a conviction will not ensue (in cases in which the actor did not act with intent to cause the result but only foresaw it as a possibility) unless the actor was sufficiently culpable to permit the imposition of criminal liability; and that therefore such a legislator has no reason to enact basic crimes of intention on the basis of the justification suggested in this chapter. I think that there is much truth in this line of argument and no doubt the need to enact basic crimes of intention on the basis of the justification suggested in this chapter may arise more frequently in a jurisdiction that adopts the English definition for recklessness than in a jurisdiction that adopts the Model Penal Code definition. Nevertheless, various reasons may be advanced for enacting basic crimes of intention in certain contexts, even within a jurisdiction that adopts the Model Penal Code's definition of recklessness. For example, it may be the case that in the context of a certain offence the legislator will be concerned with the possibility that the court or jury will be too harsh, and in too many cases of risk-taking will find that the accused was sufficiently culpable. Thus, the legislator may decide to prevent against the possibility of a conviction in cases of recklessness by enacting a basic crime of intention. Or it may be that in spite of the inclusion of a "gross deviation" element in the definition of recklessness, the legislator will be aware of the disadvantages involved in conditioning convictions upon this element, because of the moral judgment inherent in its application, and therefore in contexts in which the legislator will be ready to pay the price of refraining altogether from bringing the deterrent power of the criminal law to bear on reckless actors, he may prefer to enact a basic crime of intention over relying on the moral judgment of the court or jury.

Nor does the fact that the de minimis doctrine is recognised in the Model Penal Code (in section 2.12) yield the conclusion that there is no room for any basic crimes of intention based on the present justification in a jurisdiction that adopts the Model Penal Code. This is the case for various reasons, one of which is that the de minimis doctrine, as defined in the Model Penal Code, does not ensure that every actor who is not sufficiently culpable will not be convicted. The only subsection that might be relevant to our discussion is subsection (2), but even this subsection requires that the conduct not cause or threaten the harm or evil sought to be prevented by the law defining the offence or that it do so only to a trivial extent. However, it is reasonable to suppose that the need to enact basic crimes of intention on the basis of the present justification will arise more frequently in a jurisdiction that does not provide for the de minimis doctrine. Nevertheless, if the fact that a certain jurisdiction does not provide for the de minimis doctrine results from a principled rejection of "the principle of a threshold of culpability" itself, then naturally this jurisdiction will also reject the present suggested justification for enacting basic crimes of intention.

44   However, as the discussion in section 11.5 shows, the number of cases in which the threshold of culpability is reached is not the only relevant factor. Even assuming that in most cases of oblique intention the threshold of culpability is not reached, further questions should be raised before a decision is taken to exclude all cases of oblique intention from the scope of the offence. For example, we should inquire as to the degree of culpability generally present in those cases of (mere) foresight of certainty in which the actor *is* sufficiently culpable, and also whether we can tolerate the amount of harm that will be caused by the absence of a threat of criminal punishment for causing the result under discussion with (mere) foresight of certainty.

45   In section 11.4 I gave some examples of basic crimes of intention that may be understood in the light of the present justification for requiring intention. These offences differ in their treatment of cases of oblique intention. The offences from the

Model Penal Code brought there (example C and at note 31) require direct intention, and cannot be established by oblique intention. This is by virtue of section 2.02(2)(a) of the Code that defines purpose in terms of direct intention (see supra section 1.3.4). But the offences brought there from the proposed Canadian draft Criminal Code (examples A and B, and at note 29) *can* be established by oblique intention, by virtue of the definition of purpose in the draft code (clause 2(4)(b)). See supra section 1.3.4.

46   A third possibility is not to exempt cases of oblique intention from criminal liability, but to enact two distinct offences, one for direct intention and the other for oblique intention and to provide for a higher maximum penalty for the former. But this possibility need not be discussed here. for if the basic decision is to impose criminal liability in cases of oblique intention, then the further question whether to distinguish between direct intention and oblique intention for purposes of grading should be addressed in the light of the discussion in Part One of the book.

47   For a similar point in other contexts see supra chapter 6 at note 23; and section 9.2. In the present context, the desire not to include within the definition of the offence a vague term like "high probability" may in certain contexts lead one to take a decision that is opposite to that mentioned in the text, namely, to include all the recklessness cases within the offence (i.e., not to enact a "basic crime of intention").

Chapter 12

A Requirement of a High Degree of Culpability for Offences Enacted for Retribution Purposes

12.1 A Requirement of a High Degree of Culpability for Offences Enacted for Retribution Purposes

A common view is that the main purpose of the criminal law is to minimise harms by way of general deterrence, but that there is also a limiting condition (based on justice and fairness) according to which we should not convict and punish morally innocent people, even if doing so would contribute in some way to an increase in general deterrence. One of the implications of this view is that we will not convict agents unless they had some culpable state of mind when they acted, and it is generally held that for most crimes a conviction should be dependent upon the fact that the actor was at least reckless with regard to the elements of the offence. In addition, it is generally thought that normally recklessness with regard to the elements of the offence should *suffice* for conviction of "basic crimes".[1]

A legislator who accepts the above mentioned views, and acts upon them, enacts criminal offences for the purpose of general deterrence; and requires that the actor act with recklessness with respect to the elements of the offence – based on the view that a person must be culpable in order to *permit* us to convict and punish him. The function of recklessness is, from this standpoint, to establish that the agent is sufficiently culpable to *permit* the conviction, i.e., to fulfil the limiting condition that people who are not (sufficiently) culpable will not be convicted, or in other words, to overcome the restriction against convicting people who are not (sufficiently) culpable.

Even a legislator who thinks that general deterrence is normally the main purpose of the criminal law, may hold the view that in certain contexts it is appropriate to convict and punish for the sake of retribution (i.e., simply in order to inflict unpleasant consequences upon an offender in response to his offence, because he deserves the punishment). Such a legislator may decide, in some of the contexts in which (for some reason) the enactment of an offence cannot be justified by the goal of general deterrence, to nevertheless enact a criminal offence – solely in order to punish those who deserve to be punished. The culpability required of the actor in the last mentioned context takes on a different function than in other contexts of the criminal law. While generally the moral culpability of the actor is only needed to *permit* the conviction and punishment, in the last mentioned context the actor's culpability operates as the *justification* for the conviction and punishment. While generally the actor's culpability is only needed to overcome a restriction against punishing innocent people to promote the general good, in the last mentioned context the culpability of the actor constitutes the sole reason for punishment.[2] Now, it may be suggested that while to *permit* the imposition of punishment where it is justified by its contribution to the general good (by way of general deterrence) a certain amount of culpability is sufficient to overcome the above mentioned restriction, only a higher degree of culpability may *justify* the imposition of punishment solely for retribution purposes.[3] In other words, if we cannot justify punishment in utilitarian terms, punishment for retribution purposes should be conditioned upon the presence of a *high* degree of culpability in the agent.

If a legislator accepts the above line of thinking, and *if* he also thinks that "intention is more culpable than recklessness",[4] then he may have a prima facie reason for enacting some basic crimes of intention. For if, in a certain context, he thinks that the enactment of a certain "basic crime" will not contribute to an increase in general deterrence, but that it is fitting in that context to enact a basic crime for retribution purposes, he may require a mental state of intention to ensure that only *highly* culpable agents will be convicted of that offence. Thus, we have here a further possible justification for enacting basic crimes of intention.

The above suggested justification proceeds on the basis of several assumptions, and the denial of any of them suffices to mount a case against this justification. First, one may think that retribution alone cannot justify punishment, so that if in a certain context the imposition of punishment will not promote utility, there is no room for criminal liability in that context even if the agent is *highly* culpable. Second, one may think that the amount of culpability required to justify punishment for retribution purposes need not be higher than that required to permit punishment which is justified by considerations of utility. Third, one may say that even if a higher degree of culpability should be required for justifying punishment than for permitting it, the degree of culpability established by recklessness nevertheless suffices to justify punishment. Last, one may deny that "intention is more culpable than recklessness".[5]

I will now assume that a certain legislator accepts the assumptions on which the present suggested justification is based, and that therefore he accepts, in principle, the validity of the present justification for enacting basic crimes of intention. A further question which arises concerns whether there is any context, in reality, to which this justification may apply. It is to this question that I will now turn.

12.2   Criminal Attempts as a Possible Context for Applying the Present Justification for Requiring Intention

12.2.1 *Criminal Attempts*

It is not easy to find contexts to which the present suggested justification may apply. For if we generally view the enactment of criminal offences as being justified by the idea of general deterrence, then it is not easy to find a context in which the enactment of a criminal offence cannot be justified on this basis. But perhaps the context of criminal attempts is one to which the present justification may apply. If we think that the penalisation of attempts is not based on the idea of general deterrence, but on that of retribution, then we can apply the present justification to this context. In this manner we can explain the conventional law in many countries, that requires, for a conviction of a criminal attempt, an intention to cause the result which forms part of the *actus reus* of the completed offence. I will now turn to examine this possibility.

In many countries, an agent cannot be convicted of a criminal attempt unless he has an intention to commit the relevant completed offence, so that, in the context of result crimes, conviction of an attempt requires, *inter alia*, that the defendant intended to cause the result that forms part of the *actus reus* of the completed offence. In England, for example, section 1(1) of the Criminal Attempts Act 1981 provides, *inter alia*, that the *mens rea* of criminal attempt is that the actor acts "with intent to commit the offence". Therefore, an attempt to commit a result crime cannot be established unless the actor intends to cause the result, even if the result crime itself does not require intention for conviction. This means that, in spite of the fact that recklessness with regard to the proscribed result is a sufficient *mens rea* for most non-fatal offences against the person, the offence of criminal damage and many other offences – it does not suffice for an attempt conviction in relation to these offences.[6] This is the law even where the actor performs an act that might cause the result without further action on his part. For example, a person working on the roof of a house without warning throws a beam down onto a street. Assume that he is reckless with regard to the possibility that somebody will be wounded. Now, if somebody actually gets wounded by the beam, this person will be convicted of wounding a person (contrary to section 20 of the Offences Against the Person Act 1861), but if, by good fortune, no one gets injured, he will not be convicted of attempt to commit the offence of wounding a person because he does not intend to wound a person, but is only reckless with respect to the possibility that his act will wound someone. As a matter of fact, in the last mentioned case the person will not be convicted of any offence at all. A similar example may be found in the case where a person is reckless with regard to the possibility that his action will cause grievous bodily harm. Or take the case of a person who throws a stone near the window of his neighbour, being reckless with respect to the possibility that the window will be broken by the stone. If the window is broken, he can be convicted of the offence of criminal damage contrary to section 1(1) of the Criminal Damage Act 1971. But, if, by good fortune, nothing happens to the window, the actor will not be convicted of attempt to commit the mentioned offence because he did not intend to break the window, but was only reckless with respect to the possibility of breaking it (and he will actually not be convicted of any other offence).[7]

It is important to note that in the cases described above, the actors (in the cases in which the result does not ensue) are completely exempted from criminal liability. If English law provided for a general offence of "criminal endangerment" alongside that of criminal attempt, which would penalise cases like those discussed above, and provide for a lower punishment than in cases of attempt, then the issue of "attempts in the English law" would not be discussed in this part of the book, which is devoted to "basic crimes of intention". But because English law does not have a general doctrine of endangerment, the actors in the cases discussed above are completely exempt from criminal liability, and therefore the state of the law concerning criminal attempts is like that of "basic crimes of intention" – hence the intention requirement in the law of attempts belongs in this part of the book.[8]

The question which should be addressed now concerns whether there is any justification for requiring intention as to the result as a pre-requisite for conviction in cases in which the result does not ensue. If recklessness generally suffices for conviction throughout the criminal law, why should it not suffice in the present context?[9]

As a matter of fact, some scholars maintain that the English law concerning the mens rea of attempts is misguided, and that if recklessness with respect to the result suffices to convict of a certain result crime, then recklessness with respect to that result should also suffice to convict of an attempt to commit the same result crime.[10] Also, it seems that in Scotland the law is indeed that recklessness with respect to the result suffices for conviction of an attempt to commit a result crime in which recklessness with regard to the result suffices for a conviction.[11]

So, is there any justification for the requirement of an intention to cause the result for a conviction in cases of attempts? The requirement of intention is justified by some with a linguistic argument. It is said that in proper English, a person cannot be considered to *attempt* to cause a certain result unless he acts in order to cause it. Therefore, the argument runs, we cannot convict of an attempted wounding of a person, for example, a person who is only reckless with regard to the wounding of a person, because such a person does not *attempt* to wound.[12] But such an argument is of no help to us in our discussion. The linguistic argument may only explain why a judge who has to interpret a clause that uses the words "attempting to commit crimes" should not interpret this clause as applying to cases of recklessness with regard to the relevant result (assuming that judges are not entitled to stretch the wording of the law for policy reasons). But the argument does not give any reason based on policy or justice why the legislator should not penalise cases of recklessness. If there are good reasons for penalising cases of recklessness, then the legislator can penalise them by defining the law of attempts in such terms that make it clear that it is meant to even cover cases of recklessness, or, alternatively, by removing the word attempt from the code and replacing it with another term that is not associated with a pre-requisite of acting in order to cause the result.[13] And even if a legislator thinks that the actor who acts in order to cause a certain result is significantly more culpable than the actor in a case of endangerment – so that we cannot include cases of intention and cases of recklessness within the same offence – still such a view can only justify distinguishing between a general doctrine of "attempt" and a general doctrine of "endangerment" by providing for a higher punishment in cases of attempt than in cases of endangerment, but it cannot, by itself, justify a decision to do without a general doctrine of endangerment altogether.

One might suggest that the requirement of intention in complete attempts is intended to make up for the fact that no harm has occurred. The argument would be that in cases where the result crime is completed, the harm occurs, and therefore recklessness generally suffices for a criminal conviction. But in cases in which the harm does not occur, something should be required in order to make up for this lack and thereby to permit a conviction, and therefore a higher level of culpability is required (i.e., intention). But this "mathematical" argument is not convincing. If the existence of a doctrine of attempt is justified by reference to the general purposes of the criminal law, and if throughout the criminal law recklessness generally suffices for criminal liability, why should it not suffice in the context of attempts? The very idea that we need to make up for a lack in cases of complete attempts is problematic. In addition, if recklessness suffices for the completed offence of wounding a person, for example, why should it not suffice for a conviction if, only because of good fortune, no wounding occurs? The fortuitous fact that the beam thrown from a roof does not wound anybody does not lessen the culpability of the person who throws it, and therefore it is not clear why this fact should generate a complete exemption from criminal liability.

I will now suggest a possible explanation for the requirement of intention in the law of criminal attempts. This explanation was briefly introduced at the beginning of this section and I will now return to it.

If the penalisation of complete attempts is based on considerations of retribution, rather than general deterrence, then we can apply the present suggested justification for requiring intention to the context of complete attempts. The idea that even those who believe that the main purpose of penalising completed offences is general deterrence may agree that the penalisation of complete attempts is not based on general deterrence, may be justified by the contention that the existence of a doctrine of criminal attempts does not *add* (or does not substantially add) to the deterrence already produced by the existence of completed offences. And indeed the view that the law of criminal attempts is not based on considerations of general deterrence is a popular one. As Meehan and Currie explain: "The prospective criminal is, by definition, attempting to commit a 'target' crime, to complete his or her criminal intent and thereby achieve his or her objective. The attemptor is therefore not deterred by the serious punishment that would follow should the crime be consummated and detected. How can one possibly say the attemptor is deterred by the punishment for attempt … ?" They conclude that "deterrence is no more than a minor function of the law of attempt".[14] The same argument and conclusion are also accepted by others like LaFave and Scott[15] and the commentary to the Model Penal Code.[16] The above argument and conclusion are relevant to both complete and incomplete attempts, but my concern here is only with complete attempts.

Against the above argument, Hart claims that in some cases people might believe that if they succeed in committing the crime they will escape, but if they fail they may get caught. And in those cases the fact that attempts are punished may deter the actor from acting.[17] But others, who are aware of these kinds of cases, are not persuaded, and remain convinced that, in the final analysis, the weight assigned to considerations of general deterrence in the context of attempts is, at most, minor.[18]

Now, if we assume that punishing complete attempts does not contribute at all to an increase in general deterrence, then we cannot justify the practice of punishing complete attempts on the basis of general deterrence. But even if we accept that punishing complete attempts may contribute, to a minor extent, to an increase in general deterrence (e.g., in the cases referred to by Hart), we can still think that from a utilitarian point of view, this minor increase in deterrence cannot justify the penalisation of complete attempts. If general deterrence does not justify the penalisation of complete attempts, we may suggest retribution as an alternative justification. And if we accept this alternative justification, then we may suggest that the present suggested justification for requiring intention may explain why the law of complete attempts is limited to cases of intention (as opposed to cases of recklessness). But the argument, as introduced thus far, is a circular one. For the claim advanced above, that the penalisation of attempts does not contribute to an increase in general deterrence was *based* on the fact that current law requires intention for a conviction of attempt. In its application to complete attempts, the claim is that a person who intends to shoot another person in order to kill him – wants to kill him and expects to kill him, and therefore the sanction provided for the completed offence of murder is meant to deter him. Now, if this sanction deters him, then the fact that there is a punishment for attempted murder does not further impel him to refrain from shooting. And if the sanction provided for murder does not deter him from shooting (in spite of the fact that he wants and expects to kill) why would the fact that there is a punishment for attempted murder deter him from shooting? This argument is sound insofar as it relates to cases in which the actor intends to cause the result.[19] This, however, does not seem to be the case as regards the actor who is only reckless with respect to the result. It seems that a general law of endangerment might substantially contribute to the goal of general deterrence. In a jurisdiction in which recklessly causing death is an offence, but in which those who act recklessly with regard to the possibility that their act will cause death are not punished at all where a death does not occur, it may be the case that many people who recklessly take risks with the lives of others (and who hope that nobody will get killed) do so only because they know that if nobody is killed, they will not be subject to any punishment. They hope that no harm will occur and, therefore, are not deterred by the punishment provided for the completed offence.[20] And it is reasonable to speculate that if the law in such a jurisdiction changes, so that every person who recklessly takes a risk of harming the life of another person will be subject to punishment even if the risk does not materialise, then the number of cases in which risks of causing harm to the life of others are taken will be significantly diminished (for people will know that the moment they take the risk they are performing a criminal offence and can be punished). And if the number of such risk-takings is diminished, then the number of deaths will also be diminished. Of course, the point that was made here concerning causing death equally applies to all other result crimes. The upshot is that, if we agree with this line of thought, a law of complete attempts that penalises cases in which the actor is reckless with regard to the relevant result *can* contribute to an increase in general deterrence and, therefore, *can* be justified by reference to the goal of general deterrence. This means that we cannot apply to the context of attempts the present justification for requiring intention. In short, the popular view that the penalisation of attempts is not justified by considerations of general deterrence cannot help us in explaining why intention is required for a conviction of attempt, for the view that the penalisation of attempts is not justified by considerations of general deterrence is already based on the legal rule that intention is required for a conviction of attempt.

However, it is difficult to know for sure whether extending the law of complete attempts to cases of recklessness will bring about a significant increase in general deterrence, and whether the increase in deterrence can justify, from a utilitarian point of view, such an expansion of attempt liability. Some authors doubt that this extension of the law of attempts can be justified from a utilitarian perspective.[21] One may suggest that the mentioned extension will not bring about a significant increase in general deterrence because generally the reckless actor will not be deterred by the prospect that even if the result does not occur he will be punished, for he will estimate that if the result does not occur nobody will generally notice that he created a risk, or that even if the creation of the risk is noticed the chances that anybody will report the incident to the police, and the chances that an investigation will be carried out leading to the prosecution of the actor, will be low (since no harm has occurred).

Now, if a certain legislator thinks that the goal of general deterrence cannot justify the penalisation of complete attempts, and that this holds not only in the context of cases of intention but even in the context of cases of recklessness, he may ask himself if in the first place there is a justification for punishing complete attempts. One possible justification for punishing complete attempts is the retributive idea that people who choose to act (and do act) in a morally wrongful way should suffer, and hence be punished. If the legislator justifies punishing complete attempts on this basis, it means that in this context the culpability of the actor constitutes the *justification* for the punishment (in contrast to the context of completed offences, where the culpability of the actor is only needed in order to *permit* the infliction of punishment that is justified by the goal of general deterrence). And if he assumes, as was suggested in section 12.1, that only a high degree of culpability may *justify* the infliction of punishment for retribution purposes, and that "intention is more culpable than recklessness", then he can reasonably decide to limit the doctrine of complete attempts to cases where an intention to cause the result is present. In this manner, the justification suggested in this chapter for "basic crimes of intention" may be applied to the context of criminal attempts.

It is interesting to note that according to this explanation of the law of attempts, the reason why recklessness suffices for a conviction of wounding a person, for example, but does not suffice for a conviction of an attempt to wound a person if, by good fortune, no one gets wounded, is not based on the problematic view that if the result occurs the actor is more culpable than if the result does not occur. According to the present suggestion, in both cases the actor is equally culpable.[22] The differentiation is justified by the fact that if the result occurs, the punishment is justified by the goal of general deterrence and the culpability of the actor only serves to overcome the restriction against punishing innocent people, and recklessness is a sufficiently culpable state of mind to overcome this restriction;

but in a case in which the result does not occur, the goal of general deterrence cannot justify the punishment of the actor, and therefore, we can allow ourselves (from a utilitarian perspective) not to punish him. Indeed, when the actor is *highly* culpable, we feel obliged to punish him, for purposes of retribution, even if punishing him cannot be justified on a utilitarian basis. But since recklessness (in contrast to intention) is not a *highly* culpable state of mind, we do not punish the reckless actor for the purposes of retribution.[23] Of course, this explanation for requiring intention for conviction in cases of complete attempts can be accepted only by those who are ready to accept that the justification for punishing cases of complete attempts is a retributive one.[24]

The above line of thought, if accepted, can also be applied in another context. Under English law, an attempt to commit an offence which is triable only summarily is not a crime.[25] One possible explanation for this limitation in the scope of criminal attempts may be that the culpability inherent in attempting to commit, or committing, less serious offences is not sufficiently high to justify the imposition of punishment for retributive purposes, even when the actor acts with the most culpable state of mind with respect to the elements of the offence (however, the completed offence is penalised, as this is needed to achieve the goal of general deterrence, and the degree of culpability of the actor suffices to *permit* the conviction and punishment of the actor, which are justified by the goal of general deterrence).

It should also be noted that even a legislator who accepts the above line of thought and decides on the basis thereof to require intention for conviction of attempt (and also not to provide for a general doctrine of reckless endangerment) may still think that in the context of the most serious of harms it is justified to penalise cases of reckless endangerment. The degree of culpability of an actor depends, *inter alia*, on the degree of the harm that his action might have caused (as perceived by him at the time of the action). Therefore, when all other things are equal, recklessly endangering the life of another person is more culpable than recklessly endangering the property of another. Consequently, a legislator may think that in spite of the fact that in the context of most criminal offences (like that of damaging the property of another) only those who act with intent to cause the result reach the high degree of culpability required to justify the imposition of punishment for retributive purposes, this is not the case in the context of the most serious of harms, and that recklessly endangering the life or the bodily integrity of other persons reaches the high degree of culpability required to justify the imposition of punishment for purposes of retribution. Such a legislator may decide, then, to require intention for a conviction of attempt, but to penalise cases of reckless endangerment in the context of risks to the life or bodily integrity of other persons.[26] Actually, such a scheme is set forth in the Model Penal Code. Under the Model Penal Code, recklessness with respect to results does not suffice for a conviction of attempt.[27] Also, the Code does not provide for a "general law of endangerment" for all result crimes. However, it contains an offence of "recklessly endangering another person". Section 211.2 provides: "A person commits a misdemeanor if he recklessly engages in conduct which places or may place another person in danger of death or serious bodily injury".[28]

Thus far, I have refrained from elaborating upon the proper meaning of the proposition that "intention is more culpable than recklessness" for purposes of the present suggested justification for requiring intention for conviction of attempt. I will now turn to this point. In chapter 2, I challenged the idea that causing a bad result purposely is more culpable than causing it recklessly by bringing counter examples in which causing a result recklessly seems to be more culpable than doing so purposely. Then I suggested that we inquire as to whether when all other things, *including the motives,* are equal, causing a result purposely is more culpable than causing it recklessly. The discussion in chapters 3-6 showed that the answer to this question is not simple and that reasonable people may disagree on the subject. If the legislator thinks that when all other things are equal (including the motives) there is no difference in culpability between causing a result purposely and doing so recklessly, then he should reject the present justification for requiring intention (if in the context of the present justification the claim that "intention is more culpable than recklessness" is based on the idea that when all other things are equal intention is more culpable).[29] But what about a legislator who thinks that "when all other things are equal, causing a result purposely is more culpable than causing it recklessly"? This view, by itself, cannot justify the adoption of the present justification for requiring intention for a conviction of attempt. The present justification is based on the idea that a *high (or very high)* degree of culpability is needed in order to justify a conviction for retribution purposes, and on the assumption that in many cases (or in a sufficient number of cases) of acting with intent to cause the result, the actor reaches the high degree of culpability required to justify the penalisation of his conduct for purposes of retribution – while this is not the case concerning cases of recklessness. We can speak here of a "threshold of high culpability" that is needed in our context, and we assume that this threshold is reached in many (or in a sufficient number of) cases of intention (as opposed to cases of recklessness). Now, if the number of cases of intention in which the mentioned threshold is reached is only slightly higher than the number of cases of recklessness in which it is reached, this does not suffice to establish the suggested justification. Only if in reality there are *many (or significantly)* more cases of intention that reach the mentioned threshold than cases of recklessness, will it be reasonable to limit convictions to cases of intention.

Now, what can generate such a reality? In chapter 7 I explained that many factors determine the degree of culpability of an actor (including his motives, the specific degree of harm caused by his action etc.) and that in reality cases may differ in various respects that affect this degree of culpability. In light of this, it seems to me unreasonable to assume that the reality described above will be generated merely by the fact that when all other things are equal "intention is more culpable than recklessness". As I said earlier (in section 7.1.4) my own feeling is that this last mentioned difference in culpability (if it exists at all) is not relatively large. If so, it is unreasonable to assume that it would generate, by itself, the reality described above. However, in chapter 9, I suggested that even assuming that when all other things are equal there is no difference in culpability between intention and recklessness (or that there is only a small difference between them), it may still be the case that in reality there is a significant empirical correlation between intention and high degrees of culpability, on the one hand, and recklessness and low degrees of culpability, on the other. I suggested that this correlation may exist for various reasons. For example, it may be the case, that the motives of those who cause the result purposely are generally worse than the motives of those who cause the same result recklessly. A legislator who thinks that the mentioned correlation exists in reality, and that it generates the reality that in many (or in a sufficient number of) cases of intention the degree of culpability of the actor reaches the high degree of culpability required for punishment which is justified by the idea of retribution, and that this is not the case concerning cases of recklessness, will have a prima facie reason for requiring intention.

But note that in discussing, in chapters 9 and 11, the idea of basing the distinction between intention and recklessness on an empirical correlation, I repeatedly emphasised that it is perfectly possible that in reality the correlation between intention and higher degrees of culpability, and recklessness and lower degrees of culpability, will exist in the context of some offences, but not in the context of others (for example, because the typical motives that motivate people to act may vary from offence to offence). However, if we would like to adopt the present suggested justification to rationalise a legislative scheme (like that found in English law) of a *general rule*, applicable to all (indictable) result crimes, that conditions conviction of attempt upon the presence of a mental state of intention, then we must be ready to accept that the above mentioned empirical correlation exists not only in the context of some offences, but rather in the context of all (indictable) result crimes (or at least in a great majority of them, in which case we might be ready to ignore the minority of them, as we do sometimes when we draft rules). The idea that there is such a *general* correlation can perhaps be explained by the assumption (that should be examined empirically) that in the context of all (or most) bad results, people who act with intent to cause bad results generally act out of worse motives than people who act with recklessness with respect to the possibility of causing the same results.

However, my purpose in this book is mainly to inquire as to what legislators *should* do, and therefore we should not limit our discussion to present legislative practices. Therefore, we should be open to the possibility that the law of criminal attempts will vary according to the specific offences under discussion. Hence, if a legislator thinks that the above mentioned correlation and reality exist in the context of some offences, and does not exist in the context of other offences, it is perfectly reasonable for him to decide that conviction of attempt to commit offences that belong to the first group should require intention, but that the law will not distinguish, in the context of complete attempts to commit offences that belong to the second group, between cases of intention and cases of recklessness.[30] Of course, if a legislator thinks that the above mentioned correlation and reality do not exist in the context of any offence, then he will not be able to justify a requirement of intention for a conviction of attempt on the basis of the present line of thought.[31]

Even a legislator who thinks that in the context of all (or some) offences the number of cases of intention in which the degree of culpability of the actor reaches the *high* degree of culpability required to justify retribution is significantly higher than the number of cases of recklessness in which the actor's degree of culpability reaches the mentioned degree of culpability, has to consider alternative options before he concludes that a requirement of intention for conviction of attempt should be provided for. This is because, after all, even in the context in which the reality described above exists, there *are* cases of recklessness (albeit not many) in which the actor's degree of culpability *does* reach the mentioned threshold, so that the exemption of *all* reckless actors from conviction entails a certain price, namely, that some very wicked actors will not get the punishment they deserve.[32] One alternative option is not to require, as a pre-requisite for conviction of attempt, that the actor intend to cause the result, but to provide that in those contexts in which recklessness with respect to a result suffices to convict of the completed offence, it will also suffice for conviction of a complete attempt to commit the said offence, and to rely on the prosecution authorities that they will prosecute, in cases of recklessness, only in those rare cases in which the actor's degree of culpability is so high that it can justify punishment for purposes of retribution. Another alternative is to use a moral formula. For example, the legislator may provide that the mens rea, with respect to results, which is required for a conviction of attempt (where recklessness with respect to the result suffices for a conviction of the completed offence) is "either intention or wicked recklessness" and that "wicked recklessness" is present where the actor who is reckless with respect to the result bears a very high degree of culpability (taking into account all the factors that affect the degree of moral culpability).[33] Of course, the latter two options have their own disadvantages. The upshot is that even assuming that in the context of all (or some) offences, the correlation on which the present justification is based exists, still the final decision whether to require intention cannot be made without weighing the option of requiring intention against the other two alternative options. In section 11.5 I dealt with a similar issue. The discussion there concerned offences in the context of which most of the reckless actors do not reach the degree of culpability required to *permit* a conviction (that is justified by utilitarian considerations); while the present discussion concerns a context in which most of the reckless actors do not reach the high degree of culpability required to *justify* conviction and punishment for purposes of retribution. In the discussion in section 11.5, I discussed three options (requiring intention, relying heavily on prosecutorial discretion, and using a moral formula) that were similar in structure to the three options mentioned above in the context of the present discussion. Most of the discussion conducted in detail in section 11.5 concerning the relative advantages and disadvantages of each of the three options discussed there is relevant, with modifications, to the present discussion. I will not reiterate the arguments here, but only confine myself to mentioning that the conclusion should also be similar in the present context: That neither one of the three options is clearly better than the others. Therefore, we can conclude that if in the context of all offences (or in the context of some of them) the reality is that (taking into account all the factors that affect the degree of moral culpability) in many (or in a sufficient number of) cases of intention, the culpability of the actor is so high that it can justify the imposition of punishment for purposes of retribution, and that this is not the reality insofar as cases of recklessness are concerned, then a reasonable legislator may (but not must) decide to require intention (with respect to the result) for conviction of attempt in the context of those offences.

The conclusion is that in this chapter we succeeded in developing a potential justification for requiring intention, and in applying it to a concrete context, but it should be recalled that the validity of the suggested justification itself, and also the possibility of its being applied in the context of attempts, depends on the acceptance of many assumptions and views that were introduced throughout the discussion.

12.2.2 *Oblique Intention*

Assuming that the legislator actually decides to act upon the present suggested justification, and requires intention with respect to the result for an attempt conviction (with regard to all or some result crimes), what should he do concerning cases of oblique intention? As explained in section 12.2.1, the present justification for requiring intention is not based on a claim as to an intrinsic moral difference between intention and recklessness (i.e., on a claim that when all other things are equal, including the motives, causing a result purposely is more blameworthy than causing it recklessly). Rather it is based on empirical data and on the assumption that in reality the empirical data are such (in the context of all offences, or at least in the context of some of them) that, taking into account all the factors relevant to the degree of moral culpability, the culpability of many (or of a sufficient number) of those who act with intent to cause the result is so high that it can justify punishment for purposes of retribution, while this is not the case concerning those who act with recklessness with regard to the possibility of causing the result. Since the justification for requiring intention lies in the empirical data, the decision what to do concerning cases of oblique intention should also depend on the empirical data. The question should be whether (taking into account all the data and factors relevant to the degree of moral culpability) in many (or in a sufficient number of) cases of oblique intention, the degree of moral culpability is so high that it justifies punishment for purposes of retribution. If the answer is yes, then cases of oblique intention should be penalised, and if the answer is no, then cases of oblique intention should not be penalised (like cases of recklessness).[34]

Now, because the law governing cases of oblique intention should depend on empirical data, which may vary from offence to offence, it is possible that the conclusion will be that the law of cases of oblique intention should vary from offence to offence. This means that if we decide to require intention for a conviction of attempt in the context of all (or some) result crimes, still the law of cases of oblique intention may vary (within this group) from offence to offence.[35]

The above discussion of the law of cases of oblique intention is based on the assumption that the requirement of intention in our context does not stem from an intrinsic difference in culpability between intention and recklessness. However, as I suggested earlier in this chapter (supra at note 31) if a legislator believes, contrary to my feeling, that there *is* a *large* intrinsic difference in culpability between intention and recklessness, then he may come to the conclusion that this difference alone can generate the reality that in many (or in a sufficient number of) cases of intention the culpability of the actor reaches the high degree of culpability required for a conviction that is justified by retribution considerations, and that this is not the case concerning cases of recklessness. Now, if on the basis of the mentioned intrinsic difference, a legislator decides to require intention for complete attempts, then the decision what to do concerning cases of oblique intention should be influenced by the reason why the legislator distinguishes between intention and recklessness. In section 10.2.2, in dealing with the issue of grading offences based on the distinction between intention and recklessness, I summarised how a legislator who grades offences based on the distinction between intention and recklessness, and who bases this grading scheme on a belief in a significant intrinsic difference in culpability between intention and recklessness, should deal with the issue of oblique intention. What is said there can basically apply here, with the necessary modifications (as when I suggest there that cases of oblique intention be included within the lower offence, in the present context this should be read as a suggestion for excluding cases of oblique intention from the scope of complete attempts; and when I suggest there including cases of oblique intention within the higher offence, in the present context this should be read as a suggestion to include cases of oblique intention within the scope of complete attempts).[36]

12.3 Contexts in which Deterrence is Adequately Provided by Other Branches of the Law

Another context to which the present justification may apply may be one in which general deterrence against causing a certain harm is adequately provided for by other, non-criminal, branches of the law. In such a context, the penalisation of causing the mentioned harm will not add any (or a substantial amount of) general deterrence to that already provided by the other branches of the law, and therefore the goal of general deterrence cannot justify the enactment of an offence which penalises causing that harm. Still, the legislator may think that when the degree of culpability of the actor is very high he should be punished, for purposes of retribution, and if this legislator thinks that "intention is more culpable than recklessness", he may enact, in that context, a basic crime of intention.

The crime of defamatory libel may serve as an example for an offence to which the present line of thought may apply. There are jurisdictions that do not have a crime of defamatory libel, and there are indeed scholars who think that such a crime should not exist. One of the main arguments raised against having such an offence is that the law of torts provides a sufficient amount of deterrence against harming the reputation of people, and that the criminal law cannot make any (or a substantial) further contribution, by way of deterrence, in reducing the number of defamations. Thus, for example, criminal libel was abolished in New Zealand,[37] and libel is not a criminal offence in Scotland.[38] Also, a Canadian commission recommended that a new criminal code not include an offence of criminal libel, and one of its main arguments was that the criminal offence would not (substantially) add to the amount of deterrence already provided by tort law.[39] A consensus does not reign, however, as to whether the last mentioned argument is convincing. Many jurisdictions have an offence of criminal libel,[40] and some people think that the existence of an offence of criminal defamation is important, even in terms of general deterrence.[41] It is not my purpose here to decide whether the existence of a criminal offence of defamation can add substantially to the deterrence already produced by tort law. My interest in defamation in the present context is only that it can possibly serve as an example for a context to which the present justification for enacting a basic crime of intention may apply. So, I will proceed further in the discussion on the assumption that a certain legislator thinks that the enactment of a criminal offence of defamation cannot add anything to (or substantially augment) the deterrence already produced by tort law, and that therefore the goal of deterrence cannot justify the enactment of such an offence. Such a legislator may decide not to enact an offence of criminal defamation at all. However, such a legislator may also come to a different conclusion. He may think that in cases in which the culpability of the agent who publishes defamatory material is very high, he should be punished,[42] for purposes of retribution, even if punishing him will not bring about a reduction in the number of future cases of defamation. And if such a legislator thinks that "intention is more culpable than recklessness" he may reasonably decide to enact a basic crime of defamation which includes, inter alia, a requirement of intention to injure the reputation of the victim.[43] Of course, the offence of defamatory libel only serves here as an example, and the above line of thinking may apply to certain other offences as well.

The enactment of a basic crime of intention on the basis of the above line of thought can be justified only if one accepts several assumptions. Some of these assumptions lie at the basis of this chapter, and they were summarised supra in section 12.1. A further assumption, that is specifically relevant to the present section, is that in some contexts the penalisation of an act does not add a substantial amount of deterrence to that which is provided by the civil law. Of course, one might disagree with this assumption and say that the penalisation of an act always adds significantly to the deterrence produced by the civil law. Finally, even one who agrees in principle that the present suggested justification may reasonably lead to the enactment of a basic crime of intention, may disagree with its application to the context of defamation.[44] However, a reasonable legislator may (but not must) accept all the relevant assumptions, and enact a basic crime of intention on the basis of them. But one of the mentioned assumptions is in need of further elaboration, namely that "intention is more culpable than recklessness". What should the meaning assigned to this assumption be for purposes of the present context? The example of criminal defamation may be used in examining this question. According to the present line of thinking, the enactment of the crime of defamatory libel is justified not on a utilitarian basis but on the basis of the idea that those who publish defamatory material and who are very morally culpable – should be punished, for purposes of retribution. An exhaustive discussion of all the elements that such an offence should require will not be carried out here. Instead, the discussion will focus on the requirement of an intention to injure the reputation of the victim. The requirement of intention is justified, according to the present line of thought, on the basis of the view that in order to justify punishment for purposes of retribution, the actor should be *highly* culpable; a view that is accompanied by the belief that those who publish with intent to injure the reputation of the victim are more culpable than those who act with recklessness with regard to the possibility that the publication will injure the reputation of the victim. But what is the meaning of the last mentioned belief? On the basis of the discussion in chapter 2, we have to understand that there are, in reality, cases of publishing defamation with recklessness with regard to the damage to the reputation of the victim, in which the actor is more culpable than in certain cases in which the actor intends to injure the reputation of the victim. So the present justification should rely on a claim that in many (or in a sufficient number of) cases of intention, the publisher is so culpable that he reaches the threshold of a *high* degree of culpability that is required to punish for purposes of retribution, while such a reality is not present in the context of cases of recklessness. Now, the present suggested justification for distinguishing between intention and recklessness in our context can only be valid if in reality there are *many (or significantly)* more cases of intention than cases of recklessness in which the actor reaches the threshold of a *high* degree of culpability. What can produce such a reality? In chapter 7, I explained that many factors determine the degree of culpability of an actor (including his motives, the specific degree of harm caused by his action, etc.) and that in reality cases may differ from one another in various respects that affect this degree of culpability. As I said earlier (in section 7.1.4) my own feeling is that even *if* there is a difference in culpability between acting with intent to cause a bad result and acting with recklessness with respect to that result, when all other things *(including the motives)* are equal – still this difference is not relatively large. Therefore, it seems unreasonable to me to assume that this difference alone will generate the above described reality.[45] But in chapter 9, I suggested that even if there is no difference in culpability between intention and recklessness when all other things (including the motives) are equal (or that there is only a small difference between them) it may still be the case that in reality there is a significant empirical correlation between intention and high degrees of culpability, on the one hand, and recklessness and low degrees of culpability, on the other. As I explained there, the question whether such a correlation exists depends, first of all, on the empirical data (concerning, for example, the typical motives that lead people to engage in various courses of conduct), and it is perfectly possible that such a correlation will exist in the context of certain offences, and will not exist in the context of others. Now, a certain legislator may think that in the context of defamation this correlation exists. He may think that in this context those who act with intent to injure are (taking into account all the factors that affect the degree of culpability) *generally* more culpable than those who act with recklessness with respect to the injury.[46] And he may think that in this context many (or a sufficient number) of those who act with intent to injure are highly culpable so that the goal of retribution justifies their punishment, while only a few of those who act with recklessness reach the high degree of culpability required for punishment for purposes of retribution. Such a legislator has a prima facie reason for requiring intention in the crime of defamation. However, before such a legislator decides to enact such a requirement, he should also consider the alternatives, which are either to use a moral formula (by requiring, for example, that the actor, in cases of recklessness, act with a high degree of culpability) or not to distinguish between intention and recklessness (i.e., to include both cases of recklessness and intention within the definition of the offence) and to rely on the proper use of prosecutorial discretion, that only in rare cases will actors who act with recklessness be prosecuted.[47] The advantages and disadvantages of each of the three options were already discussed in other contexts in this book,[48] so I will not discuss them here again. The conclusion, then, is that a reasonable legislator may (but not must) enact a basic crime of intention on the basis of the present suggested justification.

Assuming that a legislator decides to enact a basic crime of intention on the basis of the present justification, what should he do concerning cases of oblique intention? A similar question was discussed in section 12.2.2, and what has been said there applies, with modifications, to the present context, so I will not repeat what was said there. I will only remark that the legislator has to estimate whether in the context of defamation, for example, in many (or in a sufficient number of) cases of oblique intention, the degree of culpability of the actor (taking into account all the factors that affect the degree of culpability) is so high that it justifies punishment for purposes of retribution, and to decide what to do concerning the cases of oblique intention on the basis of this estimation.[49] It should also be noted that the results of the mentioned estimation concerning cases of oblique intention may vary from offence to offence even within the group of basic crimes of intention that are based on the present justification for requiring intention, and that therefore the law of cases of oblique intention need not necessarily be the same in the context of all the intention crimes that belong to this group.

The discussion in this chapter has shown that a reasonable legislator may enact basic crimes of intention in contexts in which the punishment of the actor is justified based on the goal of retribution and not on that of deterrence. I have suggested two contexts in which it can be said that the infliction of punishment is not based on deterrence: that of attempts, and that of offences with regard to which it may be suggested that the criminal law does not add any (or a substantial amount of) deterrence to that provided by the civil law. These two contexts are not necessarily the only ones to which the justification suggested in this chapter may apply, and one may perhaps find further ones.[50]

12.4   A Variation of the Justification for Enacting Basic Crimes of Intention

In this section I would like to suggest a variation on the justification suggested in this chapter for enacting basic crimes of intention. According to this variation, the fact that in a certain context the penalisation of the relevant conduct does not prevent (by way of deterrence) *much* harm is still an important part of the argument for requiring intention, but (as opposed to the argument suggested in the previous sections of this chapter) the argument is not based on the idea that in such a context the punishment is solely *justified* by the goal of retribution. The present variation holds that the justification of punishment always lies in its tendency to prevent harm, and that the culpability of the actor is only needed to *permit* conviction and punishment (for there is a moral prohibition against convicting and punishing the morally innocent person). But it also adopts a principle of an inverse relation between the gain earned by punishing the actor (in terms of the amount of future harm that is prevented by punishing him), and the degree of culpability that should be required in order to *permit* the punishment. This inverse relation may be put succinctly by the following formula: "The bigger the gain earned by punishing the actor, the lower the degree of culpability that should be required to permit the punishment". If the actor is completely innocent, he should not be punished even for utilitarian purposes, because there is a restriction against convicting and punishing innocent people. But even if the actor is culpable, the amount of culpability that will suffice for a conviction may vary according to the context. If punishing him is supposed to prevent much future harm, then even a low degree of culpability will suffice to permit his conviction and punishment. But if punishing him is supposed to prevent only a small amount of harm, then a higher degree of culpability is required to permit his conviction and punishment.[51] If a legislator embraces this principle, and thinks that "intention is more culpable than recklessness", then he may come to the conclusion that it is justified to require intention for a conviction of attempt. For he may think that although punishing the actor in complete "attempts" (both in cases of intention and cases of recklessness with respect to the result) provides some additional deterrence over the deterrence provided by punishing in cases of completed offences, still this added deterrence is not large, because only in special cases does the deterrent effect of punishing attempts add to the deterrence provided by punishing in cases of completed offences. This means that the amount of harm prevented overall by punishing attempts is not relatively large, and therefore a high degree of culpability is needed to permit conviction and punishment. A similar argument may apply to the context of defamatory libel, for example. It may be said, that although the punishment of persons who publish defamatory libel provides some deterrence, in addition to that provided by the law of torts (for example, it deters poor people who are impecunious and thus are not deterred by the law of torts), still this added deterrence is not large; therefore the overall amount of harm prevented by punishing those who publish defamatory libel is not relatively large, and because of this a high degree of culpability is required to permit conviction and punishment.[52]

One advantage of the present variation of the justification is that, unlike the previous one, we do not have to ignore the additional deterrence produced by punishing attempts or defamatory libel. In the context of the previous variation, we had to adopt the view that punishment (in the contexts under discussion) is not based *at all* on the goal of deterrence. This was needed in order to establish the argument that the punishment (in those contexts) is justified by the goal of retribution. Now, if we believe that punishing attempts, for example, does not add *any* deterrence, this is not problematic. But if we think that punishing attempts adds *something* to the prevention of harms (by way of deterrence), the argument becomes problematic. In order to overcome this difficulty we had to suggest that from a utilitarian point of view, the benefits of punishing complete attempts do not outweigh its costs, and therefore we cannot, from a utilitarian point of view, justify the punishment based on the goal of deterrence: We can only justify it on the basis of retribution considerations. In contrast, in the context of the present variation we do not have to reject the possibility that punishing attempts *can* be justified, from a purely utilitarian point of view. Rather, what we have to say is that even if pure utilitarians would justify punishing all cases of attempts (including cases of recklessness), we still believe in the deontological principle that there is a prima facie prohibition against punishing people, and that this prohibition may be overridden only if the actor is *sufficiently* culpable, and we also believe that the smaller the amount of the harm that is supposed to be prevented by the punishment, the higher the degree of culpability that is required to permit its imposition – and therefore punishing attempts can be permitted only if the actor is highly culpable (i.e., acts with intent to cause the result).[53] The same can be said concerning the context of defamatory libel. Another obvious advantage of the present variation is that it can be adopted even by those who reject the very idea of punishing a person solely for the sake of retribution.

One who accepts the present line of thought may also apply it to a further context. In the previous chapter I dealt with offences that deal with harms to interests that are not considered to be very important, and suggested that the requirement of intention in the context of such offences may be justified by the idea that causing harm to those interests is not sufficiently blameworthy (to permit conviction and punishment), unless the actor acts with intent to cause the harm. But we can now suggest another explanation for requiring intention in those offences. We can suggest that because those offences protect interests that are not so important, the overall harm that is prevented (by way of deterrence) by punishing those who commit such offences is not relatively large, and therefore a high degree of culpability is required to permit the conviction. Hence, the requirement of intention.[54]

The crucial question concerning the present suggested variation is whether the basic principle on which it is based is sound. I admit that it seems illogical to some extent, because it is built on the interaction between two different kinds of considerations: utilitarian considerations (how much harm will be prevented) and deontological considerations (that only those who are sufficiently culpable should be convicted and punished). However, this phenomenon is not unique to this context. As we saw in chapter 3, many believe in the existence of some deontological prohibitions that are not outweighed by simple utilitarian calculations, but that are nevertheless outweighed when the harm that can be prevented by violating them is very large. Also, one can point toward the fact that one of the most popular philosophies of punishment asserts that we punish in order to prevent future harm (i.e., on the basis of utilitarian considerations), provided that the accused is culpable and deserves to be punished (and this is a deontological principle). According to this popular view, the whole criminal law is based on some combination of utilitarian and deontological considerations, and it might be claimed that the present suggested principle only takes us one step further. But is it only a little step? One may argue that it is not. For one may claim that although we can accept that there is a deontological restriction against convicting people unless their degree of culpability reaches a certain threshold – still the height of this threshold should remain constant (i.e., the threshold should not fluctuate according to utilitarian calculations). All in all, I think that although the suggested principle seems somewhat problematic from a logical point of view, one might find it intuitively appealing. Therefore, a reasonable legislator may (but not must) embrace it.

If a certain legislator embraces the suggested principle he may decide to enact some basic crimes of intention, provided he believes that "intention is more culpable than recklessness" in the context of the offences involved. I will not analyse here the meaning that should be given to the proposition that "intention is more culpable than recklessness" in the present context, nor will I discuss the alternative options that should be considered by the legislator before deciding to enact a basic crime of intention on the basis of the present variation, because what has been said on these issues in the discussion of the first variation discussed in this chapter (and in the previous one) can generally apply to the present variation. The same holds true concerning the issue of oblique intention.

Notes

1   See supra section 2.1.
2   In discussing the various theories of punishment, Moore refers, inter alia, to the pure theory of retribution, according to which punishment is properly inflicted because, and only because, the person deserves it; and to what he views as "by far the most usual and popular form" of the mixed theory of punishment, according to which "we do not punish people *because* they deserve it. Desert enters in ... only as a limit on punishment: we punish offenders *because* some net social gain is achieved, such as the prevention of crime, but only if such offenders deserve it. It is, in other words, the achieving of a net social gain that justifies punishment, whereas the desert of offenders serves as a limiting condition on punishment but no part of the justification". See Moore (1997) 92-93. See also Gordon (1978) 51-52.
3   Kugler (1993) 215-216. It is interesting that when authors want to convince us that the justification for punishing a person is not conditioned upon the fact that punishing him will yield some social gain in the future, they generally use examples of actors who perform very horrible actions (like brutal murders or rapes) in order to show that we intuitively feel that these actors should be punished even if we are sure that no social gain will be yielded by the punishment. See, for example, Moore (1997) 98-102, 109, 114 (but see the discussion at 184-185). Cf. Ten (1987) 47; Primoratz (1990) 142. This may suggest that the intuition that wrongdoers should suffer and hence be punished, regardless of whether the punishment will contribute to the well-being of society (by reducing future criminality) is generally present only in cases in which the actor is *highly* culpable.
4   I will not analyse and elaborate here upon the meaning of the proposition that "intention is more culpable than recklessness" for purposes of the present justification. This analysis appears infra in section 12.2.1.
5   One may also take the position that retribution is the only justification for enacting criminal offences, and that all criminal offences should be understood as being based on retributive considerations. In this case, one cannot speak of *special* contexts in which retribution forms the justification for punishment, and in which an especially

high degree of culpability should be required (but the question whether, in this case, the *general rule* should be to require intention or not, will still have to be considered).

6   Smith and Hogan (1999) 306. For a list of other countries in which the criminal law requires intention for conviction of an attempt, see Meehan and Currie (2000) 57-58.

7   Cf. Smith (1971) 66-67.

8   There are specific offences in England that penalise certain actions that are taken in certain circumstances and that require a risk that a specified harm will ensue (for a discussion of such "endangerment offences" see Ashworth (1999) 309-317). But these offences are limited to specific contexts and actions, and English law does not have a general doctrine of endangerment. Even in the contexts of a risk to life or bodily integrity there is no general offence of endangerment in English law.

9   Since in this book I am not dealing with cases of intention to perform a subsequent act, I will confine the discussion here to cases in which the actor has performed the "last act", such as those in the text involving a person who throws a beam or a stone. In other words, I am going to leave aside the issue of incomplete attempts and deal here only with *complete* attempts, inquiring as to why intent with regard to the result is required in *this* category of attempts.

10   See for example Stuart (1968) 655-662; Meehan and Currie (2000) 67-86, 354-356. Cf. Alexander (2000) 947-948. Stuart changed his mind and now thinks that intention as to the result should be required. See Stuart (1995) 598.

11   It was decided there that just as wicked recklessness is a sufficient mens rea for murder, thus it is also a sufficient mens rea for attempted murder, and commentators tend to think that recklessness suffices for an attempt conviction in the context of all crimes of recklessness. See Gordon (2000) 306-308; Jones and Christie (1996) 114. And cf. Burchell (1997) 350 on the law in South Africa. For Canadian decisions (prior to 1984) convicting of attempt in cases where the accused did not intend to cause the relevant result see Meehan and Currie (2000) 62-64. The present law in Canada, however, requires for an attempt conviction that the accused intended to cause the relevant result. See Stuart (1995) 594-598; Meehan and Currie (2000) 57-58, 64-67. For a few American cases in which courts have taken the position that a reckless disregard of human life suffices for a conviction of attempted murder see Perkins and Boyce (1982) 637.

12   See for example Williams (1983a) 408-409.

13   See Meehan and Currie (2000) 81-82.

14   Meehan and Currie (2000) 30-31.

15   LaFave and Scott (1986) 499.

16   See Model Penal Code and Commentaries (1985) Part 1, vol. 2, at pp. 293-294 stating in regard to inchoate crimes: "Since these offenses always presuppose a purpose to commit another crime, it is doubtful that the threat of punishment for their commission can significantly add to the deterrent efficacy of the sanction – which the actor by hypothesis ignores – that is threatened for the crime that is his objective. ... General deterrence is at most a minor function to be served in fashioning provisions of the penal law addressed to these inchoate crimes; that burden is discharged upon the whole by the law dealing with the substantive offenses". See also at p. 490: "It is doubtful, however, that the threat of punishment for the inchoate crime can add significantly to the net deterrent efficacy of the sanction threatened for the substantive offense that is the actor's object, which he, by hypothesis, ignores".

17   Hart (1968) 129.

18   As a matter of fact, all the authors of the sources brought above at notes 14-16 refer to such cases but still they do not change their views. Hart (ibid.) also raises the

possibility that there may be persons "who are not completely confident that they will succeed in their criminal objective, but will be prepared to run the risk of punishment if they can be assured that they have to pay nothing for attempts which fail; whereas if unsuccessful attempts were also punished the price might appear to them too high". But others may nonetheless respond that such cases are rare, and that, therefore, considerations of general deterrence play, at most, a minor role in the law of attempt.

19   And indeed the sources brought above at notes 14-16 assume that in cases of attempt the actor acts with intent to commit the completed offence.

20   Cf. Schulhofer (1974) 1539-1540: "Where the actor behaves recklessly, consciously creating an unjustifiable risk but expecting that harm will not result, he will also expect to avoid the penalty for causing harm. The severity of the latter penalty could affect his willingness to take the risk, but as the risk of harm diminishes, the actor's risk of suffering the penalty applicable in case of harm inevitably diminishes too. Hence even an actor who is fully aware of the applicable sanctions, and fully rational in his response to them, will tend to be less affected by the penalty for harm as the risk of harm diminishes. Moreover, the tendency for the deterrent effect to diminish as the risk of harm diminishes is probably reinforced by the natural inclinations of at least many people to discount even the perceived risks and to assume that they personally will not be the ones to suffer misfortunes that are, for the group, statistically inevitable. Their subjective perception of the probability of suffering the penalty in question may be far lower than the facts warrant". See also Shachar (1987) 14.

21   Smith asks: "Is society any less secure because a reckless wrongdoer escapes liability because he does not do harm?" (Smith (1971) 75). Smith and Hogan say that "on utilitarian grounds ... it is probably undesirable to turn the whole criminal law into 'conduct crimes'. The needs of deterrence are probably adequately served in most cases by 'result crimes'; and the criminal law should be extended only where a clear need is established". Therefore, they say, we can live with the fact that a person who hurls a stone, being reckless whether he injures anybody, is guilty of no offence, not even an attempt, if no one is injured (Smith and Hogan (1999) 30). Duff mentions the argument sometimes made against the extension of criminal attempts to cases of recklessness that such extension would unduly extend the scope of the criminal law and he explains the argument as being based on the claim that such extension "would subject many more citizens to the fact or threat of criminal liability, and could not be expected to bring enough benefits, in increased crime prevention, to outweigh those significant costs" (Duff (1996) 31). See also ibid. at 123: "We punish reckless or negligent conduct that actually causes some legally relevant harm; but if it does not cause such harm, it is either punished less severely or is not criminal at all. Such a practice is reasonably effective in preventing harm, since the prospect of (severe) punishment for causing harm will deter dangerous conduct generally; and we have no reason to expect that punishing conduct which causes no harm as well as, or as severely as, conduct which does cause harm would bring enough harm-preventive benefit to outweigh its additional costs". See also ibid. at 369.

22   The explanation suggested in the text also differs from the idea suggested by Duff, that there is a significant difference in moral character between the actions of reckless actors who cause the harm which they risk causing and the actions of those who do not, and that this difference in moral character explains, in part, why we criminalise the former actors and not the latter ones. See Duff (1996) 369. My explanation is not based on the claim that there is an intrinsic moral difference between the two actions, or actors.

23   The Model Penal Code's commentary states that when the actor's failure to commit
      the substantive offence is due to a fortuity, as when the bullet misses in attempted
      murder, his exculpation on that ground would shock the common sense of justice. See
      Model Penal Code and Commentaries (1985) Part 1, vol.2, p. 294. This statement is
      made in the context of attempts, i.e., concerning cases in which the actor intends to
      cause the result. The commentary does not make the same point concerning cases of
      recklessness, and indeed the code does not have a *general* law of endangerment (it
      does, however, have specific offences of endangerment in certain contexts; see infra
      the text accompanying note 28).

24   The idea that the main rationale for punishing *complete* attempts lies in retribution can
      be found in Ashworth (1987) 5-6, 17, 22-24 (the author refers to "modern
      retributivism"). For the view that retribution forms one of the rationales for punishing
      attempts see Meehan and Currie (2000) 31-33; Kremnitzer (1984) 346. Cf. Gordon
      (1978) 163. It is common to suggest that one of the important purposes of the law of
      attempts is to enable law enforcement agencies to intervene before the actor causes the
      harm. See for example Model Penal Code and Commentaries (1985) Part 1, vol. 2, p.
      294; Gordon (1978) 164; LaFave and Scott (1986) 498. But this rationale mainly
      applies to incomplete attempts, rather than complete attempts (which are the subject of
      our discussion), since in cases of complete attempts the actor has already performed
      the "last act" and no intervention (by way of arrest) is needed to prevent the harm. See
      Kremnitzer (1984) 347. Cf. Ashworth (1987) 5, 22; Ashworth (1999) 462. Another
      rationale that is suggested for punishing (both complete and incomplete) attempts is
      that the actor who attempts, but fails, to commit a certain offence, shows that he is a
      dangerous person, who is ready to commit the said offence, and therefore he should be
      treated in order to reduce the risk that he will commit this offence in the future. In
      other words, considerations of special (or individual) deterrence, incapacitation and
      rehabilitation may justify the punishment of attempts in the same way that they may
      justify the punishing of completed offences. For this rationale see for example Model
      Penal Code and Commentaries (1985) Part 1, vol. 2, at p. 294; LaFave and Scott
      (1986) 499; Hart (1968) 128-129; Kremnitzer (1984) 345-346. Those who view this
      rationale (rather than the retributive one) as lying behind the penalisation of complete
      attempts would deny the explanation suggested in the text for the requirement of
      intention in complete attempts. They might try to develop another explanation for this
      requirement, based on the claim that a person who intends to cause a bad result is more
      dangerous than one who is only reckless with respect thereto. I will not discuss this
      potential argument here, however, as this book is confined to the issue whether a
      distinction should be made between intention and recklessness based on a difference in
      the degree of *moral culpability* of the actor. It does not deal with other potential
      differences, like a difference in the degree of the *dangerousness* of the actor. For
      discussions of whether the intention requirement may be justified by arguments based
      on degrees of dangerousness of the actor, see for example Duff (1996) 181-182; Enker
      (1977).

25   Section 1(4) of the Criminal Attempts Act 1981.

26   An alternative line of thinking that may lead one to adopt a scheme similar to that
      described in the text is that the added general deterrence that may be achieved by
      penalising reckless endangerment in the context of the most serious of harms will yield
      more benefits, relative to other contexts, simply because it is expected to prevent very
      serious harms. Hence, penalising endangerment *can* be justified, in this context, based
      on the goal of general deterrence. Therefore, in this context, culpability is needed only

to *permit* the imposition of punishment, and therefore recklessness may suffice for conviction.

27 See Model Penal Code (1985), section 5.01(1)(b).

28 I am not claiming that the decisions taken by the drafters of the Model Penal Code were actually based on the line of thinking described in the text, but only that a reasonable legislator who acts on this basis may come up with a scheme similar to that found in the Model Penal Code.
One might argue that the justification suggested in this chapter cannot apply to offences in the Model Penal Code. The argument would be that this justification is based on the view that in certain contexts many reckless actors do not reach the high threshold of culpability required for punishment which is based on retribution – but that such a reality cannot exist in a jurisdiction which adopts the Model Penal Code, as the Code's definition of recklessness requires that the actor's conscious taking of the risk constituted a *gross* deviation from the standard of conduct of a law-abiding person. However, this is not a valid argument. A similar argument was made in chapter 11 (note 43), concerning the justification suggested in that chapter. The response suggested there may also apply here. Furthermore, the argument based on the Model Penal Code's definition of recklessness is significantly weaker in the present context. For the definition of recklessness in the Code is meant to set the threshold of culpability that is generally required for "normal" offences (i.e., offences based on utilitarian grounds related to crime prevention). It is therefore meant to define the degree of culpability that is required to *permit* a conviction that is based on utilitarian grounds. However, according to the present suggestion, a *higher* degree of culpability is required in offences enacted for purposes of retribution, and it is possible that in the context of certain (or many) offences, this *higher* degree of culpability will generally not be reached in cases of recklessness.

29 A different basis for this claim will be suggested later in this section.

30 In the context of offences that belong to the second group, a further decision that will have to be made is whether to include even cases of recklessness in the category of complete attempts (or, alternatively, to create a separate category of reckless endangerment for them) or not to penalise even in cases of intention. Of course, the decision need not be the same for all offences that belong to the second group. Actually, support for the basic idea of not having the same law of attempts for all crimes can be found in the English law's limitation of the doctrine of criminal attempts to indictable offences, and in the Model Penal Code's offence of "recklessly endangering another person". As was shown earlier in this section, explanations can be advanced for both the English approach and the Model Penal Code's offence which are consistent with the present suggested justification for requiring intention. On the general idea that the mens rea required for a conviction of attempt may vary according to the specific offence which is attempted, cf. Duff (1996) 142.

31 I should add here that if a legislator thinks, contrary to my view, that there is a *large intrinsic* difference in culpability between intention and recklessness, then he may come to the conclusion that, because of this difference alone, in many (or in a sufficient number of) cases of intention, the culpability of the actor reaches the required high degree of culpability and that this is not so concerning cases of recklessness. Such a legislator may, then, justify the requirement of intention for conviction of attempt on the basis of the mentioned intrinsic difference. However, it should be recalled that it is possible to argue that the intrinsic difference between intention and recklessness exists only in the context of the most heinous of moral wrongs (see supra section 7.3), or that the mentioned difference is not relevant to

offences that do not deal with harms to people, like offences against animals and offences against the state (see supra section 7.3).

32   Of course, if in the context of a certain offence *no* reckless actor reaches the threshold, no price will be paid. The fact that some actors who act with intent to cause the result do not reach the high threshold and should not be punished is not mentioned in the text as an argument against distinguishing between intention and recklessness – because the phenomenon that in rare cases people who fall within the scope of offence definitions (and do not fall within the scope of the criminal law defences) should not be convicted is not unique to the present context. The solution to this problem is to rely on the prosecutorial authorities that there will be no prosecution in such cases.

33   Another option is to require "a very high degree of culpability" even in cases of intention.

34   The present justification for the requirement of intention is based, inter alia, on the assumption that the penalisation of complete attempts does not substantially increase the prevention of harm by way of general deterrence. This surely holds for cases of oblique intention, for in these cases the actor is sure that he will cause the result, so that the punishment he may suffer if the result does not occur cannot influence his decision. Therefore, it is appropriate in the context of the present justification for requiring intention to focus, in discussing the issue of oblique intention as well, on whether punishing in cases of oblique intention can be justified on the basis of retribution.

35   The discussions conducted in section 11.6 concerning the possibility that cases of oblique intention form an "intermediate set of cases" between direct intention and recklessness, and concerning the possibility that the empirical data will justify, at least from a theoretical point of view, even the penalisation of cases of foresight of the result in high probability (and not only of cases of foresight of certainty) are relevant, with modifications, to the present context.

36   There is no consensus in the literature on the question whether oblique intention should suffice for conviction of attempt. Those who say that recklessness with respect to results should not suffice for conviction of attempt based on the linguistic argument that a person who is only reckless with respect to the death, for example, cannot be said to "attempt" (i.e. to "try") to kill, should (to be consistent) take the same position regarding cases of oblique intention, because a person who does not act *in order* to kill, cannot be said to "attempt" (or "try") to kill, even if he foresees the practical certainty that death will ensue from his action (see Duff (1996) 20-21). Yet, Williams, for example, justifies the exclusion of recklessness with respect to results from the scope of attempt liability partly on the basis of the linguistic argument, and in the same breath maintains that oblique intention should suffice for conviction of attempt. See Williams (1983a) 408-409. However, the linguistic argument is of no importance to our discussion, which is concerned not with the conventional law, but with the preferable law. Williams figures among those who think that the law of complete attempts should cover cases of oblique intention. See Williams (1983a) 409; Williams (1987) 427. This is also the position taken in the Model Penal Code. Section 5.01(1)(b) of the Model Penal Code (1985) provides that in order to be convicted of an attempt to commit a result crime (in the case of a complete attempt) it is required, inter alia, that the actor perform his action "with the purpose of causing or with the belief that it will cause" the relevant result. This means that recklessness with respect to the result does not suffice, but that either direct intention or oblique intention does suffice for a conviction. (As for the inclusion of oblique intention within the scope of complete attempts, the commentary to the Model Penal Code states that it is difficult to say what

the decision concerning this point would be under prevailing principles of attempt law, and also that only a minority of recent revisions have explicitly followed the Model Penal Code on this point. See Model Penal Code and Commentaries (1985) Part 1, vol.2, at p. 305.) Some scholars think that oblique intention should not suffice for a conviction of attempt. See, for example, Duff (1996) 370.

37   The offences of criminal libel and slander were repealed by the *Defamation Act* 1992. See Gillooly (1998) 19. It seems that the main reason for abolishing the offences was that "the civil action available for defamation provides adequate protection for defamatory statements and renders the criminal action superfluous" (Report of the Committee on Defamation *Recommendations on the Law of Defamation* (New Zealand, 1977) para. 455, as cited in : The Law Commission, Working Paper No. 84, *Criminal Libel* (1982) 80).

38   McCall Smith and Sheldon (1997) 18; *Gatley on Libel and Slander* (1998) 557. Nor does the American Mode Penal Code include an offence of defamation.

39   See Law Reform Commission of Canada (Working Paper 35) *Defamatory Libel* (1984). The commission recommends that "there should be no offence of defamation in the new *Criminal Code* or elsewhere" (p. 61). The commission mentions that some jurisdictions argue that abolition of the crime is proper because the civil remedy is adequate (p. 51), and maintains that "the merits of a case for the crime of defamation on the basis that the present crime deters where the tort does not by reason of fear of punishment appears doubtful" (p. 54). And after a long and detailed discussion, the commission concludes that "we do not feel that a crime of defamation would be able to do better that which is already done by the civil law of defamation. Nor would it seem to be an effective deterrent. Therefore, we do not feel that a crime of defamation could make a substantial contribution in dealing with the problem of defamatory publications in our society. Accordingly, we recommend that our *Criminal Code* should contain no crime of defamation, even in a restricted form" (p. 60). See also the discussion in Murphy and Coleman (1990): The fact that the law (in the United States) currently provides a civil, and not a criminal, remedy for defamation (ibid. at 110) is explained, inter alia, by the argument that "in the vast majority of cases, the private remedy of a tort suit probably works effectively to protect reputational rights. Even if damage to reputation cannot be compensated in purely economic terms, the very winning of a libel suit functions to vindicate one's reputation, and ... the threat of being sued for defamation might be sufficient to protect reputations against most serious acts of libel and slander" (p. 117). It should also be added that the argument that civil law sanctions may be considered an adequate deterrent may be invoked not only with regard to general deterrence, but also with regard to individual deterrence.

40   See *Gatley on Libel and Slander* (1998) chapters 22-23.

41   Cf. The Law Commission *Report on Criminal Libel* (1985) at 11-12.

42   Cf. The Law Commission *Report on Criminal Libel* (1985) 11: "If damage to reputation is done intentionally and with knowledge that the statement is false, then the state of mind and blameworthiness of the maker of the statement are no different in character from the person who deliberately assaults another or damages his property. He has done an act which society generally would regard as just as deserving of punishment as those acts".

43   In Israel, the criminal offence of defamation (which appears in section 6 of The Defamation (Prohibition) Law, 1965) requires that the agent publish the defamation "with intent to injure". This means that recklessness with regard to the injury that may be caused to the reputation of the victim does not suffice for conviction. For a discussion of this point see Kretzmer (1986). I do not claim that the intention

requirement was actually provided for in the Israeli offence, based on the present suggested justification for requiring intention in the offence of criminal defamation. In England, it is not clear whether the criminal offence of defamatory libel requires an intention to injure the reputation of the victim. See Smith and Hogan (1999) 719-720.

44   The legislator may think, for example, that even the most heinous publishers of defamation do not reach the very high degree of culpability which is required for punishment that is justified solely on the basis of retribution. Or the legislator may think that if we adequately define the offence by requiring, for example, that the defamation is false (and that the actor act with knowledge thereof) and that the publication is likely to seriously injure the reputation of the victim (and that the actor act with knowledge thereof), then a sufficient number of actors who will be reckless with regard to the injury to the victim (and that would fulfil all the other requirements of the offence) will be so culpable that punishing them for purposes of retribution would be justified.

45   What is written supra at note 31 is also relevant here.

46   An explanation for the view that such a reality exists may be based, for example, on the claim that those who act with intent to injure the reputation of the victim generally act from more wicked motives than those who act with recklessness. Those who act with intent to injure the reputation of the victim act many times out of spite, ill will, hatred, jealousy, revenge, the desire to remove a rival (in politics, business or work), etc.

47   Even if the legislator decides to preserve the option of private prosecution in the context of defamation, he may still condition the institution of proceedings upon the consent of the Attorney General, as was suggested in England. See: The Law Commission *Report on Criminal Libel* (1985) pp. 48 and 68.

48   See supra towards the end of section 12.2.1 and see section 11.5. The discussions there apply, with modifications, to the present context.

49   In Israel, the Supreme Court interpreted the statute that requires an "intent to injure" for a conviction of criminal defamation as requiring direct intention. Therefore, oblique intention does not suffice for a conviction of criminal defamation in Israel. See *Borochov v. Yefet* (1985), 39(3) P.D. 205. For a discussion and criticism of this decision see Kretzmer (1986).

50   For example, one may imagine that there might be a certain course of conduct that may cause some sort of harm, and even if there is no criminal sanction against engaging in such conduct, in reality people will very rarely engage in such conduct (and there is no difference, insofar as the rareness of the phenomenon is concerned, between cases in which the actor intends to cause the harm and cases in which the actor is reckless with regard the possibility that it will ensue). Given this rareness, it might be suggested that the overall harm that can be prevented by deterrence is low, and therefore the penalisation of the mentioned conduct cannot be justified by deterrence concerns. However, it may be suggested that if the actor acts with intent to cause the result, he is so culpable that he should be punished for purposes of retribution.

51   Cf. Robinson (1987) 38-39. The question whether it is justified to convict and punish an accused when the amount of future harm that is supposed to be prevented is exceptionally high even when he is completely innocent, and the question whether it is justified to convict and punish an accused where his degree of culpability is exceptionally high even if no future harm is supposed to be prevented as a result, need not be discussed here. The principle suggested in the text does not depend on a positive answer to either of these two questions. On these questions see, for example, Ten (1987) 79-81.

52 The present variation may apply to the context discussed supra at note 50, too.

53 A further advantage of the present variation is that in order to apply the previous variation to the context of attempts one has to reject the idea that the dangerousness of the actor as manifested in the attempt is a valid justification for punishment (for the sake of special deterrence, incapacitation or rehabilitation). See supra note 24. But this rejection is not essential to the present variation. For even if we accept that punishing cases of complete "attempts" (both in cases of intention and cases of recklessness) can be justified from a purely utilitarian point of view based on special deterrence, incapacitation or rehabilitation concerns, still the amount of harm prevented by way of these effects of punishment is much smaller than the amount of harm prevented by punishing completed offences (because punishing completed offences prevents harm not only by way of special deterrence, incapacitation and rehabilitation but it also prevents *much* harm by way of general deterrence). Since the amount of harm prevented by punishing completed offences is much larger than that prevented by punishing attempts, it is reasonable, according to the present argument, to require a higher degree of culpability for a conviction of attempt. Hence, the requirement of intention.

54 In chapter 11 (note 18) I referred to the fact that in certain jurisdictions, despite the principle that negligence does not generally suffice for a criminal offence conviction, it does suffice for conviction of certain offences that protect very important interests, such as human life. The explanation suggested there for punishing negligently causing death, for example, was that since the harm in this context (i.e., death) is great, even causing it negligently is sufficiently culpable to permit a conviction. In other words, the explanation was that even if we assume that the minimum degree of culpability required for permitting conviction is the same in all contexts, still in the context of causing death, even the culpability of the negligent actor reaches that degree. But if we accept the present line of thinking, we may suggest another explanation. Assuming that the punishment imposed in cases of negligently causing harms adds to the prevention of those harms (by way of general and special deterrence) we may suggest that since the amount of the overall harm prevented by punishing those who cause death, by way of deterrence, is very large (because of the high importance of life), even a low degree of culpability may suffice to permit the imposition of punishment, and therefore negligence suffices for a conviction. It is also possible to suggest that penalising cases of negligently causing death is appropriate, based on the cumulative force of two considerations: First, that because of the large amount of harm that is supposed to be prevented by the imposition of punishment, a lower degree of culpability than that which is generally required suffices to permit a conviction; second, that the fact that this lower degree of culpability (which is required in the present context) is reached is explained by the fact that the harmed interest is so important.

At the text accompanying note 28 supra, I referred to the fact that although the Model Penal Code does not have a "general law of endangerment" for all result crimes, it nevertheless exceptionally contains an offence of "recklessly endangering another person" that deals with cases of recklessly placing other persons in danger of death or serious bodily injury. I suggested there that this exception can be understood as being based on the idea that although a conviction in cases in which the result does not occur is justified only when the actor is highly culpable (because in such cases the punishment is imposed for retribution purposes), and although generally reckless actors are not highly culpable, still in the context of death or serious bodily injury even the reckless actors are highly culpable, because of the great importance of the interest that may be harmed. Now, a similar explanation of the exception may also be advanced in the context of the present variation. For we can say, in the present context, that although punishing in cases in which the harm does not occur does not add much deterrence to that provided by the completed offence – and therefore a high degree of culpability is required to permit the conviction when the harm does not occur – and although reckless actors generally do not reach the high degree of culpability that is required to permit conviction in this context, still when the harm that might be caused is great (like death) even the reckless actor reaches the high degree of culpability which is required to permit conviction. But another explanation is also possible: We may suggest that in spite of the fact that punishing in cases in which the harm does not occur does not add much to the prevention of harm (in terms of the *number* of cases in which the actor decides to refrain from acting because of his knowledge that even if he does not cause the harm he will be punished), since the deterrence in the context of the above mentioned offence is supposed to prevent very large harms (death or serious bodily injury) the overall amount of harm that is prevented by this offence is, in the final analysis, large enough, and therefore even a relatively low degree of culpability suffices to permit conviction, and this is the reason why recklessness suffices for a conviction in the context of the mentioned offence (a similar suggestion was made supra at note 26, in the context of the previous variation). Here too it is possible to suggest that penalisation is based on the cumulative force of two considerations, as was suggested above in the discussion about causing death negligently.

Chapter 13

Conclusions

13.1

In Part One of this book I discussed the issue of grading offences based on the distinction between intention and recklessness, and in chapter 10 I summarised the main conclusions of that discussion. In Part Two I discussed the issue of enacting "basic crimes of intention", and in the present chapter I will briefly summarise the conclusions of this discussion.

In chapter 2 I explained that even if we assume that intention is more culpable than recklessness, the idea of enacting "basic crimes of intention" still seems highly problematic. The main question discussed in chapters 11 and 12 was whether reasonable reasons exist for enacting basic crimes of intention. The conclusion was that in certain contexts, a reasonable legislator may (but not must) enact basic crimes of intention. A further question that was dealt with was: What should a legislator who enacts basic crimes of intention in those contexts do concerning cases of oblique intention?

13.2

13.2.1

The discussion in chapter 11 was based on the acceptance of a "principle of threshold of culpability" according to which criminal liability may be imposed only on actors who are *sufficiently* morally culpable. I suggested that a legislator who adopts this principle and who believes that "intention is more culpable than recklessness" may come to the conclusion that in the context of certain offences that do not protect very important interests, those who act with recklessness generally do not reach the threshold of culpability that is required to permit the imposition of criminal liability, as harm is only done to interests that are not very important. Such a legislator, I claimed, may reasonably decide to enact basic crimes of intention in those contexts.

In section 11.5 I examined what the proposition that "intention is more culpable than recklessness" should mean in the context of the present justification for requiring intention. I claimed that for the present suggested justification to be valid, it should be the case that in the potential contexts of its application, a great majority of the agents who act with recklessness with respect to the proscribed result (taking into account all the relevant factors that affect the degree of culpability) do not reach the threshold of culpability required for the imposition of criminal liability, while many (or a sufficient number) of those who act with intent to cause the result – do reach this threshold. Since many factors affect the degree of culpability of the actor, it seemed to me unreasonable to assume that this state of things would arise merely as a result of the fact that "when all other things are equal (including the motives) those who act with intent to cause the proscribed result are more culpable than those who act with recklessness with respect to the same result". For it seems that the difference in culpability between intention and recklessness (when all other things, including the motives, are equal) if it exists at all, is not sufficiently large to generate the above described state of things.

However, I suggested that it may be the case that in the context of certain offences an empirical correlation will exist between intention and high degrees of culpability, on the one hand, and recklessness and low degrees of culpability, on the other, and that it may also be the case that in the context of certain offences (that do not protect very important interests) the mentioned correlation will be so significant that in a great majority of cases of recklessness (as opposed to cases of intention) the actor will not be sufficiently culpable to permit the imposition of criminal liability. And *if* the just described state of affairs is present in the context of a certain offence, then the legislator will have a prima facie reason for enacting a basic crime of intention in that context.

However, before enacting a basic crime of intention on the basis of the above line of thought, the legislator should consider two further alternative options: First, to use a moral formula and, second, to refrain from requiring intention as a pre-requisite for liability, and to rely instead on the prosecution authorities, that only in rare cases will cases of recklessness be prosecuted. Each of the three options has its own advantages and disadvantages, which were discussed in section 11.5, and neither of them is clearly better than the others. This means that, in the final analysis, a reasonable legislator may decide not to enact any basic crimes of intention on the basis of the present justification. More importantly, however, a reasonable legislator *may* decide to enact basic crimes of intention, on the basis of this justification.

As was said above, the discussion does not indicate that a reasonable legislator must decide to enact basic crimes of intention on the basis of the present justification. The legislator may reject the principle of a threshold of culpability, or he may think that there is no offence in the context of which the empirical data are such that in a great majority of the cases of recklessness (as opposed to the cases of intention) the actor's culpability does not reach the required threshold. And even if he accepts that there is such an offence, he may still decide to prefer the other options mentioned above. But, as I said above, what is important here is the conclusion that if a legislator finds that there *is* such an offence, then he *may* reasonably decide to enact a basic crime of intention in that context.

13.2.2

If a legislator decides to enact some basic crimes on the basis of the present suggested justification, then he will have to decide what to do concerning cases of oblique intention. As was explained in section 11.6, the answer to this question depends on whether in the crimes under discussion the factual data are such that (taking into account all the factors that are relevant to the degree of culpability of the actor) in a great majority of cases of oblique intention the actor is not sufficiently culpable to permit the imposition of criminal liability. The law of cases of oblique intention will depend on the answer to this question, and it is possible that the answer to this question (hence the law of cases of oblique intention) will vary from offence to offence.[1]

13.3

13.3.1

In chapter 12 I suggested a further possible justification for requiring intention in basic crimes. This suggestion is based on the idea that when the imposition of punishment is based on retribution, rather than on deterrence concerns, an especially high degree of culpability should be required to justify the imposition of punishment. If we accept this view and we also think that "intention is more culpable than recklessness" then we have a prima facie reason for requiring intention in contexts in which the punishment is based on retribution. A reasonable legislator may reject this line of thought. He may think that retribution alone cannot justify the imposition of punishment, or he may reject the view that there should be any difference between the degree of culpability required for permitting the imposition of punishment (which is justified by utilitarian considerations) and that required for justifying punishment which is imposed for purposes of retribution. Or, even if the legislator accepts that there may be a justification for requiring higher degrees of culpability where the imposition of punishment is based on retribution, he may still hold the view that recklessness is generally a sufficiently culpable state of mind, even for *justifying* the imposition of punishment for purposes of retribution. But, more importantly, a reasonable legislator *may* accept the suggested justification and enact basic crimes of intention on its basis.

13.3.2

But to what context may the above suggested justification apply? The first possible context I suggested was that of complete attempts. The suggestion is that the penalisation of complete attempts does not add substantially to the general deterrence provided by the completed offences, and therefore it is not justified by the idea of general deterrence, but by the idea of retribution. Therefore, it is reasonable to require intention to cause the proscribed result for a conviction of attempt.[2]

The above line of thinking is based on the assumption that "intention is more culpable than recklessness". What is the meaning of this proposition for purposes of the present justification? It seems that in order to justify the requirement of intention on the basis of the present line of thinking, we need to accept that in many (or in a sufficient number of) cases of intention, the actor is sufficiently culpable (to justify punishment for purposes of retribution) – and that the situation differs in cases of recklessness. I suggested (in section 12.2.1) that only if in reality there are many (or significantly) more cases of intention than cases of recklessness in which the actor reaches the high threshold of culpability required in our context, will it be reasonable to distinguish in our context between intention and recklessness (by penalising cases of intention and by not penalising cases of recklessness). I further said that it does not seem reasonable to me to assume that the above described state of things will be generated merely by the fact that when all other things are equal (including the motives) intention is more culpable than recklessness (even assuming that there is a difference in culpability between them, when all others things are equal). However, if we assume that there is an empirical correlation between intention and high degrees of culpability, on the one hand, and recklessness and low degrees of culpability, on the other, it may be the case that this correlation will generate the above described state of things. Now, if the legislator thinks that the above correlation and state of affairs are present in the context of all result crimes, then he has a *prima facie* reason for always requiring intention for a conviction of attempt; but if he thinks that this state of things exists only in the context of certain offences, he may reasonably decide to distinguish between intention and recklessness (by penalising in cases of intention and by not penalising in cases of recklessness) only with regard to complete attempts to commit those specific offences, and not with regard to complete attempts to commit other offences.

But even if there are offences in the context of which the above state of affairs exists, the legislator still has to consider two alternative reasonable options before deciding to require intention for a conviction of attempt: first, to use a moral formula, and second, to refrain from requiring intention as a pre-requisite for liability, and to rely on the prosecution authorities that only in rare cases will cases of recklessness be prosecuted.

The suggested justification for requiring intention, and its application to the context of attempts, are based on many assumptions that may be rejected by reasonable people. And even one who accepts all these assumptions may still reasonably prefer one of the last mentioned options over that of requiring intention. This means that a reasonable legislator may reject the justification itself or reject its application to the context of attempts. However, more importantly, a reasonable legislator *may* accept both the justification and its application to the mentioned context, and require intention in this context.

If the legislator decides to require intention for complete attempts, in the context of all (or some) offences, what should he do concerning cases of oblique intention? Since the justification for the requirement of intention is based on an empirical correlation, the law of cases of oblique intention should depend on the empirical data relevant to the offences under discussion. For this reason, we should also be open to the possibility that the answer to the question whether oblique intention should suffice for conviction of attempt will vary according to the specific offence under discussion.[3]

13.3.3

A further context to which the justification suggested in chapter 12 may apply, is that of offences in the context of which the penalisation of the conduct does not add (substantially) to the deterrence provided by the civil law. It may be suggested that the penalisation of the conduct in the context of these offences is based on retribution, and that therefore an especially high degree of culpability should be required. Hence, the requirement of intention (for "intention is more culpable than recklessness"). I used the offence of defamatory libel as an example of an offence to which the present suggested justification may apply, for in the context of this offence it may be claimed that the penalisation of the wrongful act does not add substantially to the deterrence provided by the law of torts.

As in the context of complete attempts, distinguishing between intention and recklessness cannot reasonably be justified merely on the basis of the claim that when all other things are equal (including the motives) the actor who acts with intent to cause the proscribed result is more culpable than one who acts with recklessness with respect thereto. Distinguishing between intention and recklessness can reasonably be justified, in the present context, only on the basis of a significant empirical correlation between intention and high degrees of culpability, on the one hand, and recklessness and low degrees of culpability, on the other. That means that the present justification may only apply to offences in the context of which the factual data are such that the mentioned correlation exists.

The suggested justification itself, the idea that in certain contexts the penalisation of a certain course of conduct does not add substantially to the deterrence provided by the civil law, and the application of the justification to defamatory libel, are all based on various assumptions that can be rejected by reasonable people. Also, a reasonable legislator may decide to prefer, instead of requiring intention, one of the two alternative options mentioned in the discussion of attempts above, namely: to use a moral formula, or to refrain from requiring intention as a pre-requisite for liability and to rely on the prosecution authorities that only in rare cases will cases of recklessness be prosecuted. Therefore, a reasonable legislator may decide not to enact any basic crime of intention on the basis of the present justification. More importantly, however, a reasonable legislator *may* enact basic crimes of intention on the basis of the present justification.[4]

If the legislator decides to enact some basic crimes of intention on the basis of the present suggested justification for requiring intention, what should he do concerning cases of oblique intention? What was said on the issue of oblique intention in the last paragraph of section 13.3.2 may be applied to the present context as well. The law concerning these cases will depend on the factual data, and it is possible that it will have to vary from offence to offence, even within a group of offences in which the requirement of intention is based on the present justification.[5]

In section 12.4 I suggested a variation on the justifications suggested in chapters 11 and 12. This variation is based on a principle of an inverse relation between the amount of future harm prevented by the punishment and the degree of culpability that should be required to permit the imposition of criminal liability: the bigger the gain from punishing the actor (in terms of the amount of future harm that is prevented by punishing him), the lower the degree of culpability of the actor that should be required in order to permit the imposition of criminal liability.

13.4

Before concluding, I would like to remind the reader that the discussion in this book was confined to examining justifications for distinguishing between intention and recklessness that directly pertain to degrees of blameworthiness. Other possible potential justifications for distinguishing between intention and recklessness that are based on other kinds of considerations like, for example, that one who acts with intent to cause the result generally manifests a more dangerous character than one who acts with recklessness (and therefore he should be treated more harshly, because of considerations of special deterrence or incapacitation), are not discussed in this book and should be considered separately.

Notes

1   A legislator who, contrary to my feeling, thinks that there is a *large* difference in culpability between acting with intent to cause the proscribed result and acting with recklessness with respect to this result (when all other things, including the motives, are equal) may come to the conclusion that this difference alone can generate a state of affairs that justifies the enactment of basic crimes of intention. See chapter 11, note 35. If on the basis of this view he enacts some basic crimes of intention, then the law of cases of oblique intention, concerning these crimes, should be influenced by the reason for distinguishing between intention and recklessness. See text toward the end of section 11.6.

2   As was explained in section 12.2.1, this line of thought does not necessarily lead to the conclusion that the mens rea for complete attempts should be the same in the context of all offences. It may be the case that in the context of offences that protect against very serious harms, such as harms to life or bodily integrity, even recklessness will reach the high threshold of culpability required for punishment which is based on retribution, so that in the context of these offences – recklessness will suffice for a conviction in cases in which the result does not occur.

3   For the possibility of basing the requirement of intention in the law of attempt on the existence of an intrinsic difference in culpability between intention and recklessness, and for the implications of this possibility for the question of oblique intention, see the last paragraph of section 12.2.2.

4   For a further possible context to which the justification suggested in chapter 12 may apply see chapter 12, at note 50.

5   The discussion in the last paragraph of section 12.2.2, mentioned supra at note 3, may also be applied, with modifications, to the present context.

Bibliography

Alexander, L. (2000), "Insufficient Concern: A Unified Conception of Criminal Culpability" 88 *California Law Review* 931.

Ashworth, A. (1987), "Belief, Intent and Criminal Liability" in J. Eekelaar and J. Bell (eds) *Oxford Essays in Jurisprudence,* 3rd Series (Oxford: Oxford University Press) 1.

Ashworth, A. (1989), "Criminal Justice and Deserved Sentences" *Criminal Law Review* 340.

Ashworth, A. (1990), "Reforming the Law of Murder" *Criminal Law Review* 75.

Ashworth, A. (1995a), *Principles of Criminal Law* (2nd ed., Oxford: Oxford University Press).

Ashworth, A. (1995b), *Sentencing and Criminal Justice* (2nd ed., London: Butterworths).

Ashworth, A. (1998), "Four Techniques for Reducing Sentence Disparity" in A. von Hirsch and A. Ashworth (eds) *Principled Sentencing* (Oxford: Hart Publishing) 227.

Ashworth, A. (1999), *Principles of Criminal Law* (3rd ed., Oxford: Oxford University Press).

Ashworth, A. (2000), *Sentencing and Criminal Justice* (3rd ed., London: Butterworths).

Audi, R. (1973), "Intending" 70 *Journal of Philosophy* 387.

Bein, D. (1967), "Knowledge which Reached a High Degree of Probability" 2 *Israel Law Review* 18.

Bennett, J. (1981), "Morality and Consequences" in S.M. McMurrin (ed.) *The Tanner Lectures on Human Values,* vol. 2 (Salt Lake City: University of Utah Press) 45.

Bennett, J. (1995), *The Act Itself* (Oxford: Clarendon Press).

Brandt, R.B. (1972), "Utilitarianism and the Rules of War" 1 *Philosophy and Public Affairs* 145.

Brandt, R.B. (1985), "A Motivational Theory of Excuses in the Criminal Law" 27 *Nomos* 165.

Burchell, E.M. and Hunt, P.M.A. (1997), *South African Criminal Law and Procedure,* vol. 1 (3rd ed., by J.M. Burchell, Kenwyn: Juta).

Buzzard, J.H. (1978), "Intent" *Criminal Law Review* 5.

Card, R., Cross, R. and Jones, P.A. (1998), *Criminal Law* (14th ed., by R. Card, London: Butterworths).

Cavanaugh, T.A. (1999), "Double Effect and the End-Not-Means Principle: A Response to Bennett" 16 *Journal of Applied Philosophy* 181.

Cross, R. (1967), "The Mental Element in Crime" 83 *Law Quarterly Review* 215.

Cross, R. (1978), "The Reports of the Criminal Law Commissioners (1833-1849) and the Abortive Bills of 1853" in P.R. Glazebrook (ed.) *Reshaping the Criminal Law* (London: Stevens and Sons) 5.

Cross, R. and Jones, P.A. (1984), *Introduction to Criminal Law* (10th ed., by R. Card, London: Butterworths).

Defamatory Libel (Working Paper 35): Law Reform Commission of Canada (Working Paper 35) *Defamatory Libel* (Ottawa 1984).

Dennis, I.H. (1987), "The Mental Element for Accessories" in P. Smith (ed.) *Criminal Law: Essays in Honour of J. C. Smith* (London: Butterworths) 40.

Dennis, I. (1988), "Intention and Complicity: a Reply" *Criminal Law Review* 649.

Devine, P.E. (1974), "The Principle of Double Effect" 19 *The American Journal of Jurisprudence* 44.

Draft Criminal Code Bill (1985): See Law Commission: Codification of the Criminal Law (1985).

Draft Criminal Code for England and Wales (1989): See Law Commission: A Criminal Code for England and Wales (1989).

Duff, R.A. (1973), "Intentionally Killing the Innocent" 34 *Analysis* 16.

Duff, R.A. (1976), "Absolute Principles and Double Effect" 36 *Analysis* 68.

Duff, R.A. (1980a), "Intention, Mens Rea and the Law Commission Report" *Criminal Law Review* 147.

Duff, R.A. (1980b), "Intention, Recklessness, and Probable Consequences" *Criminal Law Review* 404.

Duff, R.A. (1989), "Intentions Legal and Philosophical" 9 *Oxford Journal of Legal Studies* 76.

Duff, R.A. (1990), *Intention, Agency and Criminal Liability* (Oxford: Basil Blackwell).

Duff, R.A. (1996), *Criminal Attempts* (Oxford: Clarendon Press).

Dworkin, R. (1993), *Life's Dominion: An Argument About Abortion, Euthanasia, and Individual Freedom* (New York: Alfred A. Knopf).

Enker, A.N. (1977), "Mens Rea and Criminal Attempt" *American Bar Foundation Research Journal* 845.

Feller, S.Z. (1970), "The Knowledge Rule" 5 *Israel Law Review* 352.

Finnis, J. (1991a), *Moral Absolutes* (Washington: The Catholic University of America Press).

Finnis, J. (1991b), "Intention and Side-Effects" in R.G. Frey and C.W. Morris (eds) *Liability and Responsibility* (Cambridge: Cambridge University Press) 32.

Finnis, J., Boyle, J. and Grisez, G. (1987), *Nuclear Deterrence, Morality, and Realism* (New York: Oxford University Press).

Fletcher, G.P. (1978), *Rethinking Criminal Law* (Boston: Little, Brown).

Foot, P. (1978), "The Problem of Abortion and the Doctrine of the Double Effect" in P. Foot *Virtues and Vices* (Oxford: Blackwell) 19.

Foot, P. (1985), "Morality, Action and Outcome" in T. Honderich (ed.) *Morality and Objectivity* (London: Routledge and Kegan Paul) 23.

Frankena, W.K. (1973), *Ethics* (2nd ed., Englewood Cliffs: Prentice-Hall).

Frey, R.G. (1983), *Rights, Killing, and Suffering* (Oxford: Basil Blackwell).

Fried, C. (1976), "Right and Wrong – Preliminary Considerations" 5 *Journal of Legal Studies* 165.

Fried, C. (1978), *Right and Wrong* (Cambridge, Mass.: Harvard University Press).

Gatley on Libel and Slander (1998), (9th ed., London: Sweet and Maxwell).

Geddes, L. (1972), "On the Intrinsic Wrongness of Killing Innocent People" 33 *Analysis* 93.

Gillies, P. (1997), *Criminal Law* (4th ed., Sydney: LBC Information Services).

Gillooly, M. (1998), *The Law of Defamation in Australia and New Zealand* (Sydney: The Federation Press).

Glover, J. (1977), *Causing Death and Saving Lives* (New York: Penguin Books).

Goff, R. (1988), "The Mental Element in the Crime of Murder" 104 *Law Quarterly Review* 30.

Gordon, G.H. (1975), "Subjective and Objective Mens Rea" 17 *Criminal Law Quarterly* 355.

Gordon, G.H. (1978), *The Criminal Law of Scotland* (2nd ed., Edinburgh: W. Green).

Gordon, G.H. (2000), *The Criminal Law of Scotland* (3rd ed., by M.G.A. Christie, Edinburgh: W. Green).

Gorr, M. (1996), "Should the Law Distinguish between Intention and (Mere) Foresight?" 2 *Legal Theory* 359.

Griffiths, C.T. and Verdun-Jones, S.N. (1994), *Canadian Criminal Justice* (2nd ed., Toronto: Harcourt Brace).

Grisez, G.G. (1970), "Toward a Consistent Natural-Law Ethics of Killing" 15 *The American Journal of Jurisprudence* 64.

Gross, H. (1979), *A Theory of Criminal Justice* (New York: Oxford University Press).

Hadden, T. (1968), "Offences of Violence: The Law and the Facts" *Criminal Law Review* 521.

Hall, J. (1960), *General Principles of Criminal Law* (2nd ed., Indianapolis: Bobbs-Merrill).

Hare, R.M. (1972), "Rules of War and Moral Reasoning" 1 *Philosophy and Public Affairs* 166.

Hart, H.L.A. (1963), *Law, Liberty and Morality* (Stanford, Cal.: Stanford University Press).

Hart, H.L.A. (1968), *Punishment and Responsibility* (Oxford: Oxford University Press).

Homicide (Working Paper 33) (1984): Law Reform Commission of Canada *Homicide,* Working Paper 33 (Ottawa).

Horder, J. (1993), "Criminal Culpability: The Possibility of a General Theory" 12 *Law and Philosophy* 193.

Horder, J. (1995), "Intention in the Criminal Law – A Rejoinder" 58 *Modern Law Review* 678.

Hudson, B.A. (1998), "Mitigation for Socially Deprived Offenders" in A. von Hirsch and A. Ashworth (eds) *Principled Sentencing* (Oxford: Hart Publishing) 205.

Huigens, K. (1995), "Virtue and Inculpation" 108 *Harvard Law Review* 1423.

Husak, D.N. (1998), "Partial Defenses" 11 *The Canadian Journal of Law and Jurisprudence* 167.

Jones, T.H. and Christie, M.G.A. (1996), *Criminal Law* (2nd ed., Edinburgh: W. Green).

Kadish, S.H. (1987), *Blame and Punishment* (New York: Macmillan).

Kagan, S. (1989), *The Limits of Morality* (Oxford: Oxford University Press).

Kamm, F.M. (1999), "Physician-Assisted Suicide, the Doctrine of Double Effect, and the Ground of Value" 109 *Ethics* 586.

Katz, L. (1996), *Ill-Gotten Gains: Evasion, Blackmail, Fraud, and Kindred Puzzles of the Law* (Chicago: University of Chicago Press).

Katz, L. (1999), "Form and Substance in Law and Morality" 66 *University of Chicago Law Review* 566.

Kenny, A. (1968), "Intention and Purpose in Law" in R. S. Summers (ed.) *Essays in Legal Philosophy* (Oxford: Basil Blackwell) 146.

Kenny, A. (1978), *Freewill and Responsibility* (London: Routledge and Kegan Paul).

Kenny, A. (1995), "Philippa Foot on Double Effect" in R. Hursthouse, G. Lawrence and W. Quinn (eds) *Virtues and Reasons* (Oxford: Clarendon Press) 77.

Kenny's Outlines of Criminal Law (1966), (19th ed., by J.W.C. Turner, London: Cambridge University Press).

Kremnitzer, M. (1984), "The Punishability of Impossible Attempts" 19 *Israel Law Review* 340.

Kremnitzer, M. (1987), "Comment" in R. Gavison (ed.) *Issues in Contemporary Legal Philosophy* (Oxford: Oxford University Press) 277.

Kremnitzer, M. (1991), "Sentencing as Art – A Response: Sentencing as a Just System" 25 *Israel Law Review* 662.

Kremnitzer, M. (1998), "On Premeditation" 1 *Buffalo Criminal Law Review* 627.

Kretzmer, D. (1986), "Intent in Criminal Libel: Statutory Interpretation or Judicial Imagination?" 21 *Israel Law Review* 591.

Kugler, I. (1993), *Foresight of a High Degree of Probability in the Criminal Law* (Ph.D. Dissertation, Jerusalem: The Hebrew University) (in Hebrew).

Kugler, I. (1997), "On the Possibility of a Criminal Law Defence for Conscientious Objection" 10 *The Canadian Journal of Law and Jurisprudence* 387.

Lacey, N. and Wells, C. (1998), *Reconstructing Criminal Law* (2nd ed., London: Butterworths).

LaFave, W.R. and Scott, A.W. (1986), *Criminal Law* (2nd ed., St. Paul, Minn.: West).

Law Commission, Working Paper No. 79, *Offences against Religion and Public Worship* (1981), (London: HMSO).

Law Commission, Working Paper No. 84, *Criminal Libel* (1982), (London: HMSO).

Law Commission, *Report on Criminal Libel*, No. 149 (London: HMSO, 1985).

Law Commission, *Codification of the Criminal Law: A Report to the Law Commission* (1985), No. 143 (London: HMSO).

Law Commission, *A Criminal Code for England and Wales* (1989), No. 177 (London: HMSO).

Mackie, J.L. (1977a), *Ethics: Inventing Right and Wrong* (Pelican Books).

Mackie, J.L. (1977b), "The Grounds of Responsibility" in P.M.S. Hacker and J. Raz (eds) *Law, Morality and Society* (Oxford: Oxford University Press) 175.

McCall Smith, R.A.A. and Sheldon, D. (1997), *Scots Criminal Law* (2nd ed., Edinburgh: Butterworths).

Meehan, E. and Currie, J.H. (2000), *The Law of Criminal Attempt* (2nd ed., Toronto: Carswell).

Michael, J. and Wechsler, H. (1937), "A Rationale of the Law of Homicide II" 37 *Columbia Law Review* 1261.

Michaels, A.C. (1998), "Acceptance: The Missing Mental State" 71 *Southern California Law Review* 953.

Mitchell, B. (1996), "Culpably Indifferent Murder" 25 *Anglo-American Law Review* 64.

Model Penal Code and Commentaries (1980): American Law Institute *Model Penal Code and Commentaries, Part II* (Philadelphia, PA).

Model Penal Code (1985): American Law Institute *Model Penal Code: Complete Statutory Text* (Philadelphia, PA).

Model Penal Code and Commentaries (1985): American Law Institute *Model Penal Code and Commentaries, Part I* (Philadelphia, PA).

Moore, M. (1997), *Placing Blame* (Oxford: Clarendon Press).

Mueller, G.O.W. (1961), "The German Draft Criminal Code 1960 – An Evaluation in Terms of American Criminal Law" *University of Illinois Law Forum* 25.

Murphy, J.G. and Coleman, J.L. (1990), *Philosophy of Law* (Revised ed., Boulder: Westview Press).

Nagel, T. (1972), "War and Massacre" 1 *Philosophy and Public Affairs* 123.

Nagel, T. (1986), *The View from Nowhere* (New York: Oxford University Press).

Nozick, R. (1974), *Anarchy, State, and Utopia* (New York: Basic Books).

Nozick, R. (1997), *Socratic Puzzles* (Cambridge: Harvard University Press).

Oberdiek, H. (1972), "Intention and Foresight in Criminal Law" 81 *Mind* 389.

Ohana, D. (1998), "Sentencing Reform in Israel: The Goldberg Committee Report" 32 *Israel Law Review* 591.

Partial Defences to Murder, Provocation and Infanticide: New South Wales Law Reform Commission *Partial Defences to Murder: Provocation and Infanticide* Report 83 (Sydney, 1997).

Perkins, R.M. and Boyce, R.N. (1982), *Criminal Law* (3rd ed., Mineola: Foundation Press).

Pettit, P. (1997), "The Consequentialist Perspective" in M.W. Baron, P. Pettit and M. Slote *Three Methods of Ethics: A Debate* (Oxford: Blackwell) 92.

Pillsbury, S.H. (1998), *Judging Evil* (New York: New York University Press).

Primoratz, I. (1990), *Justifying Legal Punishment* (New Jersey: Humanities Press International).

Quinn, W. (1993), *Morality and Action* (Cambridge: Cambridge University Press).

Rachels, J. (1986), *The End of Life* (Oxford: Oxford University Press).

Raz, J. (1986), *The Morality of Freedom* (Oxford: Oxford University Press).

Reeder, J.P. (1996), *Killing and Saving* (The Pennsylvania State University Press).

Report of the Select Committee on Medical Ethics: House of Lords *Report of the Select Committee on Medical Ethics* Session 1993-94, H.L. Paper 21 (London: HMSO).

Report of the Select Committee on Murder and Life Imprisonment: House of Lords *Report of the Select Committee on Murder and Life Imprisonment* Session 1988-89, H.L. Paper 78 (London).

Report on Culpable Homicide (1976): Criminal Law Reform Committee, New Zealand *Report on Culpable Homicide*.

Report on Recodifying Criminal Law (1987): Law Reform Commission of Canada *Report on Recodifying Criminal Law* (Ottawa).

Robinson, P.H. (1984), *Criminal Law Defenses* (St. Paul: West Publishing).

Robinson, P.H. (1987), "Hybrid Principles for the Distribution of Criminal Sanctions" 82 *Northwestern University Law Review* 19.

Robinson, P.H. (1997), *Structure and Function in Criminal Law* (Oxford: Clarendon Press).

Robinson, P.H. and Darley, J.M. (1995), *Justice, Liability and Blame: Community Views and the Criminal Law* (Boulder: Westview Press).

Roxin, C. (1996), "The Dogmatic Structure of Criminal Liability in the General Part of the Draft Israeli Penal Code – A Comparison with German Law" 30 *Israel Law Review* 60.

Russell, O.W. (1964), *Russell on Crime* (12th ed., by J.W.C. Turner, London: Stevens and Sons).

Scheffler, S. (1982), *The Rejection of Consequentialism* (Oxford: Clarendon Press).

Scheffler, S. (1988a), "Introduction" in S. Scheffler (ed.) *Consequentialism and its Critics* (New York: Oxford University Press) 1.

Scheffler, S. (1988b), "Agent-Centred Restrictions, Rationality, and the Virtues" in S. Scheffler (ed.) *Consequentialism and its Critics* (New York: Oxford University Press) 243.

Scheffler, S. (1994), *The Rejection of Consequentialism* (Revised ed., Oxford: Clarendon Press).

Schulhofer, S.J. (1974), "Harm and Punishment: A Critique of Emphasis on the Results of Conduct in the Criminal Law" 122 *University of Pennsylvania Law Review* 1497.

Scottish Law Commission *Attempted Homicide* (1984): Scottish Law Commission, Consultative Memorandum no. 61, *Attempted Homicide*.

Sentencing Reform: A Canadian Approach (1987): The Canadian Sentencing Commission *Sentencing Reform: A Canadian Approach* (Ottawa).

Shachar, Y. (1987), "The Fortuitous Gap in Law and Morality" 6 *Criminal Justice Ethics* 12.

Silving, H. (1967), *Constituent Elements of Crime* (Sprigfield, Ill.: Charles C. Thomas).

Simester, A.P. (1996a), "Why Distinguish Intention from Foresight?" in A.P. Simester and A.T.H. Smith (eds) *Harm and Culpability* (Oxford: Oxford University Press) 71.

Simester, A.P. (1996b), "Moral Certainty and the Boundaries of Intention" 16 *Oxford Journal of Legal Studies* 445.

Simons, K.W. (1992), "Rethinking Mental States" 72 *Boston University Law Review* 463.

Sinnott-Armstrong, W. (1988), *Moral Dilemmas* (Oxford: Basil Blackwell).

Smith, A.T.H. (1978), "On Actus Reus and Mens Rea" in P.R. Glazebrook (ed.) *Reshaping the Criminal Law* (London: Stevens and Sons) 95.

Smith, J.C. (1971), "The Element of Chance in Criminal Liability" *Criminal Law Review* 63.

Smith, J.C. (1978), "'Intent': A Reply" *Criminal Law Review* 14.

Smith, J.C. (1986), "Comment on *Hancock and Shankland*" *Criminal Law Review* 181.

Smith, J.C. (1990), "A Note on 'Intention'" *Criminal Law Review* 85.

Smith, J.C. (1998), "Comment on *Woollin*" *Criminal Law Review* 890.

Smith, J.C. and Hogan, B. (1983), *Criminal Law* (5th ed., London: Butterworths).

Smith, J.C. and Hogan, B. (1992), *Criminal Law* (7th ed., London: Butterworths).

Smith, J.C. and Hogan, B. (1999), *Criminal Law* (9th ed., by J.C. Smith, London: Butterworths).

Stannard, J.E. (1986), "Mens Rea in the Melting Pot" 37 *Northern Ireland Legal Quarterly* 61.

Stephen, J.F. (1883), *A History of the Criminal Law of England* (London: Macmillan).

Stuart, D. (1968), "Mens Rea, Negligence and Attempts" *Criminal Law Review* 647.

Stuart, D. (1995), *Canadian Criminal Law* (3rd ed., Toronto: Carswell).

Tak, P.J.P. (1997), "Sentencing and Punishment in the Netherlands" in M. Tonry and K. Hatlestad (eds) *Sentencing Reform in Overcrowded Times* (New York: Oxford University Press) 194.

Ten, C.L. (1987), *Crime, Guilt and Punishment* (Oxford: Clarendon Press).

Thomson, J.J. (1973), "Rights and Deaths" 2 *Philosophy and Public Affairs* 146.

Thomson, J.J. (1990), *The Realm of Rights* (Cambridge: Harvard University Press).

Tonry, M.H. (1982), "Criminal Law: The Missing Element in Sentencing Reform" 35 *Vanderbilt Law Review* 607.

Tornudd, P. (1997), "Sentencing and Punishment in Finland" in M. Tonry and K. Hatlestad (eds) *Sentencing Reform in Overcrowded Times* (New York: Oxford University Press) 189.

Turner, J.W.C. (1945), "The Mental Element in Crimes at Common Law" in L. Radzinowicz and J.W.C. Turner (eds) *The Modern Approach to Criminal Law* (London: Macmillan) 195.

Uniacke, S. (1994), *Permissible Killing* (Cambridge: Cambridge University Press).

Von Hirsch, A. (1998a), "Proportionate Sentences: A Desert Perspective" in A. von Hirsch and A. Ashworth (eds) *Principled Sentencing* (Oxford: Hart Publishing) 168.

Von Hirsch, A. (1998b), "Desert and Previous Convictions" in A. von Hirsch and A. Ashworth (eds) *Principled Sentencing* (Oxford: Hart Publishing) 191.

Von Hirsch, A. (1998c), "The Swedish Sentencing Law – The Principles Underlying the New Law" in A. von Hirsch and A. Ashworth (eds) *Principled Sentencing* (Oxford: Hart Publishing) 240.

Von Hirsch, A. and Jareborg, N. (1998), "The Swedish Sentencing Law – The Details of the New Law" in A. von Hirsch and A. Ashworth (eds) *Principled Sentencing* (Oxford: Hart Publishing) 247.

Walzer, M. (1977), *Just and Unjust Wars* (New York: Basic Books).

Wasik, M. (1979), "Mens Rea, Motive, and the Problem of 'Dishonesty' in the Law of Theft" *Criminal Law Review* 543.

Wasik, M. (1983), "Excuses at the Sentencing Stage" *Criminal Law Review* 450.

Wasik, M. (1985a), "The Grant of an Absolute Discharge" 5 *Oxford Journal of Legal Studies* 211.

Wasik, M. (1985b), "Rules of Evidence in the Sentencing Process" *Current Legal Problems* 187.

Weigend, T. (1991), "Norm versus Discretion in Sentencing" 25 *Israel Law Review* 628.

Wells, C. (1978), "The Death Penalty for Provocation?" *Criminal Law Review* 662.

Williams, G. (1961), *Criminal law: The General Part* (2nd ed., London: Stevens).

Williams, G. (1965), *The Mental Element in Crime* (Jerusalem: Magnes Press).

Williams, G. (1974), *The Sanctity of Life and the Criminal Law* (New York: Alfred A. Knopf).

Williams, G. (1978), "The Mental Element in Crime, The Law Commission's Report No. 89: (1) The Meaning of Terms" *Criminal Law Review* 588.

Williams, G. (1983a), *Textbook of Criminal Law* (2nd ed., London: Stevens).

Williams, G. (1983b), "The Problem of Reckless Attempts" *Criminal Law Review* 365.

Williams, G. (1987), "Oblique Intention" 46 *Cambridge Law Journal* 417.

Wilson, W. (1999), "Doctrinal Rationality after *Woollin*" 62 *Modern Law Review* 448.

Index